TOP STORIES 2010

ISSN 2158-3919

TOP STORIES 2010
Behind the Headlines

GALE
CENGAGE Learning

Detroit • New York • San Francisco • New Haven, Conn • Waterville, Maine • London

GALE
CENGAGE Learning™

Top Stories 2010: Behind the Headlines

Project Editors: Angus Carroll, John F. McCoy, Meghan A. O'Meara

Editorial: Sheila Dow, Kathleen J. Edgar, Jason M. Everett, Debra Kirby, Michelle Latshaw, Daniel Marowski

Rights Acquisition and Management: Robyn V. Young, Kimberly Potvin

Composition and Product Design: Cynthia Baldwin, Kristine Julien, Gary Leach

Manufacturing: Wendy Blurton, Dorothy Maki

Imaging: John Watkins

Indexing: Katy Balcer

Product Management: Leigh Ann Cusack

For product information and technology assistance, contact us at
Gale Customer Support, 1-800-877-4253.
For permission to use material from this text or product,
submit all requests online at **www.cengage.com/permissions.**
Further permissions questions can be emailed to
permissionrequest@cengage.com

Cover photographs reproduced by permission: © US Coast Guard/Corbis (firefighting boats around the *Deepwater Horizon*); AP Images/Manish Swarup (Afghan National Army soldier); AP Images/Alex Ibanez (Luis Urzua rescued); AP Images/Thanassis Stavrakis (Greek economic crisis protest); AP Images/Gerald Herbert (pelican rescue); Carlos Garcia Rawlins/Reuters (looters in Port-au-Prince); AFP/Getty Images (Iran missile test); Ali Jarekji/Reuters (veiled woman); Stringer Mexico/Reuters (Mexico drug violence victim); © Sebastião Salgado/ (Contact Press Images) (Rwandan refugees in Tanzania); Nicholas Kamm/AFP/ Getty Images (WikiLeaks homepage).

While every effort has been made to ensure the reliability of the information presented in this publication, Gale, a part of Cengage Learning, does not guarantee the accuracy of the data contained herein. Gale accepts no payment for listing; and inclusion in the publication of any organization, agency, institution, publication, service, or individual does not imply endorsement of the editors or publisher. Errors brought to the attention of the publisher and verified to the satisfaction of the publisher will be corrected in future editions.

Gale
27500 Drake Rd.
Farmington Hills, MI, 48331-3535

Hardcover: ISBN-13: 978-1-4144-8889-9   ISBN-10: 1-4144-8889-0
Softcover: ISBN-13: 978-1-4144-8890-5   ISBN-10: 1-4144-8890-4
ISSN 2158-3919

This title is also available as an e-book.
ISBN-13: 978-1-4144-8891-2
ISBN-10: 1-4144-8891-2
Contact your Gale, a part of Cengage Learning sales representative for ordering information.

Printed in the United States of America
2 3 4 5 6 7 15 14 13 12 11

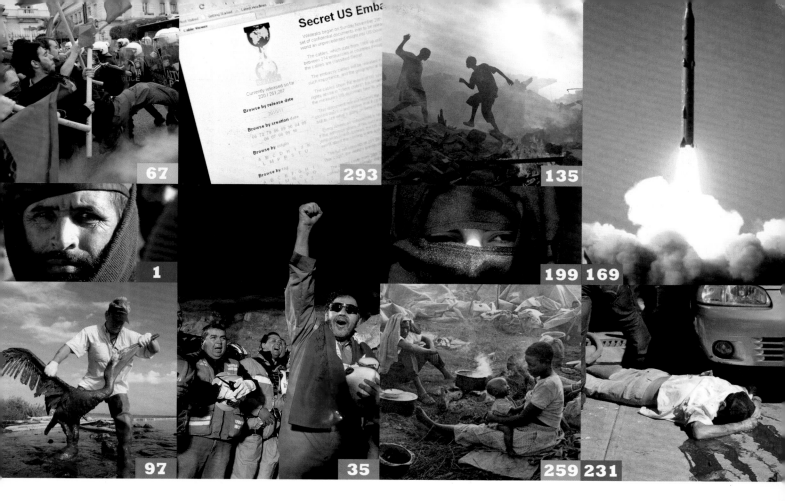

CONTENTS

Introduction . . . . *vii*

The Afghan War: *The Surge, the Taliban and Corruption* 1

Chilean Miners' Rescue: *A Dangerous Business* 35

Global Economic Crisis 67

Gulf Oil Spill: *The Business of Energy and Oily Birds* 97

Haiti: Earthquake & Aftermath 135

Iran's Nuclear Program: *Energy or Weapons?* 169

Islam in the West: *Headscarves, Mosques and Cartoons* . . . 199

Mexico's Drug War 231

Migrants, Immigrants & Refugees 259

Security in the Digital Age 293

Index *313*

INTRODUCTION

The Top Stories Series presents thought-provoking overviews of the key news events that have dominated world headlines—stories that not only captured the world's attention, but continue to impact the world today. Profusely illustrated with compelling photographs, timelines and illustrations, the issues are presented clearly and within their complex, global context.

Selecting the stories was not an easy task. Many recent stories fascinated and disturbed, haunted and inspired. From among them, ten were selected for 2010 because of their importance to the global community and because of the lessons we can learn from them. Each one lends perspective to critical concepts like community, security and responsibility.

Many are not pretty. Indeed, some are ugly, often bloody. Some illustrations will be hard to look at and some descriptions hard to read. Many images are provocative, but none are gratuitous. Each image was selected to help readers come to grips with and unravel confusing, difficult, even frightening issues.

Every effort has been made to be objective and include viewpoints from around the world. Today, we live in a world tied together economically, electronically, and environmentally. Hopefully, these stories will encourage readers to develop a larger global perspective and a deeper appreciation of wide-ranging global viewpoints.

The Editors

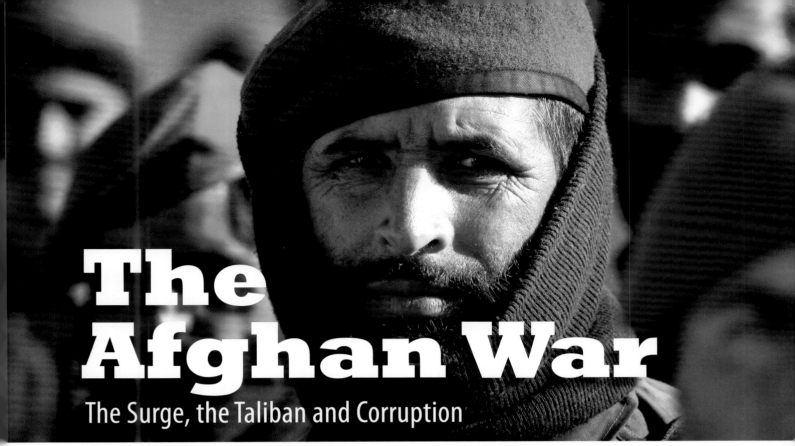

The Afghan War

The Surge, the Taliban and Corruption

AP Images/Manish Swarup.

On the morning of 18 January 2010, a group of Taliban insurgents launched a daring attack in central Kabul, the capital city of Afghanistan. The attacks began at about 10 A.M., as suicide bombers detonated explosives in front of government buildings in the central part of the city. Simultaneously another group of insurgents took over a large shopping center and attacked other government buildings, a cinema, and a hotel with rocket-propelled grenades and hand grenades.

Afghan civilians caught up in the battle told a reporter from the BBC what was happening. "We are close to the battle," said Sulaiman Aslam, who was inside the Ministry of Finance building. "I was at my computer when I heard the first big blast, then we moved into a corridor with no windows. We then heard another big blast, like a rocket launcher. Someone said our building was hit and I heard three or four of our staff were injured." Baba Jan, who was inside the Ministry of Communication and Information Technology,

said, "The Feroshgah-e-Afghan shopping centre is right in front of us, about 150 metres away. Until about 10 minutes ago the fighting was intense. With a group of colleagues, I was watching police firing on the building and saw it catch fire. Fire fighters didn't dare approach it at first the blaze was so big."

Gun battles and explosions continued for several hours, until Afghan security forces regained control of the situation at about 3 P.M. Five people were killed and seventy-one wounded in the attack. Seven of the attackers were also killed. People were soon calling it the "Day of Terror."

The United States quickly condemned the terrorist attack, the latest in a series of Taliban assaults carried out in Kabul. The ease with which the Taliban were able launch their "Day of Terror" in the heart of the capital city served to underline the need for a new strategy to combat the insurgency. It was with this in mind that U.S. President Barack Obama had announced just six weeks earlier, in December 2009, his plan to send in an additional 30,000 U.S. troops to Afghanistan. The goal of this troop increase, also referred to as the "surge," was to speed up stabilization in Afghanistan. The Americans hoped to begin withdrawing troops in July 2011, following a complete transfer of responsibility for security to the Afghan government. By 2009, American forces had been in Afghanistan for ten years. The U.S. war with Afghanistan began in 2001, when U.S. forces invaded the country in order to destroy the Taliban's ability to provide a safe haven for terrorists who had used this protection to launch attacks against the United States.

Afghanistan and the Great Powers

Due to its strategic geographic location, Af-

U.S. Army soldiers patrol near the town of Baraki Barak, Logar province, Afghanistan on 23 November 2009. Logar province is the scene of a major U.S. military surge, fuel for the argument by senior commanders that more troops and aid infusions could reverse Taliban gains in other areas of Afghanistan and ultimately culminate in victory. AP Images/Dario Lopez-Mills. ▶

ghanistan has long been the object of foreign attention. However, attempts to dominate the region by external powers have always been fiercely resisted by local tribesmen. Thus the U.S. invasion of Afghanistan in 2001 was not the first time that a Western power has sought to intervene in that country. That distinction goes back to Alexander the Great, the ancient Greek warrior who captured part of present-day Afghanistan in 328 BCE. Since then Afghanistan, often referred to as the crossroads of Central Asia, has been prey to many invaders. During ancient and medieval

Afghan security forces gather at the scene of a Taliban attack near the Afghan presidential place on 18 January 2010 in central Kabul, Afghanistan. AP Images/Ahmad Massoud.

times these invasions were led by Turks, Arabs (who brought Islam to Afghanistan), Persians, and Mongols. During the nineteenth century, Afghanistan found itself squeezed between two great expansionist powers, Britain and Russia, both of whom wanted influence in Central Asia. Diplomats referred to this struggle as "The Great Game."

At the height of its global colonial empire, Britain launched the first Anglo-Afghan War in 1839 in order to secure the northern approaches to Afghanistan. British troops, under Major General William Elphinstone, captured Kabul in 1839, but the Afghans refused to accept British rule. Three years later, in January 1842, the Afghans forced the British out of the city. In order to escape, the British, along with Indian troops in the employ of the British East India Company and still under Elphinstone's command, tried to reach the British garrison at Jalalabad, ninety miles away. But the total British force of 4,500, along with 12,500 camp followers, never made it through the mountainous terrain to Jalalabad. Harassed throughout their retreat by Afghan forces, the last sixty-five British soldiers were massacred near the village of Gandamak, thirty-five miles from Jalalabad. There was only one survi-

vor, Assistant Surgeon William Brydon, who was badly wounded but managed to reach Jalalabad on horseback.

Continuing rivalry between Russia and Britain led to the second Anglo-Afghan War in 1878. Russia, trying to exert influence in the region, had succeeded in establishing a diplomatic mission in Kabul. Britain insisted on a mission, too, but was refused by Afghan ruler Sher Ali Khan. Chafing at the rebuff, Britain launched an invasion of Afghanistan with 40,000 troops. With Britain in control of much of the country, a treaty was signed in May 1879. As part of the agreement, the British sent an envoy to Kabul, with the aim of establishing a diplomatic mission in the city. The conflict between the British and Afghans was re-ignited, however, when the British mission, accompanied by a small military escort, was massacred. Several military engagements followed, until the Afghans were finally defeated in September 1880, thus ending the second Anglo-Afghan War.

Having achieved most of their objectives, the British withdrew from Afghanistan in 1880. Afghans were given control of their internal affairs, but Britain controlled the country's foreign relations. Over the course of the next twenty years, Britain and Russia worked out between them the

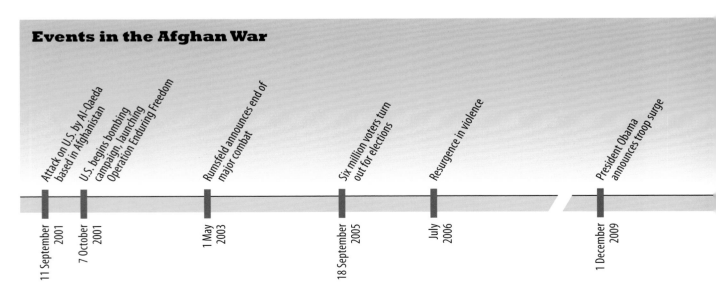

Events in the Afghan War

boundaries of modern Afghanistan. It was not until 1919 that the British ceded control over Afghanistan's foreign affairs. After formally gaining its independence in 1919, Afghanistan would remain relatively free of foreign intervention for the next sixty years.

The country became reacquainted with foreign invasion once again in 1979, when Soviet tanks rolled into Kabul. The Soviet generals in charge of that invasion, however, might well have been advised to spend some time pondering the fate of Major General Elphinstone and his doomed British army.

Soviet tanks drive through Kabul, Afghanistan on 26 April 1989 during the parade celebrating 11 years of communist revolution in Afghanistan. Richard Ellis/Reuters.

Origins of the Current War

The origins of the U.S.-led war in Afghanistan lie in the complex and bloody history of Afghanistan over the last thirty years.

With a population of 32 million, Afghanistan is a landlocked Muslim nation in south-central Asia bordered to the west by Iran, to the south and east by Pakistan, and to the north by several former Soviet republics.

During the Cold War (1945–1990) between

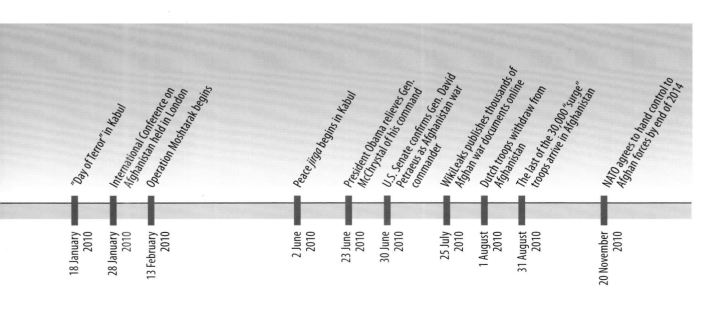

"Day of Terror" in Kabul
18 January 2010

International Conference on Afghanistan held in London
28 January 2010

Operation Moshtarak begins
13 February 2010

Peace jirga begins in Kabul
2 June 2010

President Obama relieves Gen. McChrystal of his command
23 June 2010

U.S. Senate confirms Gen. David Petraeus as Afghanistan war commander
30 June 2010

WikiLeaks publishes thousands of Afghan war documents online
25 July 2010

Dutch troops withdraw from Afghanistan
1 August 2010

The last of the 30,000 "surge" troops arrive in Afghanistan
31 August 2010

NATO agrees to hand control to Afghan forces by end of 2014
20 November 2010

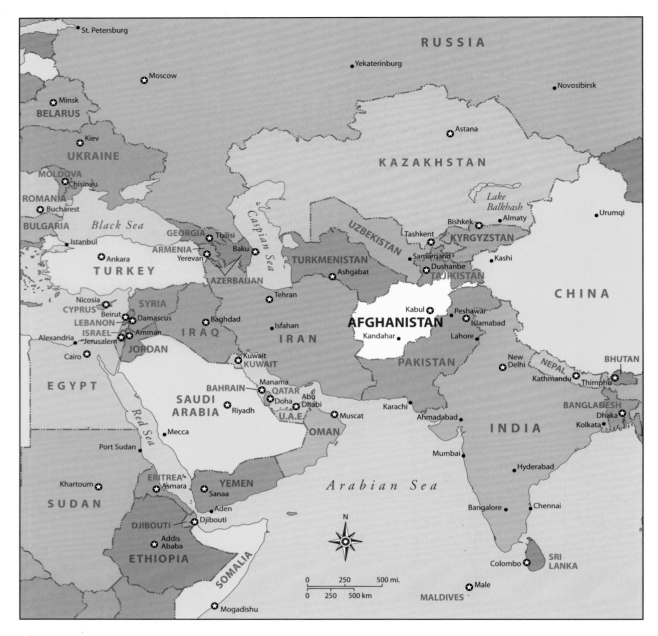

Afghanistan and the surrounding region. Illustration/XNR Productions/Cengage Learning, Gale.

the United States and the former Soviet Union, Afghanistan was strategically important to both sides of the conflict. In the north, the country bordered the Soviet Union and therefore the United States regarded it as an important buffer against Soviet influence in the region. In the late 1970s, the Afghan government asked Soviet troops to enter the country to help fight Islamist rebel groups, known as the mujahideen. (Islamists are persons who seek to establish Islam as both religion and political system in their countries.) The Soviets invaded Afghanistan in 1979 with tens of thousands of troops. Six months before the Soviet invasion, the United States, under President Jimmy Carter, had begun massive funding of the radical Islamist resistance, with the aim of countering Soviet influ-

Taliban fighters with rocket-launchers patrol the outskirts of Kandahar on 31 October 2001. Although the Taliban government was removed from power in December of that year, the Taliban-led insurgency remains a resilient foe. Mian Kursheed/Reuters.

ence in the region. The U.S. government poured hundreds of millions of dollars of cash and tens of thousands of tons of weapons and supplies to the Islamists, who in turn recruited mujahideen from Muslim countries around the world.

The Soviet invasion soon evolved into a brutal and prolonged entanglement. In 1989, after an expensive and bloody conflict, the Soviets withdrew in defeat and a variety of Islamists and warlords took over Afghanistan. They were not a united group, however. Perceiving the ruling mujahideen and local warlords as corrupt, a group of extreme Islamic purists known as the Taliban began a new rebellion and took power in 1996. They ruled Afghanistan according to one of the strictest interpretations of Muslim law ever known, violently enforcing public dress codes requiring the total concealment of women's bodies, forbidding

kite-flying, public applause at sporting events, and many other social behaviors.

The Taliban soon allied itself with the international terrorist organization al-Qaeda, which moved its headquarters into the country. On 11 September 2001, al-Qaeda carried out terrorist attacks on the United States, killing almost 3,000 people in less than two hours. The United States responded by demanding access to al-Qaeda personnel in Afghanistan, particularly Osama bin Laden, the leader of al-Qaeda and acknowledged planner of the 9/11 attacks. The Taliban refused to turn al-Qaeda leaders over to the United States.

On 7 October 2001, the United States, the United Kingdom, and Canada launched air strikes against Afghanistan. They were supported by the Northern Alliance, a loose coalition of Afghan military groups that opposed the Taliban,

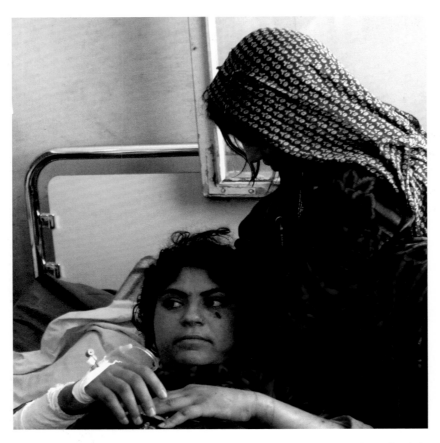

A young Afghan woman hospitalized from wounds inflicted by a U.S. air strike in Shindad province on 22 August 2008. The U.S. military acknowledged accidentally killing at least 33 civilians in the strike. AP Images/Fraidoon Pooyaa.

began to recruit new members to their cause from the general populace.

A classic guerrilla war commenced, with well-armed occupation troops from the United States and other countries pitted against an elusive insurgency drawing on religious fervor and nationalist resentment of foreign occupiers. The central government, despite a steadily growing national army, remained weak. In 2003, under a United Nations mandate, the North Atlantic Treaty Organization (NATO) took command of security operations in Afghanistan. Then, in March of that year, the United States launched an attack on the nation of Iraq. The U.S. government had intelligence that led it to believe Iraq possessed weapons of mass destruction and posed an immediate threat to the security of the United States. At first, the engagement in Iraq did not require the efforts of the military personnel stationed in Afghanistan. By 2005, however, many members of the military leadership in Afghanistan were being dispatched to support operations in Iraq.

and led the offensive on the ground. Within days, most al-Qaeda training sites had been crushed and the Taliban's air defenses had been destroyed. By November, the northern city of Mazar-e-Sharif had fallen to the Northern Alliance, and four days later, the Taliban surrendered Kabul, the capital. The Taliban surrendered Kandahar, Afghanistan's second-largest city, on 7 December 2001.

A moderate Islamist government—the official name of Afghanistan is the Islamic Republic of Afghanistan—was set up in December 2002 by the invading coalition, mujahideen leaders, and exiled Afghan leaders. However, the Taliban and al-Qaeda had not been destroyed, and bin Laden was neither captured nor killed. Instead, the Taliban and al-Qaeda withdrew into remote regions of Afghanistan and neighboring Pakistan and

In Afghanistan, local resentment of the NATO occupation grew, inflamed in part by civilian casualties resulting from U.S. and U.K. air force operations. For example, on 6 July 2008, a mistargeted U.S. air strike killed at least forty-seven members of a wedding party, including the bride, without harming any resistance fighters. In July 2007, a United Nations investigation found that pro-government and international (including U.S.) forces were responsible for more civilian casualties than the Taliban. Over the next few years, civilian casualties continued to rise, exacerbated further by suicide bombings sponsored by the Taliban.

Conflict Spreads to Pakistan

In the meantime, by 2006, the Taliban, working partly from inside Pakistan, had regrouped in the southern part of Afghanistan. According to one widely-reported analysis, by late 2007 the Taliban effectively controlled slightly more than half the country. During 2008 and 2009, the resurgent Taliban continued to make gains, forcing NATO troops to retreat, and the conflict soon spread to neighboring Pakistan.

In early September 2008, U.S. forces entered Pakistan for the first time in order to attack Taliban forces. After the raid, press reports indicated that the administration of George W. Bush had authorized U.S. raids into Pakistan when necessary to pursue militant targets. U.S. attacks inside Pakistan, involving the use of unmanned drones, continued under President Obama. Pakistan objected to the strikes on the grounds that they violated Pakistan's sovereignty. The United States claimed that Pakistan had been unwilling or unable to root out Taliban fighters and foreign militants along its border with Afghanistan, and that the attacks were necessary to protect and support U.S. troops in Afghanistan.

The Taliban seized control of the Swat Valley (just 130 kilometers northwest of Islamabad, Pakistan's capital city) in December 2008, killing hundreds of their political opponents. In order to quell the violence, Pakistan's president, Asif Ali Zardari, offered to instate Islamic law in the region in exchange for a promise from the Taliban to cease violence in the area for two years. After the Taliban continued to press toward Islamabad, getting as close as Buner, 100 kilometers from the capital, Pakistan launched a full-scale military offensive against the Taliban. The move was welcomed by President Obama, who met in May 2009 with President Zardari and Afghan president Hamid Karzai. During this meeting, Obama

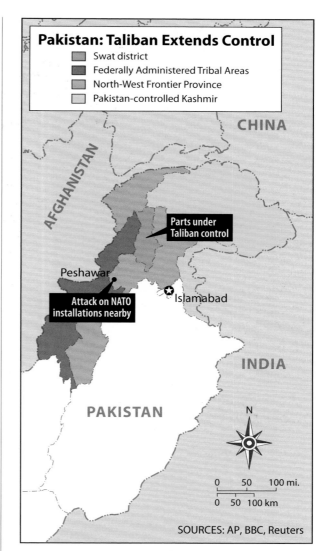

Illustration/XNR Productions/Cengage Learning, Gale.

expressed his concern over the seeming lack of progress in subduing the Taliban resurgence and stressed the need for increased cooperation between Pakistan, Afghanistan, and the United States. The Pakistani Army regained control of the Swat Valley in September 2009.

As a reaction to the growing threat posed by the Taliban, the United States moved to bolster its presence in Afghanistan. Obama ordered the first of two troop surges he would authorize in the first year of his presidency. He announced in February 2009 that 17,000 additional troops were being sent to the region, and he upped that figure to 21,000 in March. By June 2009, 10,000 of those troops had been deployed. The troop surge came at a time of increased tension between the United States and the Afghan government as a result of continued civilian casualties. The Afghan government claimed that 140 civilians were killed in a U.S. air strike in May. While the United States disputed the figure, NATO officials agreed that civilian casualties were still too high. A U.S. military report released in June 2009 provided suggestions to implement measures that would reduce civilian casualties, but the Afghan public's resentment of the U.S. military continued to mount.

July 2009 was the bloodiest month yet for the eight-year war in Afghanistan, and violence continued to escalate in August, mostly in the Helmand province, in southwest Afghanistan. Four U.S. service members were killed by a roadside bomb on 6 August 2009. Two other roadside bombs killed five civilians and five police officers. Military analysts said that a spike in violence was expected ahead of the 20 August 2009 presidential and provincial elections. The Taliban's official website urged Afghans to boycott the election, declaring that voting amounted to a show of support for the Americans. A week after the election, with about 20 percent of the votes counted, it appeared

Troop Deaths as of November 16, 2010 BY COUNTRY	
United States	1,395
United Kingdom	344
Canada	152
France	50
Germany	45
Others	233
Total	2,219

SOURCES: NATO-ISAF, iCasualties.org

Number of troops deaths for each country under NATO command in Afghanistan as of November 2010. Illustration/XNR Productions/Cengage Learning, Gale.

that Karzai had a significant lead over his chief rival, Abdullah Abdullah, an Afghan doctor and politician who ran as an independent opponent against Karzai. Abdullah alleged that the election was plagued by fraud. By the end of August, more than seven hundred fraud charges were being investigated by the Electoral Complaints Commission (ECC). Election officials had hoped to announce results by mid-September, but the large number of complaints put that goal in jeopardy, with some observers worrying that arguments about the vote count could last months. Karzai was officially declared the winner in November 2009.

However, lower-than-expected turnout and widespread alleged fraud during the 2009 Afghan presidential election seemed to indicate that the Afghan public was not confident in its government. Meanwhile, a report from General Stanley McChrystal, commander of U.S. forces in Afghanistan, to President Obama warned that the situation in Afghanistan was much worse than he had anticipated. The Taliban had gained significant momentum since June 2009, and without a dramatic increase in troop levels, the U.S. mis-

Two U.S. Navy F-18 Hornets are catapulted off the USS Carl Vinson during flight operations 25 October 2001 against targets in Afghanistan. Civilian casualties caused by airstrikes have been a deep source of tension between the U.S. and Afghan governments. Jim Hollander/Reuters.

Afghan President Hamid Karzai arrives at the Presidential Palace in Kabul, Afghanistan on 19 November 2009 to be sworn in after his re-election for a second term as president. Shah Marai/AFP/Getty Images/newscom.

sion in Afghanistan would fail. It was in this context that Obama announced in December 2009 that he had ordered 30,000 more U.S. troops to be deployed in Afghanistan within the next few months.

In late January 2010, just eleven days after the "Day of Terror" attacks in Kabul, a one-day summit on Afghanistan involving high-ranking diplomats was held in London. The participants released a statement at the end of their meeting indicating that Afghanistan might be ready to take control of security in some of its provinces by the end of 2010, and in all of its provinces within five years. The statement also touted a "refreshed" counterinsurgency effort and noted pledges from world leaders of $140 million devoted to counterinsurgency efforts. Adding to the upbeat tone, General McChrystal, speaking at a meeting of

NATO defense ministers in Turkey in early February 2010, said that security in Afghanistan, while still a concern, was improving rather than deteriorating.

The Surge Begins

The U.S. troop surge began to make itself felt in February 2010, when allied troops in Afghanistan launched Operation Moshtarak, a major offensive against Taliban strongholds in the Helmand province, particularly in the area around Marja. The offensive involved 15,000 U.S., British, and Afghan troops and was the largest joint military operation since the war began in 2001.

After a rocky start in which a dozen civilians were killed by an off-target rocket, Operation Moshtarak drove the Taliban out of the area and

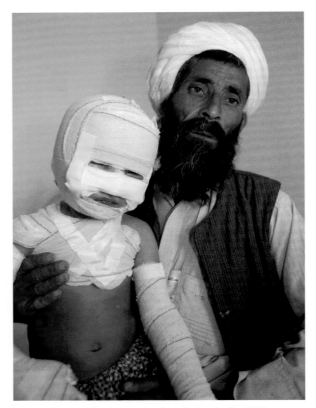

A young victim of an improvised explosive device (IED) recovers in the pediatric ward of a hospital in Kabul. The Taliban frequently targets civilians in a campaign of intimidation. Zuma Press/newscom.

was deemed a military success. However, a report issued a month later by the International Council on Security and Development (ICOS), an international policy think tank, questioned whether the United States and its allies had achieved all of their stated objectives. The aim of Operation Moshtarak had been not only to defeat the Taliban but also to win over the local people. A survey conducted by ICOS among Afghans living in Marja and other areas affected by the military operation found increased levels of hostility toward NATO. The opinions of 61 percent of those interviewed were more negative toward NATO after Operation Moshtarak than before. The interviewees were particularly angry at civilian casualties and night raids. Seven out of ten local people wanted the NATO forces to leave.

A big problem was the lack of adequate aid for civilians displaced during the operation. Thousands of people were forced to flee to refugee camps, which were soon overwhelmed by the new arrivals. Food and medical supplies were inadequate. In many cases there were no camps available and people displaced by the fighting had nowhere to go.

Most of the people interviewed by ICOS believed that the Taliban would soon return to the area. The ICOS report claimed that such negative feelings among the local population would only lead to further recruitment by the Taliban. A renewal of violence in Marja from March to June 2010, in which sniper fire and bomb explosions were daily occurrences, seemed to confirm the conclusions of the ICOS report. This was how C. J. Chivers, in a *New York Times* article in June, described the situation:

> Each day, American foot patrols move through farmers' fields and irrigated villages. And each day some are ambushed or encounter hidden

A U.S. Army soldier chats with Afghan children during a patrol in the village of Maruf-Kariz in Dand district, south of Kandahar, 19 June 2010. One of the main obstacles of the conflict in Afghanistan is winning the "heart and minds" of the Afghan people. Denis Sinyakov/Reuters.

bombs. The patrols turn into gunfights in withering heat, or efforts to dismantle the bombs or treat the wounded. Casualties accumulate with the passing weeks, for Americans and Afghans alike.

> Chivers, C. J., "What Marja Tells Us of Battles Yet to Come," *New York Times*, 2010, http://www.nytimes.com/2010/06/11/world middleeast/11marja.html?_r=2

Keeping the Coalition Together

While the U.S.-led coalition was trying to absorb the lessons of how to win the "hearts and minds" of the Afghan people, it also faced the ongoing challenge of maintaining the broad international coalition fighting the Taliban.

Coalition forces were delivered a blow in February 2010 when the Dutch government announced that it would withdraw its 2,000 troops from Afghanistan. Dutch troops departed at the end of July, ending their four-year mission, during which twenty-four of them had been killed. Although the Dutch withdrawal made little difference to the military situation, it was a concern for U.S. and NATO leaders who were aware that, partly because of rising casualties, the war was becoming unpopular in Europe. In Germany in particular, public opposition to the war was growing. A survey in April showed that two-thirds of Germans were against participation in the war. Germany had supplied more than 4,000 troops to the coalition, the third-largest commitment after the United States (90,000 troops) and the United Kingdom (9,500 troops). However, despite public protests, German Chancellor Angela Merkel told legislators in April that Germany would not withdraw its forces from Afghanistan. "We cannot expect our soldiers to be brave if we lack the courage to do what we decided," Merkel said in a speech to the German Parliament. She said that the German aim was to participate in training the Afghan army and police force until they were able to ensure the stability of their own country.

Other European countries that have supplied troops to the coalition include France (3,750),

Taliban insurgents pose in front of a burning German military vehicle in Isaa Khail village of Char Dara district of the northern Kunduz Province, 3 April 2010. A survey conducted in April 2010 showed that two-thirds of Germans were against participation in the war. Reuters.

Troops in Afghanistan
AS OF MARCH 5, 2010

United States	50,590
United Kingdom	9,500
Germany	4,335
France	3,750
Italy	3,160
Canada	2,830
Poland	2,140
Netherlands	1,880
Turkey	1,835
Australia	1,550
Spain	1,075
33 other nations	6,835
Total	**89,480**

SOURCE: NATO-ISAF

Many nations have provided troops for the NATO-led force in Afghanistan. Illustration/XNR Productions/Cengage Learning, Gale.

Italy (3,300), Poland (2,417), Turkey (1,790), Romania (1,648), and Spain (1,537). Australia, Canada, and thirty-seven other countries have also supplied troops to the coalition. In mid-October 2010 there were more than 130,000 troops under U.S. and NATO command in Afghanistan. Canada is expected to withdraw its forces in 2011, and Poland in 2012. U.S. fears that the Dutch withdrawal might open the floodgates to more European countries pulling out proved to be unfounded, but the Europeans remained reluctant to respond to persuasion by President Obama to increase their troop commitments to the war.

Corruption at All Levels of Society and Government

In late March 2010 President Obama made a surprise trip to Afghanistan to visit with troops before a planned offensive against Kandahar, a Taliban stronghold. (The offensive was later de-layed.) He also wanted to press President Karzai in person to root out corruption in his administration. With most Afghans skeptical of the power and legitimacy of the Karzai administration, the United States saw bolstering the Afghan government as a key factor in its efforts to stabilize the country. The visit came amid rising tension between Karzai and the Obama administration. The White House had cancelled a planned visit by Karzai to Washington in February 2010, reportedly because of insufficient progress against government corruption.

The problem of corruption runs deep in Afghanistan at every level of society. The country ranked 179th out of 180 on Transparency International's 2009 list of the world's most corrupt countries. Only Somalia was ranked lower. Rampant corruption has weakened the Karzai government and hampered U.S. efforts to stabilize the country. In August 2010, Senator John Kerry (D-Mass), chairman of the Senate Foreign Relations Committee, said, "Almost every analysis underscores the fact that the biggest single recruitment tool for the Taliban and the biggest single factor undermining [Afghan] government support is corruption." On a visit that month to Kabul, Kerry raised the subject with President Karzai, who had admitted in his presidential inaugural speech in November 2009 that corruption was destroying his country. In that speech, Karzai promised that the Afghan government was "committed to end the culture of impunity and violation of law and bring to justice those involved in spreading corruption and abuse of public property. Therefore, alongside an intensified judicial reform, all government anti-corruption efforts and agencies have to be strengthened and supported."

Several reports issued in 2010 brought attention to the endemic corruption in Afghanistan. One of these reports was by the United Nations Office on Drugs and Crime (UNODC), which from August to October 2009 conducted a survey in twelve towns and more than 1600 villages

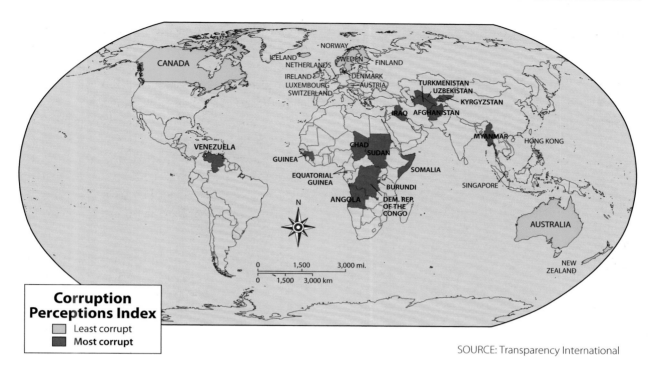

Least and most corrupt countries in the world according to the Transparency International Corruption Perceptions Index 2010. Illustration/XNR Productions/Cengage Learning, Gale.

in Afghanistan. In all, 7,600 people were interviewed.

The report produced a startling set of statistics that revealed the extent of the problem. "It is almost impossible to obtain a public service in Afghanistan without greasing a palm: bribing authorities is part of everyday life," the report stated. In 2009, according to UNODC, one Afghan citizen out of two had to pay at least one kickback to a public official. The average was about five kickbacks, and the average amount paid was $160, in a country where Gross Domestic Product (GDP) per capita is only $425 per year. The total amount paid in bribes amounted to $2.5 billion, which is the equivalent of 23 percent of the nation's GDP. The sectors most liable to bribery were police, the courts, and customs.

In an interview, one survey respondent explained how the system works:

There are people known as Employed on Com-

mission in front of each government building . . . They approach people saying that they can solve any kind of issue in a short time and then they quote the price. For example, if you need a passport or the driving license or paying taxes and custom duties they can give you the final receipt which has been processed through all official channels in matter of days which takes usually weeks. Then he takes money and of course he will distribute it with those who are sitting inside offices.

United Nations Office on Drugs and Crime, "Corruption in Afghanistan: Bribery as Reported by the Victims," September 2010, http://www.scribd.com/doc/25456453/Corruption-in-Afghanistan-Unodc.

The UNODC survey found that for ordinary Afghans, the "public dishonesty" they experienced on a daily basis was a larger concern than poverty, unemployment, or violence. Fifty-nine percent of respondents named corruption as the biggest

Afghan school girls receive treatment at a hospital in Kabul, Afghanistan 28 August 2010, after a suspected gas poisoning attack on their school in the east of Kabul. Omar Sobhani/Reuters.

problem facing the country. Eighty percent of rural Afghans said that corruption had risen over the last five years.

As Antonio Maria Costa, former executive director of UNODC, wrote in a preface to the study, "Bribery not only robs the poor and causes misallocation of resources, it destroys trust in government. When people, who earn less than $2 a day, have to bribe their way into basic services, they lose confidence in the system and look for alternative providers of security and welfare."

The statistics underline Costa's point. Sixty-five percent of respondents said they had lost trust in public services. However, many also said that it was acceptable for civil servants to ask for gifts

or money to speed up administrative procedures. The large majority of people surveyed said they never reported the corruption they experienced, and in many places, especially in the south, such issues were never raised for public discussion.

Matthew Rodieck, an American aid worker in Afghanistan who was responsible for developing the management of health care resources, saw at first hand the effects of corruption on people's health. In an October 2010 *New York Times* article, he wrote, "Corrupted decision-making processes, whether through intentional subversion of a more appropriate option or, more commonly, through the desire to influence an outcome for a tribe, family, clan, party, sect, or for monetary gain, keeps the health status of Afghans one of the lowest in the world. For Afghan women and children, corruption is particularly deadly." Rodieck used the example of the distribution of vaccines in far-flung communities to emphasize his point: "At several points along the way priorities on managing the vaccine are subverted by people demanding money for cooperation, pressuring for their own ancestral village to be seen first, or ensuring that the limited supplies be reserved for those who are prepared to pay a higher price."

Afghan women wearing the traditional burqa wait in a queue to cast their ballot outside a polling station in Kabul on 9 October 2004. Afghans elected Hamid Karzai as the country's first popularly elected president. He was re-elected, with some controversy, in 2009. Desmond Boylan/Reuters.

Corruption is also endemic at the military level in Afghanistan, and this has presented a major problem for the United States. An important U.S. goal is the training and build-up of the Afghan National Army so it can take responsibility for the country's defense, but this has been held back by Afghan inefficiency and corruption. American military trainers report that theft of fuel, weapons, and other military equipment is common. In an article in *Stars and Stripes* by Diana Cahn, Capt. Jason Douthwaite, a logistics officer with the 73rd Troop Command of the Ohio National Guard, reported that he spent much of this time trying to stop the Afghan soldiers he was training from stealing. "I feel like I am an investigating officer," he said. "It's not, 'Let me teach you your job.' It's more like, 'How much did you steal from the American government today?'" When Douthwaite tried to stop the theft of fuel, he was threatened. Another U.S. trainer, commenting on the troops he was in charge of training, said, "Everyone has their hand in the cookie jar." Afghan military units are often reportedly so poor at keeping track of who is on leave or injured that U.S. personnel spend much of their time checking that rosters are accurate. A common practice is for absent soldiers to be listed as present so that Afghan commanders can collect and pocket the wages of these "ghost" warriors.

If U.S. trainers have been frustrated with corruption in the Afghan Army, U.S. policymakers were impatient throughout 2010 with the slow pace at which President Karzai was moving on his promise to fight government corruption. The corruption directly undermined efforts of the U.S. and NATO coalition to rebuild the country. For example, billions of dollars in funds earmarked for reconstruction have been siphoned off to local warlords or have found their way to the Taliban. Misuse of funds weakens the central government, which loses whatever little trust the Afghan people still have in it. "It is a government similar to a corporation, where people are after making themselves rich," said Waheed Mozhdah, an Afghan political analyst, quoted by Sayed Salahuddin in his Reuters article "Analysis: Why Can't Afghanistan Tackle Corruption?"

One of the biggest problems is that President Karzai's political power base is weak, and he is aware that a rigorous attack on corruption will root out some of his own allies. Therefore, many analysts theorize that it is in Karzai's best political interest to turn a blind eye to some of the more egregious abuses of power. This became readily apparent in the wake of the presidential contest of November 2009, which was tainted by massive voter fraud. To remain in power, Karzai had to reward those who had made his victory possible. The issue was underlined in January 2010, when the Afghan Parliament rejected seventeen of twenty-four nominees from Karzai's list of cabinet appointments. Lawmakers objected to Karzai's list, arguing that many of the nominees had been selected not because they were suitable for the positions but because of bribery or for other illegitimate reasons.

Another major conflict over government corruption blew up in the summer of 2010. The previous year, the Afghan government, with U.S. and British support, had set up two task forces to fight corruption, the Major Crimes Task Force and the Special Investigative Unit. One of the first cases was that of Mohammad Salehi, head of administration for the Afghan National Security Council, who was arrested in July for soliciting bribes, accused of accepting a car in exchange for trying to get a suspect in another corruption case released. Karzai personally intervened in the release of Salehi, a Karzai ally. Following this incident, Karzai attempted to take control of the two task forces, saying that some of their activities violated the Afghan constitution and the civil rights of many of the officials who had been accused of corruption. Senior U.S. officials reacted negatively to Karzai's statement, which they believed would undermine anti-corruption efforts that were vital to the coalition's goals. The issue was taken up with President Karzai by Senator Kerry during his visit to Kabul in August 2010, and it appeared that Karzai may have made some concessions as a result of American pressure. "President Karzai reiterated that it was a key national security interest of Afghanistan to address corruption and its underlying causes comprehensively and across the board," Kerry said in a statement quoted in *The Washington Post*. "The president and I agreed that the work of these entities must be allowed to continue free from outside interference or political influence, including with respect to ongoing cases." (The case of Salehi was complicated in late August when *The New York Times* reported that, according to Afghan and U.S. government officials, Salehi had for years been on the payroll of the United States

An Afghan police officer eradicates poppy crops during an operation against the opium crop in Sanzeri village near Kandahar, Afghanistan on 10 April 2005. Money from the drug trade helps fund the Taliban insurgency and is also a factor in government corruption. AP Images/Noor Khan.

Central Intelligence Agency, although what he did for the agency was not known.)

The Opium Trade and Drug Addiction

A major contributor to corruption in Afghanistan is the illegal but highly lucrative opium trade. Afghanistan is the world's largest producer of opium, the main ingredient in heroin, and growing opium poppies is one of the country's main forms of agriculture. Money from the drug trade helps fund the Taliban insurgency and is also a factor in government corruption. In the Afghan police force, for example, senior jobs often go to the highest bidder, and those who secure such jobs using money from the opium trade then add to their illegal income by facilitating the shipment of the drug across the country. For several years, Presi-

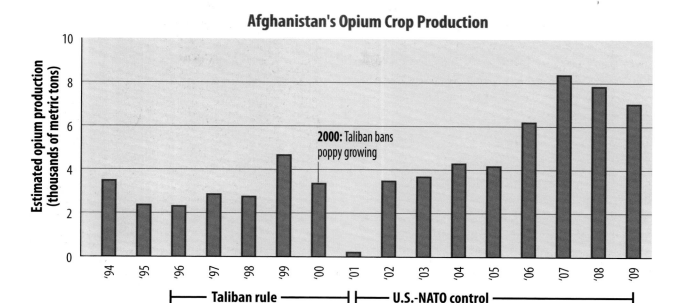

Afghanistan's Opium Crop Production

Estimated opium production of Afghanistan from 1994 to 2009. The drug heroin is made from opium derived from poppy plants. Illustration/XNR Productions/Cengage Learning, Gale.

dent Karzai's younger half-brother, Ahmed Wali Karzai, has been dogged by accusations of drug trafficking, and U.S. officials believe there is some substance in the allegations. Ahmed Wali Karzai is the head of the provincial council of Kandahar Province, the ruling body of the province containing Afghanistan's second-largest city. President Karzai, however, has so far resisted U.S. pressure to move his brother out of this powerful position.

The cultivation of opium poppies has a long history in Afghanistan, but it was not until 1979, when the Soviet Union invaded, that opium poppies became the nation's primary economic support. In the ten years of war that followed the Soviet invasion, Afghanistan's economy virtually collapsed, forcing much of the nation's population to rely on black market activities to survive. Opium provided poor farmers with a stable and comparatively lucrative crop. The opium economy, in turn, generated tax revenue for local leaders and contributed to military financing.

When the Soviet Union withdrew from Afghanistan in 1989, civil war among competing warlords continued through the mid-1990s. In those chaotic years, when Afghanistan lacked a central government, warlords, regional military commanders, and local leaders supported their operations mainly through illegal activities, and most of those activities involved opium poppies. A significant percentage of the population relied on opium poppies and the production of narcotics for their meager incomes.

In 1996, when most of Afghanistan had been taken over by the Taliban, reliance on the opium poppy was still a significant feature of the economy. But the high output of narcotics led to international complaints, and in a surprising turn, in 2000 the Taliban banned opium poppy cultivation in the parts of the country it controlled. The ban was extremely effective, reducing Afghanistan's opium production by 85 percent in 2001. For most of Afghanistan's poor farmers, however, the ban eliminated income and caused real hardship.

A heroin addict has heroin injected by a friend in Herat, Afghanistan 12 September 2010. Despite a United Nations report expected to state that opium poppy production has fallen this year, the agency says there are enough stocks to keep supplying heroin production. Raheb Homavandi/Reuters.

After the U.S.-led invasion toppled the Taliban in 2001, the interim government banned the cultivation of opium poppies, and farmers were offered compensation for getting rid of their poppy fields. But the program was ineffective; from 2002 to 2003 opium production soared. In 2006, UNODC reported that Afghanistan's production of raw opium had increased by 49 percent in just one year. It continued to rise to record levels in 2007. In that year, according to UNODC, Afghanistan produced 93 percent of the world's supply of opium, nearly 9,000 tons. Cultivating poppies, producing opium from them, and trafficking the drug provided employment for millions of Afghans and brought about $4 billion into the impoverished nation—about half of its overall gross domestic product. A significant portion of the proceeds of the opium business were gathered by the resurgent Taliban and used in its fight against NATO forces.

Over time, however, eradication policies did produce some success. By 2008, the Afghan Ministry of Counter Narcotics (MCN) announced that about twenty provinces in the north, east, and northeast parts of Afghanistan were free of poppy cultivation, while in 2007, only sixteen provinces had been poppy-free. (Afghanistan has thirty-four provinces in all.) Still, the areas that continued to grow poppies had expanded production and were able to produce as much as the entire country had produced in prior years.

Much of the heroin made from these poppies was purchased in Europe, but in recent years Pakistan and Afghanistan themselves have experienced a rise in drug addiction, and provide a new market for the homegrown heroin. In June 2010 UNODC announced that the use of opiates, such

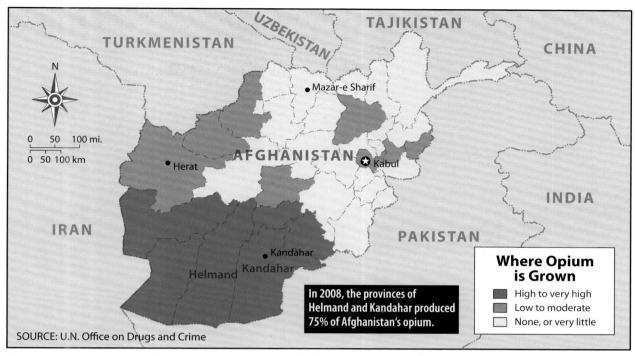

Major opium growing areas located in Afghanistan. Illustration/XNR Productions/Cengage Learning, Gale.

as opium and heroin, in Afghanistan had nearly doubled over the previous five years. The number of regular opium users increased from 150,000 in 2005 to 230,000 in 2010, while the number of heroin users jumped from 50,000 to 120,000. Nearly 3 percent of Afghans aged fifteen to sixty-four were addicted to opiates. Many children as young as four or five were addicted. Drug addiction is also a problem for recruitment for the Afghan security forces. According to a U.S. report, up to 41 percent of police recruits tested positive for drugs during their training. "After three decades of war-related trauma, unlimited availability of cheap narcotics and limited access to treatment have created a major, and growing, addiction problem in Afghanistan," said former UNODC executive director Antonio Maria Costa.

Few treatment options are available for drug addicts. The Associated Press reported on the work treatment centers in Afghanistan. One woman being treated said she had started using opium before 2001, when the Taliban ruled the country. Shirin Gul, an Afghan woman interviewed by the Associated Press, said, "I lost my brothers during the fighting and life was miserable. My brother-in-law used opium. He saw me crying and suggested I try it." Two years later she started taking heroin and became addicted to it.

Despite the extent of the drug problem, there are many critics of the eradication programs sponsored by NATO, the United States, and the United Kingdom. Critics contend that eradication programs take away the livelihoods of Afghan farmers and leave them financially desperate and with few options. President Karzai, however, strongly supported the eradication programs; the opium trade, which enriches drug traffickers and insurgents, undermines the effectiveness of the central government and threatens the long-term security and development of the country. Recognizing the economic distress that can follow eradication programs, the United States has offered incentives to farmers who stop growing opium poppies. For example, following Operation Moshtarak, the military offensive in and around Marja in February

2010, the United States promised farmers aid if they grew crops other than opium poppies. This is considered a better strategy than simply giving cash as a reward for eradicating opium, because one-time payments do not create sustainable alternatives to poppy cultivation.

In 2010, there was a sharp drop in opium production in Afghanistan, according to a September report by UNODC. Total production was estimated at 3,600 metric tons, down 48 percent from 2009. However, this presented only small cause for optimism, since the decrease was mostly due to a plant disease affecting the major poppy-growing provinces of Helmand and Kandahar. Also, the fall in production led to higher prices, thus encouraging farmers to continue to cultivate opium. The level of poppy cultivation (as opposed to opium production) remained stable in 2010, concentrated in the south and west of the country, predominantly in areas not controlled by the central government. "These regions are dominated by insurgency and organized crime networks," said Yury Fedotov, executive director of UNODC in 2010. "This underscores the link between opium poppy cultivation and insecurity in Afghanistan, a trend we have observed since 2007."

The report also noted that in 2010, eradication was at the lowest level it had been since the monitoring system began in 2005. To combat the problem of opium production, Fedotov called for the strengthening of the rule of law, the continuation of anti-corruption efforts, and greater regional cooperation, although he emphasized that the first priority must be to reduce demand:

> We must not forget the consumer side of opium's deadly equation. Unless we reduce the demand for opium and heroin, our interventions against supply will not be effective. As long as demand drives this market, there will always be another farmer to replace one we convince to stop cultivating, and another trafficker to replace one we catch.

> We need a broader strategy to support farm-

Afghan Civilian Casualties
JANUARY–JUNE 2010

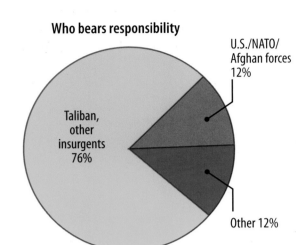

Who bears responsibility

Taliban, other insurgents 76%

U.S./NATO/ Afghan forces 12%

Other 12%

Casualties among children

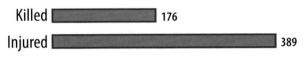

Killed 176

Injured 389

SOURCE: United Nations

Casualties among Afghan civilians during the first six months of 2010. Illustration/XNR Productions/Cengage Learning, Gale.

ers throughout Afghanistan by providing them with access to markets and a secure environment. Stability and security, combined with sustainable alternative development opportunities, will give farmers the chance to make a living without resorting to opium poppy cultivation.

"Sharp Drop in Afghan Opium Production, Says UNODC," United Nations Office on Drugs and Crime, Press Release, September 2010, http://www.unodc.org/unodc/en/press/releases/ 2010/September/sharp-drop-in-afghan-opium -production-says-unodc.html.

Change of Command and WikiLeaks

As the military operations and efforts to fight corruption continued, there was a dramatic change in personnel at the top of the U.S. army command. On the afternoon of 23 June

2010, President Obama relieved General Stanley McChrystal of his command in Afghanistan. McChrystal had been summoned to the White House to explain a *Rolling Stone* magazine article that reported disparaging and disrespectful remarks made by McChrystal and his aides about high-ranking civilian leaders in Afghanistan and in the United States, and even about Obama himself. McChrystal was replaced by General David Petraeus, a counterinsurgency expert and head of the U.S. military's Central Command. McChrystal had held his position for only one year. President Karzai publicly defended McChrystal ahead of the general's meeting with Obama, stressing that he had been a good partner.

Petraeus was confirmed in his new position by the Senate on 30 June 2010. The general had warned, during his Senate hearings, that violence in Afghanistan would intensify in the short term. Petraeus's warning was borne out on the day of his confirmation when the Taliban launched a commando-style attack on a NATO base near Jalalabad. One Afghan soldier and one NATO soldier were wounded and several Taliban attackers were killed. The perimeter of the base, however, was not breached.

In late July, the public's growing concern that the war in Afghanistan had been and continued to be mismanaged received support when more than 90,000 classified military intelligence documents pertaining to the war were published by a website called WikiLeaks. The documents themselves contain a wide range of information, some of it alarming and some of little interest. Most serious were the details of cases of civilian casualties in the war and implications that Pakistan's intelligence agency was collaborating with the Taliban. More shocking than the contents of the documents themselves, however, was the fact that so much sensitive information could find its way onto the Internet. U.S. Defense Department investigators said that a twenty-two-year-old U.S. soldier named Bradley Manning, who worked

In this 26 July 2010 screenshot of the website WikiLeaks captured in Kaufbeuren, Germany, classified secret U.S. documents about the Afghan War are published. An estimated 92,000 U.S. military records were leaked about the war that included unreported Afghan civilian deaths and secret forces to hunt down Taliban leaders. Karl-Josef Hildenbrand/Landov.

in a military intelligence office in Baghdad, Iraq, was the likely source of the leak. Manning was charged earlier in July 2010 with illegally giving WikiLeaks classified video footage of an army helicopter firing on a group of people on the ground in Baghdad.

Possibly with the damaging information from WikiLeaks in mind, Petraeus issued orders on 4 August 2010 stressing the importance of limiting civilian casualties in the Afghan War, asserting that "every Afghan civilian death diminishes our cause." Some military leaders had faulted McChrystal for emphasizing civilian protection at the expense of the safety of NATO soldiers. Petraeus's orders made it clear that troops have a right to defend themselves, but laid out details for limiting the casualties that arise from cultural misunderstanding. For example, all NATO patrols and operations now had to include involvement of Afghan military units.

By the beginning of September 2010, the final U.S. troops deployed in the surge arrived in Afghanistan, bringing the number of American troops in the country to nearly 100,000, the highest since the war began in 2001. American military leaders suggested that troop levels would

United States Support for the Afghan War

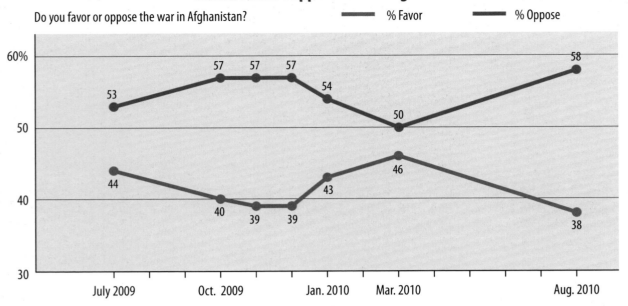

Do you favor or oppose the war in Afghanistan?   ■■■ % Favor   ■■■ % Oppose

SOURCES: Associated Press, GFK Roper Public Affairs and Corporate Communications

In 2010, more than half of all Americans reported that they opposed the war in Afghanistan. Illustration/XNR Productions/Cengage Learning, Gale.

remain high for at least another year.

However, while military leaders were gearing up for another push against the Taliban, public support for the war was declining in the United States. In mid-September, a *New York Times/CBS* opinion poll showed that only 38 percent of Americans believed the United States was "doing the right thing by fighting the war in Afghanistan now," and 54 percent said the U.S. should "not be involved in Afghanistan now." The poll's findings were in line with an *Associated Press-GfK* poll published the previous month, in which 58 percent of respondents said they opposed the war, while only 38 percent approved of the expansion of the war, an 8 percent decline since March 2010. Only 19 percent expected the situation to improve over the next year, and 29 percent thought it would get worse. However, a third opinion poll, released in September 2010 by the Chicago Council on

Global Affairs, showed a different result. A majority of the 2,500 adults surveyed said that eliminating the threat to the United States from terrorists based in Afghanistan was a goal worth committing troops to, and fully three quarters of those surveyed believed that the United States should maintain its military presence for at least two years, or even longer, to "build a stable and secure state." According to the survey, Americans also supported pursuing and killing terrorists in Pakistan, with or without permission from the Pakistani government.

The expansion of the war into Pakistan was a topic discussed by investigative journalist Bob Woodward in his book *Obama's Wars*, published in September 2010. Woodward reported that not only had U.S. forces pursued militants into Pakistani territory, but that there was a three-thousand-person CIA "army" devoted to target-

Residents on horse-led carts hurry past burning NATO fuel tankers along a road near Nowshera, located in Pakistan's Khyber-Pakhtunkhwa Province, 7 October 2010. Pakistan is under U.S. pressure to crack down harder on militants in the country. Adrees Latif/Reuters.

ing al-Qaeda and Taliban operatives throughout the Afghanistan-Pakistan border region. This paramilitary group, wrote Woodward, conducted covert missions inside Pakistan. Woodward also reported that President Obama described Pakistan as a "cancer" and that the U.S. operation in Afghanistan was designed to keep the threat posed by Pakistan from spreading.

In late September 2010, already-tense relations between Pakistan and the United States were strained even further after a NATO air strike in Pakistan reportedly killed three Pakistani soldiers. NATO confirmed that it had crossed into Pakistani territory and fired on what it believed to be armed militants. After the air strike, Pakistan blocked supply trucks from bringing supplies to NATO forces in Afghanistan. The United States apologized, and the border with Afghanistan was reopened to NATO traffic a week later. In the meantime, Taliban militants had destroyed approximately 100 NATO supply trucks.

Ethnic Tensions

A year after Karzai's controversial election victory, Afghanistan's ability to hold fair, legitimate elections was again called into question. Afghanistan's September 2010 parliamentary elections were marred by accusations of fraud. In October,

Afghan election authorities voided 1.3 million of 5.6 million votes and announced the investigation of more than 220 candidates who were suspected of possible fraud. The election drew attention to the difficulty of establishing a stable, democratic government in Afghanistan that could not only provide security for its citizens but also ensure that all the different ethnic groups and tribes in the country were adequately represented.

Afghanistan is a patchwork of distinct ethnic, linguistic, and tribal groups. The four largest are Pashtun (42 percent of the population), Tajik (27 percent), Hazara (9 percent) and Uzbek (9 percent). The Pashtuns are further divided into at least seven tribes, the Durrani, Ghilzai, Jaji, Mangal, Safi, Mamund, and Mohmand. In Af-

Different ethnic groups in Afghanistan. Illustration/XNR Productions/Cengage Learning, Gale.

Afghan President Hamid Karzai, left, prays at a meeting with tribal leaders in Kandahar city, Afghanistan, 13 June 2010. Although the Karzai administration has in many respects attempted to make itself representative of Afghanistan's ethnic mix, observers point to an ethnic imbalance in the nation's army and police that may well spell trouble for the future. AP Images/Massoud Hossaini.

ghan history, the various ethnic groups have often been at odds with each other. In the 1990s, for example, the civil war in Afghanistan pitted Pashtuns against an ethnic coalition known as the Northern Alliance, which was led by Tajiks and supported by the United States. The Taliban are mostly Pashtun, as is President Karzai. Although the Karzai administration has in many respects attempted to represent Afghanistan's ethnic mix, observers point to an ethnic imbalance in the nation's army and police that may well spell trouble for the future. As of 2010, the Afghan National Army (ANA) is dominated by Tajiks.

When the ANA was first established in 2002, it was ethnically balanced between the four major groups. However, that changed over the years, and by late 2009, Tajiks accounted for 41 percent of ANA troops, and Pashtuns, the majority ethnic group in the country, accounted for only 30 percent. Moreover, 70 percent of all battalions were commanded by Tajiks. Even in provinces dominated numerically by Pashtuns in the south and east, Pashtuns were seriously underrepresented in the ANA, largely because they perceived the ANA as dominated by the Tajiks. Tajiks speak the Dari language, whereas Pashtuns speak Pashto; the more the ANA became an increasingly Dari-speaking institution, the more the Pashtuns shunned and resented it. For their part, ANA commanders were suspicious of recruiting from Pashtuns in the southern and eastern provinces because of concerns that men from these areas were likely to have been under Taliban influence.

Some Western observers say the problem is so severe that unless something is done to restore balance in the Afghan armed forces, another civil war may be imminent. Needless to say, such an event would vastly complicate U.S. attempts to create stability in the country.

Analysts also fear that President Karzai's efforts in 2010 to reach out to the largely Pashtun Taliban and include them in the political process may reignite ethnic conflict. Talks to end the war in Afghanistan took place in October 2010 between senior members of the Karzai government and Taliban commanders who left their sanctuaries in Pakistan and traveled to Kabul under NATO protection. This development caused some anxiety among other ethnic groups who feared they would be excluded from power as Karzai attempted to reach a rapprochement with the Taliban and solidify his support among Pashtuns.

The Kandahar Offensive

While talks between Karzai and the Taliban were being planned, U.S. strategy was to continue to weaken the Taliban militarily so they would be more willing to accept a political solution to the conflict. To this end, in August 2010 American and Afghan forces began their much-delayed offensive to drive the Taliban out of their base in Kandahar Province. The offensive involved 12,000 U.S. and NATO troops as well as 7,000 troops from the Afghan security forces.

The campaign continued into October, but there were conflicting reports in the American press about its success. *The New York Times* reported a rout by coalition forces. In this version, most of the Taliban had been forced out of their traditional stronghold, many had retreated into Pakistan, and Taliban supply lines were badly damaged, limiting their ability to launch counterstrikes. Although it was uncertain whether the success of the Kandahar offensive coalition would mark a permanent turning point in the war, U.S. and NATO commanders were confident that the Taliban had been seriously weakened and would not be returning in great numbers to the area in

Two U.S. soldiers assist a wounded comrade after his vehicle struck an IED (improvised explosive device) on a road near Combat Outpost Nolen in the Arghandab Valley of Afghanistan, 23 July 2010. Bob Strong/Reuters.

the near future. The *New York Times* article quoted a U.S. commander, Lt. Col. Rodger Lemons, who believed that the Taliban were losing the stomach for a fight. "'A lot are getting killed,' he said. 'They are not receiving support from the local population, they are complaining that the local people are not burying their dead, and they are saying: 'We are losing so many we want to go back home.'"

However, just one week later, on 27 October 2010, *The Washington Post* reported almost the exact opposite about the same campaign. According to journalist Greg Miller, "An intense military campaign aimed at crippling the Taliban has so far failed to inflict more than fleeting setbacks on the insurgency or put meaningful pressure on its leaders to seek peace." Miller quoted U.S. military officials saying that the Taliban had shown great

Aid to Afghanistan

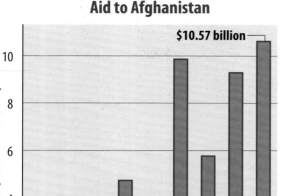

$10.57 billion

U.S. aid (billions of dollars) — Fiscal year '02 '03 '04 '05 '06 '07 '08 '09 '10

SOURCE: Congressional Research Service

U.S. aid to Afghanistan from 2002 to 2010, in billions of U.S. dollars. Illustration/XNR Productions/Cengage Learning, Gale.

resiliency in recovering from battlefield reverses and replacing commanders who had been killed or captured. The insurgents were able to melt away from the area when under pressure from the coalition and wait for an opportunity to return. According to these reports, the Taliban were confident of waiting out the coalition assault until the United States began to scale back its forces in Afghanistan in 2011.

Bringing Peace to Afghanistan

As the year 2010 drew to its close, it was unknown whether the U.S. troop surge and the offensives in Marja, Kandahar, and elsewhere had succeeded in making the Taliban more amenable to negotiating a peace settlement. U.S. war goals remained simple in outline: a stable government in Kabul that could guarantee the security of the country and deny al-Qaeda terrorists a safe haven from which to plot attacks against the United

States. However, the process of achieving that goal remained fraught with difficulty, even though the blueprint for a stable and peaceful Afghanistan had been laid out at the international conference on Afghanistan held in London in late January 2010. At that conference, attended by representatives from more than seventy countries, the Afghan government agreed to strengthen its army and police force and take control of security for the entire country within five years. The Taliban would be given incentives in the form of jobs and rural development funds to abandon their insurgency. This program would be financed by an international fund. The Afghan government also agreed to make serious peace proposals to the Taliban.

President Karzai's attempts to follow through on the promised blueprint did not meet with initial success. He organized a 1,600-delegate national peace conference (known as a peace *jirga*) in Kabul in June, but the Taliban rejected it, saying they would not consider any peace talks until all foreign troops left the country. Instead, the Taliban threatened to kill anyone who took part in the conference, and on its opening day they

Taliban Army Supreme Commander Jalauddin Haqqani is shown in this 22 August 1998 photo in Miram Shah, Waziristan, Pakistan. U.S. forces have been battling the forces of Jalaluddin and Sirajuddin Haqqani in eastern Afghanistan near Pakistan making September 2010 the most intense period of U.S. strikes since 2004. AP Images/Mohammad Riaz.

Who Is Fighting the U.S. in Afghanistan?

UZBEKISTAN

TAJIKISTAN

CHINA

Haqqani Group have expanded to Kabul and Kunar with influence across the border

AFGHANISTAN

Kunar

Kabul

North-West Frontier Province

F.A.T.A.

PAKISTAN

Islamabad

Ghazni

Hekmatyar Group of Hizb-i Islami are active in Pakistan and sometimes cooperate with the Taliban

INDIA

Afghan Taliban Mullah Omar is a leader of a network in the south and has found haven in the Quetta area

Quetta

N

0   50   100 mi.

0   50   100 km

SOURCES: ESRI, Bradford University's Pakistan Security Research Unit

This map shows the different groups fighting the U.S. and NATO forces in Afghanistan. Illustration/XNR Productions/Cengage Learning, Gale.

launched suicide attacks in Kabul near the site of the conference. Despite this setback, delegates to the *jirga* called for the release of Taliban prisoners as a goodwill gesture but also emphasized that if any Taliban wanted to participate in the peace process they would first have to renounce all connections with foreign terrorist organizations such as al-Qaeda.

The situation looked slightly more promising in October 2010, when actual talks took place between the Taliban and the Karzai government. However, these talks soon stalled because of a dispute between the other players in the peace process: Pakistan and the United States. The disagreement was over which militant groups should be included in peace negotiations. Pakistan said that the Haqqani network, whose leaders are based in North Waziristan in the Pakistani tribal areas near the Afghanistan border, should be included, but the United States disagreed because of concerns that the Haqqani are too closely linked to al-Qaeda. The Haqqani network is one of the most deadly of the militant groups in the area. It is allied to the Taliban but independent of it, and has shown itself to be capable of bold suicide attacks in Afghanistan. The network was responsible for an assassination attempt on President Karzai in April 2008, which nearly succeeded, as well as car bombings and attacks on a luxury hotel and a government building that left many dead.

The question of how to deal with the Haqqani network brought attention to the fact that the insurgent forces in Afghanistan are not under one unified command and do not speak with one voice. The Taliban itself is a confederation of ethnic Pashtuns, many of whom belong to the Ghilzai tribe. But its two factions, one based in Afghanistan and the other in Pakistan, pursue different goals and strategies. Another insurgent group, Hezb-e-Islami Gulbuddin (HIG), has been responsible for attacks on coalition forces and Afghan government targets, but is rife with internal disagreements and has also done battle with the Taliban. There were reports that the group had started its own independent talks with the Karzai government.

As President Obama prepared for a December 2010 review of his administration's Afghanistan strategy, he was confronted with a situation that was no easier than the one he faced the previous year. The year 2010 was the deadliest for U.S. forces since the conflict began in 2001. As of mid-November, 431 U.S. soldiers had been killed in 2010, up from 317 in 2009, which was the second-deadliest year. Total coalition deaths by mid-November for 2010 stood at 633, up from

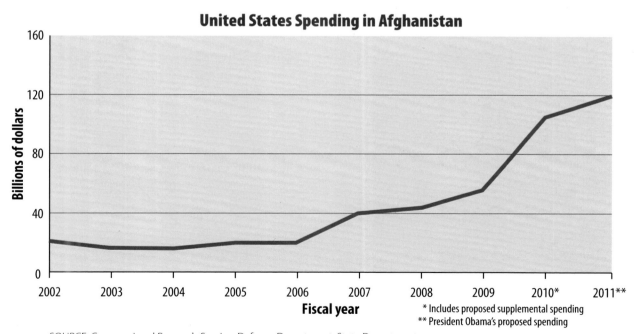

United States Spending in Afghanistan

SOURCE: Congressional Research Service, Defense Department, State Department

* Includes proposed supplemental spending
** President Obama's proposed spending

The monetary cost of the war in Afghanistan has risen substantially since 2008 as troop levels increased and fighting intensified. Illustration/XNR Productions/Cengage Learning, Gale.

521 in 2009. The war has also proved extremely costly in other ways. In fiscal year 2010, which ended on 30 September, the war in Afghanistan cost the United States $33 billion. In October, the first comprehensive audit of U.S. spending on the war revealed that the government had spent $55 billion on rebuilding in Afghanistan since the war began, but it was unable to show exactly how the money was spent. A report released by the Office of the Special Inspector General for Afghanistan Reconstruction showed that U.S. government agencies involved in Afghanistan were not properly tracking, or even recording, spending.

When Obama first announced the troop surge, he was committed to reducing the level of troops in Afghanistan beginning in July 2011. But in order to follow through on this promise, the Obama administration must demonstrate tangible progress in Afghanistan's ability to take

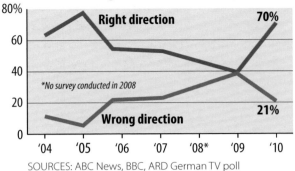

Where Do Afghans Think Things in Afghanistan Are Going?

Right direction — 70%

*No survey conducted in 2008

Wrong direction — 21%

'04 '05 '06 '07 '08* '09 '10

SOURCES: ABC News, BBC, ARD German TV poll

In 2010 a majority of Afghans felt the situation in their country was improving. Illustration/XNR Productions/Cengage Learning, Gale.

An undated photo of al-Qaeda leader Osama bin Laden, in Afghanistan. The bombings of embassies in Africa in 1998, the U.S.S. Cole in 1999, and the 11 September 2001 attacks established bin Laden and al-Qaeda as the preeminent terrorist threat to American interests. AP Images.

responsibility for its own security. In November 2010, senior figures in the administration were backing away from the 2011 deadline and citing 2014 as the year when the United States would hand over security to the Afghans. It appeared, after all, that there might be no significant reduction in U.S. forces in 2011. The administration wanted to send a message to the Taliban that the United States would continue to pursue them aggressively; so the insurgents could not simply rely on waiting things out until mid-2011 and hoping that U.S. forces would leave. This information was confirmed following a meeting during a NATO summit in Lisbon on 20 November 2010. According to an agreement reached by leaders of NATO nations at this meeting, Afghan security forces would take over control of Afghanistan's security in 2014.

Most analysts agree that a military solution to the conflict is close to impossible and that eventually a political solution must be found. But before a peace settlement can emerge, the United States insists, the Taliban must renounce violence and break all links to al-Qaeda. Some reports suggested that the Taliban might be ready to cut its ties to al-Qaeda and discuss the possibility of entering some kind of power-sharing arrangement with the Afghan government, but as 2010 drew to a close, there was little hard evidence to support this speculation. For the long-suffering people of Afghanistan, it appeared that the nine-year war would likely continue for some while yet.

Research and Exploration

"Afghanistan," *The Huffington Post,* http://www.huffingtonpost.com/news/afghanistan

This Web page contains a selection of news, photos, and opinion about Afghanistan and related issues.

"Afghanistan," *National Review Online,* http://www.nationalreview.com/news/afghanistan

This Web page contains several news articles, photographs, and opinion pieces about Afghanistan and its recent history.

"Afghanistan Country Profile," *BBC News,* 2 October 2010. http://news.bbc.co.uk/2/hi/south_asia/country_profiles/1162668.stm

This contains an overview of Afghanistan's recent history and a list of basic facts about the country.

Afghanistan Online, http://www.afghan-web.com/

This site contains a wealth of information on all aspects of Afghanistan: culture, history, politics, government, military, geography, languages, sports, travel, and many other topics.

"Afghanistan: The War Logs," *Guardian.co.uk,* http://www.guardian.co.uk/world/the-war-logs

This site contains a guide to the secret military files from Afghanistan posted online by WikiLeaks.

"Afghanistan War Videos," *PopularMilitary.com,* http://www.militarynewsnetwork.com/afghanistan-war-videos.htm

This contains videos from the frontlines of Afghanistan, featuring U.S. and allied forces, the Taliban, al Qaeda, insurgent footage, war footage, and combat footage.

"Background Note: Afghanistan," U.S. Department of State, 26 March 2010. http://www.state.gov/r/pa/ei/bgn/5380.htm

This is a detailed and authoritative account of the people, history, government, economy, education, foreign relations, and other aspects of Afghanistan.

"Country Guide: Afghanistan," *The Washington Post,* http://www.washingtonpost.com/wp-srv/world/countries/afghanistan.html

This guide to Afghanistan contains news and background notes, as well as links to photos and an interactive map.

"Gen David Petraeus Talks Strategy in Afghanistan," *Marine Corps Gazette,* http://www.mca-marines.org/gazette/gen-david-petraeus-talks-strategy-afghanistan

This contains several videos of General Petraeus discussing the war in Afghanistan.

Jones, Seth G., *In the Graveyard of Empires: America's War in Afghanistan,* New York: W. W. Norton, 2010.

Jones analyzes how the Taliban were able to make a comeback after being defeated in 2001 and how the United States can still win the war.

Loyn, David, *In Afghanistan: Two Hundred Years of British, Russian and American Occupation,* New York: Palgrave Macmillan, 2009.

Loyn brings a knowledge of history to his analysis, showing how Afghanistan has always frustrated the designs of the great powers that seek to subdue it.

Mackey, Robert, "Fighting Uphill in Afghanistan," *New York Times,* 6 October 2009. http://thelede.blogs.nytimes.com/2009/10/06/fighting-uphill-in-afghanistan/

This is a video shot in summer 2009 in Afghanistan by a British television crew near an American military base that regularly came under attack. The video shows how difficult the base is to defend.

O'Malley, Heathcliff. "Inside Afghanistan: The Sniper's Tale," *Telegraph,* 15 March 2010. http://www.telegraph.co.uk/news/worldnews/asia/afghanistan/7422208/Inside-Afghanistan-the-snipers-tale.html

This is a video of a British Army sniper in Afghanistan talking about his work in the war. There are links to other videos in a *Telegraph* series that looks at what life is like for the British Army in Afghanistan.

Chilean Miners' Rescue

A Dangerous Business

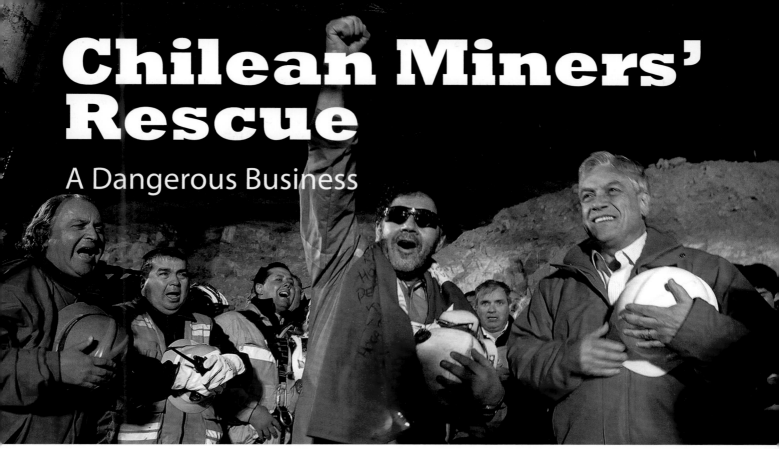

Mining is a dangerous business. During 2010, the mining industry suffered an all-too-common series of disasters. Lethal mine explosions in the United States, China, and New Zealand briefly became the focus of media attention until, in each case, the seemingly inevitable and tragic fate of miners lost was officially confirmed.

For seventeen days following the 5 August 2010 cave-in at the San José copper-gold mine located north of Copiapó, Chile, it appeared that the fate of thirty-three miners missing underground would end in similar catastrophe. There was no sign of life and only hope and dedication drove their colleagues to continue a search that many increasingly thought doomed to find only silence underground. On the seventeenth day, however, a note attached to a drill bit brought news that the men were still alive. During the following weeks and months, both rescuers and miners showed daring, courage, perseverance, and ingenuity. The dangerous and technologically complex rescue efforts mesmerized the world.

The ordeal of miners trapped deep in the bowels of the Earth—eventually televised to the world—unfolded as three dramatic rescue attempts were made.

After the note attached to the drill bit confirmed the miners were alive, Chilean officials and mine safety experts cautioned that it might take up to four months to rescue the workers. In what was subsequently described as an engineering feat to rival the accomplishments of manned space flight, teams of engineers, equipment manufacturers, drillers, and other personnel took only about half the time initially anticipated to accomplish their mission.

Seventeen days after the collapse, Chilean president Sebastian Piñera holds up a note from the miners, confirming they are still alive. Hector Retamal/AP Images.

The Rescue Effort

Organized by André Sougarret, the leader of the Chilean state-owned copper corporation CODELCO's El Teniente Mine, rescuers first attempted a detour around the massive cave-in through alternative passageways. However, each time an attempt was made, the workers found the path either blocked or unstable. One attempt was made through a ventilation shaft. However, while trying to gain entrance with the use of heavy mining equipment, another collapse occurred. Because of concerns about geologic instability in the area, further attempts to reach the miners via these means were halted. Instead, three independent drilling plans evolved, designated as Plan A, Plan B, and Plan C.

Plan A

Plan A used an Australian-built Strata 950 raise-borer drilling rig provided by South African mining company Murray & Roberts. It was the first attempt to bore a hole into the ground to rescue the trapped miners.

The raise-boring technique used by the Plan A team is known as up-reaming. In this technique, a small pilot hole is drilled while large cutting devices are attached to the drill, protruding from the bottom of the pilot hole. The cutters are used to widen the hole from the bottom up. However, this cutting action proved ineffective as the pilot hole was continually blocked or clogged with rock. Instead, the technique was modified so the hole was widened from the top down. The pilot hole was never completed by the Plan A team.

Plan C

The Plan C team used a Canadian-built RIG-421 oil-drilling rig operated by the Calgary-based Precision Drilling Corporation. The rig contained

Bundled up with blankets, relatives anxiously await news of the trapped miners on 6 August 2010, the day following the collapse. Luis Hidalgo/AP Images.

a special drill normally used for oil and gas drilling. Unlike the Plan A drill process, this technique could drill an escape shaft without first drilling a pilot hole. However, it ran into difficulties when the drill was aimed toward the small target nearly half a mile away due to the extremely hard rock. The drill was repeatedly redirected after veering off course.

Plan B: An International Success Story

The teams of Plan A and Plan C used conventional bits that worked solely through the rotation of the drill bit. However, the Plan B team used drills called downhole hammers, which contained air-powered bits that continually pounded the rock as the drill simultaneously rotated, a technology that proved successful.

In Plan B, two drilling rigs were used: the Schramm model T685 and the Schramm T130XD.

Both rigs came from U.S.-based Schramm Inc., headquartered in Chester County, Pennsylvania. The company specializes in providing mobile (truck-mounted) hydraulic rotary drilling rigs to mining, energy, geothermal, and water industrial sectors around the world. Because these rigs are mobile, the company could quickly send its trucks to the accident site.

Rig and Drill

The first step of the Plan B rescue operation used the Schramm T685, a mineral exploration rig normally used to drill water boreholes. Operated by the Chilean company TerraServices, the rig began drilling a 5.9-inch (15-centimeter) hole using the Schramm T685 WS drill. The drill bored about 98 feet (30 meters) per day.

Eight pivotal boreholes were made using percussion drills. The drills were able to bore into the rock, but not without difficulties. In several attempts, the routes of the boreholes had to be diverted from the intended routes because of rock hardness and the extreme run (intended target length or depth of the borehole) required. Adding complexity to the already tough task, the maps used during the rescue attempt proved to be out-of-date, making uncertain the estimates of the drill head's location and the best path for drilling through the rock layers.

It was critical to drill the hole accurately. The hole could not be drilled vertically because the heavy drilling rig would have had to be positioned immediately over the drilling activity, which was considered too dangerous. Consequently, the drilling occurred at an off-vertical angle. The drilling also had to avoid production tunnels that crisscrossed between the surface and the location of the trapped miners. The hard rock also wore down drill bits; during the process, one drill bit was destroyed after hitting a metal reinforcement beam.

The first breakthrough came on the seventeenth day of the rescue operation when the eighth borehole broke through a ramp near to an emergency shelter where the trapped miners were located. The hole was approximately 2,257 feet (688 meters) underground and about 66 feet (20 meters) from the miners' room. José Ojeda, one of the trapped miners, attached a note to the drill with insulation tape, which was raised to the surface and read by the rescuers: *Estamos bien en el refugio los 33*" [We are well in the shelter, the 33]. Ojeda later claimed a copyright on the widely publicized and used passage. The drill was again lowered to the miners, this time with a video camera attached. The shirtless, soiled, but alive men were seen for the first time since the mine collapse. During these first seventeen days of entrapment, the miners lived on water found near their underground location, a jar of peaches, and a two-day supply of canned tuna and mackerel. After reaching the men, rescue teams were able to provide supplies and food to the miners. Subsequently, three boreholes were used as so-called umbilical cords, nicknamed artificial pigeons, with cylindrical PVC pipes used as casing for each hole. One was used for supplies (such as dehydrated food, lights, food supplements, and medicine), a second for communications, and a third for forced air.

Center Rock Cluster Drill

After the first pivot hole was drilled successfully, two additional pivot holes were drilled nearby. Then the Schramm T130XD rig, which was nicknamed the Miracle by rescue workers, took over. The Chilean-American drilling company Geotec SA owned the rig, and Geotec Boyles Brothers operated it at the rescue site. In fact, Jeff Hart and Matt Staffel, employees of Kansas-based Layne Christensen Company, were the two drillers that manned the T130 drilling rig for thirty-three days straight. Assisting the men were two Spanish-speaking Layne employees, Doug Reeves and Jorge Herrera.

Brandon W. Fisher, the president and founder of the drilling equipment company Center Rock Inc., located in Berlin, Pennsylvania, hand delivered the specially made 28-inch (70-centimeter) hammer canisters that functioned as bits for the Schramm-made drills. Fisher remained at the site for the entire drilling operation. Each canister consisted of four air hammers and four drill bits that moved in unison. Together, the piston-driven hammers create a cluster drill. Even though the drills are not normally used to enlarge holes in mining operations, the hammers, which drive the drills into the ground, proved to be an ideal way to bore into the subsurface. Dave Singleton, president of the water resource division of Layne Christensen, stated after the successful rescue that plan B's technology and the skill of its operators shaved at least two months off the rescue effort.

The T130 drilling rig then began to enlarge (ream) the initial pivot hole—the first time to a diameter of 12 inches (30 centimeters) and a second time to 28 inches (70 centimeters). The final rescue hole allowed the miners to be lifted to safety inside the Phoenix rescue capsule.

During the drilling process, about 1,100 pounds (50 kilograms) of rock each hour fell down the borehole into the room containing the miners. The trapped miners worked in shifts around the clock to keep the passageway clear of falling debris with the use of shovels, sweepers, and wheelbarrows. In total, about 770 U.S. short tons (700 metric tons) of rock—approximately 1.5 million pounds (700,000 kilograms)—were carried off by the miners.

Phoenix Rescue Capsule

While the three rescue plans were pushing forward, the Chilean Navy constructed escape pods (rescue capsules) with design advice and help from the U.S. space agency, the National Aeronautics and Space Administration (NASA). Three Fénix (English: Phoenix) rescue capsules were built. A team of NASA engineers produced over seventy design features of the capsules, most of which were incorporated into their construction.

The steel, bullet-shaped craft used for the actual rescue was called Phoenix 2. It was 21 inches (54 centimeters) in diameter, 13 feet (4 meters) in length, weighed 924 pounds (419 kilograms) and had an oxygen supply, safety harness, voice and video communications, a clock, and an escape hatch, to name a few of its many features. It was colored red, white, and blue—the colors of the Chilean national flag. The Chilean-built rescue capsule used an Austrian-built winch and pulley system, built by OESTU-Stiettin, to lower it to the miners below (initially with rescue team members), and then to raise it (with an occupant) to the surface.

Originally, the first 330 to 660 feet (100 to 200 meters) of shaft was to be encased in steel pipes. However, after the hole was inspected with video cameras and found to be stable, only the top 184 feet (56 meters) was encased.

How the Capsule Works

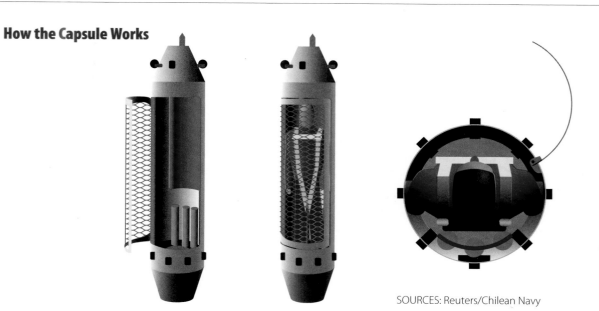

SOURCES: Reuters/Chilean Navy

The narrow rescue capsule, equipped with communications and ventilation systems, also featured an escape hatch. Illustration/XNR Productions/Cengage Learning, Gale.

Miner Alex Vega's face is seen inside the capsule as he is rescued from the mine, ending his two-month long ordeal underground. David Mercado/Reuters.

During the time when each miner was being brought to the surface—about 20 minutes—one of the biggest concerns was that the miner might have a panic attack inside the rescue capsule. A claustrophobic man had the potential to do damage to the capsule. Thus, during this time, each man inside the capsule had his pulse, temperature, and respiration measured as medical personnel looked for signs of stress.

Rescuers were also concerned that falling rocks could wedge between the hole and the capsule, halting its movement. The rescue teams said they had thought out and planned for hundreds of contingencies. In the end, the operation went smoothly, with all the miners (and recovery personnel) brought safely to the surface.

Structure of the Mine

Mining experts stated that the specific structural characteristics of the mine and the geological features at the Chilean site helped to keep the miners alive before a narrow borehole allowed food and supplies to be delivered from the surface.

The depth and length of the mine worked to the advantage of the mineworkers. Because of the depth, the miners were trapped with plenty of drinkable water. The igneous rock walls were grooved with clay that contained enough water for them to drink. Water often dripped down the walls. In addition, they were able to use bulldozers to open pockets of water.

If the workers had been located closer to the surface, little water would have been available. The Chilean Atacama Desert is often described as one of the driest places on Earth.

Because the operation mined copper and not coal, the trapped workers were not concerned with breathing in toxic gases such as carbon monoxide, nor were they worried about gas explosions caused by methane. Also, copper levels within the mine were less than 1 percent. Thus, levels of copper sulfite, which can cause irreversible eye damage and skin and respiratory irritation, were kept to a minimum.

Geology

The homogeneous nature of the soil—almost all rock with very little gravel, sand, stone, and water—and the relative dryness of the local Chilean desert environment worked to the advantage of the Plan B's cluster drill success.

The geology around the mine consists primarily of an abrasive quartzite-diorite, a medium-hard to hard, whitish-gray to dark-gray igneous rock that was formed from cooled magma. This volcanic rock was hard enough to dull the drills but not stop the high-tech methods used by the Plan B team.

San José Mine

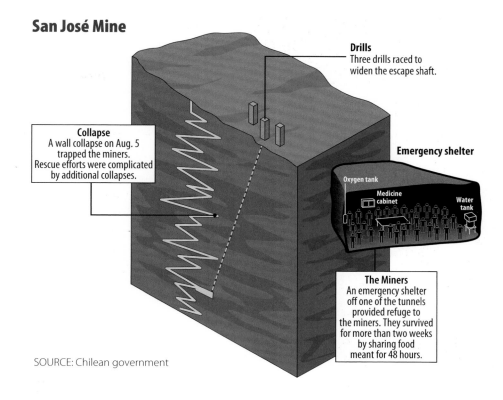

Drills
Three drills raced to widen the escape shaft.

Collapse
A wall collapse on Aug. 5 trapped the miners. Rescue efforts were complicated by additional collapses.

Emergency shelter

Oxygen tank

Medicine cabinet

Water tank

The Miners
An emergency shelter off one of the tunnels provided refuge to the miners. They survived for more than two weeks by sharing food meant for 48 hours.

SOURCE: Chilean government

The 33 miners lived underground for more than 2 months in a small emergency shelter. Illustration/XNR Productions/Cengage Learning, Gale.

The structure of the mine was considered stable overall after the initial collapse, which helped the rescue efforts. Initially, the cave-in released the stress that had built up, producing a state of equilibrium that was predicted to not change. In the end, the percussion drilling by the Plan B team was the ideal type of drilling for the hard, dry volcanic rock.

Physical and Psychological Challenges

After discovering the trapped miners, rescuers placed an immediate priority on delivering oxygen, rehydration tablets, glucose, and medicine until an extraction shaft could be completed. The miners endured many weeks of intense heat and physiological stress. Temperatures remained a humid 92°F (33.3°C). At such temperatures, humans typically need to consume more than one gallon (approximately 4 liters) of water per day.

Trapped in a multi-chambered space estimated at 530 square feet (50 square meters), the miners faced months of physiological and psychological perils similar to those encountered by astronauts and people in extreme survival situations.

According to statements made by the families of several miners, the emotional and mental stress began to build several weeks before the actual collapse. There were reports that miners had heard increasing creaking sounds in the shaft and were concerned about an impending disaster, but the miners felt that they had no recourse but to continue working and hope for the best.

Miners: A Special Group

For psychologists and those trained in special unit operations and survival, the miners constituted what is termed a self-selected group. That

Eager to see the trapped men and their underground living conditions, relatives gather to watch a video feed of the miners. Ivan Alvarado/Reuters.

is, the miners choose to do this work and are accustomed to working in harsh, cramped, dimly lit conditions for extended periods of time. The fact of self-selection, meaning having exercised the choice of putting oneself in danger and peril, made the miners as a group considerably more able than a group of average people to withstand the heat, humidity, and hostile living conditions.

The first seventeen days were the most challenging for the trapped men from a psychological

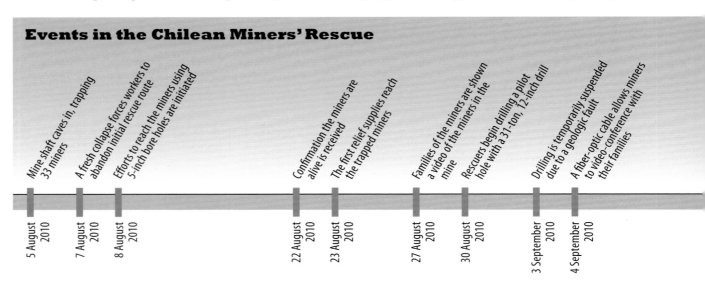

Events in the Chilean Miners' Rescue

Mine shaft caves in, trapping 33 miners — 5 August 2010

A fresh collapse forces workers to abandon initial rescue route — 7 August 2010

Efforts to reach the miners using 5-inch bore holes are initiated — 8 August 2010

Confirmation the miners are alive is received — 22 August 2010

The first relief supplies reach the trapped miners — 23 August 2010

Families of the miners are shown a video of the miners in the mine — 27 August 2010

Rescuers begin drilling a pilot hole with a 31-ton, 12-inch drill — 30 August 2010

Drilling is temporarily suspended due to a geologic fault — 3 September 2010

A fiber-optic cable allows miners to video-conference with their families — 4 September 2010 and emotional standpoint. They had no way of knowing whether rescue efforts were underway and whether they would survive. Fear and extreme hunger exacerbated their mental and physical condition.

Reactive Mode

Typical to such disasters, immediately following the roof collapse, the miners' first thoughts were of survival and of the potential impact on their families if they were to perish. In their efforts to make their plight known to the outside world, they were in a reactive mode, acting more emotionally than analytically. In desperation to gather drinking water for survival, they drained water stored in barrels designed to be used in dynamiting operations and drank the tainted substance, which caused them intestinal distress. They burned tires from mining vehicles and set off dynamite charges in an effort to attract attention above ground.

Psychologists subsequently explained these behaviors as essentially typical of desperation thinking. These early acts did more harm than good (burning tires created airborne toxins and fouled oxygen supplies), as the miners' reactive mode lowered their ability to fully assess and appreciate the longer-term consequences of their actions. Driven by extreme stress and operating on survival instincts, the miners' immediate goal, as they judged, was to do anything to increase the likelihood of their survival.

Discovery Changes Challenges for Miners

When the first probe reached them, the miners were able to send up a note indicating that they were alive and well and were safe in the emergency shelter. Psychologists who later counseled the men point to their discovery as a key moment in reducing the life-threatening levels of their stress. Assured they had not been left for dead, the miners were able to shift from reactive actions and increasingly morbid thoughts to become engaged in the shared work for survival. In many cases, care for their own peril and plight turned to thoughts about how to reassure loved ones at the surface. Physical discomforts became more bearable because the men knew supplies and communication were coming.

Setting Reasonable Expectations

The next obstacle for psychologists and rescuers to manage was the miners' initial expectation

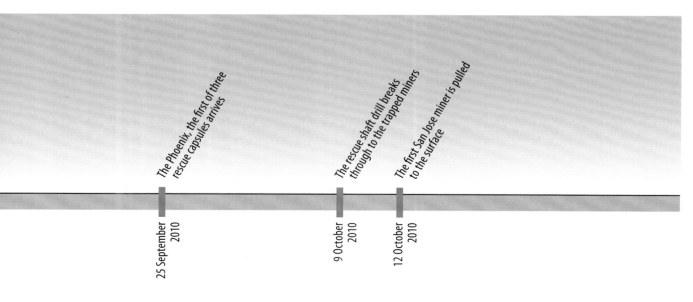

The Phoenix, the first of three rescue capsules arrives

25 September 2010

The rescue shaft drill breaks through to the trapped miners

9 October 2010

The first San Jose miner is pulled to the surface

12 October 2010

Many of the trapped miners, family members, and rescue workers relied on their religious faith to help them cope during the disaster. Here, miners bring in a statute of St. Lorenzo, the Catholic patron saint of miners, before a mass service begins at the site. Luis Hidalgo/ AP Images.

that they would be extracted quickly. Psychologists and survival specialists contend that it is normal for people under stress to set limits on how much hardship they can endure and for how long they can endure it. Setting these limits helps establish coping mechanisms (e.g., self rationalizations and bargaining exemplified by thoughts such as "If I can just endure this for x amount of time, I'll be fine.") Multiple studies have shown that when this self-limit is breached, even if external conditions have not significantly changed, people under prolonged stress can revert to early desperation thinking. Accordingly, rescue officials did not immediately tell the miners that it might take months to rescue them. As the men grew stronger (thereby pushing out the time they thought they could endure the harsh conditions), more realistic estimates of the time they could expect to be

trapped underground were provided by rescuers.

Eventually rescuers decided that the men were healthy enough to cope with the truth about their situation and that the benefits of honesty outweighed their potential negative emotional responses to learning that rescue efforts were more likely to be measured in months than days or weeks. The miners were provided photographs of drilling equipment and apprised of the progress of each rescue hole being bored. Having realistic expectations proved to diminish stress and create a healthy sense of optimism.

An Underground Society Forms

Within a short time, the miners began to coalesce into a small society and leaders emerged. They decided to make group decisions and vote on all major issues, which served to increase cooperation and to decrease some of the stress that accompanies indefinite confinement. The men worked at maintaining optimism, their own as well as that of the group. They were determined to support one another through the ordeal, leading to a far better outcome than there would have been under fragmented social conditions.

From the outset, it was determined that a key consideration for long-term survival, after assuring physical stability (medical and nutritional management), was the maintenance of emotional well-being and the management of psychological stress inherent to indefinite confinement in dark, hot, crowded conditions. An international group of psychologists and behavioral scientists from the mining industry, public and private sectors, and NASA were consulted about how to create the most optimal conditions possible for the miners, their families, and the rescue workers.

Daily Routine Critical

The behavioral health experts agreed that creating a sense of normalcy in as many aspects of the miners' lives as possible would help them survive. It was essential to have a sense of structure, purpose, and routine for each day. The shift foreman assumed a leadership role in terms of planning and authority. He established a workspace for himself and set about altering the environment so as to make it more hospitable as living quarters. He also worked to foster a sense of consistency, purpose, and order to the group's day-to-day existence. The more senior miners who had areas of expertise were encouraged to use them in the service of improving daily life and assuring safety and psychological well-being for everyone. One of the miners, an evangelical preacher, provided spiritual grounding and helped create comforting rituals for many in the group. Such rituals linked the men to their former lives above ground and played an important role in stress management. Another miner helped to create an informal support system by having the men form three-person groups tasked with mutual support and

encouragement. The more technically inclined miners created systems for storing potable (drinkable) water and disposing of human waste; others focused on managing space and supplies for bathing, daily work activities, and sleep.

Early on, the men requested clean clothing, along with grooming and hygiene supplies, as a means of increasing their comfort and affirming

Chile's Mining Minister Laurence Golborne (center) holds the pipeline used to communicate with the trapped miners. Roberto Candia/AP Images.

Chilean Miners' "Umbilical Cord"

Cylindrical PVC tubes called **"artifical pigeons"** made it possible to send food and medicine to the 33 trapped miners.

Three stages of supply in order of priority

1. **Rehydration:** glucose, mineralized water and drugs to prevent ulcers

2. **Food** in liquid form, rich in proteins, sugars and minerals

3. **Torches** and means of communication

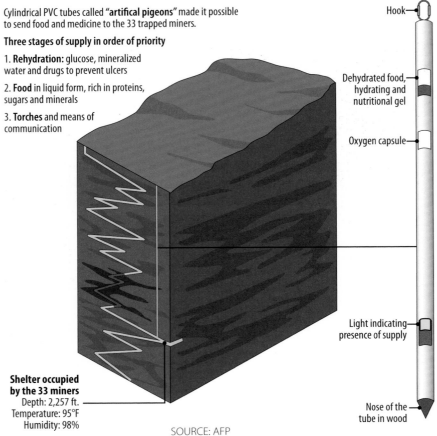

Hook

Dehydrated food, hydrating and nutritional gel

Oxygen capsule

Light indicating presence of supply

Nose of the tube in wood

Shelter occupied by the 33 miners
Depth: 2,257 ft.
Temperature: 95°F
Humidity: 98%

SOURCE: AFP

The pipe line, or "umbilical cord," carried vital food, medicines, and communication to the miners trapped far underground. Illustration/XNR Productions/Cengage Learning, Gale.

their self-control and well-being. They requested specific foods and entertainment (particularly popular were videos of soccer matches). The rescuers were advised by the mental health experts to listen carefully and respectfully to concerns and requests and to provide as many desired items as were safe and feasible.

Survival Rhythm

Common effects of long-term confinement under inhospitable conditions such as those experienced by the miners include sleep deprivation, exhaustion, and shifting of sleep-wake cycles caused by loss of circadian rhythms given confinement in total darkness. Human beings and all other animals govern their activity based on light and dark. One suggestion from psychologists and NASA consultants was to create patterns and physical locations for daily sleep, work, eating, and socializing. These arrangements helped the miners manage the stress of sustained overcrowding and hot and noisy conditions. They also maximized physical and mental health. The NASA team suggested ongoing encouragement of the miners' sense of community and advised the ground teams that the miners were likely to rebel

Camp Hope, the tent village set up for families of the miners, allowed relatives to be near the rescue operations. a11/ZUMA Press/ Newscom.

against restrictions imposed from the outside.

Experts assisted the miners with creating synchrony of sleep-wake cycles by using lighted areas for work and socializing and dark areas for sleep. They encouraged the men to retain a traditional sleep-wake pattern in order to be best able to communicate with those above ground. They also helped them to use diurnal (sleep-wake) rhythms to facilitate normative social structures involving group meals, work, and socialization through play (card games, dominoes, electronic games, and the like). They advised using the natural leaders in the group to help their peers manage themselves, their emotions, and their expectations, to facilitate and strengthen relationships among the miners, and to maintain an ongoing spirit of teamwork throughout the period of entrapment. Support of community within the mine was deemed key to maintaining the miners' sense of optimism. In addition to ongoing interaction with rescuers and family members and the maintenance of activity regimens, it was deemed important to insert elements of surprise into the men's daily routines in order to avoid boredom, depression, and anxiety, which can develop under unchanging conditions.

Managing the Miners and Families

The rescuers established a communication system so that the miners could interact with loved ones and the outside world. Experts from the military counseled family members on how to treat their away miners as soldiers. Families were also offered means of private (rather than group) telephone communication, given opportunities

The enormity of the rescue effort is seen as relatives, rescue workers, and other miners gather outside the collapsed mine on 7 August 2010. Another 15 days would lapse before they received confirmation that the trapped miners were alive. Luis Hidalgo/AP Images.

to transmit video images of themselves and their living areas, and encouraged to engage in private written correspondence with loved ones.

Their families were able to stay nearby in Camp Hope, in contact with the miners as well as the ongoing rescue efforts. This arrangement was beneficial on many levels. The proximity and access to information lowered stress levels among family members; it gave them realistic expectations and lowered their emotional stress. Rescuers emphasized that communications should be as normal as possible, focusing on routine topics such as shopping trips and children's events at school. Family members were shown how to make their communications positive and free of unrealistic or inaccurate information.

Coping with Celebrity

Media experts also offered advice on preparing the miners for their emergence as celebrities and how best to manage the radical alterations in their lives anticipated after their rescue. An important aspect of processing trauma is sharing personal stories with significant others, both family and friends and mental health professionals. Based on legal advice and a pact they made among themselves, the miners agreed not to divulge many details of their ordeal in order to preserve both their privacy and the value of potential book and movie offers. As such, they resolved not to share some experiences, typically a part of healthy readjustment.

The trapped men had been miners for varying

lengths of time; and for many of them, there was a risk that they might lose their self-definition as a result of being unable or unwilling to return to mining after their release.

Following the rescue, some miners traveled to other countries, appeared with government and world leaders, rode on parade floats, were guests on television programs, and were interviewed by journalists. Many made more money in one month than they had in several years as miners.

The miners were counseled on media expectations and intrusiveness by Eduardo Strauch, a survivor of the Uruguayan rugby team that crashed aboard Uruguayan Air Force Flight 571 in the high Andes in 1972 while en route with friends and family to a match in Santiago, Chile. Seventy-two days passed with little food, water, and medicine in freezing conditions before members of the group were able to hike out and secure their rescue. The story of the Uruguayan crash was documented in the book and film *Alive*.

Strauch and the other fifteen survivors faced intense media exposure following their unexpected rescue after being presumed dead. Media attention intensified again following revelations

In the weeks following the rescue, the miners were honored and invited to various events. In late October, they played a game of soccer with President Sebastian Piñera, other government staff, and some of the rescuers. Victor Ruiz Caballero/Reuters.

Miner Edison Pena took America by storm when he made an appearance on the *Late Show with David Letterman* and ran in the New York Marathon several weeks after being rescued. Jeffrey R. Staab/CBS/Landov.

that members of the group resorted to cannibalism, consuming the remains of some of the twenty-nine individuals who died. Strauch counseled the miners on what it felt like to be presumed lost and then to return to the world and how difficult it was to face personal questions regarding the ordeal.

The miners were given lessons in public speaking and media relations prior to their release. However, psychologists expected the loss of privacy would affect the miners in unique ways once they began acting as individuals rather than as a group. For some, the celebrity might become a stepping-stone to an improved life; for others, it could set off withdrawal and isolation behaviors. Involuntary sudden fame causes protracted loss of privacy. Sudden celebrities must deal with media presence and intrusive questions. They can face the challenge of dealing with financial and business opportunities that accompany sudden fame. Eventually, they must face the abandonment of

media that sees their experience as old news and turns to fresh newsworthy individuals and events.

Physical Problems

The miners were physically stressed by their confinement, but luckily, they were able to move freely between several large chambers. Once their survival was discovered and supplies of medicine could be delivered along with professional medical advice, their health improved. However, some prior injuries could not be properly treated, and medical care for several illnesses was limited to medication. In addition to nutritional supplements, the men received medicine to prevent thrombosis, hypertension, and other conditions related to stress.

During their confinement, the men were asked to perform a series of exercises and follow a special diet recommended by NASA. Some of the men were told they needed to lose weight in order to fit into the escape pod. Due to good leadership and organization of sanitation needs, outbreaks of infectious disease were avoided.

When initially brought to the surface the men wore sunglasses for 24 to 72 hours to allow their eyes to adjust to the light. Following rescue, some miners faced continuing physical problems such as fungal infections, partially collapsed lungs, eye damage, and related ailments. After being rescued, the miners faced potentially harmful psychological problems such as anxiety, panic attacks, depression, nightmares, and post traumatic stress disorder (PTSD).

Rescue Stories

The Foreman

Luis Alberto Urzua Iribarren, 54, was the official foreman for the shift on 5 August 2010, when

Miner José Ojeda, who wrote the note telling the world that the miners were alive, is finally brought to the surface. AP Images/Hugo Infante, Chilean Government. ▶

Rescue workers prep the Phoenix capsule before it transports the last miner, foreman Luis Urzua, to freedom. Government of Chile/Pool/Reuters.

the San José mine in Copiapo, Chile, collapsed, trapping thirty-three workers. The former soccer coach turned mining foreman knew that discipline and unity were critical for survival, but he had no idea that what started as a simple extension of his job would turn into a seventy-day shift and make him an international hero.

In the hours after the cave in, Urzua organized the men into work groups, sending some in trucks to drive slowly through tunnels to help map out the pocket they inhabited, while he ordered others to focus on finding and pooling food, water, and supplies. With military-like precision, Urzua quickly created the ration system that sustained all the men over the seventeen days before rescuers made contact; a teaspoon of tuna or salmon and a few ounces of milk every 24 to 48 hours. By the

time rescuers made contact via a 2,000-foot bore hole, the men had lost an average of about 17.6 pounds (8 kilograms) each and rations had run out 48 hours prior.

Miner Richard Villaroel told the UK-based newspaper *Guardian* that fears of cannibalism were a subtext in those last days before contact: "At that moment no one talked about it. But once [help came] it became a topic of joking, but only once it was over, once they found us. But at the time there was no talk of cannibalism." Urzua's tightly organized supervision helped to keep anxiety in check as much as possible.

Once contact was established, Urzua knew that order, with men working according to their skills and in 12-hour shifts, would be needed until full rescue could be completed. Urzua became the spokesperson for the miners and the filter for communications, conducting meetings with doctors, psychologists, and government officials to discuss rescue strategies, the miners' physical and mental health, and to make specific requests for food and supplies.

After more than two months, when initial tests of the Phoenix 2 rescue capsule showed that the equipment was ready, Urzua insisted that he be the final miner to exit, like a ship's captain remaining on a sinking vessel until all passengers and crew are evacuated. When he came to the surface, Urzua was greeted by an audience of thousands in person and more than 1 billion people watching on live television. According to the *Daily Mail*, Chilean president Sebastian Piñera greeted him first and said: "You have no idea how all Chileans shared with you your anguish, your hope, and your joy. You are not the same, and the country is not the same after this. You were an inspiration. Go hug your wife and your daughter."

The "Plan B" Drillers

For thirty-seven days Center Rock president and CEO Brandon Fisher, 38, and his manager of DHD sales & product development, Richard Soppe, were at the heart of the rescue. With the original pathways through the mine destroyed, rescuers knew they needed to create a new rescue shaft, but the physical and engineering challenges were daunting and dangerous.

Center Rock, a drilling company with just seventy-five employees in the small community of Berlin, Pennsylvania, met the challenges and made possible the rescue of the miners before a global television and Internet audience of more than 1 billion.

Center Rock was uniquely qualified to provide assistance. The twelve-year-old company provided specialized drill bits for the July 2002 Quecreek mine collapse that trapped nine miners for three days in Somerset County, Pennsylvania, and Fisher remained confident his company's equipment

After keeping the trapped miners safe and occupied during their 69-day ordeal, foreman Luis Alberto Urzua Iribarren poses with a rescuer while still underground. Ho New/Reuters.

and expertise could help to rescue the trapped miners in Chile much faster than the initially predicted estimate of four months.

Fisher flew to Chile with Soppe on 4 September 2010, and the two camped out at the mine site, ultimately spending thirty-three days guiding drill operators; coordinating with engineers, technicians, and mine officials; and focusing on creating bore holes that would be used to both send supplies to the miners and widen the shaft to shuttle the miners 2,000 feet to safety.

During the nearly six weeks he spent on site, Fisher was constantly adjusting and customizing equipment in order to deal with the terrain and obstacles, which required drilling at an angle to avoid overloading the surface around the mine entrance with heavy equipment. At one time Fisher's team broke a drill bit on a metal bar in a subterranean supporting tunnel. Fisher and Soppe slept in shifts near the drills.

The Bolivian

During the rescue effort, one Bolivian flag of red, yellow, and green waved in a field of red, white, and blue Chilean flags near Camp Hope. The flag was for Carlos Mamani, the only trapped miner not from Chile.

Mamani, 24, was also an outsider for another reason: when the San José mine collapsed it was only his fifth day on the job. Like thousands of fellow Bolivians, Mamani had come to the Chilean copper and gold mines to find work and escape poverty. Tens of thousands of his fellow Bolivians annually leave Bolivia to seek work as miners, domestic helpers, or as other laborers.

Chile and Bolivia have a long-standing border dispute that dates back over a century. Bolivia is landlocked in part due to the 1879 War of the Pacific, in which Chile claimed valuable coastline after the war with Bolivia and Peru. In the early 2000s, Bolivia and Chile frequently argued over ownership and rights to coastal access and fishing waters. Diplomatic tensions still exist between the countries.

Mamani was stuck with a group of hardy Chilean miners just as the Chilean bicentennial approached. National patriotism and pride were at fever pitch in the country, and Mamani initially feared that the stress of entrapment might fuse with nationalism, making him vulnerable as a foreigner. Instead, the miners insisted that they band together in unity. When the Chilean bicentennial rolled around on 18 September 2010 the world watched video of the miners singing the Chilean national anthem. According to the U.K.-based *Daily Telegraph*, Mamani joined in, a gesture of solidarity that gained him widespread recognition, respect, and affection among the Chilean public.

Called simply the "Bolivian" in the Chilean press, as Mamani emerged, he was greeted by his wife and the sight of Piñera and First Lady Cecilia Morel waving the Bolivian flag. Bolivian president Evo Morales missed the rescue, delayed by flight complications, but he greeted Mamani personally shortly after the rescue. Morales has promised Mamani a job and a home in Bolivia.

Political analysts speculate that the subterranean collapse may spark an easing of diplomatic tensions over water access, making the "Bolivian" an accidental ambassador of goodwill between the two countries.

Hope Above and Below Ground

For trapped Chilean miner Ariel Ticona Yanez, hope meant much more than making it back to the surface alive. The 29 year old descended into the Copiapo mine in August, expecting to return to his family at the end of what he assumed would be a normal shift. The mine collapse separated him from his pregnant wife, Elizabeth Segovia, expecting their third child and first daughter within the month.

As it became clear that Ticona would not be rescued in time to be at the birth, family, friends, and media crews stepped in and offered to document the personal experience he would not be able to share with his wife. Shortly after the miners were discovered, seventeen days into their entrapment, Ticona sent a note to his wife through the 6-inch-wide borehole used to convey food, medical supplies, and messages between the miners and rescue workers. It turns out both shared the same thought, she told Chile's Channel 13: "He thought of it there and I thought of it here in the house: She was going to be named Carolina Elizabeth, but now her name will be Esperanza Elizabeth." Esperanza is Spanish for hope.

Segovia wanted to travel to the encampment that spontaneously formed around the mine in the Atacama Desert, called Camp Hope, but Ticona sent messages urging her to stay at home and take care of herself.

On 17 September 2010, forty-three days into Ticona's confinement, Segovia gave birth to Esperanza Elizabeth Ticona, with her sister and other family members surrounding her. Photographs and videos of the birth were made available to Ticona in the mine. The thirty-second miner to be rescued, Ticona was selected for the final group due in part to his mental toughness; he told *Hello!* magazine that he coped with missing the birth of

Bolivian miner Carlos Mamani is greeted as he emerges from the rescue capsule. Chile President Sebastian Piñera stands near his side (on right) waving a Bolivian flag. Martin Bernetti/AFP/Getty Images.

Emotions ran high during the rescue operations. Here, a relative of one of the miners watches his rescue via a TV screen. Natacha Pisarenko/AP Images.

his daughter and viewing it on videotape "with the same detachment that I used to deal with everything happening down there." He noted that it was an "emotional moment" when he held Esperanza for the first time on the day of his rescue and that she is "lovely, lovely."

La Alcaldesa: *The Mayor of Tent City*

Maria Segovia is no stranger to mine accidents. She was nicknamed "la Alcaldesa," or Mayoress, for her efficient organization of the families of the trapped Chilean miners at the Copiapo mine in northern Chile. Segovia's brother, Dario, was one of those trapped during the mine collapse. Their father, also a miner, was once trapped for a week in a mining accident.

After the last trapped miner was transported to the surface, the rescue workers hold up a sign in the underground mine that reads "Mission Accomplished Chile." Government of Chile/Pool/Reuters.

Segovia organized the diverse group of relatives who congregated at the opening of the mine shaft, initially hopeful, but increasingly despondent in the early days of the rescue operation, before the miners were discovered to still be alive. On 22 August, when rescuers found a note taped to the end of a drill bit that confirmed the miners had all found a safe haven, the relatives rallied and their numbers grew. La Alcaldesa often represented the families in interviews with the media and pushed the rescue effort to move faster, threatening to organize protests if demands were not met. The UK-based newspaper the *Guardian* reported that on the fortieth day of the miners' entrapment, Segovia announced, "We're thinking about staging a protest or some other pressure tactic if they don't show us more progress." Outspoken and willing to take charge, the 48-year-old woman became the unofficial Camp Hope spokeswoman.

Camp Hope became the functional home to hundreds of family members and friends who observed the rescue process. The impromptu village was bombarded by media attention, with reporters and cameramen quickly outnumbering the camp residents. Camp Hope developed from a small group to a fully functional tent city, complete with added cell phone towers for easier communication with the outside world, a small school for children, a hair salon, sanitation services, and a clown for entertainment.

For many media commentators, the camp came to symbolize perseverance, determination, and unity heightened by national pride as Chile celebrated its bicentennial during the rescue efforts. Thirty-two Chilean flags and one Bolivian flag were erected, each one representing a trapped miner. When the rescued miners returned to the Copiapo mine site and Camp Hope on 17 October, just a few days after ascending the 2,000-foot shaft, President Piñera and some of the miners called for the San José mine and Camp Hope to become a national museum, commemorating the "Mission Accomplished Chile."

Media Frenzy Exposes Miners' Private Lives

The "*los* 33" had private lives too, some exposed by their ordeal underground. When Chilean miner Yonni Barrios Rojas listed the names of relatives and friends he wished to have greet him when he emerged, he gave the names of two women. One was his wife, Marta Salinas. The other was his mistress, Susana Valenzuela. To his surprise and chagrin, when he surfaced, his mistress rushed to his side, greeting him with kisses of relief, but his wife was nowhere to be seen.

Married for more than twenty-eight years, Barrios and Salinas are Roman Catholics, the religion of 90 percent of Chileans. Salinas leaned on her faith in the initial weeks of the ordeal, but she soon learned of her husband's five-year affair with Valenzuela when the two met at Camp Hope. The first letter Barrios sent to the surface was for his mistress, not his wife. This did not sit well with Salinas, who confronted her husband's mistress and reportedly smashed a picture Valenzuela held

Miner Yonni Barrios Rojas is greeted by his girlfriend, rather than his wife, after being rescued. Hugo Infante, Government of Chile/AP Images.

during the wait. Red Cross workers had to separate the two women.

Meanwhile, Barrios acted as the primary medical responder underground, providing care, dispensing vaccinations, and communicating with doctors above ground to help fellow miners with various conditions, including injured corneas, diabetes, and pneumonia. He asked that Salinas and Valenzuela both greet him upon his rescue according to his sister, Lidia Barrios Rojas, who told the UK-based newspaper *Daily Telegraph* that

Barrios asked "both to go up to the mine to meet him when he came out. He says quite simply that he loves them both, that they are both important to him, and he wants them to be friends with each other."

More than 1 billion people watched the 13 October 2010 rescue live on television and online around the world. Salinas did not attend the rescue. She told the *Telegraph*, "I am happy because he made it, it's a miracle of God," but she refused to do as Barrios wished. "This is very clear; it's her

Media Compares Inner Space Perils to Legendary Outer Space Heroics

During rescue operations in Chile, media commentators frequently drew hopeful comparisons to the 1970 flight of *Apollo 13*, the United States' third attempted manned lunar landing mission. The mission became the most famous near-disaster and successful rescue in NASA history. On 13 April 1970 (after launching two days earlier) when the spacecraft was more than halfway to the Moon, an explosion occurred. The crew, mission commander James (Jim) A. Lovell, command module pilot John (Jack) L. Swigert, and lunar module pilot Fred W. Haise, soon learned that several fuel and oxygen tanks had ruptured and many of the ship's systems were damaged. Hopes of landing on the Moon were lost. Instead, the astronauts faced a return trip to ↙

Earth filled with anxiety and uncertainty.

The accident of *Apollo 13* occurred fifty-six hours into the flight. At first, the crew was aware only that the fuel cells used to produce electricity were not operating properly. However, when they looked out the window and saw that the oxygen gas they needed to survive was blowing into space, the astronauts realized they faced a much larger problem.

There was nothing the astronauts could do to repair the damage. Their only hope was to ride out the journey home in the lunar module, which had life support systems designed for only two astronauts for a few days. The lunar module *Aquarius* was not built or supplied to keep three people alive for three and one-half days. Oxygen, electricity, and water all had to be conserved to last the entire journey. The cabin temperature was maintained at just above

freezing and each crewmember could drink only six ounces of water a day.

Over the next few days, the astronauts and their supporting engineers at the Mission Control Center at the Johnson Space Center, just outside Houston, Texas, scrambled to devise ways to use and manage their limited resources and power supplies for the emergency return to Earth. The astronauts performed critical maneuvers without computer backups, and ships systems were reconfigured—literally at times with duct tape—to keep the astronauts alive.

As the spacecraft finally approached Earth, the astronauts climbed back into the command module *Odyssey* and cast off the damaged service module and lunar module lifeboat. Although they operated on scant back-up power and systems, slight navigational errors could spell doom. Too steep a reentry and the capsule or me," Salinas reportedly declared. Thus, the tiny cracks in one miner's private life became a human interest story or scandal for the media coverage worldwide.

The Loneliest Man in Chile

Manuel Rodriguez, a mining safety expert with CODELCO, the state-owned copper mining company in Chile, was the first to descend the full 2,000 feet from the surface of the San José mine in the Atacama Desert at Copiapo, and the last man to emerge from the 540-square-foot pocket of space that had been an impromptu home to the thirty-three miners for seventy days. While the news media focused attention on the foreman Luis Alberto Urzua Iribarren's insistence on being the last person rescued, it was Gonzalez who technically holds two titles: the last man out and the only man to spend any time alone in the underground caverns at the Copiapo mine collapse site.

Rodriguez descended to the trapped miners in the specially constructed Phoenix 2 rescue capsule.

A Navy helicopter plucks one of the *Apollo 13* astronauts to safety after the command module splashed down in the Pacific. AFP/Getty Images.

would be consumed; too shallow a reentry would bounce the capsule off the atmosphere and back into space, where the crew would have perished. Fortunately, the calculations made by the astronauts and their ground controllers were correct. After a few tense minutes during re-entry when contact was interrupted, the crew radioed the command center to announce they had splashed down safely.

The astronauts returned home dehydrated and in varying stages of hypothermia (lower than normal body temperature), but they were alive. The "successful failure" of *Apollo 13* proved to be a celebrated NASA achievement. For rescuers over many generations and around the world, the mission offered an enduring legacy best summarized by NASA mission director Eugene (Gene) Francis Kranz, who drove engineers during rescue and recovery operations with the exhortation, "Failure is not an option!"

As part of the rescue efforts in Chile, a team of NASA doctors offered advice on nutrition and the miners' health, along with their medical and behavioral problems. Dr. Michael Duncan, a medical officer at the Johnson Space Center (Houston, Texas) led the NASA team of two medical doctors (Duncan and James Polk), one psychologist (Al Holland), and one engineer (Clinton Cragg). They also helped with suggestions on the escape pods.

After the last miner was extracted, youths and others joyfully expressed pride in their country by singing the Chilean national anthem. Mariana Bazo/Reuters.

A mere 21 inches in diameter, the capsule had wheels at both ends to help keep it centered in the tube casing and ride as smoothly as possible to ensure the safety of both the capsule and its occupant. The capsule was lighted and contained oxygen to help passengers breathe and reduce anxiety. The narrow condition of the capsule meant that some of the miners needed to lose weight before they could ascend; even with an average weight loss of 17.6 pounds (8 kilograms), some of the miners were still too wide to fit. According to CNN correspondent Karl Penhaul, a personal trainer was assigned to create exercise routines for the men, so they could "work out and slim down just to make no doubt that they're going to fit inside that rescue capsule." Doctors placed miners on liquid diets in the days before rescue not to lose weight, but to help reduce possible vomiting during the 12-to-15 minute ascent in such close quarters.

Welcomed with hugs and shouts of joy upon arriving underground, Rodriquez settled into his job of coordinating the arrival of other rescuers. The specially trained rescue unit began a triage of the miners to determine the order of ascent and to train all the miners on how to handle the psychologically perilous journey to freedom.

After the thirty-third miner, Luis Urzua, began his ascent, Manuel Rodriguez remained alone in the mine's refuge for 26 minutes, the only man to have a solo stay. As the capsule returned for its final fare, Rodriguez bowed to the video camera recording the rescue, climbed into the capsule, and rode off toward the surface to end the final chapter in a seventy-day effort that yielded, as writer Hernan Riviera Letelier noted, "the 33 crosses that never were."

Mining and Mine Safety Issues

Mining: An Ancient Practice

Mining is an ancient profession. Humans have always extracted useful materials from the ground. People living in the Stone, Bronze, and Iron Ages knew how to obtain these materials. Archaeological research has produced evidence of copper mining in Africa around 6,000 years ago and, a little later, in ancient Egypt and North America. By the time the Roman Empire reached its peak, it had established mines throughout Europe, in the British Isles, and in parts of North Africa. The earliest known scientific description of western mining operations is found in the book *De Re Metallica*, by the Saxon physician Georgius Agricola (1494–1555).

Mining technologies continue to improve. Underground mines, especially South African gold mines, can be over 2.4 miles (3.8 kilometers) deep. Mining can also be expansive. The open-pit Bingham Canyon Mine near Salt Lake City, Utah—more than 2.5 miles (4 kilometers) wide and more than 0.6 mile (1 kilometer) deep—is one of the largest industrial excavations on Earth. Mining can also take place over decades. Excavation of the Bingham Canyon pit began in 1906 and continued into the early twenty-first century, producing primarily copper with smaller amounts of gold, silver, and molybdenum.

Mining can also be environmentally destructive and result in violations of environmental safeguards such as the Clean Water Act. Across parts of Africa and South America, hydraulic surface mining operations—often unregulated open pit gold mines—create pollutants that enter nearby watersheds. Downstream residents suffer heavy metal poisoning, and the runoff damages the developing neural systems of children.

Deaths from Mining Accidents, 2008–2009

Selected Countries	2008	2009
China	3,215	2,631
Colombia	35	58
Peru	60	50
Poland	30	38
Chile	43	35
United States	53	34

SOURCES: Xinhua news agency; Chile Copper Commission, Sernageomin; MSHA; Geominas; Osinergmin; BBC

The number of mining deaths from accidents in China is far higher than that of any other country. Illustration/XNR Productions/Cengage Learning, Gale.

Mine Safety: A Global Concern

Around the world, some experts voice their concerns that mining is especially dangerous in developing industrial nations where safety issues are less important than meeting increasing production demands. At the opposite extreme, other mine experts contend that mining safety has increased tremendously over the past few decades. Although still more dangerous than other jobs, many mine safety experts insist that miners have a very good chance of surviving a mining disaster. However, their fate is often still in the hands of mine owners driven by the need to make profits for investors.

In the United States, according to the U.S. Mine Safety and Health Administration (Department of Interior), 34 deaths resulted from mining accidents in 2009 (18 deaths occurred from coal mining accidents and 16 from the mining of other substances). In 2008, 53 miners lost their lives. According to the International Federation of Chemical, Energy, Mine, and General Workers' Unions, over 12,000 mining deaths are reported annually. The union contends that many more go unreported, especially in developing and rapidly industrializing countries such as China.

China is currently considered to have one of the worst (if not the worst) records for mine safety. In 2009, China was reported to have sustained 2,631 mining deaths. In prior years, Chinese mine accidents accounted for about 80 percent of global mining fatalities. Not all accidents occur at large-scale industrial mines. Illegal, unregulated, and highly dangerous mining camps are also an increasingly global problem.

Investigation in Chile

The cause of the San José mine collapse remains under investigation. Chilean government officials stated that a roof section collapsed in the mine about 1,100 feet (350 meters) underground. Although the exact cause of the San José collapse is not known, some mine experts assert that mine collapses typically occur in tunnels that are too large to be supported or too weakly supported. Regardless of the exact cause of the San José mine collapse, the miners might have been able to escape if the mine owners had followed proper safety precautions. According to Vincenot Tobar, the head of risk prevention at the San José mine from 2004 to 2009, an area adjacent to the emergency shelter where the miners took refuge should have had an escape tunnel and safety ladder to enable escapes in the event of a mine collapse. Tobar resigned from the San José mine group in November 2009 because the mine owners repeatedly ignored his warnings about safety.

The San José Mine, owned by the San Esteban Primera Mining Company, had a checkered history concerning miner safety. Many accidents occurred at the mine during its operations, which began in 1957. Between 2003 and 2009, for instance, three deaths occurred at the mine, along with numerous accidents. One death occurred in 2007 when a mine geologist was killed at the site. The mine was closed after his relatives sued the company. The mine was reopened in 2008.

Families of some of the rescued miners are now suing the mining company for the equivalent of between $12 and $23 million in a civil case. Their lawyers claim that the mining company failed to make safety improvements to the mine, which caused the 2010 accident, and previous accidents. The families are also suing Sernageomin (the Chilean government's mining service) and the mine inspectors for a similar amount of money for allowing the mine to reopen in 2008. Following a freeze of $2 million in company assets to cover possible miner compensation claims, a Chilean bankruptcy court subsequently ordered the mine company's assets frozen to cover an initial estimate of $10 million in expenses and losses related to the accident. The company filed for bankruptcy as the result of the expenses and losses related to the accident.

After the mine collapse, Chilean president Piñera dismissed leading officials of Chile's mining regulatory agency. Piñera also publicly opened a major investigation of the agency. Piñera has promised to punish anyone found responsible for the accident. In addition, Chile's national Congress is investigating the mining accident. Eighteen mines were shut down in the days following the accident, and hundreds of others were threatened with closure. Many mines were found to be operating illegally.

A preliminary report by the Commission on Work Safety, established by President Piñera in response to the accident, contained thirty proposals, ranging from improvements in safety, health, and hygiene to better coordination of mine regulators across the country. Piñera promised that fundamental improvements would occur in how Chilean businesses interacted with their employees, citing many working conditions in mining as "inhumane."

Flames continue to burn from a ventilation shaft at New Zealand's Pike River coal mine 11 days after the first explosion. The Press/Iain McGregor/Pool/Reuters.

Chilean Miracle Set Against Another Grim Year for Miners

Contrasting with the successful rescue of the miners in Chile, 2010 proved a tragic year for American miners. In April 2010, an explosion at the Upper Big Branch mine in West Virginia killed twenty-nine miners in the deadliest mining accident in the United States in more than twenty-five years. The accident fueled a series of scientific, legal, and regulatory inquiries into the accident and current mining practices. Although the exact cause of the explosion was not known as of December 2010, it was reported that high levels of methane and carbon monoxide were present within the mine at the time of the explosion. Unlike the accident at the San José copper mine, the Upper Big Branch mine produced coal, a process that emits large amounts of methane and carbon monoxide, a combination of gases that has often proved deadly for miners. Gas pockets can suffocate miners without proper breathing equipment or adequate air supplies, as inhalation of the gas is sometimes lethal. In 2006, only one of thirteen miners who initially survived an underground explosion at the Sago mine in Tallmansville, West Virginia, survived. Facing smoke and gas fumes, the miners, some of whom relied on failed safety equipment, barricaded themselves in a chamber to await rescue.

Fortunately the trapped Chilean miners had breathable air throughout their ordeal. The U.S. miners did not. Twenty-five of the miners at the Upper Big Branch mine were initially killed in the explosion, but reportedly four men died when they did not make it into one of two available rescue chambers, which contained sufficient oxygen, food, and supplies to survive during rescue operations.

Miners face greater danger when forced to dig deeper and faster to keep up with fuel demands of rapidly industrializing countries such as China. Mine safety experts contend that the fast pace comes with a heavy price, as illustrated by the recent string of mine disasters. In January 2010, at least twenty-five miners died following an explosion and fire at a mine in Hunan Province. Just weeks later, a gas explosion at the Sunjiawan mine in Liaoning Province killed 214 people. In August 2010, miners working at the Hengxinyuan coal mine in Jixi, a city located in northeast China's Heilongjiang Province, were trapped by floodwaters. The accident happened so quickly that the only escapees were shift managers in charge of production.

Although the Chilean rescue serves as inspiration to rescue teams around the world, the reality is that the triumphant outcome is often elusive. In late November 2010, following a series of apparently methane-related explosions that rocked the Pike River coal mine in New Zealand, rescue workers continued to hope for a Chilean-like miracle until a second major explosion ended hopes of rescuing the twenty-nine missing miners. In contrast to the vertical mine in Chile, the New Zealand South Island operation consisted of a tunnel mine (essentially a horizontal tunnel dug into a hillside) lying above a seam of methane-seeping coal.

Proponents of mining argue that given the world's current dependence on fossil fuels and need for minerals critical to industrial production, there are at present no viable economic alternatives to mining. The energy budgets of most industrialized nations, even if great efficiencies and reductions are imposed, are simply beyond the generating capacities of present alternative and renewable energy sources. While critics say

Two days after the Chilean miners were rescued, a gas leak at a coal mine in China claimed more than 30 lives. Here, rescue workers prepare to enter the mine to look for survivors. imago stock&people/Newscom.

this should not deter alternative energy expansion that will lessen the need for mining, many experts accept the reality that mining operations will be critical to society for untold generations. If so, critics counter, then placing greater emphasis on mine safety becomes all the more important.

Research and Exploration

ABC News. *All 33 Chilean Miners Rescued in What Country's President Calls a "Miracle."* http://abcnews.go.com/International/chile-mine-rescue-miners-emerge-president-sebastian-pinera/story?id=11874249.

ABC News presents video of the rescue of Chilean miners along with interviews with the miners and their rescuers.

Associated Press and National Public Radio (NPR). *From Darkness to Limelight: Chilean Miners Ordeal and Assent to Freedom.* http://www.npr.org/templates/story/story.php?storyId=129398530.

An interactive photography slideshow and audio compilation of international news reporting and interviews throughout the Chilean mine disaster and rescue.

BBC News. *Jubilation as Chilean Mine Rescue Ends.* http://www.bbc.co.uk/news/world-latin-america–11485392.

BBC features an interactive presentation on the Chilean mine rescue, including demonstrations on the drilling and rescue techniques used, photos, timelines, and video diaries from the miners.

Economist. *Plucked from the Bowels of the Earth.* 14 October 2010. http://www.economist.com/node/17251964.

The *Economist* is a UK-based finance and international policy news magazine. The article discusses the Chilean government's reaction to the mining disaster.

National Aeronautics and Space Administration (NASA). *NASA Provides Assistance to Trapped Chilean Miners.* http://www.nasa.gov/news/chile_assistance.html.

Video interviews and mini-lectures by the NASA specialists who provided technical and medical expertise to the Chilean mine rescue efforts, establishing astronaut-like daily routines for the miners while underground to aid their psychological health.

Newsweek. *Back Story: Think of the Miners.* http://www.newsweek.com/2010/09/13/back-story-think-of-the-miners.html.

An infographic illustrating the size and logistical challenge of providing supplies to the trapped miners through an inches-wide borehole.

PBS *NewsHour. Chile's Mine Rescue: Costs and Benefits.* http://www.pbs.org/newshour/rundown/2010/10/cost-of-mine-rescue.html.

PBS *NewsHour* investigates the cost of the Chilean mining rescue and the impact of the rescue on Chilean society.

PBS *NewsHour. Chilean Miners' Rescue Presented Massive Engineering, Drilling Hurdle.* http://www.pbs.org/newshour/bb/weather/july-dec10/chilean2_10-26.html.

PBS *NewsHour* interviews Greg Hall, president of Drillers Supply International, who lead the drilling effort that reached the trapped Chilean miners.

PBS. *Nova. Emergency Mine Rescue.* http://video.pbs.org/video/1621938528/.

A video feature about the rescuers and rescue operations at the mine.

Telegraph. *Chile Miners Rescue as It Happened.* http://www.telegraph.co.uk/news/worldnews/southamerica/chile/8058924/Chile-miners-rescue-as-it-happened.html.

A live blog with commentary, reporting, and accompanying video footage of the Chilean mine rescue as it progressed. The *Telegraph* is a newspaper and Internet news outlet based in the United Kingdom.

Global Economic Crisis

igns pointing to an impending financial crisis in the United States were evident to many economists as early as 2007. Experts in the field were aware that the country was headed for financial trouble stemming from bad investments in mortgage loans, but no one could gauge the extent of the problem. In contrast, the general public seemed blissfully unaware that anything was amiss. Home prices across the country had been skyrocketing, especially in states like California, Nevada, Arizona, and Florida, where the average home price rose by over 80 percent between 1998 and 2006. With rates of home ownership at historically high levels (69 percent of the population owned their own homes in 2004), Americans were confident as they watched their most significant investment, their homes, continue to appreciate at almost ludicrous rates. The Dow Jones Industrial Average, an index of stocks that tracks key companies in the United States, reached an all-time high of 14,154 in October 2007, with the value of stocks climbing skyward.

In September 2008, a Wall Street icon with a history of mega-profits, the investment banking firm Lehman Brothers, suddenly collapsed. Despite speculation that the treasury department would step in to help Lehman Brothers, the U.S. government opted to let the bank fail. Worldwide financial panic ensued. The Dow Jones index plummeted by nearly 50 percent in October 2008. Lehman CEO Dick Fuld was summoned before the United States Congress and vilified by lawmakers for causing a global financial meltdown. However, Fuld explained the situation to legislators as follows:

> We are in the midst of unprecedented turmoil in our capital markets. The problems that most believed would be contained to the mortgage markets have spread to our credit markets, our

In this photo from 6 October 2008, former Lehman Brothers Holdings Inc. Chief Executive Richard S. Fuld Jr. testifies before the House Oversight and Government Reform Committee on Capitol Hill in Washington, D.C. AP Images/Susan Walsh.

banking system, and every area of our financial system. As incredibly painful as this is for all those connected to or affected by Lehman Brothers—this financial tsunami is much bigger than any one firm or industry. Violent market reactions to a number of factors affected all of the financial system. These problems are not limited to Wall Street or even Main Street. This is a crisis for the entire global economy. I will try my best to be helpful to this Committee, so that what happened to Lehman Brothers does not happen to other companies. . . .

> Fuld, Richard S. 2008. "Prepared Testimony of Richard S. Fuld, Jr." ABC News. http://abcnews. go.com/Business/storyÀid=5963581&page=1.

Legislators, however, were not impressed by Fuld's attempt at sincerity. As reported by the Wall Street Journal's MarketWatch, they tore him apart:

> "Mr. Fuld will do fine," said Rep. Henry Waxman, D-Calif., the panel's chairman. "But taxpayers are left with a $700 billion bill to rescue Wall Street and an economy in crisis...."

Said Rep. Elijah Cummings, D-Md., "I won-der how [Fuld] sleeps at night."

By October 2008, it was clear to everyone that a prolonged economic crisis had begun.

A Real Estate Boom

Mortgages, the loans people take out in order to buy homes, are large, long-term commitments. Traditionally, people applying for mortgages need to offer ample proof of their ability to take on a big financial commitment to the banks issuing these mortgages. Applicants need to provide substantial down payments—usually 20 percent of the price of the home being purchased. They also need proof of a steady income high enough to cover the mortgage payments and a good credit rating. Families often spend many years saving enough money for a down payment. But in the early 2000s, banks loosened these standards considerably. People who would never have qualified for a loan in the past were able to get approval for mortgage loans and buy homes. About 80 percent of the time, these people, called "subprime borrowers," were offered what are called adjustable rate mortgages (ARMs). These are loans on which the interest rate charged by the bank can go up or down after an initial period—usually up. Subprime borrowers got introductory interest rates that were extremely modest, lowering their mortgage payments substantially.

Countrywide, the United States' largest subprime mortgage lenders at the time, made $468 billion in mortgage loans in 2005. They offered loans that required no down payment or proof of income. At the time, the lender was lauded for helping nontraditional buyers, especially minorities, get homes of their own. The New York

Continuing to be hard-hit by the struggling economy, dairy farmers demonstrated outside the European Council headquarters in Brussels, Belgium, in July 2010. They were there to protest the lower selling prices of milk outside a meeting of European Union agriculture ministers. Yves Herman/Reuters. ▶

Stock Exchange dubbed Countrywide CEO Angelo Mozilo "American Dream builder" and featured him on the cover of *NYSE Magazine* in 2005.

Subprime lending brought enormous profits to Countrywide and other, similar lenders, and the risk seemed minimal. Home prices were rising at an unprecedented rate, and as a result, families were taking out second and even third mortgages on their homes, borrowing against the estimated value of their home.

Angelo Mozilo, founder and former CEO of Countrywide Financial Corporation, testifies before the House Oversight and Government Reform Committee in Washington, D.C., on 7 March 2008. The committee is examining the compensation and retirement packages granted to the CEOs of corporations deeply involved in the mortgage crisis. AP Images/Susan Walsh.

Many people used money from second and third mortgages for purely recreational spending: new cars, vacations, remodeling. To use a comparison that was common at the time, people were using their house as an ATM, withdrawing cash at will.

The Bubble Bursts

The housing market could not sustain the trend, and things were about to change for the worse. Economists refer to the run-up in housing prices as a "bubble," a temporary, delicate economic microcosm that can burst with the slightest pressure. Speculative bubbles have been common throughout the history of capitalism. A particularly bad one had just ended as the housing bubble began. It is known today as the dot.com bubble, and developed during the 1990s when the Internet was relatively new. Stock prices for new Internet businesses, few of which had made any money and many of whom didn't even exist yet, sold for hugely inflated prices. This was classic bubble behavior, which happens when large numbers of people become convinced that an investment is worth more than logic dictates and drive prices up further by competing with each other to purchase that investment.

Dow Jones Industrials, October 2008

10,831.07

9,325.01

8,175.77

October

SOURCE: Yahoo! Finance

A look at how the Dow Jones Industrials fell during October 2008. Illustration/XNR Productions/Cengage Learning, Gale.

Holland experienced a major financial crisis in the 1630s when the market for tulips soared to extreme heights and then abruptly crashed. At that time, tulips were relatively new to the Dutch, who prized the plants for their beauty and color. Owning tulips became a status symbol during that era, known as Tulipmania. Before the market collapsed, some bulbs were changing hands up to 10 times daily. Ultimately, the crash left many people bankrupt. This Abraham Mignon painting, like others from the Golden Age of Dutch Painting, depicts the "tulips that drove men mad." AP Images/PR Newswire.

Economists have many theories about why bubbles develop and why they burst, but they all agree that bubbles always burst. In the case of the dot.com bubble, formerly enthusiastic investors looked at their technology stocks and realized that the companies issuing the stock would never make any money. A stampede to sell followed. Prices of once-valuable stock soon fell dramatically, and many fledgling Internet companies went bankrupt. In the wake of the collapse, many investments that were viewed as promising now looked outright ludicrous. Investors had been swept up in a kind of mass irrationality, making many unwise investments look irresistible.

Much like the dot.com bubble burst in the late 1990s, the housing bubble exploded in 2006 and 2007. Housing prices fell dramatically while interest rates went up, resulting in a disastrous combination for many subprime borrowers. Previously reasonable mortgage payments suddenly became unaffordable. Worse, home owners who had taken out second mortgages found that falling home prices meant that they were unable to sell their

U.S. Foreclosure Filings

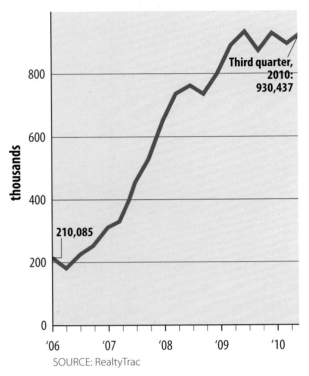

SOURCE: RealtyTrac

The number of foreclosure filings in the United States rose from 210,085 in 2006 to 930,437 in the third quarter of 2010. Illustration/XNR Productions/Cengage Learning, Gale.

homes for enough money to cover their debts. Mortgage defaults and foreclosures (in which the bank takes possession of a property after the owner defaults on loan payments) spiked, rising 42 percent from 2005 to 2006. From 2006 to 2007, foreclosures rose nearly 80 percent. Between 2006 and 2007, more than twenty-three smaller subprime lenders went bankrupt. In 2007, Countrywide and other lenders quickly tightened lending standards, ending their "no down payment" loan programs, but the damage had already been done.

Even home owners who were able to keep up with their mortgage payments and stay in their homes found themselves "under water," a real estate term meaning that they owned more on their mortgages than their houses were worth. Stories of people like Christine and Michael Canavan

became commonplace in the news. The couple bought a $250,000 house in Florida in 2005 with an adjustable rate mortgage. Their credit score was too low for them to qualify for a standard mortgage. Under the terms of their adjustable rate mortgage, they only had to pay the interest due on their loan each month, which meant they would not make any progress toward paying off the loan amount. They dutifully made their payments on time, and their credit score improved. But in 2007, just as they prepared to refinance the house with a fixed-rate loan, home prices fell dramatically.

"I had to go to (the mortgage broker) three times because our appraisal kept depreciating," Mrs. Canavan told *USA Today*. "At first he said, 'Great news, your home appraisal would be $275,000.' Within a week, the home had gone down to $240,000. When I went in to do the paperwork, I was in tears. It had dropped to $230,000 in two weeks."

The Canavans were not alone. By 2008, one in six U.S. home owners was "under water." For people who had bought their homes during the peak years of the housing bubble, the situation was even worse. According to the Wall Street Journal, 29 percent were "under water."

Countrywide, once the hero of home ownership, quickly became the villain, and the company's lax lending standards were labeled "predatory." Multiple states jumped to take legal action against the company. In a press release announcing the result of legal action against Countrywide, the attorney general of the State of Connecticut gave a rundown of Countrywide's usual way of doing business:

- Encouraging consumers to take out loans the company knew or should have known consumers could not afford.

- Improperly inflating consumers' incomes to qualify them for loans they were otherwise unqualified for.

A sheriff's deputy prepares to enforce an eviction order in California's Orange County. Lucy Nicholson/Reuters.

• Providing loans with different and more expensive terms than consumers were promised.

• Pressuring consumers into assuming mortgages with temporary, interest-only payment options when the company was aware that customers would be unable to afford the higher payments that would come due later.

• Providing variable rate loans to consumers with the assurance they would be able to refinance the loan before interest rates reset, only to later refuse to do so.

• Sending at least one consumer who was rejected for a home equity loan at one Countrywide office to another company branch, where the loan request was approved.

• Promising to help homeowners "in financial difficulty to establish suitable payment plans," but instead demanding loan modifications and repayment plans that were unsustainable, unaffordable, or unsuitable.

In 2008, Bank of America "rescued" the ailing Countrywide, acquiring it for $4.1 billion in stock.

While the real estate industry, subprime lenders, and millions of home owners suffered in 2006 and early 2007, the impact of the housing disaster seemed contained and only appeared to affect the United States. By mid-2007, however, it became clear that the global nature of the financial industry meant that financial institutions around the world had been exposed to the hazards associated with risky subprime lending practices. Large banks and financial firms had offices, operations, and investments all around the world, and therefore the housing loan crisis in the United States impacted economies across the globe.

The Waves Spread: Mortgage-Backed Securities and the Fall of Bear Stearns

Over the last few decades, banks have been packaging mortgages together and selling them as a type of investment called a mortgage-backed security, or MBS. These were attractive investments because historically, most homeowners, including subprime borrowers, make their mortgage payments on time. Even if a small percentage of the thousands of borrowers involved in an MBS defaulted, or failed to pay their mortgages, the MBS would still be valuable because the rest of the mortgages would be bringing in payments. Investors, both individuals and corporations, purchased MBSs, expecting a reasonable rate of return on their investments. Investors were aware that MBSs, similar to any other investment, carried a risk of low returns if too many homeowners defaulted. In the case of MBSs, banks that issued the mortgages profited from selling these packages, based on the belief that they no longer carried

any financial risk after unloading them to investors. The practice of selling MBSs further encouraged banks to make even riskier home loans.

As an increasing number of homeowners began to default on their loan payments around 2006, subprime lenders began to feel the impact as their cash flow began to dry up. During 2007, billions of dollars invested in MBSs evaporated. In April 2007, New Century Financial, the second largest subprime lender in the United States, declared bankruptcy when the company was unable to pay its creditors. In August 2007, Sachsen Landesbank, a German subprime lender, neared collapse before a larger bank acquired the company.

Throughout the autumn of 2007, major banks announced massive losses in investments related to mortgages. The U.S. Federal Reserve, the European Central Bank, and the central banks of several European countries injected hundreds of billions of dollars into the international banking system throughout late 2007 and early 2008 in an effort to prevent markets from failing. Even with the injection of money into the banking sector, several banks were unable to find the cash needed to remain solvent. The British government nationalized (that is, placed under government control)

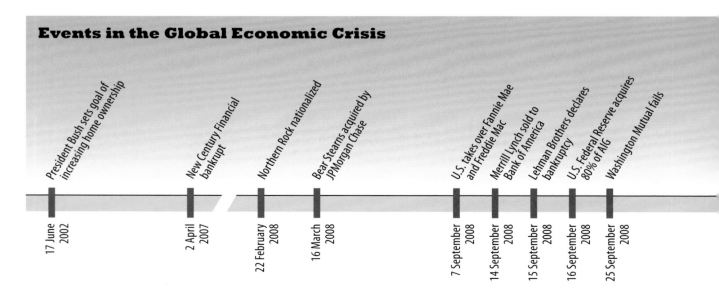

Events in the Global Economic Crisis

| President Bush sets goal of increasing home ownership | New Century Financial bankrupt | Northern Rock nationalized | Bear Stearns acquired by JPMorgan Chase | U.S. takes over Fannie Mae and Freddie Mac | Merrill Lynch sold to Bank of America | Lehman Brothers declares bankruptcy | U.S. Federal Reserve acquires 80% of AIG | Washington Mutual fails |
| 17 June 2002 | 2 April 2007 | 22 February 2008 | 16 March 2008 | 7 September 2008 | 14 September 2008 | 15 September 2008 | 16 September 2008 | 25 September 2008 |

troubled Northern Rock bank in February 2008.

In December of 2007, investment bank Bear Stearns posted massive losses from mortgage-related investments. It was only the beginning of the crisis. The head of the company, Jimmy Cayne, was forced to resign after a *Wall Street Journal* article revealed his use of marijuana and his habit of taking month-long vacations. By early March, rumors spread around Wall Street that the company was "illiquid"—that is, did not have the money to pay its investors. The company's operating cash, available through credit, dried up as other financial institutions refused to do business with Bear Stearns. In March 2008, the U.S. Federal Reserve facilitated the sale of Bear Stearns bank to JP Morgan Chase, at the close of what may have been the most dramatic disintegration of a major finance corporation yet. Bear Stearns had been valued at $20 billion. JP Morgan Chase, with Federal Reserve backing, bought the company for $2 a share, for a total of $236 million, resulting in a calamitous loss for Bear Stearns investors.

CDSs Sink AIG

As the collapse of the housing sector continued, financial firms across North America and Europe who had invested money in MBSs suffered losses. In turn, many people began to lose confidence that their investments in these companies and their products were safe. This fear was partly responsible for the rapid fall of Bear Stearns. A contributing factor to this fear was the use of credit default swaps (CDSs). A CDS is a contract that operates much like an insurance policy. It specifies that the issuer of the CDS will pay the buyer a sum if a specific event, such as a bankruptcy, occurs. In return the buyer pays the issuer a regular fee. Many financial institutions used CDSs that were tied in some way to housing prices and MBSs.

CDSs came to the attention of the public when the insurance giant AIG (American Insurance Group) was nearly destroyed by them, and required a bailout in the form of a cash loan from the government in order to survive. Simply put, AIG had promised hundreds of billions of dollars it did not have in the form of CDSs. Testifying before Congress, former AIG CEO Martin Sullivan explained the scope of AIG's CDS obligation: "From recollection, I don't believe the number got to $500 billion, but it was certainly in totality around $400 billion."

Unlike an insurance policy, CDSs are not

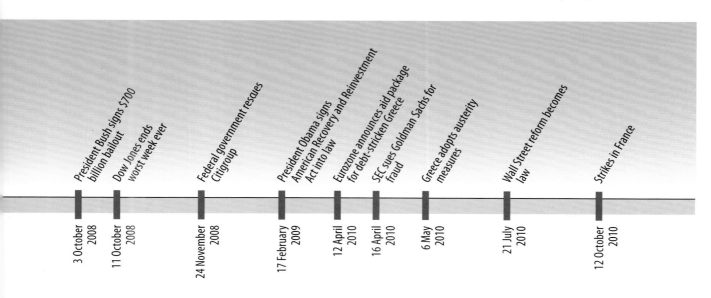

One of the signs of hard financial times—foreclosed homes—has hit many communities throughout the United States. In November 2010, CNBC reported that the states with the highest foreclosure rates included Nevada, Florida, Arizona, California, and Michigan. AP Images/Chris O'Meara.

regulated by the government. A business can issue a CDS even if it does not have enough money to pay its obligation in the event that the disaster it is insuring against does occur. After AIG's bailout, concerns arose that companies might not be able to make good on their CDS obligations. No one could know for sure which firms were at risk because the terms of the CDSs were all private, but the total amount of money in the system was enormous. In September 2008, the U.S. Securities and Exchange Commission (SEC) estimated that the global CDS market involved $58 trillion—almost three times the amount invested in the U.S. stock market.

In hindsight, many observers blamed the lack of regulation of CDSs for the trouble they caused.

Chairman of the Federal Reserve Board Ben Bernanke told a Senate committee, "AIG exploited a huge gap in the regulatory system. There was no oversight of the financial-products division." A subsidiary division "was attached to a large and stable insurance company, made huge numbers of irresponsible bets, took huge losses. There was no regulatory oversight because there was a gap in the system."

The overall effect of the housing market and CDS problems was that businesses became increasingly wary about where they invested or lent money because they had no idea how financially stable other companies were. Banks became unwilling to trade with each other, resulting in what is called a credit crunch.

September 2008: The Edge of Global Economic Collapse

Subprime mortgage losses continued during 2008 and credit tightened even further. In September 2008, the financial crisis intensified sharply, triggering major government responses around the globe. On 7 September 2008, the U.S. Treasury announced that the federal government was placing Fannie Mae and Freddie Mac into conservatorship. These two firms are government-sponsored enterprises that were responsible for nearly one-half of all mortgages in the United States. A week later, on 15 September 2008, Lehman Brothers declared bankruptcy, the largest bankruptcy filing in U.S. history. On 16 September 2008, the U.S. Federal Reserve effectively took control of AIG, the largest insurance company in the United States, after acquiring an 80 percent stake in the company in return for an $85 billion loan that allowed the company to continue operating. On 25 September, Washington Mutual became the largest bank to fail in U.S. history. European and Asian financial markets also suffered greatly.

When presidential candidate and Arizona senator John McCain cancelled a late September appearance on the *Late Show with David Letterman* and returned to Washington for an emergency session of the U.S. Senate, comedian Letterman quipped that McCain had stiffed him because "the economy is exploding, or something." In fact, Letterman was not far off the mark.

Stock markets all over the world plunged, going into full panic mode especially after Alan Greenspan, former Chairman of the Federal Reserve Board, called the crisis a "once-in-a-century credit tsunami." The events of September 2008 highlighted the worldwide impact of the financial crisis that began in the United States, and brought increased pressure on governments around the world to take action. On 3 October 2008, President George W. Bush signed a massive $700 billion bailout package called the Troubled Assets Relief Program, or TARP, designed to remove bad debts from the books of financial institutions and restore confidence in the financial system. In the months since it was approved, however, TARP for many people has become symbolic of an out of control government, throwing money at problems in the hope that an influx of cash would make things better. At the time, however, Secretary of the Treasury Henry Paulsen saw TARP as a last line of defense against the financial tsunami hitting the American economy: "Before we acted, we were at a tipping point. Credit markets were largely frozen, denying financial institutions, businesses and consumers access to vital funding and credit. U.S. and European financial institutions were under extreme pressure, and investor confidence in our system was dangerously low."

European banking and insurance giant Fortis was partially nationalized on 28 September 2008. By the end of October 2008, all three major banks in Iceland had failed and been nationalized. Similarly, in the United Kingdom three of the country's largest banks were nationalized in a £37 billion bailout. In mid-October, South Korea announced a $130 billion package to stabilize its financial institutions. The Bank of Japan injected $45 billion into Japan's banking system. The Indian central bank made $8.2 billion available to Indian banks. Despite these efforts, the international economy continued its rapid downhill slide.

Global stock markets plunged as investors lost faith in the markets and sought safer investments. By mid-October 2008, the Dow Jones Industrial Average had fallen nearly 40 percent from its record high levels in 2007. Major European indexes suffered similar declines compared to the high levels they had reached in 2007. In Asia, losses were even more severe. For example, the Chinese Hang Seng Index and Shanghai Composite Index had fallen 53 percent and 67 percent, respectively, since October 2007. The Japanese Nikkei Index was down 54 percent from its record high.

Iceland entered a severe recession when its biggest banks failed in 2008. Here, protesters express continued anger with the government's response to the crisis on 4 October 2010, lighting fires outside of parliament and pelting the building with eggs, rocks, and other objects Zuma Press/Thorvaldur Örn Kristmundsson/newscom.

The Wave Wipes Out the "Little Guy"

These complicated financial transactions between huge international financial institutions had, by October 2008, created what is now simply called "the global economic crisis." Big banks suffered on a big scale, but smaller businesses soon felt the ill effects of the risky business practices of the financial industry. Many small companies, which had come to depend on easy access to credit, struggled to stay in business. The health of small businesses is of major importance to economies around the world, as they often account for a majority of an economy's gross domestic product, or GDP, a measure of a nation's total economic

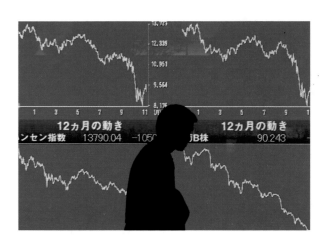

Screens at a stock brokerage in Tokyo show dismal economic news on 6 November 2008. Japan's main stock index fell 6.5 percent that day, just one in a series of declines in late 2008. Toru Hanai/Reuters.

output. In the United States, for instance, small businesses generate more than 50 percent of private GDP. Small businesses also accounted for 70 percent of new job growth in the United States in the past decade.

Following the financial crisis in 2008, it became increasingly difficult to obtain credit, for both personal and business use. Business owners found their lines of credit summarily canceled. This freeze of the credit markets had a ripple effect throughout the economy. While many homeowners were losing their houses, many companies were forced to cut jobs and tighten spending when credit sources dried up. Small businesses, which often do not have large cash reserves, were especially vulnerable to the credit freeze. Without operating capital, companies were forced to lay off workers. The loss of jobs and the fear of layoffs prompted many people to begin saving money rather than spending it, which caused sales in all industries to sag and the economic crisis to deepen. As more people lost their jobs, the housing crisis continued to worsen as even traditional mortgage borrowers with fixed rate mortgage loans (loans whose interest rate does not change) began, in large numbers, to have difficulty making mortgage payments.

The frozen credit markets in the United States and abroad have been the chief concern of government leaders and economists. A market-based economy requires access to credit in order to function. Without credit, the economy comes to a halt.

The Great Recession

By early 2009, most economists declared that the majority of the world's economies were in recession. A recession is a period of economic decline that affects gross national product, wages, employment, and other economic indicators. The U.S. economy had been in recession since December 2007. Politicians and pundits worried about

The economic crisis has impacted many families throughout the world. In Guatemala, as the economy struggled due to the financial crisis, the country declared an official state of public calamity in September 2009. AP Images/Rodrigo Abd.

a return to conditions similar to the Great Depression of the 1930s. In February 2009, newly elected president Barack Obama signed into law a $787 billion economic stimulus package called the American Recovery and Reinvestment Act, which included expanded unemployment benefits, aid to states, tax cuts, and massive government spending on infrastructure projects, education, and health care.

The effects of the recession were visible everywhere. Advertisements for a single job opening might attract a thousand applicants. In states like California and Nevada, high foreclosure rates left entire suburban neighborhoods vacant. Housing developments, malls, and public buildings stood half finished. South of Sacramento, California, a bright silver indoor mall sat in the middle of

Changes in racial hiring practices, coupled with the global economic crisis, have greatly impacted many white South Africans. Here, some of the 400 white residents of a squatter camp receive donated food. Finbarr O'Reilly/Reuters.

farm fields, brand new and completely vacant. People who had worked in construction or real estate left their jobs for good, with fading hopes that they would ever be able to return to work in those fields.

In April 2009, the leaders of the G-20 nations met in London, England, to discuss a coordinated response to the global financial crisis. The G-20 consists of major industrialized and developing nations from around the world. Gordon Brown, the prime minister of Great Britain, urged his fellow leaders to "supply the oxygen of confidence to today's global economy and give people in all of our countries renewed hope for the future."

At the conference, the G-20 leaders agreed to $1 trillion of additional stimulus spending to boost the world economy. They also announced that they would cooperate in reforming the financial industry, including instituting regulation of previously unsupervised sectors. The hope was that these measures would help to restore confidence in the financial industry and prevent a deepening of the crisis as well as avoid a repeat of it in the future.

Wobbly World Economies Struggle to Right Themselves

By August 2009, many U.S. economists were cautiously optimistic that the recession was easing, despite an unusually high national unemployment rate of 9.7 percent and double-digit unemployment rates in many states. In several European countries, the situation was worse; Spain's unemployment rate, for example, hit 18.1

Unemployment Rates

	Q1 2010	Q4 2009
Spain	19.2	19.0
France	9.9	9.8
United States	9.7	10.0
Poland	9.7	8.9
Sweden	8.8	8.8
United Kingdom	7.9	7.8
Iceland	7.4	7.8
Germany	7.4	7.5
Denmark	7.1	7.1
Japan	4.9	5.2
Switzerland	4.5	4.6
Austria	4.4	4.8
Netherlands	4.2	3.9
Norway	3.5	3.3

SOURCE: OECD

Spain topped the list of countries with the highest jobless rates in the first quarter of 2010. Illustration/XNR Productions/Cengage Learning, Gale.

percent in August 2009. Economists, however, describe unemployment as a "lagging indicator" of economic health and warn that unemployment figures tend to remain high for some time, even as other economic indicators improve.

Figures released by the British Office for National Statistics in late October 2009 showed that the economy of Great Britain had shrunk by an annual rate of 0.4 percent in the third quarter of 2009. The U.S. economy, however, grew by an annual rate of 0.9 percent, its first expansion in more than a year. Since a recession is technically defined as the contraction of the economy for two quarters in a row, any economic growth in one quarter signals the end of the recession. In late November 2009, the U.S. Department of Commerce predicted the U.S. economic growth rate would be about 2.8 percent for 2009. Despite these statistics, ordinary people had a hard

time seeing any improvement in their own lives, as jobs remained scarce and credit remained tight. Many began to regard their shrunken economic prospects "the new normal."

The Irish Republic, which was hit harder than many European nations by the economic downturn, announced in December 2009 that financial figures for the third quarter showed a 0.3 percent rise in gross domestic product, meaning that the recession was officially over. However, the country implemented extremely sharp cuts in government spending to balance its finances, and joblessness remained high.

On 9 June, the Finnish government announced that Finland's economy had dipped back into recession after a weak recovery in 2009. In the fourth quarter of 2009, the economy contracted by 0.2 percent, and in the first quarter of 2010 the economy contracted by 0.4 percent. People all over the world worried about the possibility of this kind of "double dip" recession elsewhere. A double dip recession occurs when a second period of recession follows a brief recovery from an earlier recession.

Trouble in Greece Threatens All of Europe

As the economic crisis continued, developments in Greece threatened to tear the country apart. From 1997 through 2007, Greece experienced stable economic growth averaging about 4 percent. In the wake of the global financial crisis, however, Greece dropped into a major recession that threatened not only that country but also the stability of the European Union. The government deficit in 2009 was 13.6 percent of the GDP, with public debt at 115.1 percent of GDP the same year.

By February 2010, the entire Eurozone (comprising the countries that use the euro as currency) faced a tricky dilemma as Greece edged closer to defaulting on its debts. Major governments and

Greece's Debt-Concealing Tactics That Fueled Financial Troubles

1. **Formation of European Monetary Union (1998)** To enter the EMU, a country had to meet four economic standards, all of which Greece failed

2. **Shaky fix** Greece had two years to fix its economic situation before an EMU re-evaluation; it tried to reduce deficits by mortgaging government entities, masking loans as sales

3. **'Adriadne deal'** This 2000 deal let Greece receive 355 million euros in exchange for national lottery revenues

4. **'Aiolos deal'** In 2001, Greece got 650 million euros in exchange for landing fees at Greek airports through 2019

5. **Goldman Sachs** Once part of the EMU, Greece wanted to continue domestic spending while staying within EMU rules; in 2001, Goldman Sachs helped Greece with a $15 billion bond sale following a loan-turned currency swap; Goldman got $300 million for its services

6. **Effect of debt-hiding deals** Under EMU law, disclosing such deals was not required; in 2002 the law was changed, but Greece was not required to publicize deals made before the law was enacted; the deals helped Greece improve its budget and meet its EMU targets, but hid the realities of its troubled financial situation

SOURCE: Chicago Tribune

economic powers within the bloc, such as Germany, were beginning to express a strong reluctance to bail out Greece, and some analysts were questioning the viability of the European experiment—the great institutional, political, and economic cooperation that spans the continent. The Greek debt crisis spooked international markets that were already battered by the crisis of 2008. Economists worried that if Greece was allowed to default on its debts, the world economy would plunge back into recession.

Eurozone leaders announced in April 2010 the details of a long-awaited loan package for Greece, soothing concerns about the future of the country and the value of the euro. The financial rescue plan provided Greece with up to $40 billion in loans at 5 percent interest, significantly lower than the 7.5 percent interest rate that markets were demanding. Analysts expected the International Monetary Fund (IMF), an intergovernmental body that oversees the world financial system, to offer an additional $20 billion in loans for Greece, with interest rates even lower than the 5 percent offered by Eurozone leaders.

Together, these measures stabilized the markets, but created concerns that other cash-strapped European countries, such as Spain, Portugal, and Italy, would plead for similar rescue packages. People in countries like Germany expressed outright anger at the thought of an endless line of supplicants looking for a handout.

The IMF and European Union (EU) bailout package for Greece was contingent on Greek lawmakers implementing a tough and extremely unpopular three-year austerity program. As lawmakers began debating these cutbacks in May 2010, widespread protests were held by workers opposing the proposed measures, which included raising the retirement age, reducing monthly payments to pensioners, and facilitating layoffs. Greek lawmakers voted on 6 May 2010 in favor (by wide margins) of the austerity measures.

In October 2010, the Greek government announced yet another round of austerity measures as part of its 2011 draft budget. The measures included higher taxes for businesses and an increase in the value-added tax (VAT), a tax on the estimated increase in value to a product as it moves through the manufacture and distribution

A riot policeman falls to the ground surrounded by flames after being hit with a Molotov cocktail, near the Greek parliament building on 5 May 2010. The announcement of austerity measures in Greece led to violent protests. John Kolesidis/Reuters.

processes, levied against businesses but ultimately passed on to consumers through higher prices. Officials hoped that such measures would reduce the budget deficit to 7 percent of GDP by the end of 2011, coming in below the 7.6 percent target set by Eurozone countries and the IMF as part of the nation's bailout package.

An unstable job market has made unemployment a major problem for youth and young adults just entering the workforce. According to an August 2010 survey, seven out of ten Greek college graduates between the ages of 22 and 35 wanted to find work abroad. Four out of ten were actively seeking work abroad or were pursuing further education in order to be better qualified to leave the country. In June 2010, the unemployment rate for those between the ages of 15 and 24 was a staggering 29.8 percent. For those between the ages of 25 and 34, the unemployment rate was 16.2 percent. Overall unemployment in June 2010 was 11.6 percent. Clearly, the young were feeling the heaviest strain, by far.

For the French, the Crisis Turns Even Uglier

In France, real GDP fell by 2.5 percent in 2009. In the first quarter of 2010, the economic growth rate was only 0.1 percent, with a forecast of GDP growth between 1.3 percent and 1.7 percent by the end of 2010. The unemployment rate was 9.5 percent in the first quarter of 2010, up from 9.2 percent in the third quarter of 2009. The slowdown highlighted the ongoing problem of government spending, which accounted for about

French steelworkers, dressed in their protective gear, march in Marseilles on 19 October 2010. They are participating in a nationwide strike to show their displeasure with proposed reforms to France's pension system and retirement age. Jean-Paul Pelissier/Reuters.

55.6 percent of GDP in 2009. In one effort to cut costs, the government proposed a 2010 bill to change the national retirement and pension plan by increasing the retirement age from 60 years to 62 years by 2018, with a full pension being offered at 67 years instead of 65.

An amendment would also raise the eligibility requirement for the number of years one must work and contribute to social security before retirement from 40.5 years to 41.5 years. The proposal sparked widespread outrage, resulting in protests that began in early September 2010 and continued into October, with hundreds of thousands of people marching in cities across the country. Supported through numerous labor unions,

the protests were accompanied by 24-hour strikes affecting a number of key professions and industries, including teachers and daycare workers, and workers in public transportation, construction, and the oil industry. The goal was to shut the country down utterly.

French president Nicolas Sarkozy said that he was "fully aware that this is a difficult reform. But I always considered that my duty, and the duty of the government, was to carry it out."

"The government's tactics border on fascism," one protestor responded. "The public response speaks for itself." Others responded with rocks and Molotov cocktails, or fire bombs.

Opponents of the government's proposal to increase eligibility requirements for retirement believed that the new guidelines placed an unfair burden on people who had worked part-time or been unemployed for long periods of time, especially women who had left the full-time workforce to raise children. The government maintained that pension reform was a necessary measure that could save the country 70 billion euros (about $88.9 billion). Union officials and opposition leaders proposed that the government consider alternatives, such as taxes on certain salary bonuses and higher incomes, as a way to fund the pension system.

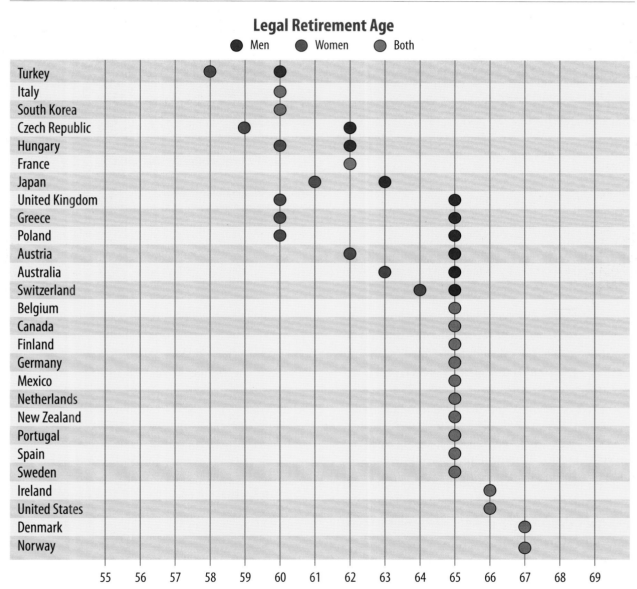

Legal Retirement Age
● Men   ● Women   ● Both

NOTE: The U.S. retirement age rises to 67 for people born after 1959. The Italian retirement age is being raised gradually from 60 to 65 by 2018.

SOURCES: OECD; The governments

French workers have strongly protested their government's plan to raise the country's retirement age to 62. This chart shows how France's retirement age compares to that of other countries. Illustration/XNR Productions/Cengage Learning, Gale.

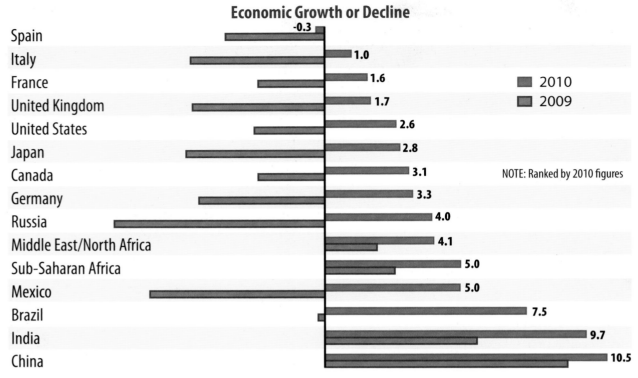

Economic Growth or Decline

Country	2010	2009
Spain	-0.3	
Italy	1.0	
France	1.6	
United Kingdom	1.7	
United States	2.6	
Japan	2.8	
Canada	3.1	
Germany	3.3	
Russia	4.0	
Middle East/North Africa	4.1	
Sub-Saharan Africa	5.0	
Mexico	5.0	
Brazil	7.5	
India	9.7	
China	10.5	

NOTE: Ranked by 2010 figures

SOURCE: International Monetary Fund

Although the world economy was predicted to grow in 2010, the United States ranked near the bottom in terms of growth while China and India were at the top. Illustration/XNR Productions/Cengage Learning, Gale.

A weeklong series of strikes beginning on 12 October 2010 resulted in serious disruptions in transportation and oil and fuel supplies, as numerous flights and trains were cancelled and nearly 4,000 gas stations ran dry. School days were disrupted as teachers and students joined the protests. Student protests in the Paris suburb of Nanterre became violent, leading police to fire tear gas to break up the crowd. Clashes between protestors and the police force also took place in Lyon and Mulhouse. The BBC reported that one opinion poll indicated that 71 percent of those surveyed supported the strikes.

Nevertheless, the new retirement age became law on 10 November 2010.

Efforts by Spain and Portugal to cut government spending met with similar push-back from labor unions in 2010. Spanish unions launched a general strike on 29 September in response to the government's plan to cut 15 billion euros from the budget. Labor leaders said the proposed reforms harmed the rights of workers in order to benefit businesses. Portugal saw its biggest strike in more than twenty years in November 2010, as workers walked off the job to protest proposed wage cuts for government employees.

Some Countries Continue to Flail While Others Thrive

On 8 July 2010, the IMF announced it was revising its global economic growth estimates for 2010 onwards, from 4.2 percent to 4.6 percent. Modest growth in developed economies and robust growth in Brazil, Russia, India, and China were cited as the causes for the revision. In fact, Brazil, Russia, India, and China, a group of developing economies nicknamed BRIC, fared surprisingly well and even thrived shortly after the worst of the global economic crisis passed. All four countries are big countries with large populations and a pool of inexpensive labor. All are predicted to have an agricultural boom in the coming decades in terms of imports, exports, and production.

A joint report by the United Nations and OECD (Organization for Economic Cooperation and Development) released in June 2010 predicted that agricultural output in BRIC nations would grow three times faster than output in developed Western nations. Brazil is on course for the biggest gains, with a predicted 40 percent expansion in agriculture by 2019. China and India are manufacturing and export powerhouses. Russia and Brazil export a range of raw materials, and Russia enjoys substantial profits from the oil

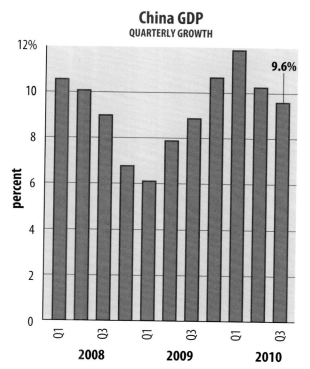

China GDP
QUARTERLY GROWTH

SOURCE: National Bureau of Statistics of China

China's quarterly growth dipped to 9.6 percent in the third quarter of 2010. Illustration/XNR Productions/Cengage Learning, Gale.

To show their displeasure with Spanish President Jose Luis Rodriguez Zapatero and other leaders, trade unionists donned masks and carried signs at the San Sebastian Film Festival in September 2010. The protester on the left depicted President Zapatero as a modern-day Pinocchio. AP Images/Alvaro Barrientos.

and gas industry. As Indian prime minister Manmohan Singh remarked in June 2009 ahead of a BRIC summit in Russia, "The countries of Brazil, Russia, India and China (BRIC) together account for 40 percent of the world's population and 40 percent of global GDP. The BRIC grouping has the potential to lead global economic growth."

However, even as the economies of BRIC countries thrive, poverty remains rampant. Simply put, economic growth in these countries does not directly translate to a higher standard of living for a majority of their citizens. A common

Although India has fared fairly well during the global financial crisis, a protest broke out in Lucknow in January 2010 when hundreds of state government workers demanded reforms to their pay system. Police officers armed with bamboo sticks sought to break up the crowd. Pawan Kumar/Reuters.

measure of standard of living is per capita GDP, or a country's gross domestic product divided by its population. Developed Western nations, though their economies struggled in 2008 and the years that followed, still had a per capita GDP seven to forty times higher than those in the BRIC countries. Economic projections show BRIC nations lagging far behind developed countries in terms of standard of living for decades to come.

In the United States in 2010, a Department of Commerce report showed that the nation's economy was growing, but more slowly than had been hoped. The U.S. economy grew by 3.7 percent in the first quarter of 2010, but growth slowed to an annualized rate of 2.4 percent in the second quarter. The slower growth has led economists to worry that high unemployment rates will persist for a long time to come.

Indeed, the U.S. Labor Department report in August 2010 showed a spike in new unemployment claims, with 500,000 new claims being filed in the week of 14 August. It was the highest weekly number in nine months. The report added to speculation that the United States may be heading toward a double dip recession, although most economists considered this an unlikely scenario because the U.S. economy was improving by several other measures. In November, the Department of Commerce said its figure for September showed the trade deficit had fallen to $44 billion due to strong sales of U.S. exports.

The Greek economy continued to contract

sharply in the second half of 2010, despite the IMF and EU rescue plan. The Greek economy shrank by 1.5 percent in the second quarter of 2010, with the GDP expected to shrink by 4 percent by the end of 2010.

Dwindling tax revenues and falling exports led many nations around the world to adopt austerity measures in 2010. Cutbacks in government spending and social benefits were met with the same kind of outrage that met similar initiatives in France, with widespread strikes by government workers and street protests in several European countries.

Things got outright dangerous for politicians who cut the budget too much. On 30 September, the government of Ecuador was almost toppled by an apparent coup attempt by police who were angry at the government's cuts in bonuses and promotions. President Rafael Correa was physically attacked as he tried to negotiate with national police gathered in the streets of Quito and forced to flee to a nearby hospital. Correa declared a state of emergency. Ecuador's state-run oil industry was hit hard by the global economic crisis and, despite rebounding oil prices, has yet to recover, by late 2010, to its pre-2008 levels.

EU leaders met in a two-day summit in October 2010 to discuss measures that would help prevent future debt crises, such as the one faced by Greece. France and Germany have offered a joint plan dubbed the Deauville Deal that would establish a permanent rescue fund and impose sanctions on debtor nations. The plan would require a change to the EU's governing treaty, which will be difficult and time-consuming.

The Major Continuing Threat: Unemployment

In the United States, the unemployment rate remained at just under 10 percent through 2009 and 2010. Recognizing that the high unemployment rate is a pressing concern and a threat to economic recovery, U.S. president Barack Obama held a "job summit" in Washington, D.C., in December 2009. The effort proved inadequate, and the Obama administration continued to try to demonstrate its commitment to stimulating job growth. On 8 January 2010, Obama announced a new set of grants to encourage jobs that create clean energy technology. He signed a bipartisan, $17.5

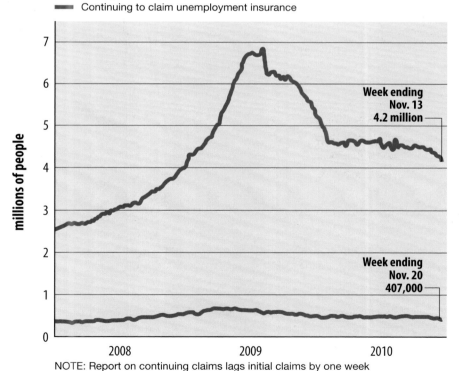

U.S. Unemployment Claims

- Making initial claim
- Continuing to claim unemployment insurance

Week ending Nov. 13 4.2 million

Week ending Nov. 20 407,000

millions of people

2008   2009   2010

NOTE: Report on continuing claims lags initial claims by one week

SOURCE: U.S. Department of Labor

Unemployment insurance claims in the United States have fluctuated significantly since December 2007, climbing to over 6 million in 2009 before decreasing to 4.2 million by mid-November 2010. Illustration/XNR Productions/Cengage Learning, Gale.

Austerity plans:

France
Plans to cut spending by 45 billion euros over three years, raise retirement age

Germany
Cut government jobs, raise tax on nuclear power

Greece
Drastic spending cuts, crack down on tax evasion and corruption within tax service

Ireland
Latest measures cut government spending by 4 billion euros, cut pay for public workers and reduced welfare

Italy
Cut public sector pay and pensions; freeze public jobs; target tax evaders

Netherlands
Budget cuts of 3.2 billion euros; includes spending on health care, immigrants, government workers

Portugal
Cut pay for top public workers and military spending, raise VAT

Romania
Wage, pension cuts

Spain
Raise taxes on the rich, cut pay for government workers

United Kingdom
New government announced its first steps, 7.2 billion euros of cuts in departmental programs

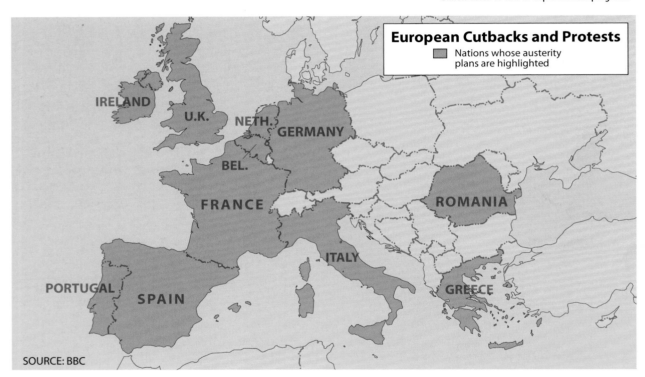

European Cutbacks and Protests
Nations whose austerity plans are highlighted

SOURCE: BBC

Throughout Europe, citizens have vigorously protested government spending cuts, pay freezes, tax increases, and other austerity measures. A look at some of those cutbacks and protests are described here. Illustration/XNR Productions/Cengage Learning, Gale.

billion jobs bill called the HIRE Act into law on 18 March. The new law contains a combination of tax cuts, business credits, and subsidies for state and local construction bonds. Nothing he did, however, made a significant difference.

On 2 November 2010, the U.S. held nationwide mid-term elections. Democrats had to defend the majorities they had won in the House of Representatives and Senate, and in state-level offices, during the presidential election cycle of 2008 that had swept Barack Obama into the presidency.

The results of the 2010 mid-term elections were a debacle for the Democrats. Republicans picked up over sixty seats in the House of Rep-

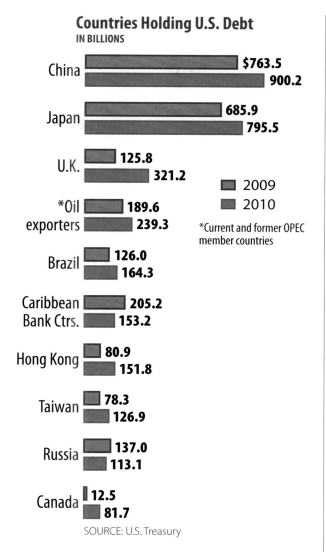

Countries Holding U.S. Debt
IN BILLIONS

China: $763.5 / 900.2
Japan: 685.9 / 795.5
U.K.: 125.8 / 321.2
*Oil exporters: 189.6 / 239.3
Brazil: 126.0 / 164.3
Caribbean Bank Ctrs.: 205.2 / 153.2
Hong Kong: 80.9 / 151.8
Taiwan: 78.3 / 126.9
Russia: 137.0 / 113.1
Canada: 12.5 / 81.7

■ 2009
■ 2010

*Current and former OPEC member countries

SOURCE: U.S. Treasury

China and Japan continue to be among the top foreign holders of U.S. debt. Illustration/XNR Productions/Cengage Learning, Gale.

resentatives, and while they did not capture the Senate, they gained enough seats in the upper house to bring them within easy striking distance of a majority in the 2012 election, when the number of Democrats defending their seats will greatly outnumber Republicans. Most striking, Republicans won sweeping victories at the state level.

Exit polls conducted during the 2010 mid-term election in the United States indicated that the condition of the economy was a dominant reason

voters had chosen to oust Democrats from power. Another factor was concern over the soaring government debt accumulated by the Obama administration and the Democratic Congress in various attempts to jumpstart the economy through direct federal spending and other forms of stimulus. The actual impact of these stimulus plans will continue to be a matter of debate for some time.

Pointing the Finger of Blame

The roots of the global financial crisis that began in 2008 stretch back several years and are complicated by many factors in addition to the risky financial decisions made by mortgage lenders. One of these was a push within the political system to increase home ownership among minority populations. In October 2002, President George Bush gave a speech in which he declared an increase in home ownership among minorities as a major goal of his presidency. "More and more people own their homes in America today," he said. "Two-thirds of all Americans own their homes, yet we have a problem because fewer than half of the Hispanics and half the African Americans own the home. That's a home ownership gap."

Bush went on to denounce traditional lending standards, citing the inability of many Americans to make a down payment as one of the reasons for the gap in home ownership among minorities. Bush wanted lenders to change traditional lending standards, easing the way for borrowers to get approved for home loans without the traditional money up front. This initiative did not meet with any resistance, and no major political figures questioned its long-term financial impact. In fact, because the idea was designed to increase minority homeownership, it was greeted enthusiastically by a wide range of people. In the end, however, lenders began making risky loans not just to minorities, but to anyone who asked, prompting the growth of the housing bubble that eventually burst in 2007.

Executives from Goldman Sachs testify before the U.S. Senate at a hearing on the role of investment banks during the financial crisis, 27 April 2010. The Securities and Exchange Commission charged Goldman Sachs with fraud on 16 April 2010. Olivier Douliery/Abaca Press/MCT.

Shady Accounting Practices

Financial policymakers also place a large part of the blame for the global economic crisis on accounting rules that made the financial health of large institutions hard to determine. Put simply, accounting rules, both in the United States and the European Union, allowed banks and financial institutions to hide risky assets from investors. They were helped by accountants willing to stretch —or even, some critics say, break —these rules to the greatest degree possible. Congress ordered the Financial Accounting Standards Board (FASB) to change rules to ensure greater transparency in financial reporting. The International Accounting Standards Board was similarly pressured by the European Commission to tighten its rules.

As Western economies regained a little momentum, the public and many political leaders expressed dismay at what appeared to be "business as usual" at some of the financial institutions that had required government assistance to stay afloat just months earlier. In July 2009, JP Morgan reported a $2.72 billion profit, while Goldman Sachs reported a $3.44 billion profit. JP Morgan had already repaid in full the $25 billion it had received in bailout funds from the government. While most analysts considered robust profits by banks to be a positive sign, the average citizen saw things differently. The idea of financiers returning to their comfortable lifestyles while ordinary people continued to suffer through hard times, in part caused by the recklessness of the same bankers, caused a lot of anger and resentment. Announcements of planned multimillion-dollar bonuses at large financial institutions further fueled the controversy. To ordinary people, it looked like outright greed.

Leaders in the United Kingdom, France, and Germany agreed that gigantic bonuses for bank-

Wall Street greed continues to anger many Americans. Here, as members of the American Bankers Association met inside a convention center in Boston in October 2010, protesters lined the sidewalk, demanding a swift end to home foreclosures. Marilyn Humphries/newscom.

ers were not only in poor taste but also financially irresponsible. German chancellor Angela Merkel, French president Nicolas Sarkozy, and British prime minister Gordon Brown issued a joint letter in September 2009 ahead of a full meeting of the G-20 nations, making clear that bankers' pay, including bonuses, should be capped. Many European Union leaders agreed that bonuses for bank executives should be regulated in some way. The United States, however, has objected to setting limits on pay. The controversy was a major topic of discussion at the meeting of the G-20 in Pittsburgh, Pennsylvania, in late September 2009.

In mid-October 2009, several U.S. banks, including JP Morgan and Goldman Sachs, announced robust profits once again. The news was enough to send the Dow Jones Industrial Average above the 10,000 mark on 14 October, its highest level in more than a year. Despite the positive financial news, the White House was quick to cau-

tion the banking industry to avoid returning to pre-crisis compensation packages. The U.S. Congress, meanwhile, pushed forward on a variety of financial regulation bills, and President Barack Obama praised a plan by the United States Treasury Department to require companies that had received government bailouts to slash the salaries of their twenty-five highest-paid employees by up to 90 percent. This proposal was the first-ever compensation cap plan by the United States government.

Learning Lessons and Moving On

On 22 April 2010, President Obama gave a speech in support of his proposed financial reform bill at Cooper Union College in New York City. In it, he assailed critics of the bill, and warned that without meaningful regulation, the United States financial system would be in danger of another crisis like the one it faced in 2008 and 2009. Obama also addressed leaders of the financial sector, calling on them to lend their support to government reform efforts for the good of the country.

The bill prompted fierce resistance by some Wall Street lobbyists, but in July 2010, the Senate gave final approval to the financial reform bill, which prompted the biggest reorganization of the U.S. financial system in decades. The new law protects borrowers from the kind of abuses that led to the subprime meltdown that started the global economic crisis in the first place. It accords the federal government the power to shut down large financial firms that are in danger of collapse; such collapse can often destroy other firms as well, and can, in a worst-case scenario, take down the entire economy. Furthermore, people who own shares in corporations will have more say over how those companies are governed. The legislation is new, however, and it remains to be seen how it will work in practice.

As 2010 drew to a close, world leaders carefully nurtured a fragile economic recovery. The IMF declared the global recession officially over in April 2010, and pointed to strong growth in Australia and industrialized Asian countries as evidence that a recovery was well under way. Still, there were worrisome indications that once-strong Western economies were still in danger. Ireland enjoyed an economic boom in the 1990s, leading financial journalists to dub it the "Celtic Tiger." However, by November 2010, Irish officials announced that Ireland had requested and accepted a bailout from the EU and IMF: a package of loans totaling $100 billion aimed at propping up Irish banks.

Americans anxious to see evidence that enormous taxpayer-funded bailouts and stimulus spending were working finally had some reason to celebrate in November 2010, when General Motors (GM) shares made a record-smashing return to the stock market. The beleaguered American car maker had gone into bankruptcy and required a government bailout in 2009. President Obama touted GM's rapid turn-around, and strong financial performances by America's other leading carmakers, at an event in an auto plant in Kokomo, Indiana, on 23 November, saying: "We're coming back. We're on the move. All three American [car] companies are profitable, and they are growing.... So here's the lesson: Don't bet against America."

Research and Exploration

The Becker-Posner Blog. http://uchicagolaw.typepad.com/beckerposner/.

> Readable explanation of economic news by a pair of famous academics.

Daniel W. Drezner. http://drezner.foreignpolicy.com/.

> Blog that combines economics with pop culture.

DQ News. http://www.dqnews.com/

> Hard information on real estate, including information that is typically kept confidential by real estate professionals.

Dr. Housing Bubble. http://www.doctorhousingbubble.com/.

> Popular blog that examines real estate in an irreverent way.

The Great Depression of 2006. http://greatdepression2006.blogspot.com/.

> Another popular blog, one that assumes we are in worse shape than many people believe.

The Housing Bubble. http://thehousingbubbleblog.com/index.html.

> Blog that examined the housing bubble as it inflated, and continues to examine the aftereffects.

Megan McArdle. http://www.theatlantic.com/megan-mcardle/.

> Daily economics news from an expert who playfully identifies herself as the world's "tallest female econoblogger."

Mortgage Fraud Blog. http://www.mortgage fraudblog.com/.

Closely tracks mortgage rescue scams and other similar fraud arising from the economic crisis.

The Mortgage Lender Implode-O-Meter. http://ml -implode.com/.

Web site that tracks bank failures and other financial disasters.

Paper Economy. http://paper-money.blogspot.com/.

Includes a great deal of raw economic data, but explains it in a readable way.

Gulf Oil Spill

The Business of Energy and Oily Birds

In April 2010, fires from an explosion sank the *Deepwater Horizon* oil rig located in the Gulf of Mexico about 52 miles (84 kilometers) southeast of the coastal city and port of Venice, Louisiana. The initial explosion killed 11 workers and seriously injured 17 others. The resulting oil-well blowout created a massive oil spill from a deep-water well located 5,000 feet (1,500 meters) below the surface that ultimately became the worst accidental marine oil spill in history.

U.S. president Barack Obama described the *Deepwater Horizon* spill (also known as the Gulf spill or BP spill) as the worst environmental disaster in U.S. history.

The spill continued to gush oil for 87 days, closing a significant portion of the gulf to fishing, fouling approximately 600 miles of coastline, and washing oil into marshes, wetlands, and inland waterways. The spill created a swath of environmental devastation—killing thousands of birds and marine animals, imperiling both local and migratory species—along broad areas of the central and northern Gulf Coast, while simultaneously delivering a crippling blow to the economic base of the region.

The Accident

Built in South Korea by Hyundai Heavy Industries, the *Deepwater Horizon* rig was classified as an ultra-deepwater, dynamically positioned, semi-submersible offshore drilling rig. At the time of the disaster, the platform was insured for $560 million (the anticipated cost of salvage and replacement) and was located within the Mississippi Canyon Block 252, also called the Macondo Prospect oil field.

The *Deepwater Horizon*, under lease to BP (formerly British Petroleum), was owned and operated by Transocean, a Swiss-based company. The

When the *Deepwater Horizon* oil rig exploded on 20 April 2010 in the Gulf of Mexico, it claimed the lives of 11 workers. The blast also marked the start of the worst accidental marine oil spill in history—a spill that lasted 87 days. John T. Fritz/McClatchy-Tribune.

rig was designed to operate in waters up to 8,000 feet deep. The rig was not yet in full production but was carrying out exploratory offshore drilling. Early engineering analysis concluded that one or more gas bubbles caused the initial explosion on 20 April 2010. Gas bubbles can work their way up a drill hole because of unusual geologic features or because of failures in safety equipment. If a gas bubble passes through the riser that connects the blowout preventer (BOP) stack and shut-off valves on the sea floor and then enters the riser connecting to the rig on the surface, the gas bubble will begin to rise swiftly, expanding as it nears the surface and pressure decreases. The expanding gas can ignite, resulting in an explosion and fire. For reasons still under investigation, shut-off valves on the rig did not contain the leaking gas or oil.

On 19 April, as part of an effort to secure the well for later production, personnel from Halliburton, an energy services corporation, completed the cementing of reinforcement casings in the well. Less than one day later, on 20 April at 9:45 p.m. central daylight time (CDT), a geyser of water, mud, and methane gas shot several hundred feet into the air over the rig's drilling floor from a

Firefighting boats surround the burning *Deepwater Horizon* on 21 April 2010. AP Images/Gerald Herbert. ▶

United States Government Flowrate Estimates
KEY ESTIMATES IN BARRELS PER DAY

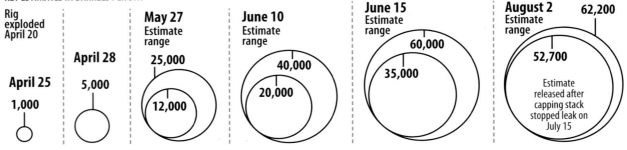

NOTE: One barrel equals 42 gallons

SOURCE: National Commission on the BP Deepwater Horizon Oil Spill and Offshore Drilling

Estimates of how many barrels of oil leaked into the Gulf per day. Scientists estimated in August 2010 that when reservoir pressures were at their highest levels during the early weeks of the spill, about 62,000 barrels (2.6 million gallons) of oil leaked from the damaged well infrastructure each day. Illustration/XNR Productions/Cengage Learning, Gale.

high-pressurized marine riser pipe attached to the wellhead below. Released gas ignited and a series of explosions followed. The explosion killed 11 workers and seriously injured another 17. Technicians struggled in failed attempts to close the blowout preventer (a valve designed to seal off a well).

In response to a distress call, the United States Coast Guard dispatched two ships, one rescue airplane, and four helicopters to the site. Within hours, response teams from BP, Transocean, and the Coast Guard were coordinating rescue and fire suppression efforts. Within 24 hours, the Coast Guard determined the incident had the potential to become a major environmental disaster for the United States. Attempts to control the blow-out failed, and fire consumed the rig.

At 3:22 p.m. CDT on 22 April, the Coast Guard log reported the sinking of the *Deepwater Horizon* rig. Oil from the sunken rig site gushed into the Gulf of Mexico. Using remotely operated vehicles (ROVs) to examine the wreckage, engineers quickly discovered at least three major leaks. Cameras aboard the submersibles showed that oil was leaking from a ruptured drill pipe near the wellhead and also from the crumpled riser pipe

that had once connected the *Deepwater Horizon* rig to the well head.

In hopes of preventing technological failures on oil rigs, some nations require redundant technologies designed to contain blowouts to be placed on every well. However, the United States, which controlled the deepwater lease in which the well was drilled, required only the BOP and no contingency plan for BOP failure.

Size of the Spill

Estimates of the volume of oil gushing into the gulf increased steadily as scientists gained access to high-resolution video of the leaking well and other data. The oil leak was initially estimated by BP at 1,000 barrels (about 42,000 gallons) of oil per day. On 21 May 2010, the national incident commander for the *Deepwater Horizon* spill established the Flow Rate Technical Group (FRTG), a government-led effort to determine the oil spill's flow rate. For several weeks, both BP and U.S. government officials clung to a spill estimate of 5,000 barrels (210,000 gallons) of oil per day. However, based on continued satellite observations and other measurements, an increasing array of experts immediately and repeatedly asserted that the rate of oil leakage was

World's Biggest Oil Spills
IN MILLIONS OF GALLONS

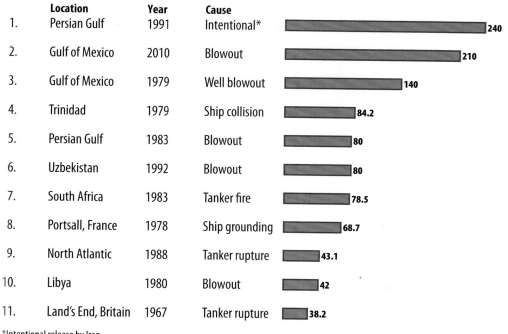

	Location	Year	Cause	
1.	Persian Gulf	1991	Intentional*	240
2.	Gulf of Mexico	2010	Blowout	210
3.	Gulf of Mexico	1979	Well blowout	140
4.	Trinidad	1979	Ship collision	84.2
5.	Persian Gulf	1983	Blowout	80
6.	Uzbekistan	1992	Blowout	80
7.	South Africa	1983	Tanker fire	78.5
8.	Portsall, France	1978	Ship grounding	68.7
9.	North Atlantic	1988	Tanker rupture	43.1
10.	Libya	1980	Blowout	42
11.	Land's End, Britain	1967	Tanker rupture	38.2

*Intentional release by Iraq

SOURCE: Oil Spill Intelligence Report

The Deepwater Horizon spill is the second biggest recorded oil spill in the world, topped only by Iraq's intentional spilling in 1991. Illustration/XNR Productions/Cengage Learning, Gale.

significantly greater. By June, continued observation of the gushing flow of oil from an overwhelmed BP containment cap system caused officials to further raise estimates of the rate of oil leakage to a range of from 35,000 barrels (1.47 million gallons) to 60,000 barrels (2.52 million gallons) of oil per day. In August 2010, scientists and engineers working for the U.S. government estimated that just prior to initially capping the well on 15 July, the rate of leakage was 53,000 barrels (2.27 million gallons) of oil per day. Because the August estimates were based on direct pressure readings taken from inside the capped well, scientists described them as the most accurate.

Scientists later estimated that when reservoir pressures were at their highest levels during the early weeks of the spill, about 62,000 barrels (2.6 million gallons) of oil leaked from the damaged well infrastructure each day. Even with an error rate estimated at plus or minus 10 percent, the new official estimates confirmed that the BP spill—estimated to total approximately 5 million barrels (210 million gallons) of oil—surpassed the estimated 3.3 million barrels (approximately 140 million gallons) of oil released during the 1979 *Ixtoc I* spill, making the BP spill the worst accidental marine oil spill in history. The *Ixtoc I* spill followed a Petroleos Mexicanos' (PEMEX) rig explosion in the Bay of Campeche (the southern Gulf of Mexico off Mexico's coast). The 2010 BP spill far surpassed the 11 million gallons of oil spilled into Alaskan waters following the 1989 grounding of the tanker *Exxon Valdez*.

By 24 April 2010, a rapidly expanding surface

Oil is shown floating in the Gulf of Mexico near Orange Beach, Alabama, in mid-June. Oily beaches kept many tourists away, resulting in a significant loss of business revenue. Kari Goodnough/Bloomburg/Getty Images.

oil slick was visible in the Gulf. The Coast Guard, which had oversight of accident and cleanup operations, reported that early efforts to reduce expansion of the slick were thwarted by heavy weather. By 14 May, the slick touched barrier islands off Louisiana's Chandeleur and Breton sounds. By 24 May, oil began to wash into Louisiana wetland areas. By June, oil washed ashore along beaches from Louisiana to Florida. One month later, observations of oil in inland waterways, estuaries, and lakes increased, including sightings of oil in Lake Pontchartrain, the large lake bordering on New Orleans and a source of water for the city.

Media Coverage: Watching and Tracking the Spill

Within days, the *Deepwater Horizon* spill became the focal point for intense and worldwide media attention. Coverage on cable and Internet news media outlets was essentially non-stop, and reporters from around the world converged on the Gulf Coast to cover various aspects of the spill. In many regards, the spill replaced the devastating January 2010 earthquake in Haiti as the preeminent global news story.

Over the following weeks and months, NASA satellite photographs—obtained from the Moderate Resolution Imaging Spectroradiometer (MODIS) mounted on the Aqua satellite and the Advanced Land Imager aboard the Earth Observing-1 (EO-1) satellite—provided evidence of an expanding surface oil slick over the northern Gulf of Mexico. Underwater photographers sought pictures of scientists using fluorometers to map and measure clouds and plumes of sub-surface oil and later layers of subsurface oil mixed with chemical dispersants. Deepwater cameras captured oil gushing from the site and broadcast them worldwide in real time. Local Gulf Coast officials became regular guests on international news programs.

Many experts asserted that clear evidence was provided from the video of the continuing underwater gusher, which produced some of the most iconic images of the disaster and which became an Internet viral sensation, that the size of the spill was underestimated. Media stories then branched

Blowout Preventer

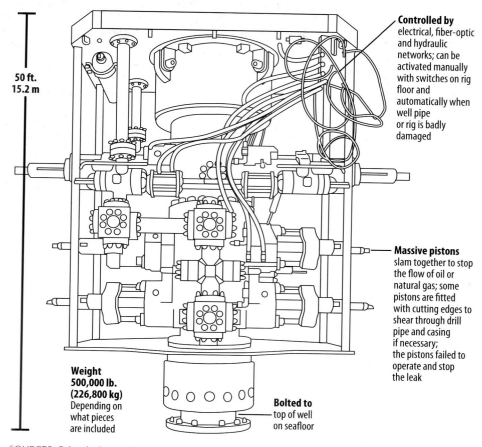

50 ft.
15.2 m

Controlled by electrical, fiber-optic and hydraulic networks; can be activated manually with switches on rig floor and automatically when well pipe or rig is badly damaged

Massive pistons slam together to stop the flow of oil or natural gas; some pistons are fitted with cutting edges to shear through drill pipe and casing if necessary; the pistons failed to operate and stop the leak

Weight 500,000 lb. (226,800 kg) Depending on what pieces are included

Bolted to top of well on seafloor

SOURCES: Orlando Sentinel, octnet.org

The blowout preventer failed to prevent or stop the oil leaking into the Gulf. Illustration/XNR Productions/Cengage Learning, Gale.

into allegations of information suppression and increasingly focused their critical attention on the government and BP responses to the spill in a manner similar to criticism levied during the failed government response to Hurricane Katrina in 2005. Many news outlets sent the same reporters back to areas and communities from which they had covered the Katrina disaster.

Containment Efforts

Stopping the spill or significantly limiting the amount of oil spewing into the gulf initially proved impossible. Automatic shut-off valves on the blowout preventer, a 50-foot stack of valves that sits on top of the wellhead, failed to operate and then failed to respond to remote commands. The blowout preventer valves are designed to close when there are sudden surges or drops in oil or gas pressure. Such surges or fluctuations in pressure are often the cause of blowout explosions. With the valves damaged or open, the oil spill continued as engineers also attempted to use robot submersibles to close the valves. While continuing efforts to stop the leak at the source, engineers immediately began to assemble oil collection domes.

Dome Setback

Pipe to ship

What happened?
Extremely cold temperatures and high pressure caused methane and seawater to turn into ice-like crystals called hydrates; the hydrates merged to plug the dome's pipe

OIL

Dome

Oil pipe from well

Sea floor

LEAK

Below surface

SOURCES: BP, USGS

A clog in BP's oil containment dome's pipe caused a setback in stopping the oil leak. Illustration/XNR Productions/Cengage Learning, Gale.

Containment domes are normally used in shallower waters and prior to the *Deepwater Horizon* spill had never been deployed at depths required to contain this type of leak. BP officials also immediately dispatched drilling equipment and two rigs capable of drilling nearby relief wells to reduce the pressure within the leaking well, thus reducing the rate and amount of oil spillage and ultimately capable of plugging the well with mud and concrete. However, engineers cautioned that drilling relief wells would take months.

Efforts to stop the leak were performed under difficult marine conditions. Rough seas hampered initial efforts to close the blowout preventer shut-off valves. The vertical column of pipes from the seafloor was so badly damaged that, akin to kinks in a hose, the twisted remains of the connecting pipe actually acted to slow the oil leak. Engineers had to proceed with caution because while attempting repairs they ran the risk of opening new leaks or inadvertently increasing the amount of oil gushing into the gulf.

Containment Dome and Siphon

Early in May, an attempt was made to place a 98-ton steel and concrete containment dome (called a top hat) on top of the largest leak. The top hat, which was four feet (1.2 meters) in diameter and five feet (1.5 meters) tall, would have attached to a drill pipe to siphon oil to a ship waiting nearby. However, this procedure failed when the pipe became blocked with gas hydrates (crystalline solids of methane gas and

How a "Top Kill" Works

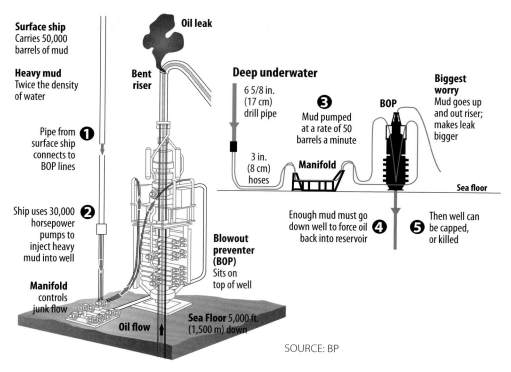

Surface ship
Carries 50,000 barrels of mud

Heavy mud
Twice the density of water

Bent riser

Oil leak

Deep underwater

6 5/8 in. (17 cm) drill pipe

❸ Mud pumped at a rate of 50 barrels a minute

BOP

Biggest worry
Mud goes up and out riser; makes leak bigger

Pipe from surface ship ❶ connects to BOP lines

3 in. (8 cm) hoses

Manifold

Sea floor

Ship uses 30,000 horsepower pumps to inject heavy mud into well ❷

Blowout preventer (BOP)
Sits on top of well

Enough mud must go down well to force oil back into reservoir ❹

❺ Then well can be capped, or killed

Manifold
controls junk flow

Oil flow

Sea Floor 5,000 ft. (1,500 m) down

SOURCE: BP

Illustration of the "top kill" procedure BP attempted in late May. Illustration/XNR Productions/Cengage Learning, Gale.

water molecules). In the second week after the attempt, the insertion of a Riser Insertion Tube Tool (RITT) between the platform pipe and the broken seafloor pipe allowed collection of a small amount of the leaking oil.

Top Kill and Junk Shot

On 25 May, the RITT apparatus was removed so a top kill technique and a junk shot technique could be attempted to permanently close the leak. Heavy drilling fluids were pumped through two lines into the blowout preventer on the seabed. The top kill technique was designed to restrict the flow of oil so that cement could be poured in to permanently seal the leak. After temporarily stopping the flow, BP announced on 29 May that the top kill method failed. The junk shot technique, which consisted of shooting shredded tire bits, golf balls, knotted rope, and certain other materials into the BOP with the intention of clogging it also failed.

LMRP Cap (BOP cap)

BP's next step was to begin using the lower marine riser package (LMRP) cap containment system. A diamond saw blade began cutting the damaged riser so that a custom-built cap could be placed on the newly cut pipe; however, the saw became stuck. With a substituted pair of shears, a successful cut was accomplished on 3 June, and a cap was attached. BP officials announced that the cut and cap procedure was capturing approximately 15,000 barrels of oil per day. However, experts quickly pointed out that this amount was obviously only a fraction of the spill continuing to gush through valves that engineers were forced to leave open in order to stabilize the cap system. Heavy seas resulting from an early-season hurricane in the southern Gulf of Mexico also interrupted surface skimming operations for more than a week.

How a "Junk Shot" Works

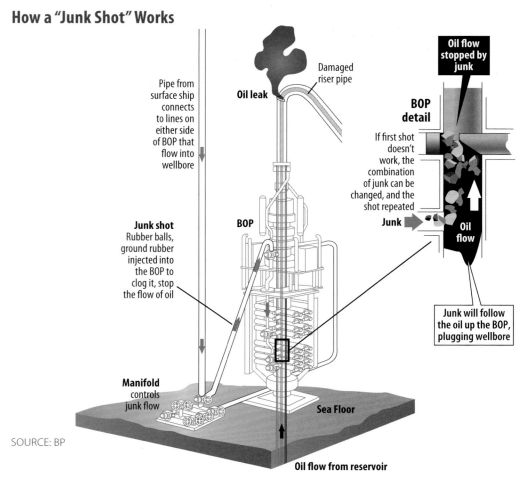

Pipe from surface ship connects to lines on either side of BOP that flow into wellbore

Oil leak

Damaged riser pipe

Oil flow stopped by junk

BOP detail

If first shot doesn't work, the combination of junk can be changed, and the shot repeated

Junk shot
Rubber balls, ground rubber injected into the BOP to clog it, stop the flow of oil

BOP

Junk

Oil flow

Junk will follow the oil up the BOP, plugging wellbore

Manifold
controls junk flow

Sea Floor

SOURCE: BP

Oil flow from reservoir

A depiction of the "junk shot" that BP used in a failed attempt to stop the oil leak. Illustration/XNR Productions/Cengage Learning, Gale.

New Cap Assembly

On 10 July, the LMRP cap was removed so that a different cap could be installed. The new cap assembly consisted of a flange transition spool and a stack of valves. Five days later, BP announced that the leak had stopped when the BOP was closed with the new cap assembly.

Static Kill

Instead of waiting for the completion of the relief wells, engineers opted to start a static kill

A remotely operated submersible vehicle works on the leaking riser pipe at the site of the Deepwater Horizon oil leak in the Gulf of Mexico in this image taken from a BP live video feed on 3 June 2010. Reuters/Landov. ▶

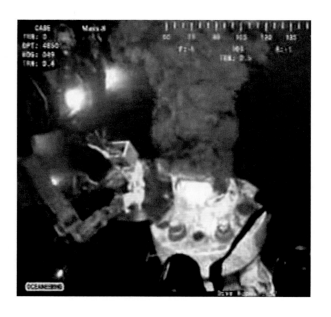

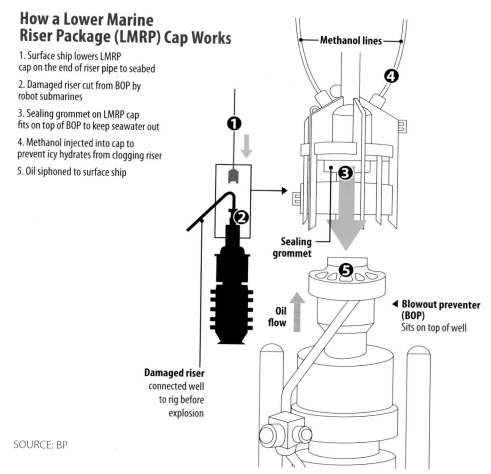

How a Lower Marine Riser Package (LMRP) Cap Works

1. Surface ship lowers LMRP cap on the end of riser pipe to seabed

2. Damaged riser cut from BOP by robot submarines

3. Sealing grommet on LMRP cap fits on top of BOP to keep seawater out

4. Methanol injected into cap to prevent icy hydrates from clogging riser

5. Oil siphoned to surface ship

Methanol lines

Sealing grommet

Oil flow

Damaged riser
connected well to rig before explosion

Blowout preventer (BOP)
Sits on top of well

SOURCE: BP

How BP's lower marine riser package (LMRP) cap was intended to capture oil that was leaking into the Gulf. Illustration/XNR Productions/Cengage Learning, Gale.

(also known as bullheading or hydrostatic kill) procedure by pumping in the sealing mixture through a modified well cap. On 3 August, BP began the static kill process. The process involved injecting several thousands of barrels of cement and mud through the containment cap and into the top of the damaged BP well. The cement plug created from the process was designed to hold back the pressure of the oil, which was estimated at about 7,000 pounds per square inch, or almost 500 times atmospheric pressure. On 9 August, BP reported that the static kill procedure was holding, and the well was temporarily sealed.

New BOP

On 4 September, the damaged BOP was removed from the site and lifted to the surface, a process that took just over one day. The FBI took possession of the damaged BOP to begin a series of forensic examinations. As an added safety measure, a new BOP was installed on the sealed well.

Bottom Kill via Relief Wells

Delayed once again by tropical weather, the long-anticipated bottom kill procedure, which involved pumping a sealing mixture through a relief well intersecting the damaged well column far

How a "Static Kill" Works

SOURCE: BP

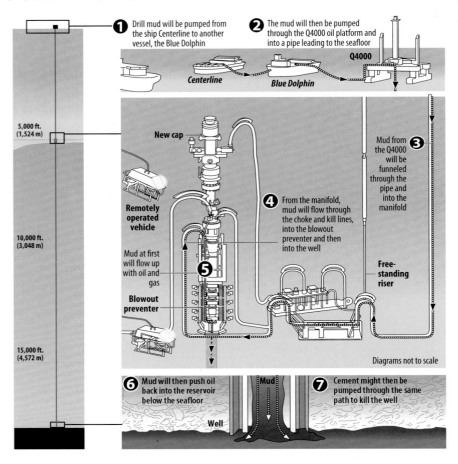

1 Drill mud will be pumped from the ship Centerline to another vessel, the Blue Dolphin

2 The mud will then be pumped through the Q4000 oil platform and into a pipe leading to the seafloor

Q4000

Centerline   Blue Dolphin

5,000 ft.
(1,524 m)

New cap

3 Mud from the Q4000 will be funneled through the pipe and into the manifold

Remotely operated vehicle

4 From the manifold, mud will flow through the choke and kill lines, into the blowout preventer and then into the well

10,000 ft.
(3,048 m)

Mud at first will flow up with oil and gas

5

Free-standing riser

Blowout preventer

15,000 ft.
(4,572 m)

Diagrams not to scale

6 Mud will then push oil back into the reservoir below the seafloor

Mud

7 Cement might then be pumped through the same path to kill the well

Well

In August, BP was able to temporarily seal the leaking well by pumping drilling mud and concrete down into the well. Illustration/XNR Productions/Cengage Learning, Gale.

below the seafloor, was completed in late August as a secondary method to permanently seal the well. The bottom kill involved pumping cement and mud from the bottom of the well, similar to the static kill technique used earlier. On 19 September, Incident Commander and Retired Coast Guard Admiral Thad Allen announced that the well was dead.

Clean Up

The federal government formed the *Deepwater Horizon* Unified Command, which includes BP and Transocean, along with numerous government agencies, to fight the environmental problems associated with the BP oil spill. At one time, the organization commanded 1,400 vessels, 20,000 personnel, and operated out of 17 staging areas.

Initial mitigation and cleanup efforts included measures to both contain and directly remove surface oil. These efforts relied on floating booms and skimmers to contain the slick until it could be pumped into container vessels. Controlled burns were used to eliminate surface oil, and boats and aircraft also applied unprecedented amounts of oil dispersants in affected areas. Teams of workers were dispatched to clean oiled beaches. In some cases, wetland areas were cleaned by hand.

Despite their efforts, Unified Command officials ultimately acknowledged that only a small percentage of oil was recovered. Aspects of the clean-up effort were also controversial because they limited citizen involvement, along with journalist and citizen access to public beaches and waters.

With the undersea oil leak stopped, the remaining surface oil slick initially appeared to dissolve quickly in the warm gulf waters. Although tar and oil continued to wash inland, by 28 July deposits on beaches diminished and became more widely dispersed and sporadic. Both observational reports and RADAR imaging showed a near complete breakdown of the surface slick across wide areas of the gulf. There were, however, still offshore areas of concentrated oil and tar balls.

By early August 2010, Jane Lubchenco, director of the National Oceanic and Atmospheric Administration (NOAA), asserted that the majority of spilled oil was accounted for and that there were no longer significant concentrations of unaccounted for oil in the gulf. NOAA officials and environmental experts were quick to clarify, however, that the full ecological impact of the spill remained unknown and that the potential for substantial long-term damage remained.

In contrast to the initial official assurances that the oil in the gulf was largely dissipated, on 17 August, researchers at the University of South Florida announced test results showing potentially toxic concentrations of submerged contaminants in areas of the Gulf of Mexico where underwater currents previously carried plumes of oil and dispersant oil emulsions. Although additional testing was required to link the oil specifically to the BP spill, plumes of oil attributed to the spill were previously observed in test areas. In September 2010, oceanographic researchers announced the discovery of a deep layer of oil, several inches thick, hovering near the ocean floor in the Gulf of Mexico. The scientists also discovered in the oil at depths of one mile or more a layer

Remotely operated undersea vehicles work to cut and cap the riser pipe at the site of the Deepwater Horizon oil leak as it continues to spew oil into the Gulf of Mexico in early June. Reuters/Landov.

of dead shrimp and other species normally found near the ocean surface. Although the oil exhibited weathering characteristics that fit with the oil known to come from the damaged Macondo well, additional testing was required to link conclusively the massive oil spill with the discovered sunken oil layer. The report was one in a series of findings that contrasted with government and BP claims that the spilled oil had been degraded by chemical dispersants and by the bacteria that typically digest the oil that naturally seeps into the warm gulf waters.

Federal officials commissioned a scientific survey and assessment of the amount of oil potentially remaining in the Gulf of Mexico, along with an assessment of potential environmental impacts. Initial plans called for funding of the NOAA-coordinated study from a $500 million pledge by BP for oil spill related scientific research. The study is designed to eliminate confusion over conflicting claims regarding the fate of spilled oil, especially concerning the submerged oil appearing in underwater plumes. In October 2010, researchers discovered additional thick layers of degraded oil near the gulf seabed in areas extending 140 miles from the spill site. As always, molecular fingerprinting was required to definitively trace the degraded crude oil to the BP spill. Separate teams of researchers discovered oil and traces of chemical dispersants in underwater sediment samples and in blue crab larvae.

A number of efforts continue in order to minimize damage and remediate existing damage to bays, estuaries, and wetlands, including the controversial construction of protective sand berms.

Containment Booms

Many miles of floating containment booms were used to prevent surface oil from moving into mangroves, marshes, and other ecologically sensitive areas. These booms extended to about one to four feet (0.3 to 1.2 meter) above and below the water line in places.

Skimming and Controlled Burns

The U.S. Coast Guard used dozens of skimmer ships to collect oil that was on the surface waters of the Gulf of Mexico. Skimmer vessels were also used to contain oil in preparation for controlled fires.

After the slick at first moved northward toward wetland sections of the Louisiana coast, the U.S. Coast Guard (USCG) began setting controlled fires to parts of the slick in order to delay or diminish movement of oil into shallow water. Although such burns can eliminate 50 to 95 percent of the oil, they are not without environmental risk or cost. Oil residues still cause pollution and marine animals and birds, including the endangered Kemp's Ridley sea turtle, were reportedly killed by the fires and toxic fumes.

Dispersants

Dispersants are detergent-like chemicals that break up oil slicks. The molecular nature of the dispersants (one part of the molecular structure of dispersants has a polar affinity to water, the other end a non-polar affinity to oil) allows dispersants to surround and coat small droplets of oil. Oil remains on the inside of the oil-dispersant glob in contact with the non-polar parts of the dispersant molecule. On the surface of the glob, the polar portions of the dispersant molecules allow the glob to drop out of the spill and mix with water (a polar substance). Ultimately, the oil-dispersant globs drop to the sea floor. Over thousands of years, those globules that do not wash up on beaches are consumed by microorganisms.

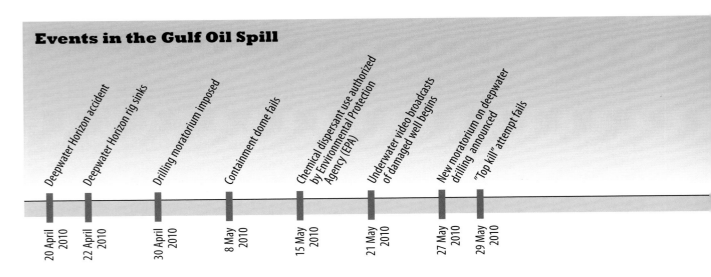

Events in the Gulf Oil Spill

Deepwater Horizon accident — 20 April 2010

Deepwater Horizon rig sinks — 22 April 2010

Drilling moratorium imposed — 30 April 2010

Containment dome fails — 8 May 2010

Chemical dispersant use authorized by Environmental Protection Agency (EPA) — 15 May 2010

Underwater video broadcasts of damaged well begins — 21 May 2010

New moratorium on deepwater drilling announced — 27 May 2010

"Top kill" attempt fails — 29 May 2010

To illustrate the extent of the oil found on the surface of Barataria Bay on the 45th day of the spill, a reporter put his hand in an oil patch on the water. Julie Dermansky/Photo Researchers, Inc.

Chemical dispersants are used to accelerate the way that oil is naturally dispersed in water following oil spills. Specific, artificially made dispersants used on the gulf oil spill included Corexit EC9500A and Corexit EC9527A. Although many marine experts expressed disagreement or caution, according to their manufacturer (Nalco), "[Corexit 9500] is a simple blend of six well-established, safe ingredients that biodegrade, do not bioaccumulate, and are commonly found in popular household products. COREXIT products do not contain carcinogens or reproductive toxins. All the ingredients have been extensively studied for many years and have been determined safe and effective by the EPA."

Some dispersants have, however, proven toxic to marine organisms. In addition, dispersed oil globules can also be highly toxic. By June, U.S. Environmental Protection Agency (EPA) officials expressed concern about the untested toxicity of dispersants used to reduce the surface slick. EPA officials ordered changes in the types of dispersants used and, at one point, issued a ban on the use of some types of dispersants. Experts contend that it will take years to measure the full impact of the unprecedented use of dispersants, including the first-ever application of dispersants underwater. Dispersants were sprayed by ROVs directing dispersants into the oil gushing from the BOP and various caps.

Marine wildlife experts warned against indiscriminate use of dispersants because some dispersants are toxic to marine organisms. In addition, dispersed oil globules can also be toxic to fish. Concentration is the key to a tricky environmental trade-off; cleanup engineers and crews rely on

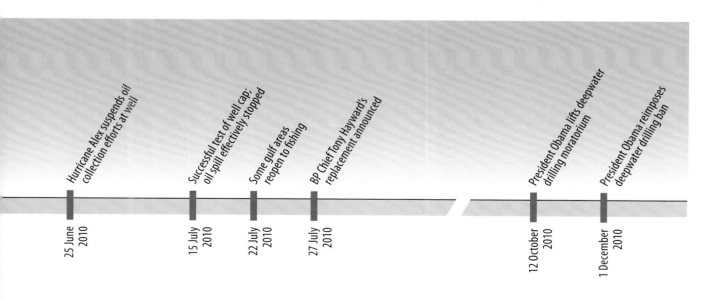

Hurricane Alex suspends oil collection efforts at well — 25 June 2010

Successful test of well cap; oil spill effectively stopped — 15 July 2010

Some gulf areas reopen to fishing — 22 July 2010

BP Chief Tony Hayward's replacement announced — 27 July 2010

President Obama lifts deepwater drilling moratorium — 12 October 2010

President Obama reimposes deepwater drilling ban — 1 December 2010

Controlled burns, such as this one conducted in mid-July, were used to eliminate surface oil in the Gulf of Mexico. AP Images/Gerald Herbert.

the dilution of dispersants and dispersed oil to minimize levels of toxicity. Federal agencies, including NOAA, normally monitor applications of dispersants through the Special Monitoring of Applied Response Technologies (SMART) program.

Ultimately at least 1.1 million gallons of chemical dispersants were applied to the spill.

On-shore Clean Up

Oil from the spill washed ashore on beaches in Louisiana, Mississippi, Alabama, and Florida. Sand contaminated with oil was often scraped or buried. Buried oil was the subject of subsequent deep cleaning efforts.

As of November 2010, at least 11,000 people were still working to clean Gulf Coast shores.

Oil patties and tar balls continued to periodically wash ashore along gulf beaches. The highest number of cleanup workers was estimated to be about 48,000 throughout the many months of shoreline cleaning. As of 27 October 2010, about 93 miles (150 kilometers) of shoreline still had moderate to heavy oil present, with most of the oiled coastline in Louisiana. An additional 483 miles (779 kilometers) of shoreline had light-to-trace amounts of oil present, with about 226 miles (365 kilometers) in Louisiana, 119 miles (192 kilometers) in Florida, 78 miles (126 kilometers) in Mississippi, and 60 miles (97 kilometers) in Alabama. Cleanup efforts are expected to be completed, with respect to deep beach cleaning of oil in Pensacola, Florida, Orange Beach, Alabama and Gulf Shores, Alabama, in 2011.

The Gulf's Natural Recovery Systems

Although it may require decades, the Gulf of Mexico and its ecosystem have an enormous restorative capacity. Microbial life devours an estimated 1,000 barrels of crude oil naturally seeping into gulf waters each day, and microbes flourishing in the warm gulf waters quickly devoured significant amounts of oil. However, there are differences in scientists' estimates of how much oil was consumed. While composed primarily of hydrocarbons, crude oil contains thousands of other chemicals in trace amounts, and bacterial responses to the particular crude spilled vary. Some bacteria consume selected elements of crude, leaving residues for other bacteria or for slower physical degradation. The rate at which microbes feed on oil is also related to levels of other nutrients present such as nitrogen, phosphorus, and iron.

Several species of prokaryotic microorganisms are responsible for devouring the petroleum hydrocarbons emanating from natural seafloor seeps of oil and gas found around the world. A challenging question for marine scientists is whether the microbial population explosion in the Gulf of Mexico will create larger hypoxic regions devoid of oxygen and life. Such dead-zone areas already existed in the gulf prior to the spill, but experts feared that the spill will expand the number, area, and depth of such zones.

The abundance of oil may also alter the population balances among microbes and have lasting impacts on their evolutionary development. There are also unanswered question as to how the microbes that normally feed on oil will respond to the partially emulsified oil in large undersea oil clouds and plumes. Microbiologists initially defended the use of dispersants because reducing the droplet size of the spilled oil created a larger

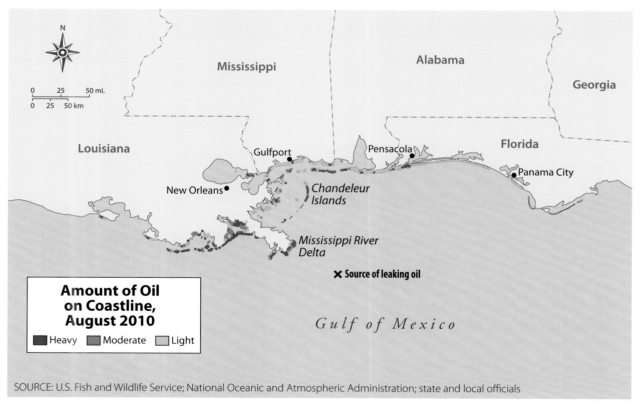

Amount of Oil on Coastline, August 2010
■ Heavy ■ Moderate □ Light

✕ Source of leaking oil

Gulf of Mexico

SOURCE: U.S. Fish and Wildlife Service; National Oceanic and Atmospheric Administration; state and local officials

The federal government reported varying amounts of oil on coastlines in Florida, Alabama, Mississippi, and Louisiana in August. Illustration/XNR Productions/Cengage Learning, Gale.

Trying to keep the oil from washing up on shore was a difficult task. Here, a worker uses a vacuum hose in an attempt to capture some of the oil that is closing in on Port Fourchon, Louisiana, in late June. Joe Raedle/Getty Images.

surface area upon which microbes could feed.

Complicating the analysis are the natural checks on the growth of bacteria. For example, as a consequence of the higher bacterial counts, predatory bacterial viruses and protozoa not normally pathogenic to humans, but normally effective in stabilizing the populations of pathogenic bacteria, also increased in numbers.

Following the *Exxon Valdez* spill in 1989, the percentage of petroleum-consuming microbes in contaminated waters soared to ten times normal levels.

Scientists also expressed uncertainty about how long it would take the Gulf of Mexico to recover. Evidence of the *Exxon Valdez* oil spill can still be found in coastal areas of Alaska. Scientists have previously measured adverse environmental impacts and food-chain disruptions extending for decades following other large spills around the world. In one case, botanists working in Mexico discovered damage to plants more than 30 years after a major spill. Biologists still note abnormalities in the behavior of crabs and other species in Buzzard's Bay, Massachusetts, more than 40 years after a nearby fuel oil spill. Subsurface oil pockets—lacking the oxygen needed by a number of microorganisms that degrade oil over time—can contaminate spill areas for decades. The oil pockets impair nesting habitats and release low levels of hydrocarbon toxins into sand, soils, and water supplies. Both acute destruction and slow poisoning of protective vegetation can also spur coastal erosion.

Environmental Impact

Overview

Throughout the spill, the bulk of the slick remained at sea, elongating eastward in the gulf's clockwise circulation pattern. As the oil moved eastward, so did the extent of emergency declarations. NOAA models predicted that the slick,

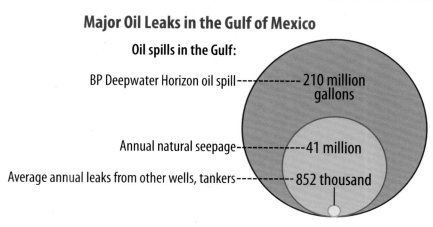

Major Oil Leaks in the Gulf of Mexico

Oil spills in the Gulf:

BP Deepwater Horizon oil spill --------------- 210 million gallons

Annual natural seepage -------------- 41 million

Average annual leaks from other wells, tankers ----------- 852 thousand

SOURCES: NOAA and International Maritime Organization

The BP oil spill as compared with others sources of oil in the Gulf of Mexico. Illustration/XNR Productions/Cengage Learning, Gale.

caught in the gulf's loop current, could ultimately impact the Florida Keys, enter the Gulf Stream, and move up the East Coast of the United States. On 16 May 2010, NASA and NOAA satellite imagery confirmed that a large section of the oil spill moved southeast from the site of the spill to enter the loop current. However, because of the rapid dispersion of oil at sea, no large surface spill moved significantly southward in the loop current.

By June 2010, the surface slick extended over most of the northern Gulf of Mexico. Oil washed into ecologically sensitive marshlands in Louisiana. Predicting precise landfalls and the degree of damage to specific areas proved difficult. Oil slicks are generally not consistent in thickness; most of a discernable slick is a thin sheen that can dissipate to create gaps in the slick area. However, within

oil slicks are areas of thicker oil that pose substantial threat to wildlife, coastal environments, and the economies of impacted areas. Estimating what portion of a visible spill might dissipate before reaching shore is also complex and subject to wave action, distance to the shore, and other variables. Wave action can churn the slick, hardening and clumping oil so that globs sink to the ocean floor. However, such globs of oil can wash up on beaches and contaminate coastal areas for weeks and months following a spill.

While still at sea, the slick killed and threatened birds, marine mammals, plankton, and species of fish that lay eggs at the surface.

Wildlife Impacts

Throughout the spill, federal agencies worked with state governments in Texas, Louisiana, Mississippi, Alabama, and Florida to coordinate efforts to mitigate potential damage. Immediately following the discovery of the spill, Louisiana officials ordered placement of containment booms near environmentally vulnerable coastal areas, including the Pass-a-Loutre Wildlife Management Area used by several migratory bird species.

As damage to the coastal environment visibly worsened, the Associated Press reported that workers helping to recover wildlife on Louisiana's East Grand Terre Island, found birds "coated in thick, black goo" and brown pelicans "drenched in thick oil, struggling and flailing in the surf." Areas of the wetlands system—supporting a complex array of wildlife, including seabirds and wading birds; speckled trout; shrimp; whooping cranes; wood storks; songbirds; sea turtles, including the endangered Kemp's Ridley turtle; along with untold numbers of lower life forms—were

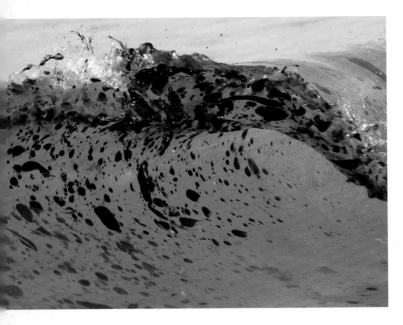

It was only a matter of time before oily waves brought the crude oil from the *Deepwater Horizon* spill to shore. Large amounts of oil battered many coastal areas along the Gulf of Mexico, leaving a slick mess in its wake. AP Images/Dave Martin.

covered with oil, and subsurface oil moved into inland waterways.

In June 2010, U.S. Fish and Wildlife Service officials reported a spike in the number of dead and oil-stained birds. By 15 July 2010, wildlife officials and pathologists conducting necropsies on dolphins, sea turtles, and other species noted anomalies in the numbers of deaths and in the areas where dead marine life was collected. In some cases, animals were found far from their normal habitat areas.

The exact number of fish, marine mammals, birds, and other forms of wildlife killed or injured by the spill is unknown. Experts contend that it will take several years of study, perhaps decades of study, to fully assess the environmental and ecological impact of the spill, especially on species with extensive damage to eggs and larvae. Wildlife officials point out that in comparison with worst case scenarios based on the size of the spill, however, the death toll on birds and other marine

mammals is initially far lower than expected. However, wildlife experts continue to assert that official estimates of injured and recovered wildlife are far lower than actually occurred and that estimates fail to account for observable reductions in many wildlife populations in the spill region.

Human Health Concerns

Along the Gulf Coast bordering the spill, residents frequently reported a light acrid smell in the air. Some reported respiratory irritation. The EPA began specialized monitoring and reporting of potentially toxic air pollution created by the volatile petroleum compounds released from the spill. Public health officials expressed a range of concerns about health impacts. Surgeon General Regina Benjamin said that scientific predictions ranged from little or no toxic effect (especially from short-term exposure) to levels of serious concern for long-term health impacts. Complaints among coastal residents, along with workers cleaning the oil both on land and at sea, included skin rashes, headaches, nausea, and irritation in the throat and eyes. Several workers also experienced heat stress due to working in hot and humid conditions.

Although the composition of crude oil varies somewhat according to its source, crude oil is a naturally occurring brown or black liquid that is composed of a mixture of hydrocarbons and other organic compounds. Crude oil is toxic, flammable, and contains volatile organic compounds (VOCs) that have known adverse effects on human health, including benzene, a carcinogen, and polycyclic aromatic hydrocarbons (PACs), which are toxic to the central nervous system. A substantial portion of the volatile components of petroleum, about 25 to 40 percent of the total volume of spilled oil, dissolved in the water column as oil rose to the surface or evaporated at the surface. People are exposed to oil-spill toxins through direct contact with oil on the skin, by breathing VOCs and other chemicals released into the air, or by coming in contact with oil-contaminated sand, soil, water, or food. Multiple exposure paths

Cleaning oily birds is a delicate and difficult task. Here, several women team up to clean a brown pelican that was rescued after being exposed to the *Deepwater Horizon* spill. AP Images/Charlie Riedel.

can occur simultaneously. All adverse reactions to oil are dependent upon both the duration of the exposure and a person's particular susceptibility to the particular toxins in the oil.

Hundreds of workers and coastal residents were treated for various medical problems during the cleanup that were initially attributed to exposure to the oil spill, including mixtures of oil and dispersants. Symptoms observed included nausea, vomiting, coughing, chest pain, respiratory stress, headaches, and dizziness. Health experts stated that such symptoms were common in people exposed to oil spills. For example, after the 1989 *Exxon Valdez* oil spill in Prince William Sound, Alaska, hundreds of workers cleaning Alaskan

shores, marshes, and oiled waterways complained of skin rashes, dizziness, headaches, and nausea. Some experienced longer-lasting symptoms, including shortness of breath, muscle aches, and neurological problems, including numbness and tingling of the extremities. Experts also claimed that workers later showed higher rates of chronic airway diseases than normally occur.

Public health officials along the Gulf Coast continue to monitor communities affected by the *Deepwater Horizon* spill. Data-collection efforts are designed to identify and document potential longer-term consequences of oil exposure, such as kidney damage, birth defects, and cancer.

Covered in oil, a loggerhead sea turtle struggles to survive. A conservation group hoped it would be able to clean and save the animal. Alan Spearman/The Commercial Appeal/Landov.

Along with fouling marine and coastal ecosystems, offshore oil spills pose potential long-term health hazards. Regarding the *Deepwater Horizon* oil spill, information on potential long-term health impacts remains conflicting and inconclusive. Moreover, not all impacts are physical or easily observable. Public health experts warn that disaster-related stress also carries an emotional and mental health toll. After the *Exxon Valdez* spill, a study published in the *American Journal of Psychiatry* showed that residents living in areas impacted by the spill were more likely to suffer mental health problems than the general population.

Impacts on a Culture under Stress

Although high levels of mental and emotional stress are expected during a natural or technological disaster, the *Deepwater Horizon* oil spill impacted an area whose vulnerable population, social infrastructure, and culture was still recovering from hurricanes Ivan, Katrina, and Rita.

Benjamin Springgate, a physician and public health researcher at Tulane University in New Orleans, estimated that over 30 percent of people in the impact zone of Hurricane Katrina experienced symptoms of anxiety, depression, or other mental illness after the storm and also predicted that the impacts of the *Deepwater Horizon* oil spill on the mental health of coastal residents will be a long-lasting concern. The most frequent symptoms of stress-related mental disorders are feelings of hopelessness, disturbances in sleep patterns, lack of concentration, mood swings, irritability, inability to make productive decisions, nightmares or persistent memories of disturbing or frightening events, and general anxiety.

Pubic health officials along the Gulf Coast are also employing innovative and culturally sensitive advertising and intervention techniques to help reach people who may be experiencing symptoms of stress but are unlikely to seek help. Pubic health officials have sought and encouraged participation by volunteers and professionals with knowledge of local multilingual immigrant cultures, including many close-knit fishing communities in which Vietnamese or Spanish may be the primary language for many residents.

The U.S. Department of Health and Human Services created a $10 million fund to track *Deepwater Horizon*-related illnesses. More than 14,000 oil spill workers have volunteered to participate in a similar study for the Centers for Disease Control and Prevention (CDC).

Economic Impact

Extending eastward into Florida waters, the surface slick spotted white-sand beaches vital to local tourist-based economies. Fishing bans resulted in crippling economic hardship and apocalyptic predictions for the future of a gulf seafood industry integral to the regional economy and deeply entwined with the culture of the region. Businesses failed due to lack of tourism. Fishermen and an array of businesses were put at the mercy of a BP compensation fund that the media continually described as inefficient and insufficient to provide meaningful relief. Ultimately, the BP-run reimbursement system was replaced by a BP-funded, but independently administered, relief fund, the Gulf Coast Claims Facility, run by Kenneth Feinberg, the generally lauded administrator of the fund for compensating victims of the 9/11 terrorist attacks on the World Trade Center in New York. Because economic vitality is closely linked to consumer perceptions, BP countered with a large advertising campaign both to promote its own image and to reduce losses to coastal tourism.

The spill also posed both environmental and economic peril to the white sand beaches and communities along the Alabama and Florida coasts. Beach closures damaged tourist-sensitive local coastal economies still struggling to fully recover from a string of intense hurricanes and

Dolphin Deaths Pose Challenges for Scientists

In addition to helping measure and remediate devastating impacts on the environment and wildlife, scientists also face an array of continuing challenges. Along with securing new data, scientists must take into account the influence of natural factors and preexisting phenomena. For example, media reports of dolphin deaths in the northern Gulf of Mexico in May 2010 were quickly attributed to the oil spill. However, there was an observed spike in bottlenose dolphin deaths in the region prior to the oil spill. In March 2010, one month before the spill, wildlife officials recorded more than three times the normal number of dead bottlenose dolphins. NOAA officials declared the deaths an "unusual mortality event" and ordered an investigation. Although oil residues are highly toxic to marine mammals and significant deaths and damage were observed, pathologists conducting necropsies did not definitively link subsequently observed bottlenose dolphin deaths directly to the oil spill prior to June 2010. Scientists are also investigating alternative causes, including the influence of an abnormally cold winter, possible paralytic shellfish poisoning, or deaths caused by viruses such as the Morbillivirus.

Experts contend that such scientific rigor, at times unyielding to personal perceptions, political correctness, or popular media influences, is critical to determining the full extent of the damage caused by the spill. Incontrovertible scientific evidence strengthens claims made against parties responsible for the spill—making it difficult for them to escape legal accountability—and also strengthens efforts to find effective solutions.

At a protest in New Orleans, Louisiana, in late May, hundreds of demonstrators rallied against BP and offshore oil drilling in general. Julie Dermansky/Photo Researchers, Inc.

tropical storms over the last six years. Expenditures on clean-up efforts funneled money into affected areas, but the benefit of these expenditures for local workers and communities remains controversial.

Fishing

The slick crippled the regional seafood industry, destroying or closing oyster beds and prime fishing grounds for shrimp and crab. On 2 May 2010, federal and state agencies instituted temporary bans on commercial fishing from the mouth of the Mississippi River to the Florida Panhandle. By 22 June 2010, the fishing ban extended over 33 percent of the Gulf of Mexico. Unable to fish, many skippers of shrimp boats

and other fishing vessels volunteered to assist in cleanup efforts.

A March 2009 report by BP that analyzed further oil exploration in the Gulf of Mexico, "Initial Exploration Plan Mississippi Canyon Block 252 OCS-G 32306," stated that "no adverse activities are anticipated" to the fishing industry or fishing habitats in the event of an offshore oil spill in the Gulf of Mexico. Just over a year after the report, the fishing industry in the northern Gulf of Mexico was virtually shut down as a result of the *Deepwater Horizon* oil spill.

On 29 April 2010, Louisiana governor Bobby Jindal declared a state of emergency and opened an emergency shrimping season to allow fishermen to harvest shrimp before the oil slick reached the Louisiana coast. On 2 May, NOAA closed federal waters between the Mississippi River and Pensacola Bay—an area comprising 6,814 square miles (17,650 square kilometers)—to commercial and recreational fishing and shrimping. By 21 June, the growing and shifting oil slick closed 86,985 square miles (225,290 square kilometers) of the gulf, approximately 36 percent of federal waters in the gulf, including some of the most lucrative commercial fishing and shrimping areas.

In addition to lost revenue produced by the closure of fishing waters over the summer of 2010, the gulf seafood industry remains hampered by consumer concerns over the safety of seafood. Many consumers throughout the United States have expressed fear of contamination of seafood from oil and chemical dispersants. A 24 September 2010 report in the *Christian Science Monitor* stated that safety concerns and the closures could cut revenue of the gulf's $10.5 billion fishing industry in half over the next few years. The report also noted that Alaskan fisherman claimed that the reputation and sales of the Alaskan fishing industry did not recover from the *Exxon Valdez* oil spill for more than a decade. As of November 2010, BP had pledged to spend

$78 million promoting Louisiana seafood and tourism and $20 million to promote Florida seafood. BP remains in negotiations with the states of Alabama and Mississippi over similar measures.

Tourism

The *Deepwater Horizon* oil spill occurred during the height of the summer travel season for Gulf Coast communities, forcing many travelers to cancel plans for vacations in the area. According to 2008 statistics, the most recent available, tourism along the Gulf Coast is a $34 billion per year industry that supports 400,000 jobs.

A July 2010 study conducted by Oxford Economics for the U.S. Travel Association revealed that tourism-related economic losses associated with the oil spill could total $22.7 billion over three years. The study analyzed current spending habits and effects of past crises on tourism. According to the study, the effects of a crisis on tourism typically extend well beyond the resolution of the crisis because public perceptions are slow to adjust. The study's best-case scenario claimed that the effects of the oil spill would last fifteen months and result in $7.5 billion of lost revenue.

Clean-Up Costs

In November 2010, BP estimated that its total costs associated with the *Deepwater Horizon* oil spill would reach $40 billion. This figure includes the cost of sealing the well, claim disbursements to affected industries, clean-up costs, and other expenses. Although BP had forecast a cost of $32 billion, the company revised their estimate upwards by $8 billion in November 2010.

A November 2010 report by the Government Accountability Office (GAO), the auditing and financial investigative office of the U.S. Congress, stated that BP had reimbursed federal and state agencies $581 million for clean-up costs incurred by state and federal agencies and billed to BP. Over $518 million of this amount reimbursed federal payments out of the federal Oil Spill Liability Trust Fund, a fund established to cover the

Despite the oil-stained sands of Orange Beach, Alabama, some tourists decided to take in some sun anyway. Julie Dermansky/ Photo Researchers, Inc.

clean-up and environmental restoration costs associated with oil spills. The fund allows the federal government to spend money for these operations and then seek reimbursement from the oil company responsible for the spill. The fund, however, features a liability cap of $1 billion, which the GAO warned could be exceeded with the *Deepwater Horizon* oil spill.

Moody's Analytics estimates that the Gulf Coast region will lose 17,000 jobs by the end of 2010. Moody's Analytics estimates that this job loss would be offset to some degree by the creation of jobs associated with oil spill clean up. Many residents of affected communities, however, counter that many of the clean-up jobs created in the wake of the oil spill have gone to out-of-state workers, not local workers left unemployed as a result of the oil spill.

Responsibility

Government

A broad array of oil industry analysts, regulatory experts, and media commentators charge that a culture of lax government oversight and corrupt relationships between government and corporate entities must shoulder some responsibility, even if indirect, for the gulf oil spill. The assertion is echoed in an increasing number of government reports and in preliminary presidential commission investigative findings establishing that the lack of regulatory authority exerted by the U.S. Department of the Interior's Minerals Management Service (MMS) fostered an energy industry culture that increased risk factors related to the engineering practices resulting in the blowout and spill. The harshest critics conclude that in many regards there was a total lack of meaningful government oversight, leaving the energy industry free to exorcise its own rules. Such self-regulation inevitably yields to corporate cultures where higher-risk ventures are justified by higher profits.

Since its creation in 1982, MMS had the responsibility for managing the oil and gas industry in the United States. MMS was responsible for the inspection and oversight of wells, including offshore wells, to ensure that all wells complied with environmental and safety regulations. MMS also leased federal land to energy companies, which provided one of the federal governments largest sources of revenue. Essentially, MMS collected billions of dollars each year from the industry that the agency was tasked with regulating.

A 2008 report by the inspector general of the Department of the Interior found numerous instances of unethical and criminal conduct by MMS employees, including accepting gifts from energy companies and other conflicts of interest. The findings established a culture of corruption and lax oversight traceable to practices dating at least as far back as the 1990s, subsequently made increasingly risky by a political culture emphasizing deregulation.

Following the Gulf of Mexico oil spill, an investigation revealed that MMS employees even allowed energy company officials to fill out MMS inspection reports on oil wells in the Gulf of Mexico. Requirements to file contingency plans in the case of disaster were waived or ignored, and energy companies were allowed to submit drilling operations reports and disaster response plans for the gulf that were literally copies of plans designed for drilling operations in Alaska and other environments dramatically different from the gulf. For example, several spill response plans allegedly designed for the gulf were found to contain bizarre references to plans to protect and lessen damage to species that exist only in arctic waters, copies of response plans between allegedly competing companies were found to be copies essentially differing only in the corporate coversheet stapled over the plan. Critics cited such examples as evidence that such plans were simply token responses to a government agency unconcerned with meaningful protection of people and the environment.

In the aftermath of the Gulf of Mexico oil spill, Secretary of the Interior Ken Salazar and other agency officials restructured MMS. The Department of the Interior claimed that MMS did not have enough inspectors to carry out all of its inspection duties. Salazar split the regulatory and royalty collection functions of MMS into three separate divisions: the Bureau of Ocean Energy Management, the Bureau of Safety and Environmental Enforcement, and the Office of Natural Resources Revenue. On 27 May 2010, Elizabeth Birnbaum, director of MMS, announced her resignation. In June 2010, Salazar renamed MMS as the Bureau of Ocean Energy Management, Regulation, and Enforcement.

BP

BP has pledged to cover all costs related to the *Deepwater Horizon* oil spill, even though the company is not required to do so under federal or state laws governing compensation for oil spill-related damage. BP would likely be found liable for damages under other civil laws, however, although injured parties would have to sue in order to recover damages. As of November 2010, BP had pledged $40 billion to cover costs associated with the oil spill, including clean up and economic injuries. BP officials, however, admitted that the November 2010 estimate would not necessarily reflect their final costs once the full extent of damage is known. JP Morgan analysts estimate that BP could be liable for up to $69 billion in damages from the oil spill if courts determine that BP was grossly negligent.

Sub-Contractors

Although BP has pledged billions of dollars to cover costs associated with the *Deepwater Horizon* oil spill, BP likely will seek to recover some of its costs from sub-contractors and co-owners of the oil well. BP indicated that litigation was likely when the company released the results of its four-month investigation into the cause of the oil spill. The report stated that "multiple companies and work teams" contributed to "a complex and interlinked series of mechanical failures, human judgments, engineering design, operational implementation and team interfaces" that resulted in the oil well explosion and subsequent oil spill.

Transocean, the owner of the drilling rig, and Halliburton, the company attempting to seal the well with cement, are likely litigants. Anadarko Petroleum and Mitsui—35 percent owners of the oil well—are also likely to be targets of litigation. By the end of October 2010, BP had billed $4.3 billion to sub-contractors and co-owners. BP

The grandson of one of the oil rig workers killed in the *Deepwater Horizon* explosion mourns the loss with other family members at a memorial service in Louisiana in early May. Carol Guzy/Washington Post/Getty Images.

partners have indicated that they will withhold payments pending further investigations.

Repercussions of the Gulf Oil Spill

U.S. Energy Policy

The U.S. Energy Information Administration, a government energy policy and research think tank, estimates that the United States consumes more than 21 million barrels (882 million gallons) of petroleum-based products each day. Nearly half of the daily petroleum consumption in the United States is in the form of gasoline, primarily used in the nation's 215 million motor vehicles. Almost 90 percent of that gasoline is produced in U.S. refineries, many of which are

Locations of Ultra-Deepwater Drilling Rigs, 2010

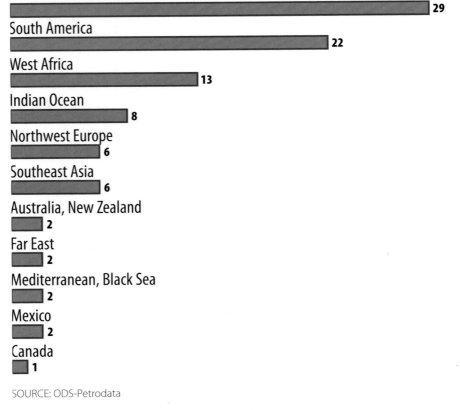

United States (Gulf of Mexico) 29

South America 22

West Africa 13

Indian Ocean 8

Northwest Europe 6

Southeast Asia 6

Australia, New Zealand 2

Far East 2

Mediterranean, Black Sea 2

Mexico 2

Canada 1

SOURCE: ODS-Petrodata

Location of ultra-deepwater oil rigs in 2010. Illustration/XNR Productions/Cengage Learning, Gale.

coastline from Delaware to Florida to new oil exploration and drilling. The *Deepwater Horizon* leak and oil spill led several political candidates and elected officials to reconsider their position on expanding areas for offshore drilling.

Deep-sea Drilling

The oil spill renewed the controversy on the environmental risks of offshore drilling for oil and gas reserves. Following the spill, President Obama formed a commission to investigate the cause of the oil spill and to evaluate both the industry and government response to the disaster. White House officials pledged changes in industry oversight, and Obama specifically criticized what he characterized as a "cozy relationship" between government regulators and oil industry representatives.

located in states bordering the Gulf of Mexico. Crude oil extracted from U.S. lands or offshore areas, however, accounts for only 35 percent of the crude oil processed in U.S. refineries.

Deepwater wells are the most prolific wells in the Gulf of Mexico. As of 2007, deepwater drilling provided 70 percent of the oil from federally managed areas in the gulf. The United States recently moved to expand areas off of the nation's coastline available for offshore oil drilling. On 31 March 2010, the U.S. government proposed opening large areas of the eastern Gulf of Mexico and waters off of the Atlantic

The U.S. government declared a six-month moratorium on drilling new offshore wells deeper than 500 feet while the presidential commission conducted an investigation of the spill. In 2010, approximately 600 wells in the Gulf of Mexico operated at depths greater than 500 feet. Such deepwater operations accounted for 80 percent of gulf oil production. The moratorium became the subject of litigation and a number of federal court orders and interventions, as it initially stopped new work on 33 deepwater drilling rigs. Operations at existing wells were not affected by the moratorium. After establishing new rules related to safety, certification, and licensing, the moratorium on new deepwater oil and gas drilling was removed on 12 October 2010. In early December however, the Obama administration announced that it would continue the ban on new offshore wells as part of the next five-year drilling plan.

Impact on BP

In addition to a massive rescue and search effort for the 11 missing crew members, BP and dozens of supporting companies and agencies dispatched engineers to the site of the disaster. BP sent more than 1,000 emergency personnel to attempt to plug the leaking undersea oil.

The U.S. government named BP the responsible party in the disaster, asserting that a U.S. law enacted in 1990 made BP responsible for all clean-up costs. BP accepted responsibility for the spill and agreed to pay all clean-up costs, but added that the accident was not entirely the company's fault because the rig's owner and operator was another company, Transocean, and that operations potentially related to the explosion and spill were carried out by additional contractors.

The White House later announced plans to develop a comprehensive Gulf Coast restoration plan. President Obama directed BP officials to establish an escrow fund (a dedicated reserve fund), under the control of a third party not accountable to BP, which must be dedicated to paying compensation and other damage claims. BP officials subsequently announced that they would place $20 billion in escrow toward the compensation fund. BP pledged to pay $5 billion to the fund each year for the next four years. The fund is not intended to cover fines or clean-up costs. BP also established funds to partially compensate people who lost work during the drilling ban and to fund scientific research to monitor environmental impacts of the spill.

President Barack Obama (center) meets with National Incident Commander Adm. Thad Allen (left) and Mississippi Gov. Haley Barbour in mid-June to discuss issues pertaining to the *Deepwater Horizon* oil spill response. AP Images/Charles Dharapak.

Executives representing the companies involved in the *Deepwater Horizon* oil spill were called to appear before the U.S. Senate Committee on Environment and Public Works in May. They were asked to explain the "cascade of failures" that led to the spill. From left to right: Lamar McKay, president and chair of BP America; Steven Newman, president and chief executive officer of Transocean Limited; and Tim Probert, president of Global Business Lines and chief health, safety and environmental officer for Halliburton. AP Images/Pablo Martinez Monsivais.

Although both BP and government officials initially downplayed the importance of determining the exact volume and extent of the spill, industry and environmental experts said accurate measures were key to planning and assessing remediation efforts. With potential penalties under the U.S. Clean Water Act ranging from $1,100 per barrel upwards to $4,300 per barrel in cases of gross negligence, a wide array of experts claimed that accurate assessments of the spill were legally, politically, economically, and environmentally important.

Federal scientists ultimately estimated that the multifaceted containment efforts recovered less than 20 percent (about 800,000 barrels) of the oil spewed from the well. Based on August 2010

recovery figures and spill estimates, in addition to other losses and costs related to the spill, BP and other responsible parties also face total fines ranging from approximately $4.4 billion to $17.2 billion, even if fined only for the estimated 4 million barrels of unrecovered oil. Legal experts argue that the actual range of potential fines facing responsible parties will be substantially greater. Adverse judgments in civil actions could easily eclipse the maximum fines ultimately imposed on responsible parties.

Immediately after the spill, BP's stock value plummeted. Its chief executive officer, Tony Hayward, also became a lightening rod for media and pubic criticism following a string of public relations gaffes that made him appear insensitive to the plight of Gulf Coast residents. After telling a reporter on 30 May 2010 that "no one who wants this thing over more than I do; I'd like my life back," at least one member of the U.S. Congress called for his resignation. Three weeks later, images of Hayward on board his yacht *Bob* racing in a regatta off the Isle of Wight were widely reported. Hayward was replaced as CEO of BP by Mississippi-native Bob Dudley on 27 July 2010.

Safety and Government Oversight in the Gulf

Several official investigations of the spill were conducted, including the *Deepwater Horizon* Joint Investigation (conducted by the Minerals Management Service and Coast Guard) and an investigation by the National Academy of Engineering. In addition, President Obama announced the creation of the bipartisan National Commission on the BP *Deepwater Horizon* Oil Spill and Offshore Drilling and charged the commission with investigating the incident.

In the months after the spill, the government also made changes to the agencies that regulate and oversee oil leases and drilling in U.S. waters. Interior Secretary Ken Salazar abolished the Minerals Management Service, which was accused of granting drilling leases without sufficient environmental impact reporting. A new oversight organization, the Bureau of Ocean Energy Management, Regulation, and Enforcement was created to regulate offshore drilling and evaluate new drilling projects.

Investigations into the *Deepwater Horizon* sinking provided tentative conclusions that a series of technical and human failures resulted in the massive gulf oil spill. The National Commission found that the spill occurred largely as a result of missteps on the part of BP, Halliburton and Transocean. Congressional hearings produced documents and testimony that showed the reliability of deepwater technology and the ability to handle "worst-case scenarios" are questionable, at best. In addition, lax government inspections and improper relationships between government regulators and oil representatives have also been revealed and reported during ongoing investigations.

In July 2010, four major oil companies (Chevron, ConocoPhillips, ExxonMobil, and Royal Dutch Shell) voluntarily pledged $1 billion to create the Marine Well Containment Company (MWCC), an entity charged with creating and maintaining an emergency response team to handle future deepwater oil spills in the Gulf of Mexico.

Other Oil Disasters

According to the U.S. Federal Minerals Management Service, there have been more than 850 reported fires and explosions related to oil exploration and production in the Gulf of Mexico since 2001. Small spills are not uncommon from the string of offshore rigs that dot the Gulf Coast. However, federal records indicate that prior to the *Deepwater Horizon* spill there had not been a confirmed spill in excess of 1,000 barrels into the Gulf of Mexico since 1996.

Oil spills are, however, a global problem with a long history. Examples of disastrous oil spills include the following accidents involving oceanic supertankers: (1) the *Torrey Canyon*, which ran aground in 1967 off southern England, spilling about 129,000 tons (117,000 metric tons) of crude oil; (2) the *Metula*, which wrecked in 1973 in the Strait of Magellan and spilled 58,000 tons (53,000 metric tons) of petroleum; (3) the *Amoco Cadiz*, which went aground in the English Channel in 1978, spilling 253,000 tons (230,000 metric tons) of crude oil; (4) the *Exxon Valdez*, which ran onto a reef in Prince William Sound in southern Alaska in 1989 and discharged 39,000 tons (35,000 metric tons) of petroleum; (5) the *Braer*, which spilled 93,000 tons (84,000 metric tons) of crude oil off the Shetland Islands of Scotland in 1993; and (6) the *Prestige*, which split in half off Galicia, Spain, in November 2002, spilling about 67,000 tons (61,000 metric tons) of crude oil. All

Eight Errors Leading to Deepwater Horizon Explosion

Well integrity was not established, or failed

1. Annulus cement barrier didn't isolate hydrocarbons

2. Shoe track barriers didn't isolate hydrocarbons

Hydrocarbons entered well undetected and well control was lost

3. Negative pressure test was accepted although well integrity hadn't been established

4. Influx wasn't recognized until hydrocarbons were in riser

5. Well control response actions failed to regain control of well

Hydrocarbons ignited rig

6. Diversion to mud gas separator resulted in gas venting onto rig

7. Fire and gas system didn't prevent hydrocarbon ignition

Blowout preventer failed

8. Blowout preventer emergency mode didn't seal well

SOURCE: BP

Rig

Riser ④

Water

Blowout preventer

Wellhead   Sea floor

Rock layers   Well casing

NOTE: Diagram not to scale

Oil reservoir

In the opinion of BP, a series of problems and mistakes throughout the *Deepwater Horizon* led to the Gulf oil spill. Illustration/XNR Productions/Cengage Learning, Gale.

of the tankers involved were of the older single-hull design. Newer regulations require reinforced hulls on tankers.

Significant oil spills have also occurred from offshore drilling or production platforms as the result of mechanical or operational failure. In 1979 the *Ixtoc I* exploration well had an uncontrolled blowout that spilled more than 551,000 tons (500,000 metric tons) of petroleum into the Gulf of Mexico. Smaller spills include a 1969 spill off Santa Barbara in southern California, when about 11,000 tons (10,000 metric tons) were discharged, and the *Ekofisk* blowout in 1977 in the

The massive *Exxon Valdez* oil spill in southern Alaska in 1989 dumped 39,000 tons of petroleum into Prince William Sound. As part of the extensive cleanup, workers used steam cleaning equipment to remove oil from various affected areas. Accent Alaska.com/Alamy.

North Sea off Norway, spilling a total of 33,000 tons (30,000 metric tons) of crude oil.

Pipeline accidents also create oil spills. A leak from a hole in an oil pipeline at Prudhoe Bay, Alaska, is estimated to have released between 200,000 and 300,000 gallons of crude oil in early 2006. Sub-zero temperatures made repairs, in which a steel sleeve was placed around the pipeline and welded into place, and cleanup difficult. Later that year, the discovery of extensive corrosion in the 30-year old Prudhoe Bay pipeline system, which sends oil to the Trans Alaskan Pipeline, led to a complete shutdown of that oilfield while 16 miles (26 kilometers) of the 22-mile (35-kilometer) long pipeline were replaced.

Large quantities of petroleum have also been released during warfare. Because petroleum and its refined products are important economic and industrial commodities, enemies have commonly targeted tankers and other petroleum-related facilities during wars. For example, during World War II, German submarines sank 42 tankers off the East Coast of the United States, causing a total spillage of about 460,000 tons (417,000 metric tons) of petroleum and refined products. There were 314 attacks on oil tankers during the Iran-Iraq War of 1981–1987, 70 percent of them by Iraqi forces. The largest individual spill during that war occurred when Iraq damaged five tankers and three production wells at the offshore *Nowruz* complex, resulting in the spillage of more than 287,000 tons (260,000 metric tons) of petroleum into the Gulf of Arabia. An Israeli air attack on an oil-fired power plant in Lebanon released about 15,000 tons of oil into the Mediterranean Sea during the 2006 Hezbollah-Israel conflict.

The largest-ever spill of petroleum into the marine environment occurred during the 1991 Persian Gulf War. Iraqi forces deliberately released an estimated 0.6-2.2 million tons (0.5-2 metric tons) of petroleum into the Persian Gulf from several tankers and an offshore tanker-loading facility known as the *Sea Island Terminal*. An additional 700 production wells in Kuwait were sabotaged and ignited by Iraqi forces in January 1991. The total spillage of crude oil was 46–138 million tons (42–126 metric tons). Much of the spilled petroleum burned in atmospheric conflagrations, while additional amounts accumulated locally as lakes of oil, which eventually contained 5.5–23 million tons (5–21 metric tons) of crude oil.

World Energy

On 15 June 2010, President Barack Obama delivered a speech from the White House oval office that called upon Americans to use the gulf oil spill crisis as a springboard toward a national energy policy aimed at reducing the need for foreign oil and risky offshore drilling. Obama characterizing the need to develop alternative energy sources as a "national mission."

Fossil Fuel Production & Consumption

Most of the world's energy still comes from fossil-fuel-based energy production. Fossil fuels are buried deposits of petroleum, coal, peat, natural gas, and other carbon-rich organic compounds derived from plants and animals that lived many millions of years ago. Over long periods of time, pressure generated by overlying sediments and heat from within Earth concentrated and modified these remains into usable energy resources. Fossil fuels, once consumed, are effectively gone forever. Nonrenewable fuels such as coal and petroleum began to be widely

No Spotlight on Spills in Developing Nations

Nigeria has had a troubled history with oil exploration. Most of the nation's oil is taken from the Niger River delta region, home to several ethnic minorities. The Ogoni and Ijaw peoples, both of whom have been negatively impacted by oil spills or incidental environmental damage from drilling and exploration, have protested oil industry operations in the region for over 20 years. In 1995, nine Ogoni people were executed by government officials after they protested oil drilling on their traditional lands. Under Nigerian laws, some revenues from land-based drilling are supposed to be invested in the 36 Nigerian states. However, there are few laws governing revenues from the majority of Nigerian oil wells, which are off shore.

The world's rural and developing regions are particularly vulnerable to oil spills. Lack of government stability undermines environmental and safety regulation of oil industries. When spills occur, developing nations are often less equipped to rapidly respond with containment and clean-up efforts. It is often more difficult to identify which companies are responsible for a spill or for impacted citizens to hold those companies liable through legal proceedings. Furthermore, spills in rural developing regions receive less attention from international media than spills that affect populated areas in developed nations.

In addition to industrial oil spills resulting from exploration, a controversial United Nations report issued in 2010 also attributed many spills in developing nations to internal violence and crime.

used starting with the Industrial Revolution in the late 1700s. Some renewable energy sources, including hydropower and wood, remained in use even after the Industrial Revolution, though their share of the energy supply dwindled. For many decades, coal and oil easily supplied nearly 90 percent of the industrial world's energy.

In 2010, global oil demand exceeded 85.37 million barrels a day, a 1.1 percent increase from demand in 2009. The United States, the world's largest national consumer of oil, consumed an average of 21 million barrels of oil per day. As the world's most populous nations, including China and India, increase development, global oil demand is expected to increase by over 25 percent by 2025.

Conventional, Unconventional & Unrecoverable Reserves

There are substantial amounts of oil reserves remaining on Earth. However, for an oil resource to be exploited, it must be both technically and economically recoverable. The technology must exist to extract and refine the resource to make it useable. The discovery, extraction, and refinement must not make the final oil product cost more than consumers can afford. These considerations make some forms of oil deposits more attractive for exploiting than others. Conventional resources, such as wells on land or at sea, are the most cost effective to recover and are the most heavily exploited types of oil resources worldwide. These conventional oil reserves comprise only 30 percent of Earth's known remaining oil reserves. Oil sands and bitumen make up 30 percent, heavy oil 15 percent, and extra heavy oil 25 percent of global oil deposits.

Conventional oil reserves are extracted through drilling wells. Unconventional resources include extra oil shales, oil or tar sands, heavy oil, and natural bitumen. Oil from unconventional resources requires specialized production methods; it cannot be recovered through traditional drilling. Obtaining usable petroleum products from these deposits is more expensive, increasing consumer prices. Typical oil wells on land or at sea cost between $100,000 and $100 million to construct. Extracting unconventional oil costs considerably more, and most of the world's remaining untapped oil reserves are from unconventional sources.

U.S. offshore oil reserves may contain as much as 85.9 million barrels of oil. A large amount of these reserves, however, lies outside the proposed areas for new exploration. Some of these reserves may also lie in areas where drilling is not commercially feasible. Most of the proposed areas for new drilling will not produce oil until at least 2015. Furthermore, in 2007, the Energy Information Administration (EIA), a division of the U.S. Department of Energy, estimated that offshore drilling would not affect oil prices until approximately 2030.

Global Connections, Geopolitical Consequences

Global energy consumption is uneven. Africa, which has about 14 percent of the world's people, consumes 3 percent of its energy, while the United States, with 5 percent of the world's people, consumes 25 percent of its energy—over twenty times more per person. The United States is the world's largest user of oil. Since it uses more than it can produce domestically, it must import petroleum and natural gas from other parts of the world. Relying on imported, oil-based fuels can create dependence on hostile nations, balance-of-trade deficits, and provoke conflict.

Oil reserves are geological phenomena, scattered across the globe in various concentrations. The Middle East contains most of the world's largest oil deposits. Almost all of its current, active extraction occurs with conventional drilling, making Middle East oil potentially cheaper than other sources. The world's oil-rich countries—predominantly Middle East nations, North African nations, and the South American nation of

World Oil Reserves with Production & Consumption Rates

Rank	Country	Reserves[1] (billions)	% World	Production[3] (billions/year)	% World	Years Left	Consumption[3] (billions/year)	% World
1	Saudi Arabia	264.8	22.4%	3.9	12.6%	67.3	.88	2.8%
2	Iran	137.0	11.6%	1.5	4.9%	89.9	.62	2.0%
3	Iraq	126.0	10.6%	.9	2.8%	144.7	.22	.7%
4	Kuwait	99.4	8.4%	1.0	3.2%	99.4	.13	.4%
5	Venezuela	81.0	6.8%	1.0	3.2%	83.9	.27	.9%
6	Russia	76.0	6.4%	3.6	11.5%	21.3	1.00	3.4%
7	U.A.E.	68.1	5.8%	1.1	3.6%	61.3	.19	.6%
8	Nigeria	37.2	3.1%	.8	2.5%	46.9	.10	.3%
9	Libya	36.5	3.1%	.7	2.2%	53.3	.10	.3%
10	Canada[2]	25.2	2.1%	1.2	3.9%	20.5	.84	2.7%
11	United States	21.3	1.8%	3.1	3.1%	6.9	7.12	22.8%
12	Qatar	20.0	1.7%	.4	1.4%	45.6	.04	.1%
13	China	18.0	1.5%	1.5	4.6%	12.5	2.86	9.2%
14	Brazil	12.5	1.1%	.9	2.8%	14.3	.91	2.9%
15	Algeria	11.9	1.0%	.8	2.6%	14.9	.11	.3%
	Top Fifteen	1,035.0	87.4%	22.3	71.6%	46.3	15.46	49.6%
	World Total	1,184.2	100%	31.20	100%	37.9	31.2	100%

[1] World Oil, year end 2007 estimates, in barrels (1 barrel = 42 U.S. gallons).

[2] Excludes unrecoverable or unconventional reserves.

[3] Production and Consumption numbers from U.S. Energy Information Administration, also in barrels.

Each country's size in the map above is proportional to its proven oil reserves. There is a great disparity between reserves and consumption: the United States has less than 2% of the world's oil reserves but consumes almost 23% of the world's oil production. Conversely, the top five oil-rich countries in the Middle East have almost 60% of the world's reserves but consume only 6.5% of world production. Based on today's reserves and consumption rates there are less than 40 years of oil left. Illustration/XNR Productions/Cengage Learning, Gale.

Venezuela—banded together to form the Organization of the Petroleum Exporting Countries (OPEC). OPEC regulates the amount of petroleum products that its members refine and export, thus insuring stable and often higher prices for oil and gasoline in the global marketplace. OPEC policy has significant economic effects on countries that depend on importing its oil, from the price of auto gasoline to the cost of transportation for food.

The transportation of oil can also be a source of geopolitical conflict. Oil extracted far from where the companies intend to refine the product must be transported, often across international waters or through transboundary pipelines. A national or private company of one country may own a drilling lease or prospect in another country. It may use a pipeline that crosses yet other countries to bring the oil to refineries in the first nation. All of these countries will likely receive some economic benefit from the oil production, but those benefits are often disproportionate and can breed discord.

Research and Exploration

American Association for the Advancement of Science (AAAS). "The Science of the Oil Spill." http://news.sciencemag.org/oilspill.

The American Association for the Advancement of Science (AAAS) presents science-based articles on the fate of the oil spilled into the Gulf of Mexico, the safety of the dispersants used on the oil, and the effect of the oil spill on marine life.

BP. "A Community Fights Back." http://bp.concerts.com/gom/gulfcoasttourism100110.htm.

BP, the corporation that has assumed responsibility for the *Deepwater Horizon* oil spill along with BP's subcontractors, presents a video on the recovery efforts of Gulf Coast seafood and tourism.

Guardian. "Deepwater Horizon: BP's Efforts to Control the Gulf of Mexico Oil Spill." http://www.guardian.co.uk/environment/interactive/2010/may/20/deepwater-horizon-gulf-oil-spill-gulf.

The *Guardian*, a daily newspaper from Manchester, United Kingdom, features an informative, animated presentation on the various techniques used to prevent the flow of oil into the Gulf of Mexico and cap the well.

MSNBC. "Disaster in the Gulf." http://www.msnbc.msn.com/id/36947751.

MSNBC presents an interactive timeline on the *Deepwater Horizon* oil spill.

National Geographic Channel. "Gulf Oil Spill." http://channel.nationalgeographic.com/episode/gulf-oil-spill-5488/Overview#tab-Videos/08211_00.

The National Geographic Channel presents a video detailing the efforts of the U.S. Coast Guard to rescue workers from the *Deepwater Horizon* oil platform and extinguish the fire that engulfed the platform.

National Oceanic and Atmospheric Administration. "Education Resources: Gulf Oil Spill." http://www.education.noaa.gov/Ocean_and_Coasts/Oil_Spill.html.

The National Oceanic and Atmospheric Administration (NOAA) presents an educational web portal, featuring information gathered from across NOAA publications about the Gulf of Mexico oil spill and its effects on oceans, coastal areas, marine life, and other topics.

National Oceanic and Atmospheric Administration: Office of Response and Restoration. "Deepwater Horizon/BP Oil Spill Response." http://response.restoration.noaa.gov/dwh.php?entry_id=809.

The Office of Response and Restoration, an office of the National Oceanic and Atmospheric Administration (NOAA), features scientific information on the emergency response to the Gulf oil spill and natural resource restoration.

National Public Radio. "Gulf Oil Spill: Complete Coverage." http://www.npr.org/series/126475680/gulf-oil-spill-complete-coverage.

National Public Radio (NPR) features ongoing coverage of the *Deepwater Horizon* oil spill, including audio reports, interactive maps, and videos.

National Public Radio. "Morning Edition: How Will the Gulf Oil Spill Affect Human Health?" http://www.npr.org/templates/story/story.php?storyId=128008826.

National Public Radio presents an audio story on the potential physical and psychological effects of the *Deepwater Horizon* on residents of Gulf Coast communities.

New York Times. "Tracking the Oil Spill in the Gulf." http://www.nytimes.com/interactive/2010/05/01/us/20100501-oil-spill-tracker.html.

The *New York Times* features an interactive map that provides day-by-day tracking of the Gulf oil spill from 22 April to 2 August 2010.

Restore the Gulf. "RestoretheGulf.gov Homepage." http://www.restorethegulf.gov.

RestoretheGulf.gov is the U.S. government's official website for information on the Gulf of Mexico oil spill response, news, current operations, and other up-to-date information. The website includes contact information for people affected by the oil spill who want assistance in filing a claim with insurance companies or federal, state, or local agencies.

Reuters. "Gulf of Mexico Oil Spill." http://www.reuters.com/subjects/gulf-oil-spill.

Reuters, a worldwide news service, features information from across the Gulf Coast about the effects of the *Deepwater Horizon* oil spill.

Southern Oral History Project. "Documenting the Gulf Oil Spill." http://oilspillstories.tumblr.com.

The Southern Oral History Project presents interviews with people affected by the gulf oil spill to assess the effects of the oil spill on their lives.

the.News. "Impact of the Deepwater Horizon Spill." http://www.pbs.org/newshour/thenews/thevote/story.php?id=17563&package_id=634.

the.News, a youth-oriented news service of MacNeil/Lehrer Productions, the producers of the Public Broadcasting Service's *PBS Newshour*, presents a video chronicling the impact of the oil spill on the Gulf region.

Times-Picayune. "2010 Gulf of Mexico Oil Spill." http://www.nola.com/news/gulf-oil-spill/.

The *Times-Picayune*, a daily newspaper from New Orleans, Louisiana, presents news stories, editorials, photographs, and maps of the Gulf of Mexico oil spill with a focus on New Orleans and the Louisiana coast.

U.S. Coast Guard. "Visual Information Gallery." http://cgvi.uscg.mil/media/main.php?g2_itemId=1034589.

A U.S. Coast Guard video chronicling the release of 32 sea turtles that had been treated for oil exposure from the Gulf of Mexico oil spill.

Haiti: Earthquake & Aftermath

Carlos Garcia Rawlins/Reuters.

On 12 January 2010, a devastating 7.0-magnitude earthquake struck Haiti, causing catastrophic damage and loss of life, and leaving an estimated three million people in need of emergency aid. The earthquake was the strongest to hit the country in more than two hundred years.

Estimates of the death toll climbed rapidly. Haitian President René Préval said that rescue workers collected more than 200,000 bodies from collapsed buildings in the first five weeks following the quake, with tens of thousands more missing or buried in rubble still too thick or unstable to clear. Dead bodies were piled in almost impassable streets and carted to mass graves. The numbers of dead precluded efforts to identify the majority of bodies. In 90-plus-degree heat, with a lack of water, food, and basic sanitation, medical care and disease prevention became prime issues for rescue and recovery teams. Hundreds of thousands of survivors, unable or afraid to move back into damaged homes, camped in streets and parks.

Powerful aftershocks interrupted desperate rescue attempts for more than a week following the initial earthquake. Global media focused on Haiti, with around-the-clock coverage of increasingly miraculous survival stories contrasting with the deepening desperation of survivors. Although survival beyond four days without water is rare in such disaster situations, especially among the injured, the rapid collapse of buildings created pockets of survivors, some of whom had limited access to food or water. By the beginning of February, however, the United Nations (UN) declared that rescue operations were at an end and that further efforts would be directed toward recovery operations.

Although official estimates vary, Préval later estimated that the death toll ranged between 220,000 and 300,000 people. While an exact

Rescue workers pull a woman from a collapsed cathedral in Port-au-Prince 19 January 2010, six days after the devastating earthquake. © Katie Orlinsky/Corbis.

death toll may never be fully determined, international disaster and relief experts contend that the earthquake was likely the most lethal natural disaster in modern history, surpassing the estimated 220,000 to 250,000 people killed as a result of the 2004 Indian Ocean tsunami.

The Earthquake's Destructive Power

The epicenter of the earthquake was near the Haitian capital of Port-au-Prince, which suffered extensive damage. More than 80 percent of the buildings in the city were destroyed or rendered unusable. Haiti's National Palace, Parliament, and the headquarters of the UN peacekeeping forces were severely damaged or destroyed. Medical services were severely hampered by the collapse of most hospitals and clinics. Most of the buildings and homes in Haiti were not specially reinforced to withstand the horizontal stresses encountered during an earthquake. Many buildings were constructed of un-reinforced concrete, with walls of stacked blocks rather than vertical columns supporting roofs. Under horizontal stress, the concrete walls collapsed, literally exploding into dust, and roofs crumpled and then came crashing down. In the aftermath of the earthquake, clouds of white concrete dust—similar to those seen in New York after 9/11—choked the Haitian capital.

A van avoids a large crack in the road near Petit Goave, Haiti. The earthquake ravaged the country's already fragile infrastructure. Al Diaz/MCT/Landov. ▶

Even reinforced structures such as the UN headquarters were no match for the massive quake.

In addition to loss of life, relief agencies estimated that more than 250,000 homes were destroyed by the earthquake and that approximately 1.5 million people were forced to live in makeshift camps with inadequate shelter and sanitation. Concerns over the lack of shelter and sanitation for the homeless continued throughout 2010.

Immediate Impacts and Response

The earthquake killed key leaders and destroyed important cultural landmarks. President Préval reported the death of Hedi Annabi, chief of the UN mission in Haiti. More than one hundred UN workers also lost their lives. A significant number of UN aid and security workers stationed in Haiti lived at the collapsed Hotel Montana. The National Cathedral was destroyed, and Catholic archbishop Msgr. Joseph Serge Miot was killed in the collapse of an archdiocese building. Church buildings across the heavily Catholic country were reduced to ruins.

The day following the earthquake, UN Secretary General Ban Ki-moon declared the Haitian capital of Port-au-Prince to be in a state of civil collapse and urged the international community "to come to Haiti's aid in this hour of need." Even prior to Ban Ki-moon's appeal and within hours

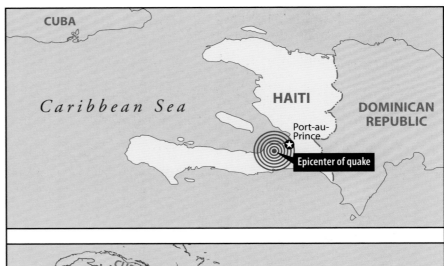

SOURCE: USGS

The epicenter of the 7.0-magnitude earthquake was near the Haitian capital of Port-au-Prince, which suffered extensive damage. Illustration/XNR Productions/Cengage Learning, Gale.

of the earthquake, the United States promised full military and civilian aid. Non-governmental agencies (NGOs) and nations from around the world, including Canada, Russia, China, Israel, and several European Union countries, immediately dispatched rescue and relief services to Haiti.

UN officials released emergency funds and sent a response team to coordinate humanitarian relief efforts in Haiti. World Bank President Robert B. Zoellick and International Monetary Fund (IMF) Managing Director Dominique Strauss-Kahn pledged the support of their institutions

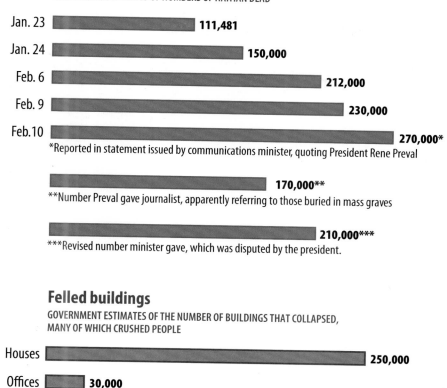

Death and Destruction in Haiti
CONFLICTING ESTIMATES OF NUMBERS OF HAITIAN DEAD

Jan. 23 — 111,481
Jan. 24 — 150,000
Feb. 6 — 212,000
Feb. 9 — 230,000
Feb.10 — 270,000*

*Reported in statement issued by communications minister, quoting President Rene Preval

170,000**

**Number Preval gave journalist, apparently referring to those buried in mass graves

210,000***

***Revised number minister gave, which was disputed by the president.

Felled buildings
GOVERNMENT ESTIMATES OF THE NUMBER OF BUILDINGS THAT COLLAPSED, MANY OF WHICH CRUSHED PEOPLE

Houses — 250,000
Offices — 30,000

It was difficult for Haitian officials to quantify exactly how much damage was inflicted by the earthquake. Illustration/XNR Productions/Cengage Learning, Gale.

for use. While inland hospitals fared better, they were without electricity and supplies of fuel for generators were in short supply. Amputations were performed in the street and in the rubble of collapsed buildings as workers struggled to free trapped victims. Morphine to control pain was often unavailable. Common trauma encountered by health workers included crush injuries, broken bones, head injuries, open fractures, and piercing injuries from flying glass and steel. Burns from ruptured stoves and gas lines were also common. Lack of operational medical facilities and supplies turned many otherwise survivable injuries into fatalities. For example, crush injuries often lead to significant protein release into the bloodstream that threatens kidneys and other vital organs. Although the crush injuries themselves are not necessarily lethal, victims often die from metabolic shock or trauma without proper care.

to aid both relief and recovery efforts. The World Bank quickly authorized 100 million U.S. dollars in emergency grants. UN World Food Program director Josette Sheeran ordered immediate airlifts of food. By 4 February, more than one billion dollars of international aid had been pledged to relief and recovery efforts in Haiti.

The UN World Health Organization (WHO) quickly dispatched experts in mass casualty management, public health, and sanitation to Haiti. Medical teams of doctors, nurses, and other health care workers also headed for the disaster area, but commonly encountered a lack of facilities and supplies. All three of the Médecins Sans Frontières (MSF; Doctors without Borders) hospitals already operating in Haiti were destroyed or unfit

During the week following the earthquake, Haiti, already on the edge of social unrest, experienced scattered outbreaks of looting, gunfire, and violence. Jobs also were in short supply. Although accounts of disruptions at supply centers were reported, UN officials continued to emphasize that the overall situation was safer and calmer than had been anticipated. By early February, however, a number of street protests over slow food distribution and alleged corruption among some responsible for relief efforts were reported. The UN's Haitian mission, which included 7,000 peacekeeping troops and 2,000 international police prior to the earthquake, assumed responsibility for security. At their peak in early February 2010, approximately 20,000 U.S. troops were also assigned to recovery and rebuilding efforts in Haiti. After weeks of controlling the airport and port facilities at the request of both Haitian and UN relief officials, U.S. forces began the process of returning control to a reorganizing Haitian government in late February.

By July 2010, Haitian police reported that sexual assaults and other forms of violence had risen dramatically following the earthquake's devastation of communities. Women and girls living in temporary housing or on the streets were especially vulnerable to criminal attacks. In areas with surviving buildings, more than a dozen people routinely crowded into rooms built to accommodate only three or four people. Although schools across the country gradually reopened, often in temporary facilities stocked with books and supplies from other countries and cultures, they were often overloaded with students and with survivors seeking shelter.

Earthquake Predictions and Dynamics

For more than a decade, geologists predicted that the stresses building over the

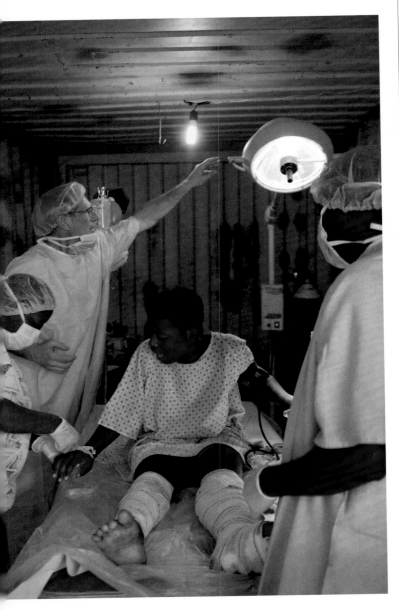

A man with leg injuries is treated by Médecins Sans Frontières (MSF) staff at the makeshift Trinity clinic, across the street from MSF's collapsed hospital, in Port-au-Prince, in the days after the quake. MSF had been operating in Haiti since 1991 and was able to treat patients within moments of the earthquake. AP Images/VII/Ron Haviv.

Haitian President René Préval and his wife, Elisabeth Préval at the 23 January 2010 funeral mass for Haiti's Archbishop Joseph Serge Miot, who died in the earthquake. Al Diaz/MCT/Landov.

Survivors Gave Desperate Rescue Workers Hope

Covered with dust, scrapes, and mud, images of two-year-old Redjeson Hausteen Claude captivated the world when he was pulled alive and relatively uninjured from the wreckage of his home in Port-au-Prince on 14 January 2010, almost three days after the Haiti earthquake. Photos of Redjeson clinging to his Spanish and Belgian rescuers, and then smiling and reaching for his waiting mother circulated throughout world media, and documented a rare victory for frantic rescuers who were running out of time to find survivors in the rubble.

Daphnee Plaisin and Reginald Claude spent the previous two days and nights separating the rubble of their home by hand in an attempt to reach their son. They described his cries as a guiding force, loud and strong at first, but becoming quieter as his condition weakened. When they were unable to move the large concrete blocks and metal sheets that trapped

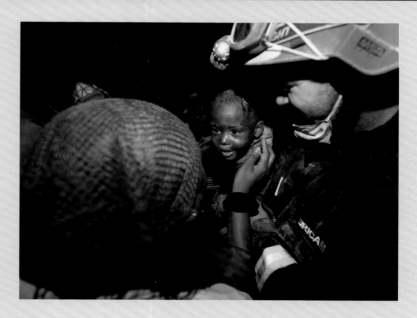

Redjeson Hausteen Claude is reunited with his mother after being pulled from his collapsed home by a Belgian and Spanish rescue team. AP Images/Gerald Herbert.

their son, members of a joint Spanish and Belgian fire rescue team stepped in to help. After hours of painstaking, exhausting work removing the heavy obstacles one by one in the remains of the dangerously unsound structure, dramatic photographs captured the moment when Spanish rescuer Félix del Amo pulled the child from the rubble.

Despite widespread damage to infrastructure, including major roads and airports, within 48 hours of the disaster more than 20 countries managed to set military troops, medical workers, and rescue teams on the ground in Haiti. Their top priorities during the first week were finding and reaching survivors, administering medical aid, and providing food and water to almost one million displaced people in need.

two-hundred-plus years since the last major earthquake emanating from the fault system in Haiti would eventually result in a potentially catastrophic earthquake or a series of several smaller quakes. In 2006, American geophysicists predicted that seismic shifts could result in a major earthquake up to a magnitude of 7.2 on the Richter scale. At the 18th Caribbean Geologic Conference held in

Santo Domingo, Dominican Republic, in March 2008, geologists openly discussed the fact that the fault system around Haiti was "locked" and had failed to move significantly for more than forty years. Such locked faults must eventually move to relieve tectonic stresses. The conference report argued that "built-up stress and energy in the earth could one day be released resulting in an

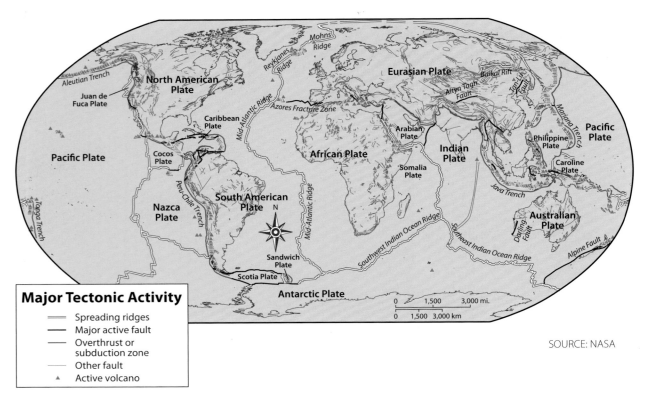

Major Tectonic Activity

≡ Spreading ridges
— Major active fault
— Overthrust or subduction zone
— Other fault
▲ Active volcano

SOURCE: NASA

Major ridges, faults, and volcanic centers of the last one million years. Global tectonic stresses make earthquakes common and inevitable. Illustration/XNR Productions/Cengage Learning, Gale.

earthquake measuring 7.2 or more on the Richter Scale." In September 2008, the Haiti-based newspaper *Le Matin* published an article predicting that there was a high risk of imminent major seismic activity in or near Port-au-Prince.

Even though geologists can sometimes identify fault areas under stress, they do not yet have the capability to predict exactly when another quake might occur. Earthquake warnings for specific areas may range over decades or centuries, but global tectonic stresses make earthquakes common and inevitable.

The January 2010 Haiti earthquake took place about six miles deep along the Enriquillo-Plantain Garden Fault that runs from near Montego Bay in Jamaica to the southern tip of Hispaniola (the Caribbean island divided into Haiti and the Dominican Republic). The Enriquillo-Plantain

Garden Fault is a vertical fault primarily stressed by movement of the Caribbean Plate.

The Enriquillo-Plantain Garden fault system is one of several faults along the boundary between the Caribbean and North America tectonic plates. In the area of Haiti, the plates slip past each other along an east-west line of contact. Following the January 2010 earthquake, scientists rushed to estimate residual stress levels in the faults around Haiti. According to the U.S. Geological Survey (USGS), only a 31-mile-long (50-kilometer-long) surface stretch of the fault line moved several feet from pre-quake locations, but the portion of the fault beneath Port-au-Prince remained intact. This means that the risk of future earthquakes in the region remains high. GPS tracking devices now monitor surface movements at recording stations located along the fault line, but there were no monitoring stations in Haiti prior to the quake.

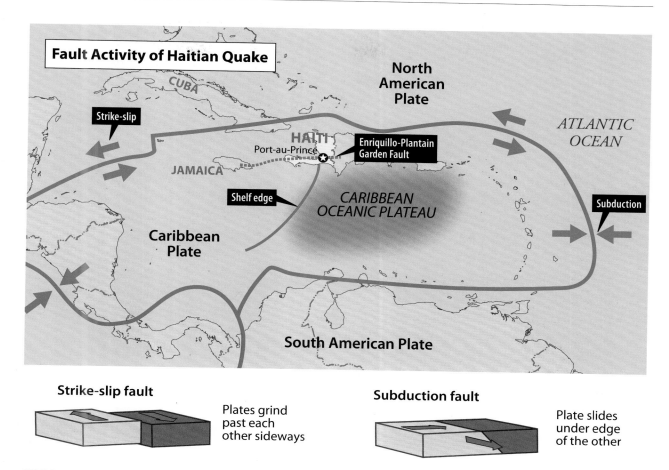

Strike-slip fault

Plates grind past each other sideways

Subduction fault

Plate slides under edge of the other

SOURCE: USGS

The Haiti earthquake took place about six miles deep along the Enriquillo-Plantain Garden Fault that runs from near Montego Bay in Jamaica to the southern tip of Hispaniola (the Caribbean island divided into Haiti and the Dominican Republic). Illustration/XNR Productions/Cengage Learning, Gale.

A Difficult Road to Recovery

In late April 2010, initial recovery efforts moved into longer-term reconstruction phases. Many foreign medical teams returned to their home countries. Although conditions gradually improved in some areas, throughout 2010, large segments of the population lived day-to-day on ration cards and meager subsistence diets. More than 460 temporary relocation sites transformed into semi-permanent tented or tarped communities. In many cases, residents had no option to return to destroyed homes. While many survivors were fortunate to find space to live in camps for internally displaced persons, others slept in open fields. Rural relief centers were stressed by a lack of supplies and staff and were overwhelmed with the large influx of people needing shelter, food, and medicine. Basic sanitation remained an urgent concern. In many camps, raw sewage ran through open areas where survivors cooked and children played nearby.

Life in the camps placed residents at greater risks associated with extreme weather. In July 2010, storms lashed temporary camps along coastal areas, destroying tents and knocking out makeshift power systems. Relief officials were

People displaced by the earthquake live in makeshift tents on the grounds of the International Club in Port-au-Prince. More than one million Haitians live under tarps and tents in cramped and unsanitary conditions. Alison Wright/National Geographic Stock.

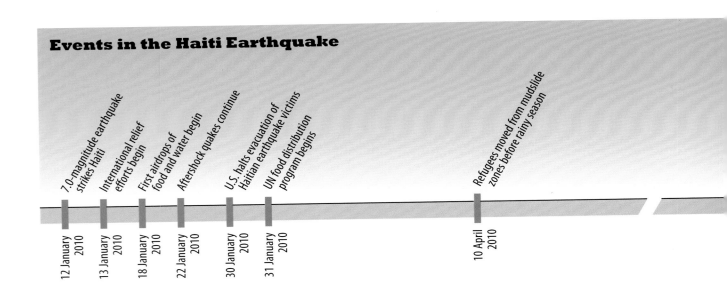

Events in the Haiti Earthquake

7.0-magnitude earthquake strikes Haiti

International relief efforts begin

First airdrops of food and water begin

Aftershock quakes continue

U.S. halts evacuation of Haitian earthquake victims

UN food distribution program begins

Refugees moved from mudslide zones before rainy season

12 January 2010

13 January 2010

18 January 2010

22 January 2010

30 January 2010

31 January 2010

10 April 2010

forced to evacuate sites at risk of landslides. These and other problems added to the difficulty in establishing basic social infrastructure, including providing consistently clean water and food, adequate waste disposal and sanitation facilities, and building new clinics and schools.

Shifting populations presented ongoing problems. Prior to the earthquake, approximately one third of Haiti's 10 million people lived in Port-au-Prince or its immediate suburbs. UN officials estimated that 400,000 to 600,000 people from Port-au-Prince fled the city for surrounding areas in the immediate aftermath of the earthquake. The exodus initially eased pressure on relief camps located in the city, but placed a burden on settlements in surrounding areas. Many outlying towns also suffered severe earthquake damage. Many who fled then drifted back to Port-au-Prince or other larger coastal towns looking for jobs or aid.

Access to smaller towns and remote areas was frequently complicated by rain, which made dirt roads impassable. Large trucks normally deliver food and medical supplies, but in times of heavy rain and stormy weather, smaller four-wheel drive vehicles were required to navigate otherwise impassable roads.

Continuing Public Health Struggles

Many medical facilities in Haiti, especially outside the capital of Port-au-Prince, operated without laboratories and dependable power sources. Accordingly, doctors and nurses relied on their own experience and observations to make correct diagnoses. Many survivors of the January 2010 earthquake congregated into internally displaced persons (IDP) camps, where providing basic sanitation was a continuing challenge. In such cities as Pétionville, Freres, and Cité Soleil, relief and health workers report that up to 50 percent of children suffered from acute diarrhea.

Given the scope of the disaster and Haiti's lack of resources, most Haitians remain dependent on outside medical aid. Prior to the earthquake, extreme poverty in Haiti kept over-the-counter medicines like aspirin and acetaminophen out of the reach of many Haitians. A dozen tablets of either preparation could easily cost one week's salary. Following the earthquake, with needs increased and the availability of medicine limited, health care workers struggled to provide a range of care, from critical, life-saving operations, to the most basic medical aid and medicine.

Malnutrition, dehydration, vitamin deficiency problems, and reports of nursing mothers unable

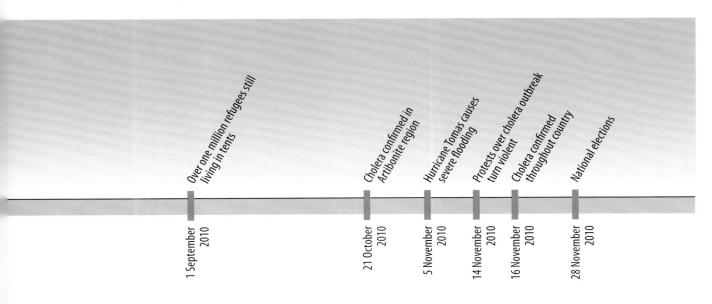

Over one million refugees still living in tents — 1 September 2010

Cholera confirmed in Artibonite region — 21 October 2010

Hurricane Tomas causes severe flooding — 5 November 2010

Protests over cholera outbreak turn violent — 14 November 2010

Cholera confirmed throughout country — 16 November 2010

National elections — 28 November 2010

A funeral for a cholera victim in Drouin (Grande Saline), in the Artibonite province, north of Port-au-Prince, Haiti, on 23 October 2010. Andres Martinez Cesares/EPA/Landov.

to produce sufficient breast milk were common. Infants forced to eat mashes of various foods that their immature digestive systems could not tolerate or fully process resulted in an increase in diarrhea, which hampered the development of immune systems needed to fight off an array of potentially fatal illnesses.

In May 2010, following an outbreak of diphtheria that spread rapidly in Port-au-Prince and its surrounding temporary housing camps, WHO, the UN Children's Fund (UNICEF), and Haitian health authorities launched an emergency vaccination campaign. The outbreak started with reports from Camp Batimat, a temporary housing camp in the Cité Soleil district. Prior to the start of vaccination efforts, health experts estimated that thousands of people were exposed to diphtheria bacteria via coughing. Some cases of

diphtheria, especially cases involving infection of the lower respiratory tract, can be life threatening. The diphtheria outbreak and emergency vaccination program was an addition to programs that have already vaccinated nearly 900,000 people housed in temporary camps following the earthquake. Diphtheria is endemic (nearly always present) in Haiti. One of the last cases of diphtheria recorded in the United States was traced to a traveler returning from Haiti in 2003.

Cholera Epidemic Strikes

In October 2010, cholera was reported in Haiti. Cholera is an acute intestinal infection caused by the bacterium *Vibrio cholerae*. Infection can cause rapid dehydration of the body, which can prove fatal within a few hours. Cholera is transmitted by contaminated food and water. It is endemic in countries where there is inadequate sanitation and access to clean water. Quarantine and isolation measures were put in place to halt the outbreak. Medical teams rushed to the rural areas where the initial cases of cholera were reported. Within days, however, the death toll mounted, with thousands of sick people seeking care from an already stressed health care system struggling to recover.

Cholera was first identified in Artibonite, a poor, rural valley region about 60 miles north of Haiti's capital city of Port-au-Prince. Thousands of refugees flooded into the region after the January earthquake. The Artibonite River serves as a source for water for bathing, washing, drinking, and sewage disposal by the community's inflated population, and initial investigations pointed to contamination in the river as the source of the cholera outbreak.

Hurricane Tomas brushed the island of Hispaniola in early November, resulting in flooding that caused at least eight deaths, and complicating the task of providing clean water to relief camps. As roads flooded, relief convoys bogged down. People fleeing from flooded areas increased congestion on the few passable roads in some areas. Heavy flooding effectively cut off some mountain towns and villages from clean food, clean water, power, and medical supplies. Although Hurricane Tomas caused less direct damage than initially feared, the country's infrastructure remained battered and the population vulnerable. Flooding from Hurricane Tomas was also blamed for helping to spread contaminated water that, in turn, helped expand the cholera outbreak.

Members of a Chinese medical team examine the water quality at an aid post in Port-au-Prince in February 2010. With a cholera outbreak beginning in October 2010, experts continued to examine water sources and networks in the captial and elsewhere to make sure that people had access to clean water for drinking, bathing, and washing clothes and food. Wu Xiaoling/Xinhua/Landov.

Cholera's deadly diarrhea and vomiting can be treated with proper oral dehydration therapy, intravenous fluids, and antibiotics. Although public heath officials estimated that sufficient supplies of fluids and antibiotics were initially on hand to fight the growing outbreak, treatment is also labor intensive, demanding many health care workers to care for the sick. Treatment for those who become more severely ill requires health care workers who are trained in fluid and electrolyte management and who know how to provide personal care to exhausted patients with frequent diarrhea, which must be kept from contaminating the local water supply in field conditions. The flooding related to Hurricane Tomas hindered the distribution of supplies and personnel at a time critical to stopping the cholera outbreak while the numbers of cholera victims remained relatively small.

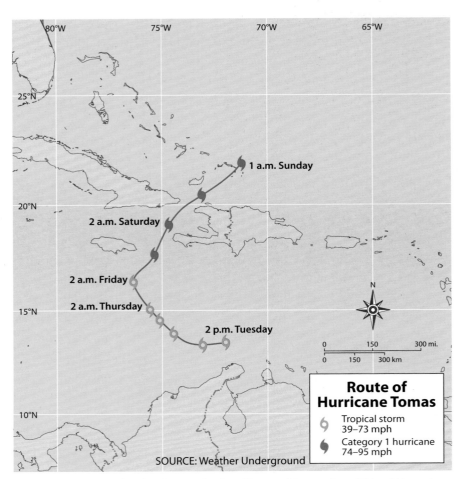

Hurricane Tomas passed within about 140 miles of Port-au-Prince early on Friday, 5 November 2010. The storm caused widespread floods, wind damage along the far edge of Haiti's coast and is blamed for the deaths of at least eight people. Illustration/XNR Productions/Cengage Learning, Gale.

Cases of cholera were quickly reported within seven of Haiti's ten departments: Artibonite, Centre, Nord, Nord-Ouest, Nord-Est, Ouest, and Sud. According to WHO, most troubling to health officials was a reported rise in cases in the Cité Soleil community of Port-au-Prince, a crowded, impoverished slum of about 300,000 people who do not have modern sanitation or dependable access to clean water.

Even prior to Hurricane Tomas, there were scattered but unconfirmed reports of a handful of cases of cholera in Haiti's densely populated capital, Port-au-Prince, where more than one million people still lived in tarpaulin-draped, makeshift tents in crowded camps and with limited access to clean water or adequate waste-disposal facilities. Epidemiologists scrambled to determine whether there was a source of contamination in the capital or whether the cholera was carried by people coming to the city in search of food, water, or treatment.

Clean water and effective sanitation are the most effective preventive measures against cholera. Chlorination of water, boiling of water in

Demonstrators run past burning tires during a protest over the cholera epidemic in Port-au-Prince, 18 November 2010. AP Images/Emilio Morenatti.

households, and the construction and maintenance of latrines are basic measures that can help achieve these goals. High standards of personal hygiene and food preparation can also reduce the spread of the disease. However, these everyday considerations can become major obstacles in crowded and temporary relief camps. In cramped and unhygienic conditions—often with insufficient number of toilets, faulty toilets, or toilets placed too close to water supplies—diarrheal symptoms are common, and so health care workers initially faced the additional challenge of trying to quickly determine whether cases were simple dysentery or related to the more dangerous cholera outbreak. On 8 November 2010, cholera was confirmed in a four-year-old child in Port-au-Prince who had not traveled to any of the cholera-active areas of the island, leading officials to suspect that the outbreak had taken hold in the capital city.

Thousands of Haitians also work in neighboring Dominican Republic, crossing the border and returning to Haiti often. As many people with cholera do not exhibit severe symptoms, WHO officials expected the outbreak to inevitably spread to the Dominican Republic, despite the fact that the Dominican Republic tightened border controls with Haiti. Officials anticipated fewer cases of cholera in the Dominican Republic because of widespread access to improved sanitation, and organized medical teams and supplies in order to prepare to respond to an outbreak. Despite precautions, on 16 November, the first case of cholera in the Dominican Republic was reported in a man returning from Haiti.

Cholera, a Global Killer

Cholera is an acute intestinal infection caused by the bacterium *Vibrio cholerae*. *V. cholerae* belongs to the *Vibrio* genus of Gram-negative bacteria. The term Gram-negative refers to the way in which a bacterium absorbs visualizing stains under a microscope for identification purposes. *Vibrio* species exist as straight or curved rods in watery environments. These bacteria use a whip-like projection called a flagellum to propel themselves. *Vibrio* species prefer marine environments and grow best in the presence of salt. They are one of the most common organisms in the surface waters of the world.

Transmission of *V. cholerae* is through the fecal-oral route, which, in practical terms, means the consumption of, or contact with, food and water contaminated by fecal matter. *V. cholerae* is hard to avoid

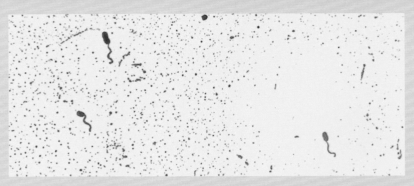

An electron microscope image of group of Vibrio cholerae bacteria. Center for Disease Control/McClatchy-Tribune.

in places where sanitation is poor and access to clean water for drinking or washing is limited or nonexistent.

The most important treatment for cholera is fluid and electrolyte (salt) replacement to treat the losses caused by diarrhea and vomiting. Oral rehydration fluid, containing glucose and salts dissolved in water, is the most common form of this treatment, and is given continually in small amounts by mouth as tolerated. Eighty percent of all cases of cholera can be treated in this way, and the treatment needs to be continued until the diarrhea stops. Intravenous administration of fluid is often necessary, and antibiotic treatment has been shown to shorten the duration of the disease.

Treatment of cholera is simple, but labor intensive, and relies on

By 20 November, deaths from the cholera epidemic in Haiti totaled more than 1,100 and more than 18,000 people were hospitalized with the disease.

Unfounded rumors, disproved by genetic testing, that the cholera outbreak was possibly imported by relief and security forces from countries where cholera is endemic (in particular, Nepal) touched off violence in parts of Haiti among protestors who feared that the contamination was a deliberate attempt to eliminate earthquake survivors and thus reduce demands on the international community. Additional protests occurred around newly established cholera treatment centers, as local citizens feared that the presence of the clinics would bring the disease into their neighborhoods.

The Economics of Recovery and Rebuilding

Many nations and groups, including the G7, canceled international debts so that Haiti could use its funds for rebuilding. Within weeks of the earthquake, cancellation and forgiveness of Haiti's international debt reached more than $1.2 billion.

Countries Reporting Cholera in 2009

CASE-FATALITY RATE

- 5% or greater
- 1–4.9%
- 0–0.9%

SOURCE: World Health Organization

Cholera is endemic in countries where there is inadequate sanitation and access to clean water. An estimated 3–5 million cases and over 100,000 deaths occur each year around the world. Illustration/XNR Productions/Cengage Learning, Gale.

restoring the fluids lost by the body. However, even this simple treatment may not be available in very poor countries. The best approach to preventing cholera lies in better sanitation—improving public health through adequate sewage disposal and cleaning up the water supply. In many less developed countries such as Haiti, this is a difficult challenge to meet because it requires political stability and increased investment in the national infrastructure.

More sobering, however, were assessments by the Inter-American Development Bank that the estimated cost of rebuilding Haitian infrastructure could approach $14 billion over the next decade.

Despite the initial international outpouring of aid, by late 2010, Haiti was still waiting to receive much of the promised aid. By March 2010, the international community had pledged more than $5.3 billion to aid the reconstruction of Haiti. However, by July 2010, more than six months following the earthquake, less than 10 percent of the promised aid had been disbursed to victims or programs designed to help victims.

Some payments were slowed by internal politics in donor nations, but in some cases, pledges of aid never materialized or were diverted to other disasters and causes. International officials continued to express concern regarding the slow payment of promised financial help for Haiti. Relief groups and workers renewed protests over interference and bureaucratic inefficiency in delivering aid, including the imposition of import taxes on some relief and recovery supplies.

Differences in the availability of funds for short-term versus long-term aid also emerged, hindering the transition from relief to long-term recovery and rebuilding efforts. For example, despite sending hundreds of millions of dollars in short-term emergency aid, by July, the United States had not disbursed a significant portion of the $900 million pledged to assist reconstruction efforts. International aid organizations were, in many cases, also slow to release funds to Haiti. However, governments around the world and several international aid organizations consistently argue that the Haiti reconstruction effort will take years to complete and that releasing all of recovery and reconstruction funds at once would be imprudent and create massive waste. Many government and NGO leaders have also stated a desire for the Haitian government to exercise better control of reconstruction efforts and articulate a comprehensive reconstruction plan before releasing the bulk of their financial aid.

"Haiti at a Crossroads," a June 2010 report issued by the U.S. Senate Foreign Relations Committee, also criticized the Haitian government for failing to more effectively manage recovery efforts.

Managing Recovery: The Haitian Government Response

The Interim Haiti Recovery Commission (IHRC) was created to oversee Haiti's recovery and reconstruction efforts. The IHRC adopted a Haiti Recovery Plan, which guides the IHRC's actions related to recovery and reconstruction efforts. The IHRC works with the Haiti Reconstruction Fund (HRF). The HRF is a partnership between the government of Haiti and the international community, including governments, NGOs, and the private sector. The HRF coordinates and allocates contributions from the international community to projects and programs. The IHRC must approve all funding for HRF-supported projects and programs.

Critics argued that the Interim Haiti Recovery Commission (IHRC) did not proceed quickly enough to provide aid for hundreds of thousands of Haitians. Critics also charged that the Haitian government was ineffective and too slow to

Top Ten Countries Donating Money to Haiti
AS OF DECEMBER 3, 2010

United States	$1,177,417,441
Canada	$162,829,447
Spain	$72,277,006
Japan	$71,664,000
Saudi Arabia	$50,000,000
Sweden	$37,351,986
France	$36,136,891
United Kingdom	$33,272,548
Germany	$32,854,285
Norway	$29,070,011

SOURCE: U.N. Office for the Coordination of Humanitarian Affairs

Top donor countries and amounts pledged to Haiti. By July 2010, more than six months following the earthquake, less than 10 percent of the promised aid had been disbursed to victims or programs designed to help victims. Illustration/XNR Productions/Cengage Learning, Gale.

respond to the tragedy, and rebuilding efforts have languished. In the six months immediately following the earthquake, the government constructed only enough shelters to house less than 0.2 percent of displaced Haitians. Government officials countered that reconstruction of buildings and infrastructure could not take place in earnest until the rubble from the earthquake was cleared. Independent analysts and engineers observed that at the current pace rubble removal will take years to complete.

International Coordination

International relief and recovery efforts are managed by a diverse group of organizations, many coordinated by the UN Office for the Coordination of Humanitarian Affairs (OCHA).

A man walks among the rubble of his home that was destroyed in the earthquake in the Fort Nationale neighborhood of Port-au-Prince. The earthquake killed and injured thousands and left more than a million people living in makeshift camps. AP Images/Ramon Espinosa.

Founded in 1991, OCHA's mission is to help the international community respond to emergencies. The agency works with humanitarian organizations and governments to coordinate aid efforts. OCHA's goals are to alleviate suffering after natural disasters or conflicts, help governments and organizations prepare for and respond to emergencies, and facilitate solutions for effective aid distribution.

High-Profile Fundraising

A number of special groups and organizations were formed specifically to help raise funds for relief and recovery efforts in Haiti. For example, former U.S. Presidents Bill Clinton and George W. Bush joined efforts to raise money for the victims of the earthquake. On 16 January 2010,

U.S. President Barack Obama met with Clinton and Bush at the White House and asked them to spearhead an effort to raise private-sector funds for Haiti relief and rebuilding efforts. The former presidents founded the Clinton Bush Haiti Fund to provide immediate relief aid and investment in initiatives chartered to foster economic growth and improve the quality of life in Haiti.

The Clinton Bush Haiti Fund is modeled on the relief effort led by Bill Clinton and former U.S. President George H.W. Bush following the December 2004 tsunami in South Asia. A massive earthquake off the western coast of Indonesia triggered a tsunami that devastated coastal areas in fourteen countries that left millions homeless. Ultimately, their involvement helped raise more

Haiti's President René Préval, second from left, former President George W. Bush, second from right, and former President and UN special envoy for Haiti Bill Clinton, left, arrive at the earthquake damaged Presidential Palace in Port-au-Prince, 22 March 2010. AP Images/ Jorge Saenz.

than $1 billion for relief, reconstruction, and economic development projects in the countries affected by the tsunami. Clinton's participation in Haiti earthquake relief efforts was also a continuation of his long-term interest in the island nation. In May 2009, UN Secretary-General Ban Ki-moon named Bill Clinton the UN Special Envoy to Haiti. Clinton launched an initiative to raise $300 million to assist Haiti in rebuilding efforts after more than $1 billion in damage was caused by a series of hurricanes and tropical storms in 2008.

Regional Responders

Regional economic response to the earthquake in Haiti centered on the Caribbean Community, or CARICOM, an organization of independent states and dependencies in the Caribbean region. The fifteen-member CARICOM was established by treaty in 1973 to promote economic cooperation and trade among its members, advance a united foreign policy on international issues affecting the Caribbean region, mediate trade disputes among members, and aid development in the region's poorest areas. The organization, which originally focused on the creation of a common economic market for Caribbean states, expanded in 2001 to include the Caribbean Court of Justice. CARICOM is currently based in Georgetown, Guyana, an English-speaking Caribbean state on the northern coast of South America.

Haiti first applied to join CARICOM in 1997, joined in 2002, and was admitted as a full member in 2006. Haiti is the poorest CARICOM member, but as of 2006 its population was greater than all of the other fourteen CARICOM member states combined. It is the only French/Haitian Creole-speaking member of the organization.

One of CARICOM's goals is to help Haiti rebuild trade-related infrastructure.

Funding Shortfalls

Many organizations reported dramatic differences between pledges of assistance and funds received, a situation made more difficult by general global economic recession with uneven recovery in many nations. The problem was not unique to Haiti, just more acutely exposed by the scale of need in Haiti. For example, the UN Central Emergency Response Fund (CERF) was created to enable more rapid deployment of humanitarian assistance to those affected by conflict or natural disaster. The fund is supposed to boost early response to humanitarian crises, with a special emphasis on underfunded countries or people. CERF is funded by donations from UN-member governments, independent corporations, aid organizations, non-governmental organizations, and individuals. When established, the fund was intended to reach $500 million; however, the fund continues to struggle to secure actual payment of pledges. As a result, CERF could fully fund only a portion of its efforts in Haiti.

Media Coverage and Fundraising Impacts

The Haiti earthquake demonstrated the importance of mass media and social media in shaping public response to a disaster. Aid organizations say the response established the Internet and social media as powerful tools to allow, promote, and organize global response to a crisis.

The 24-hour news cycle created by cable news stations and the Internet requires a constant supply of new material that ideally contains photos or videos. When the earthquake struck, the mainstream media had a limited presence in Haiti and was unable to get reporters on the ground quickly afterwards due to destroyed airports and ports. The mass media, therefore, turned to social media for reporting. Video reports from bloggers and photos shared over Twitter, Facebook, and other social media sites provided the world with many of the first images and stories of the Haiti earthquake.

The BBC (British Broadcasting Corporation), for example, used posts from Twitter to augment the stories of reporters. The iReport section of CNN's website featured hundreds of video reports, photos, and news stories supplied by users in Haiti. Launched in 2006, iReport allows users to upload videos, pictures, and stories onto the website. While CNN verifies some of the user-generated content, most remains unverified, and CNN notes whether or not individual content has been verified. Some of the first images of the Haiti earthquake to appear in mainstream media coverage originated on iReport. The website of *The Guardian*, a newspaper based in Manchester, United Kingdom, featured a live blog of relief efforts and the earthquake aftermath. The blog featured embedded, user-generated photos and videos and reports from citizens and journalists in Haiti. Media experts argued that the inclusion of user-generated content on iReport and *The Guardian*'s website demonstrated the increasing use of citizen-based journalism to amplify both television and newspaper coverage of major events.

While many experts cited extensive traditional and new media coverage as a key factor fueling fundraising, critics countered that the use of graphic images, including those showing the bodies of dead or injured children on several news media sites, was exploitative, failed to observe journalistic standards, and lacked purpose. Many journalists, however, defended the inclusion of such images because the graphic images presented

Mackenson Magloire holds his rations for the day from a food distribution conducted by the Brazilian Battalion and the U.S. Army in Cite Soleil, Haiti. Al Diaz/MCT/Landov.

the true scale of the catastrophe and the level of human suffering.

As news spread about the extent of the earthquake to a wider audience, charitable organizations received a flood of donations. A large portion of the donations was contributed via text-message campaigns. Backed by the U.S. State Department, White House, and government and social media sites around the world, the fundraising effort spread quickly—becoming "viral" in Internet jargon—to raise millions of dollars for relief efforts. The Red Cross telephone texting appeal quickly became the leading fundraiser in the organization's history. The Red Cross received $2 million in donations in the first 24 hours and ultimately raised over $30 million via text-message donations.

Throughout 2010, social media sites provided direct help to earthquake relief workers and victims. Even when overall transmission capacity was inconsistent, small pockets of connectivity remained in Haiti following the earthquake because many cell phone towers have generators to provide emergency power. Some cell phone users accessed social media sites that sprang up within hours of the first shocks or communicated with Twitter sites via still-functioning text message services. Online volunteer efforts included groups that compiled post-quake maps of areas that helped rescuers pick through rubble. Online groups also formed to provide volunteers fluent in French and Haitian Creole to translate and post missing persons information. For example, Facebook contains many sites listing and seeking missing people.

The online aid effort for Haiti also set new records in terms of amounts of money raised and in the diversity of online involvement. Organizers of "Hope for Haiti Now" set a new record for disaster relief telethons, and a special rerecording of the 1985 charity single "We Are the World" with contemporary artists was released to benefit Haiti relief efforts. Aid professionals argue such diversity provides a broader base of people with personal interest and "ownership" in Haiti's long-term recovery efforts. Experts also argue that the level of involvement of social media in relief and recovery efforts in Haiti was both innovative and unprecedented in terms of scale.

The Haitian community in the United States also spearheaded numerous fundraising efforts to benefit Haiti in the aftermath of the earthquake. Haitian musician Wyclef Jean (who attempted to qualify as a presidential candidate for November elections) and Raymond James, Jean's uncle and the Haitian ambassador to the United States, called for earthquake relief donations to Jean's Yéle Haiti Foundation, a charitable organization. By June 2010, Yéle Haiti Foundation had raised more than $9 million for earthquake relief efforts.

In the United States, more than half of all households made private contributions to relief and recovery efforts. In some countries, including Canada, private contributions were greater than initial government pledges. In response, Canadian officials ultimately pledged to match the level of private contributions.

Disaster Exposes Haitian Infrastructure and Social Vulnerabilities

Haiti is considered the poorest nation in the Western world. Approximately half of the citizens of the French and Creole-speaking nation live in crowded cites near the coast. Eighty percent of Haitians live in poverty, and nearly half are classified as illiterate. Police and medical infrastructure are stressed under normal circumstances, and fire

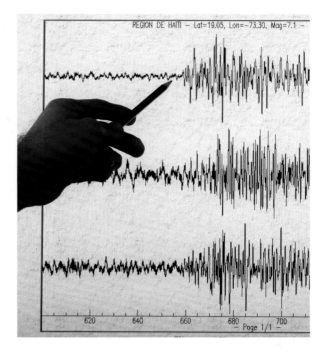

The siesmograph reading of the Haiti earthquake. The quake ranks as one of the deadliest in history. Zuma Press/newscom.

and paramedic services are essentially nonexistent for much of the population. Violent political unrest and crime are common, and Haiti is plagued by high rates of AIDS and outbreaks of infectious disease. Extensive deforestation makes hillsides prone to mudslides, and the island suffered damage from a series of tropical storms and hurricanes over the last decade.

Poverty is at the root of differences between nations in terms of their ability to prepare for and cope with disaster. As is often the case, disasters expose fragility in government and social infrastructure. The poorest and weakest often suffer the greatest.

A mountainous central region divides the Caribbean island of Hispaniola into Haiti in the west and the Dominican Republic in the east. While buildings shook in the Dominican capital of Santo Domingo, a country with greater resources, developed infrastructure, and social stability, there were no reports of major damage, deaths, or injuries.

The destruction caused by the Haiti earthquake,

Destruction in Concepcion, Chile, on 2 March 2010 following a massive earthquake which killed more than 720 people and left most of the population without water, food and electricity. AP Images/Jonne Roriz.

both economically and in terms of casualties and human suffering, stands in stark contrast to the effects of the 27 February 2010 earthquake off the coast of Chile. The 8.8-magnitude Chilean earthquake was over five hundred times more powerful than the Haitian earthquake, yet deaths from the Chilean earthquake were measured in hundreds compared to the hundreds of thousands killed in the Haitian earthquake.

Chile was better prepared for an earthquake and the relative wealth of Chile lessened the impact of the stronger Chilean earthquake. Since 1900, Chile has experienced seven earthquakes of 8.0 magnitude or greater, including the strongest earthquake ever recorded. Consequently, Chile implemented strict building codes, even for low-income housing. In contrast, Haiti had not experienced a major earthquake in more than two centuries and enforced few building codes.

A number of design and construction standards in Chile require incorporation of special features designed to reduce earthquake damage. Many building codes in Chile require some form of a "strong columns, weak beam" system that utilizes reinforced vertical concrete columns that are further strengthened by steel framing. Reinforced concrete beams then join columns to create more earthquake resistant floors and roofs. While beams may break during an earthquake, steel reinforcement allows columns to continue to stand and support floors and roofs. As a result, buildings are designed to stay at least partially erect during an earthquake, and not "pancake" or flatten as easily as the buildings constructed in Haiti.

Although the devastation was significant and

widespread in Chile, the country is a modernized and industrialized nation. That fact, combined with the geological characteristics of the Chilean quake, reduced the death toll and percentage of destruction in comparison with the January 2010 Haitian earthquake. Although the earthquake that struck Chile was hundreds of times stronger than the Haitian earthquake, it was also far deeper, muting some of the surface damage. The Chilean earthquake also took place in the well-studied subduction zone along the western coast of South America. The Peru-Chile trench marks where the Nazca plate is subducted beneath the South American plate. The strongest earthquake in recorded history, a 9.5 Richter scale-magnitude quake centered off the coast of Chile in May 1960, killed an estimated 2,000 people.

The reconstruction effort in Haiti will cost an estimated $14 billion or more, which is double Haiti's 2008 gross domestic product (GDP) of $6.9 billion. In contrast, the economic damage in Chile—estimated at $15 billion—represents only a fraction of Chile's 2008 GDP of $169.5 billion. Furthermore, Chile, which has one of the most stable economies in Latin America, had amassed a $15 billion savings fund.

Haitian Cultural Origins

The small nation of Haiti is located on the western portion of Hispaniola, sharing the island with its neighbor to the east, the Dominican Republic. The small nation is bordered on its north by the Atlantic Ocean and by the Caribbean Sea to the west and south. Although the country also has a low coastal plain in the west, Haiti has a largely mountainous terrain, with three separate ranges running north, south, and east. The country's climate is tropical, with generally warm temperatures throughout the year ranging from 21.1° to 32.2°C (70°F to 90°F). The country has two rainy seasons (April to June and October to November) and hurricanes are common between June and November.

Haiti's history helps explain its unique culture.

While indigenous peoples lived on the island for centuries, Christopher Columbus' first expedition landed on Hispaniola in 1492 and brought the first Europeans to the island. Columbus claimed the island for Spain, but over the following two centuries, the island became a favorite haven for pirates. French buccaneers settled on part of the island that would later become Haiti. French colonists arrived after the Treaty of Ryswick in 1697 formally ceded the western third of Hispaniola to France.

The French colony grew wealthy from trade in sugar, coffee, tobacco, and African slaves. In 1793, slavery was abolished in the colony, which the French called Saint-Domingue (not to be confused with Santo Domingo or the Dominican Republic, also located on Hispaniola). Many white French, mixed ethnicity, and free black slave holders fled to Cuba and Louisiana with their slaves, spreading Creole culture that became an important influence in both places.

Saint-Domingue declared its independence in 1804 after a slave revolt wrested power from French landlords and government officials. Haiti, the new nation, became the second in the Western Hemisphere, after the United States, to gain independence from a European colonial power. With a large Afro-Caribbean population, Haiti was also the first black-ruled modern nation.

By 2000, 95 percent of Haiti's population was of African descent with the remaining 5 percent mixed-race and white. The 1987 constitution established Haitian Kreyol (Creole), a French-derived local dialect with African and English influences, as the primary national language. French, spoken by about 10 percent of the population, became the nation's secondary language but was often still used by government elites. In recent decades, the infusion of international media on the island and large waves of immigration to Canada and the United States have increased the prevalence of English in the island nation.

Haiti's unique language makes aid efforts more difficult, as few people outside of Haiti speak Haitian Kreyol. Although the spoken dialect is prevalent within the nation, literacy rates are low, making transmitting written information or instructions—even in Kreyol—to large groups of people difficult. During relief efforts following the January earthquake, the BBC established multilingual broadcasting services to help disseminate news and disaster relief instructions.

Haiti has also suffered endemic poverty for decades. The nation's infrastructure lacked before the 2010 earthquake. Many Haitians, especially those living in the poorest urban areas, did not have daily access to fresh, piped water or sanitation systems. The nation's poorest urban residents lived in ad-hoc communities of temporary housing built from scrap materials. Accurate

People reach out to catch books, donated by the Cuban government, during an 2 October 2010 distribution in Port-au-Prince. Haiti's education system was nearly destroyed by the quake. AP Images/Ramon Espinosa.

population estimates of these areas were difficult to obtain. When the earthquake struck, it was impossible to know immediately how many people from such a community were missing. Aid workers encountered difficulty assessing and planning for the number of people in these neighborhoods, many of which were devastated by the quake and needed immediate aid.

Haitians tend to embrace mysticism and a sizable portion of the population is distrustful of some types of formal medicine. 70 percent of residents are Catholic, and a growing minority is Protestant. Within Catholic parishes are those "serving the lwa" (lwa, or loa, are spirits or angels) who practice a hybridized religion of Catholicism and African beliefs that is known as voodoo or vodoun. Many Haitians hold spiritual and cultural beliefs that claim spirits or spells affect human health. Such beliefs sometimes keep people from seeking medical attention when needed. In the aftermath of the earthquake, doctors encountered cultural and economic prejudices against handicaps and a reluctance from patients and family members to consent to amputation unless the patient was gravely ill, even if there was no way to save the damaged limb.

United States Involvement with Haiti

Although a former French colony, some historians and political scholars argue that the long history between the United States and Haitian people fuelled intense interest and concern over the earthquake and its aftermath. That relationship has also shaped a connection that will be highly influential in Haiti's recovery and future role among other nations.

A large Haitian immigrant population now lives in the United States. According to the latest figures from the U.S. Census Bureau, in 2008 546,000 Haitian immigrants lived in the United States The number of Haitians currently living in the United States represents a significant increase from the 408,000 immigrants in 2000 and 218,000 in 1990. Between 100,000 and 200,000

Haitian immigrants currently live in the United States on a temporary or unauthorized basis. Following the earthquake in Haiti, the U.S. Department of Homeland Security announced that the agency would extend Temporary Protected Status (TPS) to all temporary or unauthorized Haitian immigrants living in the United States as of 12 January 2010. TPS status is granted to immigrants of countries experiencing extraordinary conditions, including armed conflict or natural disasters. Haitian immigrants receiving TPS status will be allowed to work in the United States for 18 months and will not face deportation during that period.

Throughout the twentieth century, the United States and Haiti shared a tense relationship, with the United States often exerting influence over its neighbor to the south. In 1910 and 1911, the U.S. Department of State backed a group of U.S. investors in a takeover of Haiti's treasury and only commercial bank. The United States supported these moves in order to protect American economic interests and limit the influence of a small but economically powerful German community in Haiti. Between 1911 and 1915, political unrest in Haiti resulted in six presidential changes and numerous political assassinations. In July 1915, Haiti's pro-American president General Jean Vilbrun Guillaume Sam executed 167 political prisoners. A mob removed Sam from the French embassy, dismembered his body, and paraded his body parts through the streets of Port-au-Prince. Rosalvo Bobo, who opposed American influence in Haiti, then became president of Haiti.

On 28 July 1915, U.S. President Woodrow Wilson sent 330 U.S. Marines to Haiti to protect American economic interests there. With an anti-American government in power, the United States and France feared that Haiti would not repay its debts to those nations. Within weeks of the invasion, U.S. forces seized Haitian customs houses, banks, and the treasury. Under American control, 40 percent of Haiti's national income went to pay

A man carries medication for sale in Haiti. A black market emerged for food and medicine within weeks of the earthquake. Alison Wright/National Geographic Stock.

debts to the United States and France, crippling the Haitian economy. The United States installed a puppet government, maintained veto power over all policies, and installed American military governors in Haiti's provinces.

In 1918, about 40,000 Haitians revolted against U.S. military rule. The United States sent military reinforcements to suppress the rebellion, resulting in the death of about 2,000 Haitians. By the early 1920s, the American representatives began working closely with Haitian leaders to improve infrastructure in Haiti, including building over 1,000 miles of roads, nearly 200 bridges, hospitals, schools, and irrigation and water systems. In 1930, Sténio Vincent, a critic of American occupation, became president of Haiti. U.S. President Herbert Hoover investigated the effects of the U.S. occupation and began to place more Haitians in positions of power. In August 1933, the United States agreed to withdraw troops from Haiti and completed the withdrawal in 1934. The United States, however, maintained control over Haiti's economy until the late 1940s.

Following the U.S. occupation, Haitian leaders tended to be skeptical of U.S. interference in Haitian affairs. Haitian president François "Papa Doc" Duvalier developed a tense relationship with the United States over its support of the Dominican Republic. Duvalier embezzled tens of millions of dollars of U.S. humanitarian aid intended for the Haitian people. Following the assassination of U.S. President John F. Kennedy in 1963—which Duvalier claimed was the result of a curse he placed on Kennedy—the United States began to regard Duvalier as unstable, but nonetheless an ally against Communist-controlled Cuba. In the 1980s, the United States pressured Jean-Claude "Baby Doc" Duvalier, who became president following his father's death in 1971, to resign.

Although the United States claims it has promoted democracy and economic development in Haiti, critics and scholars argue that the promotion was conducted with a heavy hand. U.S. President Bill Clinton ordered U.S. troops into Haiti under the terms of a UN resolution in 1994 to re-install Haitian President Jean-Bertrand Aristide. Aristide, Haiti's first democratically elected president of modern times, had been ousted by a military coup in 1991. Following Aristide's re-election in 2001, a 2004 rebellion, accusing Aristide of

A resident walks between destroyed buildings in downtown Port-au-Prince. Poor building construction and rapid urban growth lead to high fatalities in the downtown area. Alison Wright/National Geographic Stock.

widespread assassination and corruption, removed him from power. Aristide claims that the United States led the rebellion against him, but the United States denies these charges. In February 2004, an interim government took office to organize new elections under the auspices of the UN Stabilization Mission in Haiti (MINUSTAH). Continued violence and technical delays prompted repeated postponements, but Haiti finally did inaugurate a democratically elected president and parliament in May 2006. Haiti's political situation remains unstable, with 2010 national elections eventually held in late November 2010 during a cholera epidemic.

U.S. relations with the Haitian people have at times been strained, shaping the interests of those seeking to enter the United States and those who gain entrance. Although the United States has in general traditionally encouraged immigration from many different countries of the world, restrictive immigration measures and informal types of discrimination have periodically reflected fears about the impact of large numbers of migrants from particular countries or ethnic groups. In the past, especially during the 1980s and 1990s, asylum seekers from Haiti have been regarded mainly as economic migrants rather than genuine refugees. As a result, asylum seekers from Haiti during years of dictatorship were the target of restrictive admissions policies designed to deter further migration from Haiti to the United States.

In the 1990s, the U.S. government chose to

regard the majority of the Haitian "boat people" (refugees who travel by boat) as economic migrants from a poverty-ridden country, rather than refugees fleeing a brutal regime. With the exception of small numbers of particularly vulnerable migrants, such as HIV-positive refugees, the majority of the boat people were intercepted at sea and interviewed by immigration officers on board U.S. vessels. Until 1991, almost all were returned to Haiti, as they could not demonstrate a well-founded fear of persecution. In the 1990s, asylum interviews were also held at the U.S. naval base at Guantánamo Bay, Cuba. Camps at Guantánamo Bay were also used as a safe haven for those who were deemed to be genuine refugees, but who were not permitted entry to the United States. The safe haven policy had been successful in U.S. immigration policy in terms of restricting the entry of vast numbers of Haitian nationals to the United States, while at the same time conforming to the requirements of international refugee law. The UN High Commissioner for Refugees (UNHCR) had approved the safe haven proposals as providing protection within the framework of the UN Refugee Convention. Many Haitians chose to return voluntarily to their country when it became clear they would not be granted asylum in the United States.

Land Ownership Disputes

Years of political instability and corruption, combined with a government deeply entrenched in a system of rewarding political loyalty over merit, fostered a society in which a large amount of the land lots on Haiti are claimed by multiple

A man gets a haircut in a makeshift barbershop in Port-au-Prince, 3 March 2010. The shop is on the grounds of the Petionville Club golf course, home to tens of thousands of earthquake survivors. Al Diaz/MCT/Landov.

A store burns in the distance on a rubble-lined street in downtown Port-au-Prince. The 7.0 magnitude earthquake destroyed large parts of the Haitian capital, including many hospitals and health facilities, and several urban centers elsewhere in the country. Al Diaz/MCT/Landov.

title-bearing owners, often making it difficult to determine who has the dominant legal claim of ownership. This has raised a host of problems for those who are homeless and displaced from the earthquake. Landowners, fearing that squatters would lay claim to temporary shelter campgrounds, at times attempted to reclaim land by evicting the otherwise homeless. Because some of the camps contained thousands of people, these eviction attempts were met with threats of violence, with camp residents chasing away eviction notice messengers with sticks and machetes. The government has been pushed to speed up relocation efforts, but in order to establish a second camp elsewhere or begin construction of more permanent shelters at any location, officials must

first determine who owns the land for the new site and whether or not the owner is willing to rent or sell the land. A secondary concern is that new construction projects may not provide adequate housing for the sheer number of homeless and displaced Haitian people. In some areas, the rows of simple, single-family, wood-framed shelters that the government would like to build will not accommodate the same number of people that once lived in the neighborhood, where extra, unstable levels were sometimes added to homes to accommodate multiple families. Even some prefabricated shelters supplied through aid organizations have been larger than the homes that some families occupied before the quake.

A nun hangs a serum bag on a tree for patients suffering cholera symptoms in Robine, Haiti, 23 October 2010. A spreading cholera outbreak in rural Haiti threatened to outpace aid groups as they stepped up efforts hoping to keep the disease from reaching the camps of earthquake survivors in Port-au-Prince. AP Images/Ramon Espinosa.

Continuing Difficulties

At the close of 2010, Haiti remained dependent on foreign aid, a large portion of its population still in temporary shelters, where despair and disease are close companions. What started as tremor in the earth fractured an already fragile political, social, and medical infrastructure. Both Haitian officials and international observers fear that violence in Haiti—whether driven by need, fears of cholera, or political unrest—opens a dangerous chasm through which the country could fall into chaos. Hope for the Haitian people rests on their ability to keep the peace, and for the world to maintain the compassion and interest in the plight of the Haitian people even as other events compete for the world's attention.

Independent media and observers reported violence, chaos, and confusion surrounding the conducting of Haiti's first general election since the January earthquake, which took place on 28 November 2010. At some voting stations, including the damaged Lycee Pétionville (a school in Pétionville), election officials and independent monitors were forced to count paper ballots by candlelight. Wide swings in predictions and polls, many regarded as dubious by international monitors, were used to bolster claims of election fraud. One dozen of the 18 candidates for president joined to petition the governing election council to nullify election results. Although candidates called for peaceful protests, violence erupted in several locations as angry protestors demanded that the election results be nullified and another election held. Despite allegations of fraud and destruction of ballots at more than 50 voting centers,

Haitian election officials vowed to recognize the results of the election as official. The results of the election promised to remain in dispute, however, even following certification.

Mounting fears and tensions related to the cholera epidemic also continued to threaten aid delivery and long-term recovery efforts in late 2010. Some aid workers cancelled missions. More than 500 tons of food aid was allowed to spoil as a result of civil unrest following the general election. As the year closed, U.S. Centers for Disease Control and Prevention (CDC) and Pan American Health Organization (PAHO) experts expressed concerns that cholera would become endemic in Haiti and that any program to deal effectively with the outbreak would take many months or years. Experts also claim that the number of cases and deaths related to cholera is vastly underreported, in part because victims in isolated rural communities are often neglected in official Haitian reports. Infectious disease experts also predict the current outbreak will not be the last, and that fresh outbreaks will occur during the next few years.

Despite the bleak realities and assessments of troubles ahead, many people remain dedicated to the creation of a more stable, healthy, and prosperous Haiti. While some aid groups withdrew people and programs, others like Médecins Sans Frontières (Doctors Without Borders) renewed their pledge to not abandon the Haitian people in their time of great need, and the NGO *Terre des Hommes* (TDH) joined the Swiss organization Save the Children to create new programs to tackle cholera in rural areas and to more effectively distribute supplies and aid.

Research and Exploration

American Red Cross. "International Disaster Response: Earthquake in Haiti." http://www.redcross.org/Haiti

The American Red Cross has been actively involved in the overall global Red Cross response to the cholera outbreak, providing personnel, urgently needed supplies, and chlorine for clean water.

BBC. "Animated Guide: Earthquakes." http://news.bbc.co.uk/2/hi/science/nature/7533950.stm

An animated demonstration from BBC news of the geological science behind earthquakes and how they happen.

BBC. "Voices from Haiti." http://news.bbc.co.uk/2/hi/americas/8518856.stm

A collection of six short video interviews from the BBC news of people struggling with the earthquake's aftermath, including residents, aid workers, and military personnel.

CNN. "Haiti: 360°" http://www.cnn.com/interactive/2010/01/world/haiti.360/index.html

Video of the aftermath of the quake in the Haitian capital city of Port-au-Prince from the American news organization CNN.

Frontline. "Economy of a Tent City." http://www.pbs.org/wgbh/pages/frontline/haiti/view/economy_tent_city.html

A short video feature about a former golf course that became a tent city after the January 2010 earthquake. The reporting focuses on the economy within the temporary settlement.

Frontline. "The Quake." http://www.pbs.org/wgbh/pages/frontline/haiti

Video and written reports from Haiti focusing on aid efforts after the January 2010 earthquake. Frontline is a television and online newsmagazine produced in the United States by the Public Broadcasting Service (PBS).

National Geographic-Eye in the Sky News. "Nature's Fury: Earthquakes." http://www.nationalgeographic.com/eye/earthquakes/earthquakesintro.html

An introduction to earthquake science featuring an animation of how earthquakes happen.

Pan American Health Organization (PAHO). "Cholera Outbreak in La Hispaniola, 2010." http://new.paho.org/hq/images/Atlas_IHR/CholeraOutbreak/atlas.html

An interactive map detailing the cholera outbreak in Haiti according to location, number of cases, deaths, weather patterns, and available health facilities, provided by the PAHO, a division of the World Health Organization.

The New York Times. "The Destruction in Port-au-Prince." http://www.nytimes.com/interactive/2010/01/14/world/20100114-haiti-imagery.html

Satellite photos from GeoEye allow for a comparison of the capital city before and after the earthquake.

The Washington Post. "Old and Poor in Haiti Suffer Mightily after the Quake." http://www.washingtonpost.com/wp-dyn/content/article/2010/03/12/AR2010031202050.html

A written and video feature about Haiti's poor and disabled in the aftermath of the January 2010 earthquake.

The Washington Post. "Six Weeks in Haiti." http://www.washingtonpost.com/wp-dyn/content/article/2010/04/15/AR2010041504675.html

Natasha Archer, a resident in internal medicine and pediatrics at Brigham and Women's Hospital/Children's Hospital in Boston, describes her six-week volunteer shift with Partners in Health at Haiti's largest hospital.

UNICEF. "UNICEF Haiti Stresses Cholera Prevention in Overcrowded Districts of Port-au-Prince." http://www.unicef.org/infobycountry/haiti_56930.html

United Nations Children's Fund (UNICEF) Health Specialist physician Mireille Tribie discusses UNICEF's strategy for combating cholera in Haiti.

USGS. "Earthquake Hazards Program." http://earthquake.usgs.gov/

Provides up-to-date information and maps of the day's global earthquake risk, activity, and history of past earthquakes from the United States Geological Survey (USGS). Observers can also report earthquake activity in their area in real-time.

USGS. "Latest Earthquakes in the World." http://earthquake.usgs.gov/earthquakes/recenteqsww/Quakes/quakes_all.php

A real-time index of all quakes in the United States, and all quakes above 4.0 in the world, for the past seven days. Information on historically significant quakes is also available.

Iran's Nuclear Program
Energy or Weapons?

AFP/Getty Images.

For decades there has been speculation about whether Iran is trying to build nuclear weapons. The building blocks are clearly in place, but intelligence agencies in the United States, France, Germany, Israel, and the United Kingdom vary in their estimates about how long it could take Iran to put the pieces together to produce a nuclear weapon. More importantly, there are key differences of opinion about Iran's intentions regarding the applications of its nuclear power. Without a diplomatic resolution, international security experts fear that military action and conflict are inevitable, despite the potentially disastrous consequences.

As international intentions and suspicions mounted throughout 2010, Iran consistently de-nied allegations that its nuclear program was intended for anything but legitimate and peaceful purposes. United Nations Secretary-General Ban Ki-moon has publicly warned Iranian officials, however, that the burden of proof of such peaceful intent is on Iran.

International acrimony and mutual mistrust continued to mount. The International Atomic Energy Agency (IAEA), the United Nations independent nuclear affairs monitoring agency, voted at the end of 2009 to censure Iran for its concealment of an enrichment plant discovered near the city of Qom. The IAEA board also demanded that Iran suspend construction of the facility. Agency leaders stated they had "serious concern" about potential Iranian military ties to its nuclear development program. The action

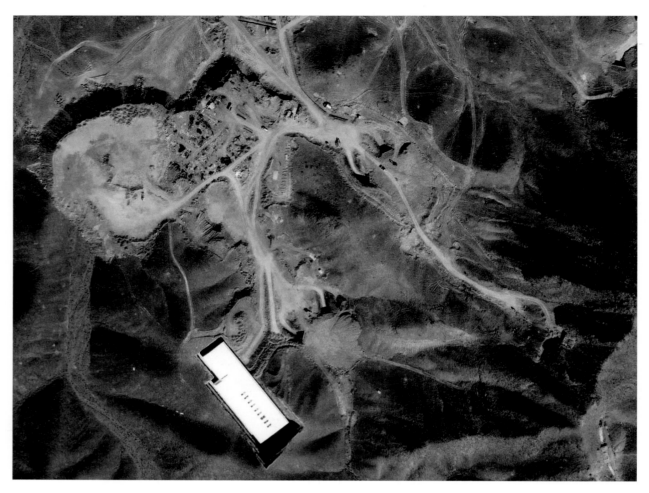

A secret uranium enrichment site near Qom, Iran, was revealed in September 2009. AP Images/GeoEye.

capped a year of reports contending that Iran had failed to provide sufficient information and access to IAEA inspectors, and that Iran's lack of cooperation thwarted efforts to alleviate international concerns over Iran's nuclear program. IAEA officials also asserted that Iran had clearly not suspended enrichment-related activities that increase its capability to produce nuclear weapons, contrary to UN Security Council resolutions.

In 2010, a series of IAEA reports on Iran's nuclear program showed IAEA officials' increasing frustration with what they saw as Iran's lack of cooperation with IAEA rules and inspections.

Current Status of Iran's Nuclear Program

In September 2010, the UN Security Council released an IAEA report accusing the Iranian government of failing to fully cooperate in producing documents related to Iran's nuclear program. The report also cited Iran's refusal to allow inspections of enrichment facilities and equipment that the IAEA insists are needed to gauge the intent of Iran's nuclear program. Iran has barred experienced IAEA inspectors' access to existing facilities and also refused to discuss alleged steps it has taken to develop missiles capable of carrying a nuclear warhead. The IAEA report asserted that Iran is increasing its nuclear fuels stockpile and has produced more than 6,000 pounds of enriched uranium that with further enrichment could be sufficient to produce two crude nuclear weapons.

The September 2010 report was significant because prior IAEA assessments maintained that Iran's stock pile of uranium ore and slightly enriched uranium remained below the levels of enrichment needed to produce a nuclear weapon. IAEA experts had already stated that Iran's technology was advanced enough to support a higher enrichment program quickly capable of producing weapons-grade material.

Iran's continued development of enrichment capacity is a key technical element in the controversy. With minor modifications, the same technology required to enrich uranium to levels required for use in civilian power plants can be used to enrich uranium to weapons-grade levels. Accordingly, as Iran continues to develop its enrichment capacity, the international community demands closer monitoring to ensure the technology is not diverted to weapons production.

Proponents of sanctions or direct military action against Iran argue that the IAEA assessment means that Iran is edging slowly toward the final steps needed to develop a nuclear weapon. Critics of sanctions or military action argue that Iran continues to operate within its rights to develop nuclear power, and that the IAEA assessment shows that Iran has not yet committed itself to becoming a nuclear power.

Iran and its neighbors. The city of Qom is the location of a once-secret uranium enrichment plant. Illustration/XNR Productions/Cengage Learning, Gale.

Iran's Policies and Positions

Iranian President Mahmoud Ahmadinejad has consistently denied that Iran has a secret nuclear weapons program and has insisted that its nuclear facilities and activities are intended only for the peaceful production of nuclear energy. In January 2008, Iran's Supreme Leader, the Ayatollah Seyyed Ali Khamenei, told then-IAEA director Mohamed ElBaradei that Iran opposed the production of nuclear weapons based upon Shari'a, or Islamic law.

In late August 2009, IAEA experts declared that they were at an impasse with Iranian officials who were unwilling to further comply with international efforts to verify the status and intent of Iran's nuclear program. In early September 2009, Ahmadinejad declared that while Iran was prepared to continue talks with representatives of world powers, including the United States, negotiations regarding Iran's right to have a nuclear development program were "finished." Ahmadinejad specifically asserted that Iran would not abandon its uranium enrichment programs.

Iran frustrated negotiators at the end of 2009 with rapid changes in policy regarding a potential deal to send the bulk of its nuclear fuel to Russia or another IAEA-monitored country for enrichment to levels usable in nuclear reactors. The proposed transfer would eliminate Iran's need to advance its enrichment capabilities, reduce Iran's capacity to quickly produce a nuclear weapon, and allow more time for diplomacy regarding the future of Iran's nuclear program.

According to the Islamic Republic News Agency, the Iranian Cabinet issued orders on 29 November 2009 to begin construction and site selection for ten new uranium enrichment sites. According to the news reports, the Iranian nuclear agency was directed to immediately begin construction work at five new enrichment sites, and

was further directed to locate five additional sites for new enrichment facilities.

In May 2010, a Non-Proliferation Treaty (NPT) review meeting at the United Nations brought renewed global attention to reducing and preventing the spread of nuclear weapons worldwide and to the standoff between Iran and the IAEA over Iran's nuclear program intentions. A NPT review conference is normally held every five years to address issues and compliance disputes related to the treaty. Although representatives from the United States, Israel, and several other Western governments walked out in protest, Ahmadinejad spoke to the conference to reiterate that, in Iran's view, the country did not need IAEA or world approval for what he described as Iran's intentions to use nuclear technology only for peaceful purposes.

2010: Shifting Policies, Escalating Tensions, and New Sanctions

2010 began with Iran ignoring an ultimatum by the United States to accept the multinational

Uranium Enrichment Process

Uranium ore

1. Mining, refining
Ore is purified to a powder called yellowcake

Yellowcake

2. Conversion
Yellowcake is turned into a gaseous uranium compound

Uranium gas

3. Enrichment
Gas is treated to increase amount of unstable form of uranium in it

4% — Low-enriched uranium hexafluoride *Used for reactor fuel*

90% — Highly-enriched uranium hexafluoride *Used for weapons*

4. Reconversion
Gas is converted to uranium dioxide, a solid

5. Fabrication
Shaped into fuel for power plants or weapons

SOURCE: Uranium Information Center (Australia), Encyclopaedia Britannica, Reuters

The five steps needed to enrich uranium into fuel for nuclear power or weapons. Illustration/XNR Productions/Cengage Learning, Gale.

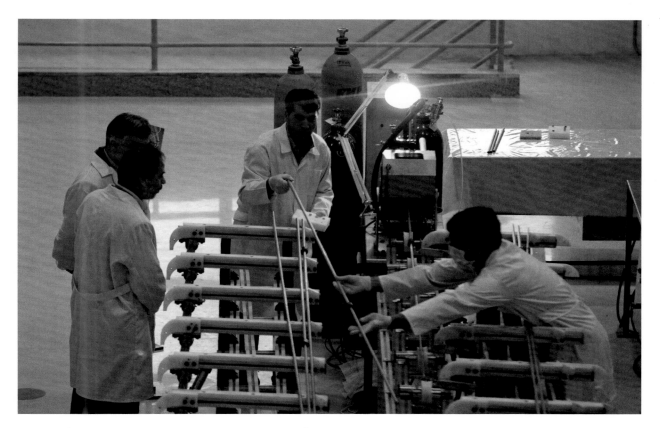

At Iran's Isfahan uranium conversion plant, located south of Tehran, employees move nuclear fuel rods in April 2009. Caren Firouz/Reuters.

plan to enrich its nuclear fuel outside of Iran. In January 2010, Iran notified the IAEA that the country would only consider a simultaneous exchange of lightly enriched uranium for more highly enriched uranium that took place within Iran's borders. Iranian officials then publicly threatened to develop additional uranium enrichment programs if the West did not accept an Iranian counterproposal.

In early February 2010, Ahmadinejad seemingly reversed position again and announced that Iran would agree to ship uranium abroad for enrichment. In making this apparent policy shift, however, the Iranian president declared that his country would enrich uranium to higher levels on its own if enriched fuel was not returned to Iran. Less than one week later, Iran again hardened its official stance toward the proposed external enrich-

ment offer, and on 8 February 2010, IAEA officials received an official Iranian communiqué announcing Iran's intent to enrich uranium to levels approaching 20 percent. Iranian officials confirmed their intent to immediately begin enrichment, but insisted that their plan was to develop fuel rods for a reactor used to produce medical isotopes. Nuclear experts widely agree that enriched fuel rods are difficult to convert into weapons material and that 20 percent enrichment is insufficient to sustain the fission reaction needed to produce a nuclear explosion. However, analysts point out that the technology and skills gained in the enrichment process are fundamentally identical to the process of further enriching uranium for use in nuclear weapons. Moreover, enrichment of uranium to 20 percent levels would significantly reduce the time needed to produce a nuclear weapon.

The announcement of Iran's intention to further enrich its uranium stockpile spurred fresh calls for tougher sanctions from the United States, France, Russia, and other world powers. Russia's shift in position was significant. Along with China, Russia had previously resisted calls for tougher sanctions.

On 18 February 2010, the IAEA submitted a quarterly summary to the United Nations Security Council expressing concern that Iran may be using its openly declared civilian nuclear program to cover up a military nuclear weapons program. The report was the first issued by the IAEA after Yukiya Amano assumed leadership of the agency. According to Associated Press (AP) and *Agence France-Presse* reports, the report offers the IAEA's most direct assessment that Iran has not made full disclosure of its work towards developing a nuclear weapon. The report states that evidence collected to date "raises concerns about the possible existence in Iran of past or current undisclosed activities related to the development of a nuclear payload for a missile."

The IAEA report concluded that Iran's weapons research had continued beyond a date specified in a 2007 U.S. National Intelligence Estimate (NIE) that such activities had stopped.

The IAEA report also contained information on the state of Iranian uranium enrichment equipment and facilities. IAEA analysts say that problems with centrifuges at Iran's Natanz enrich-

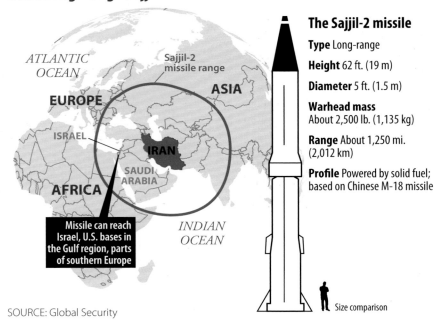

Iran's Long-Range Sajjil Missile

ATLANTIC OCEAN
EUROPE
ISRAEL
AFRICA
Sajjil-2 missile range
ASIA
IRAN
SAUDI ARABIA
INDIAN OCEAN

Missile can reach Israel, U.S. bases in the Gulf region, parts of southern Europe

The Sajjil-2 missile

Type Long-range

Height 62 ft. (19 m)

Diameter 5 ft. (1.5 m)

Warhead mass About 2,500 lb. (1,135 kg)

Range About 1,250 mi. (2,012 km)

Profile Powered by solid fuel; based on Chinese M-18 missile

Size comparison

SOURCE: Global Security

Iran's Sajjil-2 missile has a range of approximately 1,250 miles (2,012 kilometers), making it capable of reaching Israel and India, among other countries. Illustration/XNR Productions/Cengage Learning, Gale.

ment site have resulted in limiting and slowing uranium enrichment. Late in 2010, intelligence experts concluded that Iran's problems with its centrifuges could have been the result of a computer virus deliberately designed to disrupt the computer-controlled centrifuges. No party immediately claimed responsibility for constructing or planting the virus.

At the slowed rate of enrichment, construction of a nuclear weapon would take several years. However, experts caution that slowdowns in centrifuge operation might also help Iran disguise the secret development of more centrifuge sites that would drastically shorten the time needed to construct a bomb. The IAEA report also reiterated prior concerns that Iran has conducted tests on potential nuclear detonators and researched designs of nuclear warheads capable of being mounted on current Iranian missiles.

In April 2010, Iranian Foreign Minister Ma-

UN Security Council Sanctions on Iran

Expand arms embargo on Iran	Control of Iranian activities abroad	Measures against Iranian banking sector
• Including: sale of battle tanks, combat vehicles, artillery systems, aircraft, warships, missiles, missile systems	• Including: ban on uranium mining, technical assistance for enrichment, missile related activities • Provision for cargo inspections in any port or at sea, seizure of prohibited items	• Block on financial transactions, including insurance linked to nuclear weapons proliferation • Ban on licensing any Iranian banks abroad linked to weapons proliferation

SOURCE: AFP

In June 2010, the UN Security Council imposed sanctions on Iran that included an expanded arms embargo as well as financial and shipping restrictions. Illustration/XNR Productions/Cengage Learning, Gale.

nouchehr Mottaki announced plans to hold separate and direct talks with members of the UN Security Council over the potential nuclear fuel swap deal. Mottaki also expressed Iran's intention to have indirect talks with the United States. The international community generally regarded this offer as a stalling tactic. The United States pushed for new and tougher sanctions.

New Sanctions

The five permanent, veto-wielding members of the Council—the United States, the United Kingdom, France, Russia, and China—subsequently agreed to level new sanctions against Iran. In June 2010, the Security Council voted to institute a fourth set of sanctions against Iran. The tougher sanctions are designed to bring pressure on Iran to more fully comply with IAEA inspections and slow the progress of Iranian nuclear fuel enrichment programs. The Security Council vote was not unanimous, with non-permanent Council members Brazil and Turkey voting against additional sanctions. The government of Lebanon

abstained. Iranian officials immediately denounced the sanctions and said Iran would not change its current policies.

The new sanctions further restrict or forbid the sale of technical equipment used in nuclear fuel processing, especially equipment that can enrich fuel to levels required for military use. The sanctions also further restrict trade and financial transactions involving the Islamic Revolutionary Guard Corps, the security group within Iran that manages the nuclear development program.

International Interests and Policies

European nations and the United States have jointly declared that if Iran developed a nuclear weapon it would destabilize regional and world security. United Nations (UN) sanctions on Iran are designed to force compliance with UN resolutions and IAEA inspection requests.

Israel's Position: A Nuclear-armed Iran is Unacceptable

Israel views the possibility of an Iranian nuclear weapon as a threat to its existence due to repeated warnings by Iran that it would destroy Israel. Although Israel does not confirm its status as a nuclear power, it does not deny that it has nuclear weapons. Because Iran has openly denied Israel's right to exist and has repeatedly threatened to annihilate the country, Israeli officials indicate that their patience with Iran regarding openness about its nuclear program is limited.

In June 2008, Shaul Mofaz, then Israel's Deputy Prime Minister and former Minister of De-

Iran's continued nuclear ambitions led U.S. President Barack Obama to sign a bill imposing further sanctions against the nation in July 2010. AP Images/J. Scott Applewhite.

fense, warned that if Iran continued to develop nuclear weapons, Israel would attack Iran. Israel has repeatedly pledged to take whatever military action it deems appropriate to ensure its security and has mounted conventional weapons attacks against suspected nuclear facilities in Iraq and Syria in the past. Mofaz called on the UN Security Council and the international community to use "drastic measures" to dissuade Iran from developing nuclear weapons.

In July 2009, remarks by U.S. Vice President Joe Biden gained widespread coverage when some commentators argued that Biden's remarks indirectly signaled that the United States would not interfere if Israel decided to bomb Iran's nuclear facilities. Israeli Prime Minister Benjamin Ne-

tanyahu has indicated that Israel may launch air strikes against Iranian nuclear facilities to prevent Iran from developing a nuclear weapon. Biden insisted that Israel was a sovereign nation, and that the United States cannot "dictate to another sovereign nation what they can and cannot do."

Within days, U.S. President Barack Obama sought to diffuse the tension by stating that the United States had not given Israel the go-ahead to launch a military strike on Iranian nuclear facilities. In subsequent remarks, U.S. Secretary of State Hillary Rodham Clinton asserted that the United States would consider formally extending a "defense umbrella" over allies in the Middle East if Iran continued to fail to comply with international demands for more openness regarding their

This alleged Syrian nuclear site was targeted by Israeli airstrikes in 2007. Illustration/XNR Productions/Cengage Learning, Gale.

nuclear program and intentions. In traditional diplomatic and military usage, a defense umbrella promises use of American military assets to thwart an attack or act in reprisal to an attack upon an ally.

Iranian officials responded the next day by stating that they would respond in a full-scale and decisive manner to an Israeli attack.

The United States: Conflicting Interests and Intelligence

In 2002, the possibility that Iran was concealing a program to produce nuclear weapons became an international issue when Iranian dissidents publicized the existence of secret nuclear facilities. The IAEA began inspections of Iran's facilities later that year. In its role as lone remaining military superpower, and because of its recent enmity with Iran and assumed influence on Israel, the United States assumed a unique position with regard to monitoring and resisting Iran's apparent interest in becoming a nuclear power. U.S. interest and ties to Iran's nuclear program were also

grounded in the historical origins of Iran's use of nuclear power.

Iran's Nuclear Program Origins

Iran's first nuclear technology was obtained as a gift from the United States under the Atoms for Peace program begun by President Dwight Eisenhower in 1953. The Atoms for Peace program eventually came to be seen as a grave mistake by the United States, which has since sought to recover the nuclear fuel dispersed around the world by the program. It has not always been able to do so because of political change. The post-revolutionary Islamist Iranian state inherited an already sophisticated nuclear power program.

Despite Iranian denials, the declassified portion of a 2005 U.S. National Intelligence Estimate expressed "high confidence" among all sixteen U.S. intelligence agencies that Iran was "determined to develop nuclear weapons." In response, the United States successfully secured UN Security Council resolution 1696, passed in 2006, demanding that Iran "suspend all enrichment-related and reprocessing activities."

Debate about the intent of the Iranian nuclear program and Iran's capacity to produce a nuclear weapon intensified in 2007 following the release of a declassified portion of another U.S. NIE asserting a "high confidence" that Iran had not produced weapons-grade uranium or plutonium and that "[Iran] halted its nuclear weapons program" in 2003. The NIE also expressed uncertainty as to whether "[Iran] currently intends to develop nuclear weapons."

The 2007 NIE was also later contradicted by independent IAEA reports concluding that Iran had continued work potentially related to nuclear weapons development. The IAEA reports also stated that additional information was needed before drawing final conclusions about Iranian intentions. The 2007 NIE was subsequently reviewed and eventually discounted by the Obama Administration when in December 2009, admin-

To show its military strength, Iran displays its Shahab-3 missile in 2008. The image of Iranian leader Ayatollah Ali Khamenei is featured prominently above the missile. AP Images/Hasan Sarbakhshian.

istration officials were quoted as saying that presidential advisors no longer trusted the contentious 2007 NIE.

British, French, and German officials also disputed the 2007 U.S. NIE, asserting there was sufficient intelligence evidence indicating that Iran's military research had resumed or had never halted.

Perhaps more importantly, another IAEA report, the IAEA's confidential "Possible Military Dimensions of Iran's Nuclear Program" leaked early in 2010, tentatively concluded that Iran has acquired "sufficient information to be able to design and produce a workable implosion nuclear device" using highly enriched uranium. The IAEA report went on to assert that Iran had collected information from unauthorized or rogue nuclear experts around the world and had performed extensive research and testing on the actual design and manufacture of critical weapons components. The report declined to speculate about the success or failure of Iran's programs. According to the report, Iran's programs, in operation since 2002, appear "aimed at the development of a nuclear payload to be delivered using the Shahab-3 missile system," which is estimated to have sufficient range to reach targets in the Middle East and parts of Europe.

U.S.-Israeli Relations

At the core of disputes between the United States and many Muslims is the degree of support—especially military aid—that the United States extends to Israel every year. While Israel has acted on its own in the past when it felt threatened, across the Arab and Islamic world there is a strong perception that Israel would only strike against a perceived nuclear threat from Iran if it had at least the tacit approval of the United States. This linking of Israeli actions with U.S. attitudes or policy has been pervasive in the Middle East for many years.

Along with diplomatic initiatives directed toward Iran, some of which have caused concern in Israel, President Obama has proposed increasing defense aid to Israel, including aid to purchase and develop anti-ballistic missile systems. This is part of a strategy by U.S., European, and Israeli officials to counter a potential Iranian nuclear threat.

During the administration of President George W. Bush, the United States refused to negotiate until Iran ceased all enrichment activities in accordance with Security Council Resolution 1696. In 2009, President Obama opened the door to negotiations with Iran about its nuclear program.

International Concerns

Skepticism over Iran's nuclear intentions and frustration at its lack of cooperation with the IAEA continues. Although Iran consistently asserts that its nuclear program is intended only to develop nuclear power for civilian use and denies that it plans to develop nuclear weapons, French President Nicolas Sarkozy scoffed at Iran's claims that its nuclear program is not intended to produce weapons, asserting during a September 2009 UN Security Council meeting that "No one can seriously believe that the aims of these activities are peaceful."

Russia's President Dimitry Medvedev has stated that it is the shared responsibility of the United States and Russia to prevent nuclear weapons proliferation in Iran and other parts of the world, but he is supportive of Iran's right to develop a

In November 2010, Russian President Dmitry Medvedev (right) met with Iranian President Mahmoud Ahmadinejad in Baku, Azerbaijan, to discuss Iran's nuclear program. Ria Novosti/Dmitry Astakhov/Reuters.

peaceful nuclear power program. Medvedev met with Ahmadinejad in November 2010 for the first time following Russia's historic statement of support for UN sanctions against Iran.

In November 2010, a WikiLeaks online publication of U.S. State Department internal cables, some of them classified as secret, shed new light on widespread diplomatic infighting related to the Iranian nuclear program. WikiLeaks is a nonprofit organization that makes sensitive and classified information available to the public via its website. The U.S. State Department initially registered no objections to the authenticity of the content. Leaked materials indicated that several Middle Eastern nations voiced substantial concern over Iran's alleged nuclear ambitions. According to accounts based on advanced access to the leaked materials granted to a handful of respected American and European news organizations, among the most inflammatory allegations not specifically denied by the United States were attempts by Arab leaders to urge the United States to use military force to halt Iran's nuclear program. Many of the comments directly contradicted public positions.

One series of cables revealed that King Abdullah of Saudi Arabia reportedly urged the United States in 2008 to use military force to destroy Iran's developing nuclear program, asking the United States to "cut off the head of the snake" before Iran developed an operational nuclear weapon. In 2009, Bahrain's King Hamad also asked the United States to consider using military force against Iranian nuclear facilities.

Following the disclosure of the comments, expert analysts expressed little surprise at the fears of an Iran with nuclear weapons underlying the comments by Arab leaders, especially given the longstanding tensions between Arabs and Persians, and between Sunni and Shiite Muslims.

The leaked diplomatic cables also revealed that U.S. experts and diplomats thought there was sufficient evidence to argue that Iran obtained advanced longer-range ballistic missile technology purchased from North Korea that would extend Iran's missile target range to at least Moscow, and into several cities across Western Europe. Other cables revealed that such capability, along with concessions on defensive missile placements by the United States, brought Russia into the group of nations calling for tougher sanctions against Iran. The Russians have not, however, severed the their contracts to provide equipment and support to Iran's allegedly civilian nuclear facilities.

Other leaked U.S. diplomatic cables revealed that in May 2009, Israel's defense minister Ehud Barak asserted that only about 18 months remained in which "stopping Iran from acquiring nuclear weapons might still be viable." According to a classified cable sent by the U.S. ambassador to

Controversial Iranian President Mahmoud Ahmadinejad. AP Images/Saman Aghvami.

Israel, James B. Cunningham, however, Barak also expressed reservation that "any military solution would result in unacceptable collateral damage." Collateral damage is a term commonly used to describe unintended destruction or death (usually civilian) resulting from an operation.

The cables cited a meeting in 2005 where United Arab Emirates military leaders—in conference with then head of the U.S. Central Command, Gen. John P. Abizaid—asserted that Ahmadinejad "seemed unbalanced, crazy even," according to one cable cited by the *New York Times.*

The leaked cables also revealed a practicality in securing the greater cooperation of China in leveling tougher sanctions against Iran. China's exceptionally rapid industrial expansion depends on a constant supply of foreign oil, much of it from Iran. The diplomatic communications revealed an allegedly successful U.S. scheme to have the Saudi government increase its supply of oil to China in order to make China less dependent on Iranian oil. The scheme was discussed as important to China's subsequent agreement to allow and participate in new UN-backed sanctions against Iran.

Internal diplomatic communications revealed that Bush and Obama administration officials and experts expressed reservations that a military strike would only delay Iran from obtaining a nuclear bomb and further galvanize anti-U.S. sentiment and hatred in the region.

Iranian President Mahmoud Ahmadinejad dismissed the leaks as a ploy by American intelligence services to damage relations between Iran and its neighbors.

Nuclear Weapons

Nuclear weapons are by far the most destructive weapons ever created. Although often lumped with biological and chemical weapons as "weapons of mass destruction," the destructive potential of chemical weapons and biological weapons pales in comparison to the devastation wrought by nuclear weapons. Because nuclear weapons present a unique threat, they inspire a singular conglomeration of international fears, threats, treaties, secrets, and monitoring activities.

The first country to detonate a nuclear weapon was the United States. After secret development by the Manhattan Project, the United States tested its first nuclear explosive on 16 July 1945. On 6 and 9 August 1945, the United States used nuclear weapons to destroy two Japanese cities, Hiroshima and Nagasaki, in an effort to end World War II.

Fission and Fusion Bombs Fuel the Cold War

German physicist Albert Einstein did not know it at the time, but when he published his Special Theory of Relativity in 1905 he provided the world with the basic information needed to build nuclear weapons.

One aspect of Einstein's work (embodied in the famous equation $E=mc^2$) stated that the amount of matter of an object (i.e., its mass) is equivalent to a specific amount of energy. The exact amount of energy in an object equals its mass multiplied by the square of the speed of light. The speed of light is a mind-boggling 300,000 km/sec (186,282 miles per second), so even a small piece of matter contains a vast amount of energy. A baseball-size sample of uranium-235, for example, can explode with as much energy as 20,000 tons of TNT—and this involves the conversion of only a tiny fraction of the uranium's mass into energy. One pound of explosive material in a fission weapon is approximately 100,000 times as powerful as one pound of TNT.

The energy released through nuclear fission, the splitting of the atomic nucleus, was the source of power for the first atomic bomb, built in the United States during World War II by a large team of scientists led by U.S. physicist J. Robert Oppenheimer. This secret research and development program was dubbed the Manhattan Project. The first atomic bomb was detonated in Alamogordo, New Mexico, on 16 July 1945. Three weeks later, on 6 August, 1945, a United States bomber, the *Enola Gay*, dropped a four-ton atomic bomb containing 5.4 kg (12 lbs.) of uranium-235 on the Japanese city of Hiroshima. Seventy thousand people died as a direct result of the blast. Within two months, nearly twice that many were dead from blast injuries and radiation. Three days later, on 9 August, a bomb containing several pounds of plutonium was dropped on Nagasaki, Japan. Thirty thousand people died in the seconds following the explosion, and more later. The Japanese surrendered the next day, ending World War II.

These first nuclear weapons were atomic bombs, known as A-bombs, and they depended on the energy produced by nuclear fission for their destructive power. However, scientists like U.S. physicist Edward Teller knew even before the first atomic bomb exploded that the fission weap-

A French nuclear weapons test in French Polynesia, 1971. ©STOCKFOLIO®/Alamy.

ons could be used to create an even more powerful explosive, now known variably as a thermonuclear device, hydrogen bomb, or H-bomb. This weapon gets it power from the energy released when atoms of the hydrogen isotopes deuterium or tritium are forced together, a process called nuclear fusion. Starting a nuclear fusion reaction is more complicated than setting off a fission reaction; the former requires the heat produced by a fission bomb used as a detonator to explode the fusion bomb. The United States tested its first hydrogen bomb on November 1, 1952. It exploded with the force of 10.4 megatons, which is the equivalent of millions of tons of TNT and is 450 times more powerful than the bomb dropped on Nagasaki. Three years later, the Soviet Union exploded a similar device.

For the next 40 years, the United States and its allies raced against the former Soviet Union to build more nuclear weapons. Each side produced tens of thousands of nuclear weapons. The end of the Cold War and the breakup of the Soviet Union in the early 1990s led to a significant decrease in the numbers of nuclear weapons in the world; however, the U.S. and the Russian Federation still possess thousands of nuclear weapons.

An average modern nuclear weapon is twenty times more powerful than the bombs that destroyed Hiroshima and Nagasaki; one such bomb could effectively destroy a large metropolitan area containing millions of people.

Nations with Nuclear Weapons

Since World War II, no nuclear weapon has been used in war, but other nations have acknowledged developing or are assumed to possess nuclear weapons. Listed by year of first known or suspected nuclear test, the countries include the Soviet Union (1949), the United Kingdom (1952), France (1960), China (1964), India (1974), Israel (possibly c. 1979), South Africa (possibly c. 1979, in collaboration with Israel), Pakistan (1998), and North Korea (2006). South Africa dismantled its nuclear arsenal before signing the Nuclear Non-Proliferation Treaty in 1991 and has not possessed nuclear weapons since that time. After the disintegration of the Soviet Union in 1990, all of its nuclear weapons were inherited by Russia, the dominant successor state.

Proliferation of Nuclear Weapons

The main international legal instrument for preventing nuclear proliferation—the spread of nuclear weapons—is the Nuclear Non-Proliferation Treaty (NPT or sometimes NNPT) of 1968. The NPT allows nuclear powers to keep their weapons as long as they promise to eliminate them at a still unspecified future date. In the meantime, the five original nuclear powers—the United States, Russia, Britain, France, and China—promise to provide aid to the rest of the world for the devel-

opment of civilian nuclear power. The treaty is the basis for international monitoring and inspections conducted by the IAEA.

The technologies required to produce nuclear power and nuclear weapons largely overlap, although the former is intended to provide a source of power for energy and non-military uses. Both require enrichment technology and procedures that extract and concentrate uranium-235 (^{235}U), an isotope capable of sustaining a nuclear chain reaction, from raw uranium ore that contains 99 percent uranium-238 (^{238}U), an isotope incapable of sustaining the chain reaction needed to produce a nuclear explosion. The percentage of enrichment required for use in weapons is much higher than the levels needed to produce nuclear reactor fuel.

Current Nuclear Arsenals

As of 2010, four countries known or assumed to have nuclear weapons—India, Israel, North Korea, and Pakistan—are not parties to NPT. The international community assumes that Israel has nuclear weapons, but Israel does not confirm or deny these claims. North Korea denounced and withdrew from the NPT in 2003.

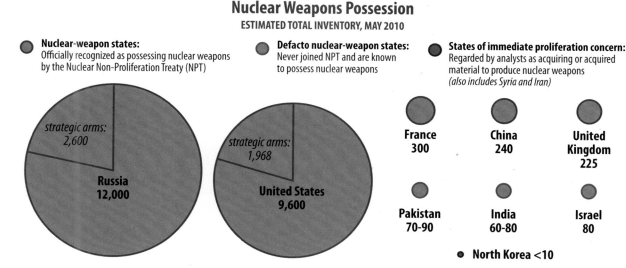

Nuclear Weapons Possession
ESTIMATED TOTAL INVENTORY, MAY 2010

Nuclear-weapon states:
Officially recognized as possessing nuclear weapons by the Nuclear Non-Proliferation Treaty (NPT)

Defacto nuclear-weapon states:
Never joined NPT and are known to possess nuclear weapons

States of immediate proliferation concern:
Regarded by analysts as acquiring or acquired material to produce nuclear weapons
(also includes Syria and Iran)

strategic arms: 2,600

Russia 12,000

strategic arms: 1,968

United States 9,600

France 300

China 240

United Kingdom 225

Pakistan 70-90

India 60-80

Israel 80

● **North Korea <10**

SOURCES: Bulletin of the Atomic Scientists, Pentagon, White House Press Office Arms Control Association, Federation of American Scientists

Russia and the United States lead the world in total nuclear inventory. Illustration/XNR Productions/Cengage Learning, Gale.

The most recent country known to develop a nuclear weapon was North Korea. On 9 October 2006, North Korea conducted a test that produced a small nuclear explosion that most experts termed a technological failure. Nevertheless, the general consensus was that North Korea proved itself capable of building crude nuclear weapons, and the United Nations Security Council imposed sanctions on North Korea to discourage further nuclear technology development.

Nuclear Treaties and Diplomacy

In April 2009, President Obama pledged his administration's efforts to renew the push for U.S. ratification of the 1996 Comprehensive Nuclear Test-Ban Treaty, which aims for better security and monitoring of nuclear materials and provides a ban on the development of weapons-grade materials. As of December 2010, 151 countries had officially ratified the Test-Ban Treaty. Among declared nuclear states, the United States and China have signed but have not ratified. Israel also has signed but has not ratified. Countries with declared nuclear weapons that have not signed include Pakistan, India, and North Korea.

In October 2009, the Norwegian Nobel Committee awarded President Obama the Nobel Peace Prize for what they cited in their press release announcing the award as his "extraordinary efforts to strengthen international diplomacy and cooperation between people." The press release also indicated that the organization attached "special importance to Obama's vision of and work for a world without nuclear weapons."

Presidents, prime ministers, and senior foreign policy officials from 47 nations attended an April 2010 Nuclear Security Summit in Washington, D.C. that dealt with an array of nuclear weapons related issues, and that resulted in agreements to proposals aimed at reducing the risk of nuclear terrorism. Iran was not invited to the summit. World leaders agreed to participate in a four-year program for developing common standards related to the security of nuclear materials, including standards for storage, tracking, and inspection of plutonium and highly enriched uranium. The goal of the plan is to support the work of the IAEA rather than replace or supplant the agency.

Presidents Obama and Medvedev signed a new Strategic Arms Reduction Treaty (START) on April 8, 2010. The two major nuclear powers agreed to lower the number of deployed strategic warheads and launchers and create a new inspection system. The U.S. Senate ratified START on 22 December 2010.

Action to limit arms also proceeded at the UN. In a move that analysts concluded was aimed at Israel's widely assumed but unverified possession of nuclear weapons, the Non-Aligned Movement bloc, comprised of 118 UN member nations, pushed for the establishment of a nuclear weapons-free zone in the Middle East. The Non-Aligned Movement also demanded that all countries with nuclear power submit to weapons inspections by the United Nations. Following the Obama administration's announcement of a new U.S. policy promising not to use nuclear weapons against states complying with the NPT, member states of the Non-Aligned Movement expressed opposition to parts of the policy, especially provisions that penalize countries that opt out of the NPT. Non-aligned members also oppose plans to establish a UN-controlled and guarded repository of nuclear fuel.

On 5 May 2010, in a surprise to many analysts, the United States, the United Kingdom, France, Russia, and China issued a joint statement of support for creating a nuclear-weapons-free zone in the Middle East. The five permanent UN Security Council members statement reiterated their mutual support for full implementation of the 1995 NPT, which calls for making the Middle East a nuclear-weapons-free zone. The U.S. described such a zone as a future goal, but one which could ultimately force Israel to disclose and disband its assumed nuclear weapons. Israel maintains that it

The Bushehr nuclear power plant in southern Iran in late October 2010. AP Images/Majid Asgaripour.

would only disarm following a Middle East peace agreement, and the United States has expressed support for this position. With regard to the Iranian nuclear program the statement asserted that the "proliferation risks" associated with the current Iranian nuclear program continue to remain a "serious concern."

In October 2010, Russian and Iranian engineers completed loading enriched uranium fuel rods into the Bushehr nuclear plant. Although a significant step toward energy production, nuclear security experts downplayed the significance in terms of Iran's capacity to produce a nuclear weapon. Iran has already demonstrated the technical capacity to enrich uranium beyond the level used in civilian reactors. Moreover, any attempt to further enrich the fuel rods would be difficult to conceal from external monitoring by the IAEA and other agencies.

It is clearly not Iran's capacity to produce a weapon alone that worries the international community, according to analysts. For example, Japan possesses a strong civilian nuclear-power program, with approximately one third of its electricity needs met by nuclear power. It has favored a plutonium-based nuclear system that relies on separating plutonium from spent reactor fuel for re-use. Such separated reactor-grade plutonium is potential bomb material. Since the 1970s Japan has admitted having the capability to make nuclear weapons, but Japan has renounced the development and possession of nuclear weapons. By 2004 Japan's bomb-grade plutonium stockpile stood at 29.3 metric tons, enough to make approximately 3,500 nuclear weapons. Japan's nuclear-weapons capabilities thus greatly exceed Iran's. However, because of compliance with IAEA monitoring, Japan's nuclear program is not a subject of international controversy.

International fears regarding Iran's nuclear ambitions, both real and perceived, are grounded in existing geopolitical tensions that are understood only in the context of the history of Iran and the evolution of its culture, policies, and place in the modern world.

Iranian Culture and Politics

Iran, with a population of over 72 million people, is a geographically large country in south-central Asia, ruled since 1979 by a revolutionary, fundamentalist Islamist government. Islamists are Muslims who support government enforcement of their interpretations of Muslim law.

Early History of Iran

In 1925 Reza Khan overthrew Ahmad Shah Qajar to become Reza Shah Pahlavi, the imperial leader of Persia. In 1935, Persia officially requested that other nations refer to it as Iran, the name that inhabitants of Persia had long used to describe their region. Persia was the name given to the region by ancient Greeks that was then adopted by other Europeans.

During World War II, Reza Shah's alliance with the Axis powers led to post-war occupation by Britain and Russia, as the two nations divided Iran into spheres of influence. In 1951, a power struggle between Pahlavi and Iranian Prime Minister Mohammad-Ali Foroughi followed a parliamentary vote to nationalize the oil industry that, at the time, was dominated by the British owned Anglo-Iranian Oil Company. Following the invasion of Iran by Soviet, British, and Indian forces, Reza Shah was forced into exile and was replaced as Shah of Iran by his son, Mohammad Reza Shah Pahlavi. A 1953 coup in Iran, orchestrated by the U.S. Cental Intelligence Agency (CIA) and Britain's MI6 (Secret Intelligence Service agency in charge of supplying foreign intelligence to Britain), led to the installation of Mohammed Mossadegh as Iran's new Prime Minister and the exile of Mohammad

Reza, who returned to power after Mossadegh was arrested and charged with treason. By 1963, Mohammad Reza began the White Revolution, a campaign to modernize the country by implementing policies governing land, social, and economic reform. To squelch opposition to his reforms, Mohammad Reza relied upon state secret police, who were often accused of employing brutal and repressive tactics.

The Modern Monarchy

Mohammad Reza Shah's movement to modernize Iran was funded by vast oil revenues; however, inflation, government corruption, and a growing income gap eventually led to widespread unrest by 1976. In addition, modernization policies began to alienate the conservative Muslim clergy in the country. By 1978, approximately 60,000 foreigners resided in Iran. Their influence upon dress, culture, and entertainment, along with the Mohammad Reza's modernization policies, created the perception among religious fundamentalists that Iran was sacrificing its Islamic values and cultural identity.

Mohammad Reza boldly announced on 2 March 1975 that the multi-party system in Iran was abolished and that government control was granted to the Rastakhiz Party. This action sparked international outrage and concern about fascism and human rights abuses in Iran.

Protests and unrest spread into secular segments of Iranian society—including a middle class led by intellectuals, lawyers and secular politicians—and led to a campaign of protest against Mohammad Reza in the form of letters, declarations, and resolutions calling for the restoration of constitutional rule.

The Iranian Revolution

In 1978, a series of protests signaled the beginning to the end of Mohammad Reza Shah's rule in Iran. Protests began after an article appearing in the newspaper *Ettelaat* questioned the piety and loyalty of the Ayatollah Ruhollah

After 14 years in exile, the Ayatollah Khomeini returned to Iran in 1979. AP Images.

Khomeini. Although in exile, Khomeini was considered the country's spiritual leader by many Shiite Muslims in Iran. The accusation against Khomeini was not received well and resulted in orchestrated demonstrations and strikes. From exile, Khomeini issued proclamations calling for the overthrow of Mohammad Reza Shah and continued protests. His supporters declared their goal of creating an Islamic state with Khomeini as its leader. One such protest took place in September 1978 at the public prayers to commemorate the end of Ramadan, the Muslim month of fasting. An assembly of approximately 100,000 quickly turned into a protest against Mohammad Reza. The protests continued for several days until martial law was declared in Tehran and eleven other cities. 9 September 1978 became known as "Black Friday" when troops fired into the crowds at Tehran's Jaleh Square and killed at least eighty-seven people.

The killings further escalated the violence of the protests as the opposition became radicalized and began to target symbols of the Mohammad Reza's modernization program. Nightclubs and movie theaters, viewed as symbols of moral corruption, were bombed. Considered agents of economic corruption, banks were likewise targeted, as were police stations, which for the opposition represented political corruption.

The protests form the core of what is termed the Iranian Revolution, a series of mass demonstrations against the Iranian monarchy, culminating in the abdication of Mohammad Reza Shah.

In October 1978, Khomeini, recently expelled from Iraq, reestablished his headquarters

During the hostage crisis in Iran, one of the American captives (blindfolded with hands bound) is taken by militant students and shown to a crowd that gathered outside the seized U.S. embassy in 1979. AP Images.

in France outside of Paris. This new location afforded Khomeini better exposure in the world press, as well as better communication with his followers in Iran. In November 1978, leaders of the National Front, an opposition political party, met with Khomeini and issued a statement calling for the removal of Mohammad Reza and the creation of a new government in Iran. At this same time, Mohammad Reza began to negotiate with moderate oppositions, some of whom were

also members of the National Front. After meeting with Mohammad Reza, National Front leaders arranged to form a government as long as the Shah left Iran.

On 16 January 1979, Mohammad Reza Shah departed Iran. The more moderate National Front leadership could not, however, gain the support of Khomeini and other fundamentalist Muslim leaders, known as Mullahs.

In February 1979, the Ayatollah Ruhollah Khomeini returned to Iran after fourteen years in exile. By the end of March 1979, Khomeini successfully led a movement to replace Iran's constitutional monarchy with the Islamic state that exists today.

The Iranian Islamic State

Ayatollah Khomeini created a new governmental structure, placing himself at the top as "Supreme Leader," a position he occupied until his death in 1989. His rule and legacy continue to have vast implications for Iran.

Although the post-revolutionary constitution created a presidency, the constitution declares that the supreme leader has final say in internal and foreign policies and control over the armed

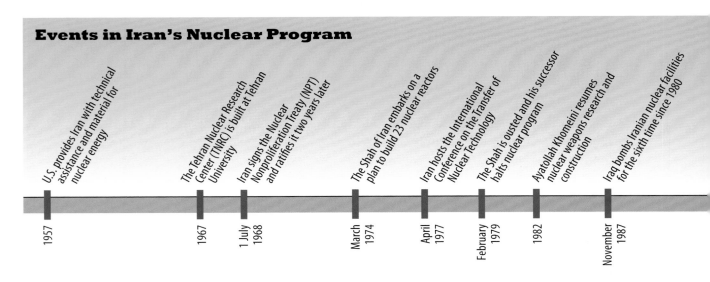

Events in Iran's Nuclear Program

U.S. provides Iran with technical assistance and material for nuclear energy — 1957

The Tehran Nuclear Research Center (TNRC) is built at Tehran University — 1967

Iran signs the Nuclear Nonproliferation Treaty (NPT) and ratifies it two years later — 1 July 1968

The Shah of Iran embarks on a plan to build 23 nuclear reactors — March 1974

Iran hosts the International Conference on the Transfer of Nuclear Technology — April 1977

The Shah is ousted and his successor halts nuclear program — February 1979

Ayatollah Khomeini resumes nuclear weapons research and construction — 1982

Iraq bombs Iranian nuclear facilities for the sixth time since 1980 — November 1987 forces. Thus, while Iran retains the impression of a democracy it remains, in essence, a religious theocracy.

Even under President Mohammad Khatami, who served from 1997 to 2005 and was considered by analysts to be relatively liberal, efforts to further freedom of expression and create a civil society in Iran were continually hindered by the supreme religious authority. Ayatollah Ali Khamenei became Iran's Supreme Leader following Khomeini's death in 1989. According to internal U.S. diplomatic intelligence made public in 2010, Khamenei is assumed to be suffering from leukemia. Accordingly, by December 2010, there was open international speculation about an upcoming shift in supreme leadership of Iran.

Many international analysts conclude that Iran has, since Khomeini's death, wavered between allowing social liberalization and repressing reforms. The situation is complicated by a number of institutions that run parallel to those of the Iranian state. The Revolutionary Guard, a branch of the Iranian army that remains loyal to Iran's religious elite, also control the operation and security for Iran's nuclear program. The *Basij* are a volunteer religious police force founded by Khomeini's order that at times act as vigilantes and assume the responsibility of protecting the country from such Western-style "decadent" behavior as watching Western television (via illegal satellite link) or inappropriate dress (e.g. a woman not wearing a headscarf in certain areas). Since the 2005 election of President Mahmoud Ahmadinejad, a former member of the *Basij,* Iran has witnessed a return to stricter interpretations of Islamic social structure.

Iranian Society and Culture

Although its wealth was distributed unevenly, pre-revolutionary Iran was one of the most prosperous countries in the Middle East. Decimated by its bitterly fought war with Iraq (1980–88) and Western sanctions—both indirect consequences of its revolution—Iran experienced a marked deterioration in its wealth in the 1980s and 1990s. Oil production, its main source of income, fell and unemployment soared.

Economic hardships are worst for the most vulnerable members of Iranian society, including women, children, the elderly, and the poor. Unemployment is particularly high among Iranian youth, fueling renewed generational tensions. At the same time, Iran's leaders claim that the revo-

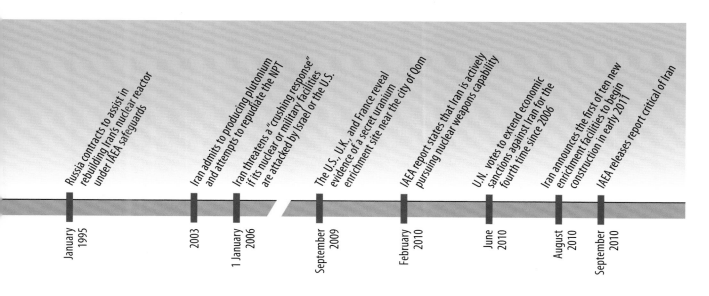

Russia contracts to assist in rebuilding Iran's nuclear reactor under IAEA safeguards — January 1995

Iran admits to producing plutonium and attempts to repudiate the NPT — 2003

Iran threatens a "crushing response" if its nuclear or military facilities are attacked by Israel or the U.S. — 1 January 2006

The U.S., U.K., and France reveal evidence of a secret uranium enrichment site near the city of Qom — September 2009

IAEA report states that Iran is actively pursuing nuclear weapons capability — February 2010

U.N. votes to extend economic sanctions against Iran for the fourth time since 2006 — June 2010

Iran announces the first of ten new enrichment facilities to begin construction in early 2011 — August 2010

IAEA releases report critical of Iran — September 2010

lution created a generous social policy, in which food and fuel subsidies and state housing are available to the poor and needy.

Anti-American and Anti-Western Sentiment in Iran

Critics contend that one of the defining characteristics of the Iranian revolution was its xenophobia (fear of, or contempt for foreigners), particularly its anti-Americanism, which has had enormous consequences for the country's foreign policy. For anti-Shahist protesters, hostility towards the monarch and the United States were indistinguishable. This hostility was exploited by Iranian opposition leaders. The Shah later blamed foreign governments for exacting his downfall.

Anti-Americanism culminated in November 1979 when a group of Khomeini-inspired students gathered at the U.S. embassy in Iran to protest. The students subsequently invaded the lightly guarded embassy and seized sixty-six hostages (thirteen women were released soon thereafter and one male hostage was released later due to illness). The United States retaliated by freezing billions of dollars of Iranian assets, but an unrepentant Khomeini issued his own demands in return for freeing the hostages. The standoff lasted 444 days, and included a disastrous attempted rescue by U.S. military forces in which a helicopter accident killed eight U.S. servicemen. The mission was aborted before the remaining hostages were released.

By then the crisis had arguably come to define U.S. President Jimmy Carter's term of office, and by many accounts cost him any chance at re-election. Iran was transformed from being one of the United States' closest allies to being one of its prime enemies. Economic sanctions have remained in place ever since.

Through the Iran-Iraq War the United States provided military and intelligence assistance to Iraq in an attempt to bring about Iran's defeat and unseat Khomeini. Iran, for its part, has often remained combative, funding the Lebanese militia Hizbollah, which has since conducted terrorist and paramilitary operations against U.S. military targets.

Iran's international anti-Western image compounded by the so-called "Rushdie Affair" when, in 1989, Ayatollah Khomeini issued a *fatwa* (a religious edict) against British novelist Salman Rushdie, calling for him to be killed for his allegedly blasphemous book, *The Satanic Verses.*

In January 2002, President Bush named Iran as part of what he called the "Axis of Evil" for acting as a state sponsor of terrorism. Although the European Union (EU) has made efforts to normalize relations with Iran, the West's view of the country remains largely defined by U.S. distrust of Iran for its hostilities toward Israel, its alleged intent to develop nuclear weapons, its alleged interference in the U.S.-led war and occupation in Iraq, and what the United States characterizes as Iran's support for terrorist operations.

Geopolitical Realities and Iran's Nuclear Program

Sunni and Shiite Disputes

Islam consists of two major sects, the Sunnis, who comprise approximately 85 percent of the worlds Muslim population, and Shiites, who make up approximately 13 percent of the world's Muslim population. Shiites enjoy majority status in Azerbaijan, Bahrain, Iran, and Iraq. Significant Shia populations exist in Afghanistan, Albania, Lebanon, Pakistan, Syria, Turkey, and Yemen. Despite a bloody early history, Sunnis and Shiites lived in relative peace throughout most of the twentieth century. During the last several decades, however, the Sunni–Shiite conflict has intensified, with tens of thousands of people killed in sectarian fighting.

The split of Islam into Sunni and Shia sects occurred after the death of the prophet Muhammad in 632 AD, when a debate arose over who would take Muhammad's place as leader of the faith. Sunnis, which means followers, asserted that any qualified, spiritual man chosen by the

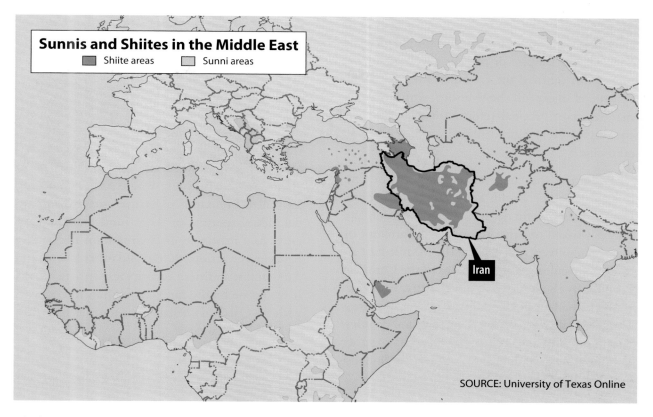

Sunnis and Shiites in the Middle East

☐ Shiite areas   ☐ Sunni areas

Iran

SOURCE: University of Texas Online

In both Iran and Iraq, the vast majority of Muslims are Shiites. Sunni Muslims predominate elsewhere in the Middle East. Illustration/XNR Productions/Cengage Learning, Gale.

Muslim community could become caliph, the supreme ruler and successor of Muhammad. The Sunnis favored Abu Bakr (c. 572–634) to become caliph. Other Muslims claimed that only a direct descendant of Muhammad could serve as caliph, and, therefore, they favored Muhammad's cousin and son-in-law, Ali ibn Abu Talib (c. 599–691), as caliph. Supporters of Ali became known as Shi-at-Ali, or partisans of Ali, which eventually was shortened to Shiites.

Sunni and Shia sects share common beliefs but with a few important distinctions. Both sects accept the Five Pillars of Islam—monotheism, daily prayer, alms giving, fast during Ramadan, and pilgrimage to Mecca—although Shiites add three additional rituals. Sunnis and Shiites also accept that Muhammad was the messenger of Allah, and both sects accept the Qur'an as a sacred text. In addi-

tion to the debate over succession of Muhammad, Sunni and Shia Muslims have several important differences in their beliefs. One such difference is the dispute over the nature of the Mahdi, or the prophesied redeemer of Islam. Shiites believe that their twelfth imam, or religious leader, Imam Muhammad al-Mahdi, is the Mahdi. Shia doctrine holds that al-Mahdi will be revealed in the future and become the savior of humanity. Sunnis believe that the Mahdi will come to earth, but they reject the belief that al-Mahdi is the mahdi.

After the schism of Islam, Sunnis and Shiites battled for decades over control of people, land, and resources. Sunnis eventually won the struggle for superiority. Throughout the following centuries, the sects assassinated rival religious and political leaders and killed civilians. Sunnis, who greatly outnumbered Shiites, carried out most of the attacks. During the sixteenth and seventeenth centuries, the Sunni Ottoman Empire battled the Shia Safavid Empire of present-day Iran. In the nineteenth century, the Ottoman Empire, which controlled most of the Muslim world, implemented constitutional reforms that asserted the equality of every citizen regardless of religion or ethnicity.

Following the collapse of the Ottoman Empire at the end of World War I, Sunnis and Shiites lived in harmony for decades. Initially, Sunnis and Shiites worked together to oppose the attempt by European powers to secularize the Middle East after Europe colonized the remains of the Ottoman Empire. By the mid-twentieth century, European countries had granted independence to most areas of the Middle East. Over the next several decades, Sunni and Shia religious leaders worked together to oppose Arab nationalism, a secular nationalist push for a unified Arab state.

By the 1970s, a rift developed in the peaceful relationship between Sunnis and Shiites. No one event triggered the renewed fighting between Sunnis and Shiites. Several Islamic scholars argue that sectarian fundamentalism replaced the unifying ideas of anti-colonialism and anti-Arab nationalism of the early twentieth century. The Islamic Revolution of Iran in 1979, when the Shia cleric Ayatollah Khomeini came to power, emboldened Shiites and threatened Sunni dominance in the Middle East.

During the 1980s, governments perpetrated most of the sectarian violence, primarily to quash perceived sectarian rebellions. In 1982, the minority Shia government of Syria killed between 10,000 and 25,000 Sunnis during the Hama Massacre. Under former Iraqi dictator Saddam Hussein, the minority Sunni-led government of Iraq killed tens of thousands of Shiites, including ethnic Kurds, who Hussein viewed as a threat to his power. Iraq's prolonged war with Iran also carried ethnic and religious overtones.

By the mid-1990s, non-state actors became the source of most sectarian violence. The Sunni Taliban of Afghanistan killed thousands of Shia civilians, including 8,000 people during a 1998 attack on Bamiyan and Mazar-i-Sharif. Al-Qaeda (a loose international association of groups or cells dedicated to achieving the goals of radical Islam through threats and terrorist acts) and other anti-Shia groups sponsored attacks on Shiites in Afghanistan and Pakistan, where sectarian violence has killed thousands of people over the last two decades. Experts cite these fundamental differences as a reason to draw important distinctions between the actions of Iran and other Islamic fundamentalist entities. Security experts assert that it would be highly unlikely for Iran to cooperate with Al-Qaeda with regard to transfer of nuclear technology or weapons.

According to published portions of National Security Estimates, evaluation of the normally hostile relationship between Islamist groups with Shiite and Sunni Islamist groups remains an intense area of intelligence interest, especially with regard to the acquisition of nuclear materials or weapons. In June 2009, during an interview broadcast on the Al Jazeera network, Mustafa Abu al-Yazid—described as a leader of Al-Qaeda—underscored international concern. Al-Yazid claimed that if nuclear weapons came under the control of Al-Qaeda, the group's leadership would seek to use, and condone the use of, nuclear weapons against the United States and other pro-Western countries.

Iran and Arab-Israeli Conflict

Although Iranians are Persians and not Arabs, they join with Arab states in most of the aspects of the ongoing Arab-Israeli conflict, a many-sided dispute over national identity in the Middle East that has global consequences.

Israel is a small democracy at the eastern end of the Mediterranean Sea. In 2007 Israel's population was 7.3 million, and ethnic demographics included 75.8 percent Jews and 19.7 percent Arabs.

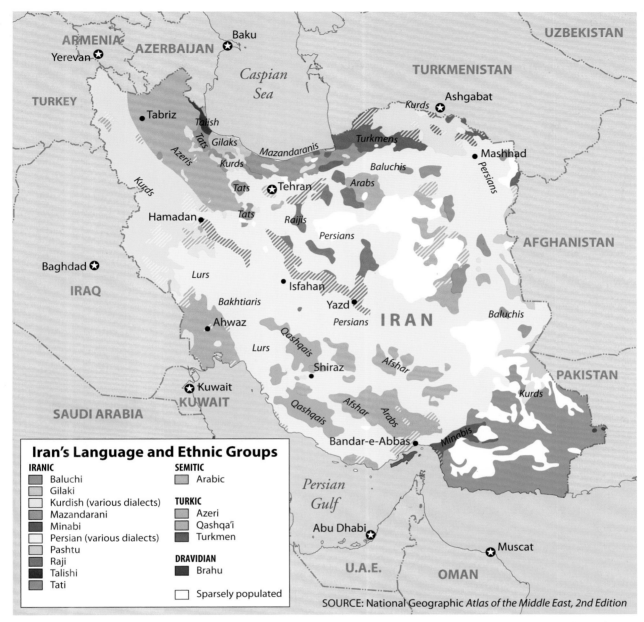

Iran's Language and Ethnic Groups

IRANIC
- Baluchi
- Gilaki
- Kurdish (various dialects)
- Mazandarani
- Minabi
- Persian (various dialects)
- Pashtu
- Raji
- Talishi
- Tati

SEMITIC
- Arabic

TURKIC
- Azeri
- Qashqa'i
- Turkmen

DRAVIDIAN
- Brahu

- Sparsely populated

SOURCE: National Geographic *Atlas of the Middle East, 2nd Edition*

Persians and Azeris are the largest ethnic groups in Iran, while most of its Middle Eastern neighbors are dominated by Arabs. Illustration/XNR Productions/Cengage Learning, Gale.

The term "Arab" denotes persons descended from tribes inhabiting the Arabian Peninsula or persons speaking the Arabic language. By this definition, there are about 250 million Arabs worldwide, most found in the group of countries occupying North Africa and the western part of the Middle East. Most Arabs are Muslims, but a significant minority (about 10 percent) in the Arab Middle East are Christians. Many are secular, or not identified with any religion.

Disputes with Israel center on Israel's right to exist on territory that was the ancient homeland of the Jews but which in recent centuries was inhabited primarily by Arabs. Israelis tend to see

Israeli authorities assert that they will protect their nation against nuclear threats from Iran like they have done in the past with Iraq and Syria. Shown here is the Tammuz nuclear reactor in Iraq, which was bombed by Israel in 1981 and also hit during the Gulf War in 1991. Ramzii Haidar/AFP/newscom.

their country as a democratic, enlightened, much-needed refuge for Jews, relentlessly attacked by Arabs and judged unjustly by most of the world; Arabs tend to see Israel as a racist colony founded on the expulsion of Arabs from their homeland, Palestine, and unjustly supported by the United States. Not all Israelis and Arabs hold these exact views, of course, and there are different apects for each viewpoint relating to the core disputes.

Most Israelis, as well as many non-Israeli Jews and other supporters of Israel worldwide, see Israel as a refuge for Jews that was made necessary by the Holocaust, or Shoah, the Nazi state-sponsored, systematic genocide of 6.6 million Jews during World War II. But the project of creating a Jewish state in Palestine, the territory between the Mediterranean and the Jordan River,

dates to the late nineteenth century, when the Zionist movement began.

Central to the ongoing Arab-Israeli conflict is the question of Palestinian statehood. During the Israeli war of independence, about 80 percent of Arabs living in the territory that is now Israel (about 700,000 people) fled, fearing attacks by Israeli militants. Palestinians refer to their expulsion from Israel as the *nakba* or "disaster." The refugees and their descendants, the Palestinians, today reside in the coastal Gaza Strip to Israel's south and along the west bank of the Jordan River, to Israel's east.

In 1949 the UN arranged a cease-fire in Israel, setting a boundary around it known as the Green Line. In 1967, during the Six-Day War fought between Israel and Egypt, Jordan, and Syria, Israel extended its borders beyond the Green Line, into the Gaza Strip and the West Bank, and began building settlements there. These areas are known as the Occupied Territories. Many Arabs view the Israeli occupation of the Occupied Territories as having as its ultimate goal the further expulsion of the Palestinians and the annexation of their lands to an expanded Israel.

Several wars have occurred in the Arab-Israeli conflict: the war of Israeli independence in 1948, the war with Egypt in 1956, the Six-Day War of 1967, the Yom Kippur War of 1973, and the Israeli invasions of Lebanon in 1978, 1982, and 2006. Many smaller-scale military actions have also been taken. As of the early 2000s, despite decades of peace talks, the situation was little changed from earlier decades, with entrenched hostilities, racism, and radically divergent claims of fact dividing Israel from the Arab world.

The majority international view of the Arab-Israeli conflict is that both sides have acted illegally and aggressively at different times. As manifested in UN General Assembly and Security Council vote counts, the international consensus often opposes official Israeli policies. For example, the Security Council, in resolutions 446 (1979), 452 (1979), 465 (1980), and 471 (1980), has declared that Israel's West Bank settlements are illegal. However, the international consensus also rejects the claim of some extreme Arab militant groups (such as Hamas and Hezbollah) that Israel has no right to exist. These two elements of the international consensus—Israel's right to exist and the imperative that it withdraw from the Occupied Territories—were first expressed by the Security Council soon after the 1967 war in which Israel took the territories. In resolution 242 (11 November 1967), the Council called for both "(i) Withdrawal of Israel armed forces from territories occupied in the recent conflict" and "(ii) … respect for and acknowledgement of the sovereignty, territorial integrity and political independence of every State in the area and their right to live in peace within secure and recognized boundaries free from threats or acts of force."

Iran does not recognize the state of Israel, contributing to regional tension. Moreover, calls for the destruction of Israel by Iranian leaders, along with denials of the reality of the Holocaust, continue to escalate tensions and the possibility of war.

The Israeli World View

Foreign policy experts argue that Israel's world view is a product of post-Holocaust Israeli politics. Following the Holocaust, more than 100,000 Jews fled displaced persons camps in Europe and emigrated to British-controlled Palestine—an area that now forms Israel, Jordan, and the Palestinian Territories—against the wishes of the British government. Following the establishment of Israel in 1948, Israeli citizens, many of whom were Holocaust survivors, pledged that "never again" would Jews be the target of genocide or unprovoked attacks.

Israel's Prime Minister Benjamin Netanyahu's own world view has, in the past, led him to take hard-line positions on numerous issues, including the Israeli-Palestinian conflict, Israel's relations with Arab nations, and Iran's pursuit of nuclear weapons, the latter of which does not come

without provocation. In 2005, Iranian President Mahmoud Ahmadinejad stated in a speech to the World without Zionism conference that Israel "must be wiped off the map."

Netanyahu too has made controversial comments. Between 2006 and 2008, he compared Iran's nuclear weapons program to Nazi Germany and the Holocaust. In 2006, Netanyahu stated, "It's 1938, and Iran is Germany, and Iran is racing to arm itself with atomic bombs." In 2007 and 2008, Netanyahu stated that Germany started a global conflict and then sought atomic weapons, whereas Iran is seeking atomic weapons and will then start a global conflict.

The actions of Iranian leaders in support of those who deny the Holocaust also stirs Israeli passions. Many experts familiar with the people and history of Israel contend that it is impossible to overestimate how seriously such denial about the realities of the Holocaust wounds the collective Israeli psyche and fosters resolve to never again allow the wholesale extermination of the Jewish people. In addition to the Jewish victims of the Holocaust, Nazi policies also led to the killing of over 5 million others, including ethnic Poles, Romani, religious minorities, homosexuals, political dissidents, and prisoners of war. There is no legitimate scholarly debate over whether the Holocaust occurred, nor any evidence that mitigates its horror. The Holocaust is, in fact, one of the most heavily documented events in history, with tens of thousands of supporting eyewitness testimonies, documentary footage, official Nazi records, and dozens of extermination camps discovered by liberating Allied forces, which even now contain the remains of Holocaust victims in mass graves. Still, some Iranian leaders, including Ahmadinejad, have openly embraced those who claim that the Holocaust did not take place and those who claim that the extent of the Holocaust is exaggerated in the West to create sympathy for Israel.

Israel maintains that Iran's heated rhetoric toward Israel—with threats to wipe Israel off the

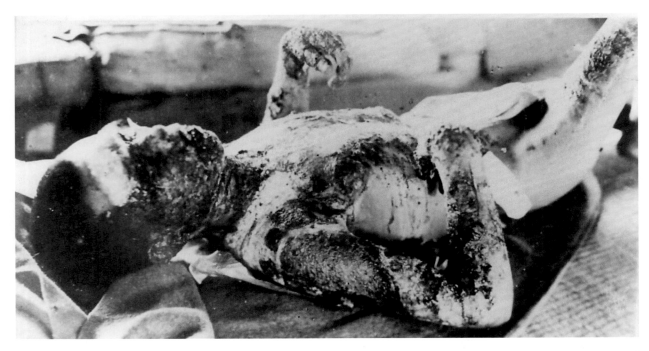

A horribly burned victim of the atomic bombing of Hiroshima, Japan. The incredible destructive force of nuclear weapons—and the long-term effect of radiation—puts them in a class by themselves. Approximately 140,000 people were killed or injured by the single American nuclear weapon used at Hiroshima, many more suffered long-term problems from radioactivity. Roughly 11 square kilometers of the city were destroyed. EPA/Landov.

map and its open support for organizations that deny Israel's right to exist—fully justify maximal defense efforts by Israel. Some maintain that such rhetoric even justifies preemptive military strikes against Iran by Israel—with or without U.S. aid or approval—should diplomacy fail to offer assurances of the peaceful nature of the Iranian nuclear program.

Toward an Uncertain Future

Although Iran continues to maintain that its nuclear program is devoted toward peaceful purposes, Israel, along with many in the West, remains openly skeptical. Each side in the dispute asserts evidence and claims in support their respective positions.

While the United States and Iran continue to be the prime adversaries pitted against each other in diplomatic circles, many experts insist that the

security interests of Israel may drive Israel to act with or without international sanction. In September 2007, Israeli jets struck a facility in Syria that Israel and the United States claimed was a nuclear reactor built with North Korean aid for the purpose of making nuclear weapons. Israeli officials and experts deal very openly and with great military practicality about the nature of a potential war or significant military encounter with Iran.

By definition all nations reserve the right to arm themselves, but nuclear weapons represent a special case because of their incredible destructive power. Indeed, most nations have signed the NPT, foregoing the right to develop nuclear weapons in exchange for the promise that they will not be attacked with nuclear weapons by any signatory that has them. Only a handful of countries (India, Pakistan, Israel and North Korea) have not signed or have withdrawn from the NPT. Iran is a party to the NPT but has been found in noncompliance. The rest of world does not question whether or not Iran has the right to develop nuclear energy, but is concerned about where it might lead.

Without continued diplomacy, international cooperation, and ultimately Iranian concessions with regard to greater IAEA access and monitoring, the result of failed diplomacy regarding Iran's nuclear program and ambitions may lead to military conflict, heightened regional tensions and instability, and possible wider war that polarizes an always somewhat tenuous peace among world powers.

Research and Exploration

ABC News. *Iranian President on Nuclear Program,* May 5, 2010. http://abcnews.go.com/GMA/video/iranian-president-nuclear-program–10560253.

ABC News features a video interview with Iranian President Mahmoud Ahmadinejad on the future of Iran's nuclear program.

ABC News. *Israel's PM on Iran's Nuclear Program,* April 19, 2010. http://abcnews.go.com/GMA/video/benjamin-netanyahu-irans-nuclear-program–10412732.

ABC News' *Good Morning America* presents video of an exclusive interview with Israeli Prime Minister Benjamin Netanyahu on Iran's nuclear program.

BBC. *Q&A: Iran Nuclear Issue.* http://www.bbc.co.uk/news/world-middle-east-11494946.

The BBC presents information on recent events involving Iran's nuclear program in an informative question and answer format.

Center for Strategic and International Studies (CSIS). Cordesman, Anthony H. and Abdullah Toukan. *Options in Dealing with Iran's Nuclear Program,* March 2010. http://csis.org/files/publication/100323_Options_todealwith_Iran.pdf.

A report from the Center for Strategic and International Studies analyzes Iran's nuclear program and possible responses by other countries, including diplomacy, deterrence, and preemptive strikes.

Council on Foreign Relations. *Iran's Nuclear Program.* http://www.cfr.org/publication/16811/irans_nuclear_program.html.

The Council on Foreign Relations, a nonpartisan think tank and publisher, examines Iran's nuclear program, including Iranian threats and the world's response.

C-SPAN. *Iranian Nuclear Program.* http://www.c-spanvideo.org/program/295570-1.

C-SPAN presents a video of Congressman Howard Berman, Chairman of the Foreign Affairs Committee of the U.S. House of Representatives, discussing Iran's nuclear program and its impact on regional and world security.

Federation of American Scientists. *Uranium Production.* http://www.fas.org/programs/ssp/nukes/fuelcycle/centrifuges/U_production.html.

The Federation of American Scientists, a nonpartisan group of scientists dedicated to security issues, details the processes used to produce and enrich uranium.

The New York Times. Iran's Nuclear Program. http://www.nytimes.com/info/iran-nuclear-program/#the-bush-response.

The New York Times presents detailed information on the history of Iran's nuclear program, the response to Iran's nuclear program by the United States and Israel, and ongoing debates about sanctions against Iran.

PBS: *Frontline/World. How to Become a Nuclear Superpower: The Dangerous World of Nuclear Proliferation.* http://www.pbs.org/frontlineworld/stories/iran403/howto.html.

Frontline/World, an in-depth news analysis show on PBS, presents an interactive graphic describing the ways in which a country may acquire nuclear weapons.

U.S. Nuclear Regulatory Commission. *Uranium Enrichment.* http://www.nrc.gov/materials/fuel-cycle-fac/ur-enrichment.html.

The U.S. Nuclear Regulatory Commission, the government agency responsible for nuclear safety in the United States, provides a description and diagrams on uranium enrichment.

The Washington Post. Getting Iran to Agree to Talk about its Nuclear Program Proves Difficult, November 13, 2010. http://www.washingtonpost.com/wp-dyn/content/article/2010/11/13/AR2010111304158.html?

The Washington Post examines the difficulties in persuading Iran to rejoin talks with other nations about Iran's nuclear program.

The Washington Post. Netanyahu Says Iran Needs to Know "All Options" Open. November 9, 2010. http://www.washingtonpost.com/wp-dyn/content/video/2010/11/09/VI2010110906907.html.

In a videotaped interview with *Bloomberg,* a New York-based news service, Israeli Prime Minister Benjamin Netanyahu discusses Iran's nuclear program.

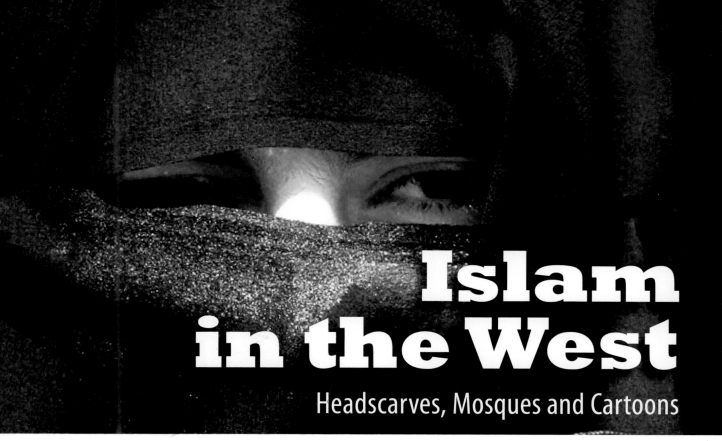

Islam in the West

Headscarves, Mosques and Cartoons

Murfreesboro, Tennessee, a city of about 100,000 people thirty-five miles northwest of Nashville, is not the sort of place that is featured in the national headlines very often. It's a fast-growing city, though, and it also happens to have a thriving Islamic Center that serves the local Muslim community. The Islamic Center has been in Murfreesboro for over a decade, and during that time it has attracted no more attention than any other place of worship in the city. But all that changed in 2010, when word got out that the Center was expanding because its existing premises, an office building, were not big enough to accommodate the up to 1,000 people who attend regular Friday prayers. The Center planned to build a new, much larger facility on a fifteen-acre field that it owned. The new Center would include a prayer room, community room, and classrooms.

The first sign of trouble came in January, 2010, when the sign that the Center had placed at the new property was vandalized: the words "Not Welcome" were spray-painted on it. Over the next few months it became clear that there was considerable public opposition to the building of the new center in Murfreesboro, even though the project had been approved by Rutherford County authorities in May 2009. At a packed public hearing of the Rutherford County Board of Commissioners in June 2010, many residents of the city expressed their misgivings. Some feared the Center would pose a threat to public safety and might be used for military training. Others wanted to know more about the officers and advisers of the Center and how it was being financed. Some of the views expressed were extreme, but not a single voice was raised in support of the proposal.

Later that month the issue was injected into

Lou Ann Zelenik, a Republican candidate for U.S. Congress from Tennessee's 6th District, speaks in Murfreesboro, Tenn., on 18 February 2010. In a statement 24 June 2010, Zelenik said plans to build a mosque in Murfreesboro pose a threat to the state's moral and political foundation. AP Images/ Aaron Thompson.

the congressional election campaign when Lou Ann Zelenik, one of the Republican candidates for Tennessee's 6th congressional district, denounced the planned Islamic Center in strident terms. Zelenik said she was opposed to building what she called "an Islamic training center," and described the proposed center as part of a political rather than religious movement that was "designed to fracture the moral and political foundation of Middle Tennessee."

Opposition to the Center took an even uglier turn in August, when heavy construction equipment at the proposed site was set on fire and destroyed. Police said it was a case of arson. Gas was poured over the equipment to start the fire. The arson incident spread fear among the Islamic community in Murfreesboro. The very next day,

as CBS was filming a news segment about the fire, five gunshots were fired near the site. No one was hurt in either of these incidents, but people were worried. Some Muslims in Murfreesboro were reluctant to send their children to school out of fear of what might happen. The alarm spread to mosques in Nashville, and several of them, concerned that trouble in Murfreesboro might spill over into their city, requested police surveillance.

Islamophobia on the Rise

The incidents involving the Murfreesboro mosque were not the only recent examples of what commentators refer to as Islamophobia in the United States. Islamophobia is a relatively new word referring to discrimination against or hostility toward those of the Islamic faith. The term was first used in government policy in 1997 when Britain's Runnymede Trust, a self-described "independent research and social policy agency" devoted to promoting cultural diversity, published a report titled *Islamophobia: A Challenge for Us All.* In this report, the trust outlined eight common beliefs of Islamophobes: Islam is "unresponsive to change"; Islam does not share common values with other cultures; Islamic culture is inferior to Western culture and marked by sexism and barbarism; Islam is violent and pro-terrorism; Islam is a political/military ideology; Muslim criticisms of the West are invalid; hostility towards Islam justifies discrimination against Muslims; and hostility towards Islam is natural and normal. The term Islamophobia conveys the growing tension and hostility between Islam and the West throughout the twenty-first century.

In an article for *Time* magazine, Bobby Ghosh elaborated on the increasing hold of Islamophobia in the United States in 2010:

> The arguments marshaled by Islam's detractors have become familiar: Since most terrorist attacks are conducted by Muslims and in the name of their faith, Islam must be a violent

creed. Passages of the Qur'an taken out of context are brandished as evidence that Islam requires believers to kill or convert all others. Shari'a laws requiring the stoning of adulterers or other gruesome punishments serve as proof that Muslims are savage and backward. The conclusion of this line of reasoning is that Islam is a death cult, not a real religion, so constitutional freedoms don't apply to it.

> Bobby Ghosh, "Islamophobia: Does America Have a Muslim Problem?" *Time*, 19 August 2010, http://www.time.com/time/nation/article/0,8599,2011798,00.html.

Islamic scholars and others are quick to point out that such portrayals are a caricature of Islam and bear little relation to the faith practiced by a billion people around the world. The Council on American-Islamic Relations (CAIR) notes that "Muslims follow a religion of peace, mercy and forgiveness that should not be associated with acts of violence against the innocent." However, the long and often contentious relationship between Islam and the West has far-reaching historical, cultural, and religious roots. The controversy and conflict between Islam and the West in the twenty-first century is yet another chapter in this history.

Many of the attitudes described in the definition of Islamophobia were apparent in the hostility toward mosques and people of Islamic faith that seemed to sweep across the United States in 2010. In February in Sheboygan County, Wisconsin, local residents protested when Muslims numbering no more than 100 applied for a permit to use a former health food store as a prayer space. (The permit was later granted.) In Temecula, California, when the Muslim community of about 150 families had outgrown its meeting space at a warehouse and wanted to build a mosque and community center, protesters rallied outside an existing mosque. Some of the protestors had brought their pet dogs with them because they had been told that Muslims hate dogs. (In Islam, dogs are regarded as

What Is Shari'a?

In the U.S. midterm elections in November 2010, voters in Oklahoma overwhelmingly approved a ballot initiative banning the use of Shari'a law in the state's courts, although the measure was quickly subjected to legal challenges.

What is Shari'a law and why has it become controversial in the United States?

Shari'a law is a part of the legal system in many Muslim countries. It is derived from the Qur'an and the Sunna (traditional Islamic customs and practices developed over the centuries).

Shari'a has attracted attention in the West because it calls for harsh punishments for crimes, including amputation of hands for robbery, stoning to death for adultery, as well as flogging, exile, and execution for other crimes. These punishments are, however, not common, and most Islamic countries, while retaining such measures in theory, opt for more lenient punishments. The strictest interpretation of Shari'a law is practiced in Saudi Arabia.

Shari'a law is also criticized in the West because of its unequal treatment of women in matters of inheritance and social standing, including marriage and child custody.

However, millions of Muslims support Shari'a law because they believe it ensures that people are able to conduct their lives under divine guidance.

In Britain, where there is a growing Muslim minority, the use of Shari'a tribunals governing marriage, divorce, and inheritance, has been officially allowed since 2008, as long as both parties agree to it. Criminal law, however, remains entirely within the British legal system.

ritually unclean.) One demonstrator held a sign that read, "Mosques are Monuments to Terrorism." In Florence, Kentucky, when Muslims planned on building a mosque in the area, an anonymous flier that circulated widely at the time contained the sentence, "Americans need to have this stopped." The implicit assumption behind such sentiments is that there is something "un-American" about being a Muslim in the United States, even though the people who want to build the mosques in the examples cited above are overwhelmingly American citizens.

The Park51 Project

By far the biggest controversy over the building of mosques in 2010 surrounded a development called Park51. The planned Islamic community center and mosque would be located near the former location of the World Trade Center in New York City. This was controversial because the militant Islamic group al-Qaeda destroyed the World Trade Center in the 9/11 terrorist attacks. The thirteen-story building that would house the proposed Islamic center had been bought in 2009 by a group of Muslims led by Imam Feisal Abdul Rauf, founder and CEO of the American Society for Muslim Advancement (ASMA). The building had formerly housed a Burlington Coat Factory store but had been abandoned after 9/11.

In July and August, as the project moved closer to approval by New York City authorities, the controversy intensified. Opponents of

Location of Proposed Mosque at Ground Zero

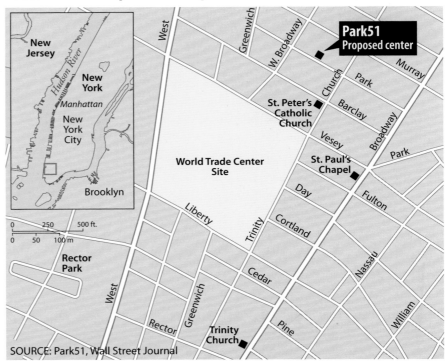

The proposed location of the "Ground Zero Mosque" is shown in relation to the World Trade Center site and other religious centers. Illustration/XNR Productions/Cengage Learning, Gale.

the mosque, which would actually be two blocks away from Ground Zero (the site of the 9/11 attacks), started referring to it as the Ground Zero mosque. Most Americans regard Ground Zero, where nearly 3,000 people had died, as sacred ground. There was widespread anger among opponents of the Ground Zero mosque at the idea that the people who wanted to build the mosque at that site were of the same religion as the terrorists who carried out the attack.

Various politicians and advocacy groups also voiced shock and dismay at the plan. Former vice presidential candidate Sarah Palin said the plan "stabs hearts," and she called on "peace-seeking Muslims" to reject it. Former Republican speaker of the House of Representatives Newt Gingrich said the plan was an "assertion of Islamist triumphalism." It would be "like putting a Nazi sign

U.S. Public Opinion on Mosque in NYC

As you may know, a group of Muslims in the U.S. plans to build a mosque two blocks from the site in New York City where the World Trade Center used to stand.
Do you favor or oppose this plan?

AUGUST 6–10, 2010

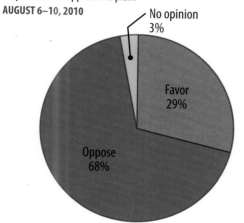

No opinion
3%

Favor
29%

Oppose
68%

SOURCE: CNN/Opinion Research Corporation

Two-thirds of Americans opposed the "Ground Zero Mosque" in early August 2010. Illustration/XNR Productions/ Cengage Learning, Gale.

next to the Holocaust Museum." Other politicians who opposed the plan included former Massachusetts governor Mitt Romney and Senator John McCain. Many families of 9/11 victims were also opposed to the location of the Islamic center, saying that it was insensitive to their feelings.

In a move that surprised many commentators, the Anti-Defamation League, a nonprofit organization that defines fighting anti-Semitism and all forms of bigotry as its fundamental goal, publicly opposed the project, saying it would cause the relatives of the 9/11 victims more pain. The organization quickly reversed its position after it was widely accused of hypocrisy and anti-Muslim bigotry.

Opponents conceded that the Muslim group had a legal right to build the mosque, but believed nonetheless that the project should be moved elsewhere. Among those who advocated this position were Democratic National Committee chairman Howard Dean and Senate Majority Leader Harry Reid. President Barack Obama also commented on the issue, noting that he supported the

developers' "right to build a place of worship and a community center on private property in lower Manhattan," although he later qualified that remark, saying he was commenting only on the group's legal rights, not on the wisdom of going ahead with the project.

Supporters of the plan characterized the opposition as being motivated by Islamophobia and hopes for short-term political gain. New York City mayor Michael Bloomberg gave a speech firmly

New York Mayor Michael Bloomberg voices his support for the proposed mosque near the World Trade Center site on 3 August 2010. City Council Speaker Christine Quinn and local religious leaders stand behind him. AP Images/Seth Wenig.

Rev. Terry Jones at the Dove World Outreach Center in Gainesville, Fla., 30 August 2010. Jones created an international controversy when he announced he would burn copies of the Qur'an to mark the anniversary of the 11 September 2001 terrorist attacks. AP Images/John Raoux.

supporting the project, saying that New York City had a unique heritage of religious tolerance and openness, and that the building of the community center and mosque would honor that heritage.

Other supporters of the mosque included former president Bill Clinton and Republican senator Orrin Hatch. Hatch, a Mormon from Utah, pointed out that in 2000, local people in Belmont, Massachusetts, had opposed the building of a Mormon temple there. The temple had been built, however, and Hatch said he would always support the right of legitimate religious groups to build places of worship on property they owned.

Public opinion polls during the summer consistently showed that a majority of Americans, both nationally and in New York, opposed the

building of the center. In a July Rasmussen Reports poll, 54 percent of Americans opposed the center; only 20 percent supported it. A CNN poll in August produced similar results, with a margin of 68 percent to 29 percent. However, two polls, conducted by Quinnipiac University and by Marist Poll, showed that although New York City residents overall opposed the plan by a wide margin, people in Manhattan, the borough where the center was to be built, supported it by a double-digit margin.

By mid-August, the controversy over the planned New York City Muslim center and mosque appeared to have added to the surge of anti-Muslim sentiment in the United States. Protesters rallied against the planned building of mosques in cities in California and Georgia. A very small Florida church called the Dove World Outreach Center even planned a "burn the Qur'an" event for 11 September 2010. The church's pastor, Rev. Terry Jones, described Islam as a "violent and oppressive religion that is trying to masquerade itself as a religion of peace, seeking to deceive our society." On 9 September, Jones agreed to cancel his plan to burn the Qur'an because, according to him, the Park51 developers had agreed to relocate their planned community center. However, the Park51 developers said they had no intention of relocating the project. As of December 2010, construction on the project had not commenced.

American Muslims: Demographics and Integration

The intolerance toward the building of mosques set many people thinking about American Muslims. How many Muslims are there in the

United States? How well are they integrated into mainstream American society?

Estimates of the number of American Muslims vary widely. According to the Council on American-Islamic Relations there are an estimated seven million Muslims in the United States. This is higher than many other estimates. The Pew Research Center, for example, estimated in 2009 a figure of 2.9 million American Muslims. One reason the figures vary widely is that the U.S. Census is not permitted to ask questions about religious affiliation, and estimates rely on different methodologies. The total population of the United States in 2010 was over 308 million, meaning that Muslims account for 2 percent of the United

People in Istanbul, Turkey hold copies of the Qur'an during a demonstration against U.S. pastor Terry Jones's plan to burn the Qur'an, 19 September 2010. Stringer Turkey/Reuters. ▼

States population at most.

Researchers agree that the number of American Muslims is increasing, largely due to immigration. The Pew Research Center estimated in 2007 that two-thirds of American Muslims are foreign-born. Over one-third (37%) come from Arab countries, while 27 percent come from South Asian countries such as Pakistan, India, Bangladesh, and Afghanistan. Thirty-nine percent have come to the United States since 1990. Of native-born American Muslims, more than half are African American, and African Americans make up 20 percent of U.S. Muslims overall.

A 2007 Pew Report titled "Muslim Americans: Middle Class and Mostly Mainstream" presented a positive picture of Muslim Americans and their assimilation into American society. The study found that Muslim Americans were "largely

Mistrust of the West in the Muslim World

Many Americans were stunned by the 11 September 2001 attacks, especially by the scenes of jubilation and expressions of satisfaction in parts of the Muslim world. Many were left wondering: "Why do they hate us so much?"

The history of the relationship between the western world and the Islamic world is complex. The discussion surrounding the modern clash is peppered with the language of campaigning on both sides. Some historians see such language as simply rhetoric. Others argue that though the disputed issues are primarily secular in nature, they continue to reflect religious concerns that have historically dominated contact between the Islamic world and the West, beginning with the Crusades.

The Crusades were a series of military campaigns lasting from the eleventh to the thirteenth century. By the time of the first Crusade in 1095, Arab Muslims had conquered the area of Palestine on the eastern shores of the Mediterranean Sea. Their conquests included the city of Jerusalem, which they had wrested from Christians in the seventh century, and by the end of the eleventh century, Muslim expansion threatened the Byzantine Empire in the area of modern Turkey. The Byzantine leader sent for help from the Roman Catholic pope who sent Western European armies to defend the Byzantines and recapture Jerusalem. In 1099 Christian forces captured Jerusalem and massacred the local Muslim population in the first of many Crusades conducted through the late 1200s. The Crusaders slowly lost control of their principalities until their last defeat in 1302.

The Crusades left a major mark on world history and had a significant impact on the growth of religious prejudice among both Christians and Muslims. Although the Crusades opened up much commerce between Europe and the Middle East and led to the inclusion of advanced Islamic thought in the sciences and medicine in European circles, the relationship between Christians and Muslims changed fundamentally as a result. The crusaders were never permanently successful in controlling the Holy Lands, and Muslim peoples forever regarded the Crusades as brutal attacks by Christian armies.

In modern times, anger at the West in the Muslim world stems partly from multiple instances of interference by Western powers in the affairs of Muslim nations, especially in the Middle East. Before World War I, most of the Middle East was under control of the vast and powerful Ottoman Empire, a Muslim regime. The Ottoman Empire was on the losing side of the war, and disintegrated after 1918, leaving much of its former territory in the hands of the victors. Arab groups were delighted to have British help in driving out the Ottomans, but the British were reluctant to leave once the war was over. France and Britain regarded

assimilated, happy with their lives, and moderate with respect to many of the issues that have divided Muslims and Westerners around the

New York City firefighters look at the destroyed facade of the World Trade Center 13 September 2001, two days after terrorist attacks destroyed the site. Many people's views of Islam and Muslims have been colored by these attacks. Chris Hondros/Getty Images. ▶

territories freed from the Ottoman Empire as the spoils of war and asserted their control over many parts of the region. As a result, resentment toward Europe mounted in the Middle East. This sentiment intensified further after the United Nations pushed for the creation of Israel at the conclusion of World War II without the consent of the Palestinian Arabs who were already living in the area. Israel's subsequent territorial expansion in the 1960s and the West's customary support for Israel have further intensified the anger of Arabs in the Middle East.

This anger was increasingly directed at the United States as the country rose to the status of a superpower during the Cold War. With the United States and the Soviet Union engaged in a struggle for dominance around the world, many developing nations found themselves used as pawns between the two countries. In some cases, the United States government backed repressive, undemocratic regimes primarily because of their anti-Communist, anti-Soviet stance. The people in countries repressed by these regimes—including Muslim nations such as Iran and Indonesia—tended to form unfavorable opinions of the United States as a result of this policy. These unfavorable feelings were heightened by the belief that United States foreign policy was often motivated not only by fear of communism but by a growing thirst for the oil reserves in many Muslim nations.

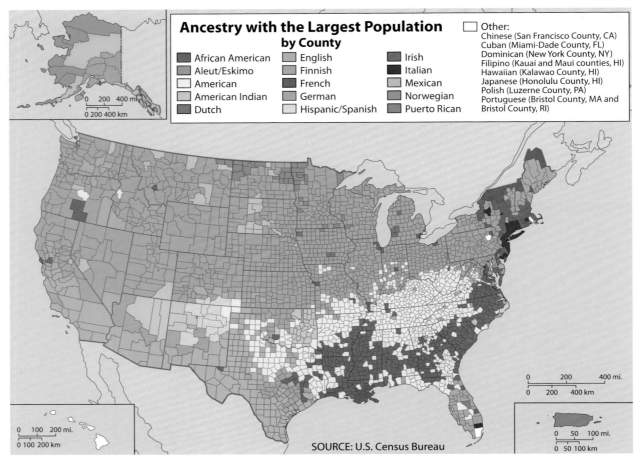

Ancestry with the Largest Population
by County

African American · English · Irish
Aleut/Eskimo · Finnish · Italian
American · French · Mexican
American Indian · German · Norwegian
Dutch · Hispanic/Spanish · Puerto Rican

Other:
Chinese (San Francisco County, CA)
Cuban (Miami-Dade County, FL)
Dominican (New York County, NY)
Filipino (Kauai and Maui counties, HI)
Hawaiian (Kalawao County, HI)
Japanese (Honolulu County, HI)
Polish (Luzerne County, PA)
Portuguese (Bristol County, MA and Bristol County, RI)

SOURCE: U.S. Census Bureau

U.S. Census Bureau map depicting the most commonly reported ethnic background of the residents in each county as of 2000.. Illustration/XNR Productions/Cengage Learning, Gale.

world. Muslim Americans are a highly diverse population. . . . Nonetheless, they are decidedly American in their outlook, values, and attitudes. Overwhelmingly, they believe that hard work pays off in this society." Pew found that income levels among Muslim Americans were comparable to that of the general population. For example, 41 percent reported annual household incomes of $50,000 or more; the comparable figure for the general population was 44 percent.

In March 2009, the Gallup Center for Muslim Studies released a poll based on a randomly selected sample of American Muslims. The poll found Muslim Americans to be very diverse, highly religious, and generally better educated than the general population. Forty percent reported

having a college degree, compared to 29 percent of the general population. Like the earlier Pew study, the poll found that in terms of income, American Muslims were roughly on par with the American population as a whole. Forty-one percent described themselves as "thriving," compared to 46 percent of the general population. Fifty-six percent described themselves as "struggling."

Gallup also found signs of cultural or social alienation, especially among the young. For example, only 51 percent of young Muslims (age 18–29) were registered to vote, compared to 78 percent of young Protestant Americans and 73 percent of young Jewish Americans. Young Muslims were also less likely than other groups of young people to be satisfied with the area in

How Much Do Americans Say They Know about Islam?

	Nov. 2001	March 2002	July 2003	July 2005	Aug. 2007	Aug. 2010
A great deal	6%	5%	4%	5%	7%	9%
Some	32%	29%	27%	28%	34%	35%
Not very much	37%	37%	39%	36%	33%	30%
Nothing at all	24%	28%	29%	30%	25%	25%
Don't know	1%	1%	1%	1%	1%	0%

SOURCE: Pew Research Center, August 19–22, 2010
Figures may not add to 100% because of rounding

A slightly higher percentage of Americans believed they knew "a great deal" or "some" about the Muslim religion in August 2010 then they did in November 2001. Illustration/XNR Productions/Cengage Learning, Gale.

which they lived and with their jobs. Forty percent of young Muslims reported that they were "thriving," the lowest level of any youth group surveyed, and young Muslims were the only group of young people in which a majority (51%) rated current economic conditions as poor. Young Muslims were also more likely than other groups of young people to say they experienced a lot of anger the day before.

Significantly, many of these findings surveyed young Muslims who came of age after the terrorist attacks of 9/11. Many surveys and other data have shown that in the wake of 9/11, it has become more difficult to be a Muslim in the United States. In the 2007 Pew survey, for example, 53 percent of Muslims expressed such a view, and a majority also complained of being unfairly singled out by the government for surveillance and monitoring. There has also been a rise in anti-Muslim hate crimes since 9/11.

Attitudes toward Islam have not improved over the last few years. A poll conducted by the Pew Research Center in August 2010 found that only 30 percent of Americans held a favorable view of Islam. This was down from 41 percent in 2005. Thirty-eight percent held an unfavorable view (up from 36 percent in 2005). Thirty-five

percent said that Islam was more likely than other religions to encourage violence, while 42 percent believed that Islam did not encourage violence more than other religions. This represented a marked change in views since 2002, when a Pew poll recorded figures of 25 percent (Islam encourages violence more than other religions) and 51 percent (does not encourage violence more than other religions).

The negative perceptions of Islam were also reflected in the recent rise in discrimination against Muslims in the workplace. In the year ending 30 September 2009, the Equal Employment Opportunity Commission (EEOC) received a record 803 complaints from Muslims, up 20 percent from the previous year. The complaints included harassment by other workers and disputes over the wearing of headscarves and the taking of prayer breaks.

In August 2010, the EEOC announced that it was suing JBS Swift, a meatpacking company in Greeley, Ohio, and Grand Island, Nebraska, for discrimination against Somali Muslim employees. In a press release the EEOC reported the nature of the case:

The complaints allege that supervisors and

coworkers threw blood, meat, and bones at the Muslim employees and called them offensive names. The complaint filed in Colorado alleges that there was offensive graffiti in the restrooms at the Greeley facility . . . which included comments such as "Somalis are disgusting" and "F..k Somalians", "F--k Muslims, and "F-⁴k Mohammed." The suit filed in Nebraska alleges that supervisors and coworkers made comments to Somali employees at the Grand Island facility such as "lazy Somali" and "go back to your country."

U.S. Equal Employment Commission, "EEOC Sues JBS Swift for Religious and National Origin Discrimination in Colorado and Nebraska," EEOC, 31 August 2010, http://www.eeoc.gov/eeoc/newsroom/release/8-31-10.cfm.

One interesting finding of the August 2010 Pew poll was that Americans, while continuing to hold unfavorable views of Islam, also say they know little about it. Fifty-five percent say they do not know very much (30%) or know nothing at all (25%) about the Muslim religion and its practices. Only 9 percent say they know a great deal. Aware of this lack of knowledge about their faith on the part of non-Muslims, many Islamic centers have, over the past few years, begun to organize "open houses" in which non-Muslims are invited into mosques to join with Muslims in prayer and discussion. Muslims hope that the open houses will help to dispel negative stereotypes about Islam. For example, The Islamic Center of Murfreesboro, which has faced such hostility to its building plans, hosted several "educational seminars" for non-Muslims, beginning in May 2010. The goal, as described on the Center's Web site, was "to spread knowledge about Islam in our community. . . . The ultimate goal is to improve diversity in Murfreesboro via knowledge and respect of one another, and create a healthy diverse community for everyone to live in." In October 2010, hundreds of mosques and Islamic centers across the United States offered "open houses" in an attempt to increase understanding and acceptance of Islam in their communities. In New York City, twenty mosques participated in an open-house program titled "A Week of Dialogue," intended to counteract the negative publicity surrounding the proposed Islamic center and mosque near Ground Zero.

Echoes of Past Anti-Catholicism

Many Muslims realize that the road to full acceptance in the United States may be a long one. Some may draw consolation from the fact that many other religious and immigrant groups have faced severe discrimination in the past. Roman Catholics, for example, experienced discrimination for more than a hundred years in largely-Protestant America. Catholics in the nineteenth and early twentieth century—many of them Irish immigrants—faced arguments similar to those used against Muslims today, such as: Catholicism is not compatible with democracy; Catholics are loyal to the pope, not to the United States, and are therefore not true Americans.

The Know-Nothing movement that flourished in the 1850s was particularly virulent in its anti-Catholic sentiment, mainly targeting Irish immigrants and native-born people of Irish origin. Know-Nothings believed that Catholics should not be eligible for U.S. citizenship, and they stirred up mobs to attack and burn Catholic churches and cathedrals across the country. In Cincinnati in December 1853, for example, a mob of six hundred men armed with weapons marched to the cathedral, intending to set it on fire. The police managed to disperse the mob before major damage had been done. In Maine in 1854, a Catholic priest was dragged from his church and tarred and feathered.

The justifications used for violence against Catholics is viewed by some as a forerunner of today's anti-Muslim sentiment, that sometimes views Muslims as loyal not to America but to some

This 1840s cartoon charges Irish and German immigrants to the United States with stealing elections, by showing a keg of Irish whiskey and a barrel of German beer running off with the ballot box. Fotosearch/AFP/Getty Images.

other foreign state, or to a transnational terrorist organization. Some of the wildest expressions of anti-Muslim feeling—the idea often heard in 2010 that the Muslims are planning to take over the U.S. government and impose Shari'a law on the country—have parallels in past anti-Catholic bigotry. A case in point is that of Sidney J. Catts, governor of Florida from 1917 to 1921, whose anti-Catholic stance was well known. At the time, World War I was raging in Europe, and the United States would soon join the conflict in alliance with Great Britain and France against Germany. In Florida, anti-German feeling, as well as anti-Catholicism, was running high. Catts claimed that German Catholic monks who had settled in

St. Leo, in Pasco County, Florida, were stockpiling weapons with which they planned to arm Florida's African Americans to create a general rising in favor of Germany. According to Catts, this would prepare the way for the pope, who would soon be forced to flee Italy, to invade Florida, move the Vatican to San Antonio, near St. Leo, and close down all the Protestant churches.

A hundred years later, it is hard to imagine that such an absurd scenario could be taken seriously. However, many people at the time did. Anti-Catholicism was justified as a matter of national security and an important part of the effort to preserve the American way of life. It is not difficult to see

Vandals defaced gravestones of French Muslim soldiers in this World War I cemetery at Ablain-Saint-Nazaire, France, on 6 April 2008. They also left a severed pig's head and inscribed graves with anti-Islam slogans. Sami Belloumi/Maxppp/Landov.

the parallels with today's Islamophobia. For most of the first decade of the twenty-first century, the United States has been fighting two wars, both of them—in Iraq and Afghanistan—in Islamic countries. Muslims in the United States must therefore, so goes the most extreme of the Islamophobic arguments, be on the side of America's foreign enemies and be plotting terrorist attacks in the United States as a prelude to taking over and destroying the American way of life.

Anti-Catholic bigotry continued into the twentieth century. In the early 1920s, such sentiments were noticeable for example in Birmingham, Alabama, a city that would later become a battleground in the civil rights movement of the 1950s and 1960s. Writing about anti-Semitism and anti-Catholicism in the South, Charles P. Sweeney pointed out that although Catholics

amounted to only 5 percent of Birmingham's population of 200,000:

> [T]he good people of Birmingham have been led to believe that Catholics are plotting control of the city, state, and national governments in the name of the Pope, that they seek the destruction of the public schools, and that they are a menace to the existence of the home as the basic unit of organized society. So firmly do the great majority of inhabitants believe these things that they go to the polls and elect men to public office on the single issue of protecting the Government and the community from Popery.

Charles P. Sweeney, "Leo Frank and Bigotry in the South," The Nation, 6 April 2009. http://www .thenation.com/article/leo-frank-and-bigotry-south.

The parallels between the two situations were highlighted in 2010, when more than one congressional candidate in the U.S. midterm elections in November thought it advantageous to take up a blatantly anti-Muslim stance in order to advance his or her chances of winning. Anti-Catholic sentiments largely faded away after World War II, and in 1960, John F. Kennedy became the first Catholic to be elected president of the United States. The nation is many years away from electing its first Muslim president, but thoughtful Muslims have expressed their belief that anti-Muslim sentiment will likely go the way of anti-Catholicism. However, they also acknowledge that Muslims have a role to play in encouraging increased tolerance towards their religion. Hadia Mubarak, a former president of the National Muslim Students Association, wrote about the dilemma facing her generation of Muslim Americans:

> How do we demonstrate our commitment to Islam is integral to our American identity? How do Muslims demonstrate that acts of worship—wearing headscarves, taking off work at noon on Friday to attend congregational prayers, building mosques, etc.—do not undermine our patriotism or pride in being American? The path ahead is arduous and demanding. Through bridge-building, civic participation, and political empowerment, Muslim Americans must define their own identity within American culture.
>
> "Muslim Americans: A National Portrait: An In-Depth Analysis of America's Most Diverse Religious Community," Muslim West Facts Project/Gallup Center for Muslim Studies, 2009, http://www.muslimwestfacts.com/mwf/116074/Muslim-Americans-National-Portrait.aspx.

The Case of Germany

Although Muslim Americans may have experienced a rise in anti-Muslim sentiment over the last few years, the overall position of Muslims in

German Chancellor Angela Merkel and German State Minister Maria Boehmer pose in front of the Ottoman-era Sultanahmet Mosque, also called the Blue Mosque, in Istanbul, Turkey, 30 March 2010. Merkel has stated that Germany has failed to properly integrate immigrants into the German culture. Osman Orsal/Reuters.

the United States is markedly better than their counterparts in Western Europe. While American Muslims are on par with the general population in terms of income and generally consider themselves to be part of mainstream U.S. society, a Pew Global Attitude survey in 2006 showed that Muslims in Britain, France, Germany, and Spain

Thilo Sarrazin, a German central bank board member, holds his book *Germany Abolishes Itself: How We Are Risking The Future of Our Nation* during a news conference in Berlin, Germany, 30 August 2010. Sarrazin sparked outrage over remarks stereotyping Muslims and Jews in his book. AP Images/Gero Breloer.

lagged behind the rest of the population in that respect. In Germany, for example, 53 percent of Muslims reported annual incomes of less than 18,000 euros, compared to 35 percent of non-Muslims.

In Germany, Pew found that a majority (51%) of Muslims thought that Europeans were hostile to Muslims, and only 34 percent of Germans said that immigration from the Middle East and North Africa (i.e. Muslim immigration) was a good thing, compared with 59 percent who considered it a negative. German Muslims were also far more likely than Muslims in other Western European countries to want to remain distinct rather than assimilating to the majority culture. Fifty-two percent of Muslims took this view,

which was also taken by a large majority (76%) of German nationals.

The perception that Muslims in Germany form a group apart from the mainstream, and that such a situation produces negative consequences for the nation as a whole, made international news in October 2010. German Chancellor Angela Merkel, who leads Germany's largest political party, the Christian Democratic Union (CDU), bluntly told a meeting of young CDU members in Potsdam that multiculturalism in Germany, in which people of different cultural backgrounds learn to live harmoniously together, had failed. Quoted in the *Christian Science Monitor*, Merkel said that at "the beginning of the 1960s our country called the foreign workers to come to Germany and now they live in our country. . . . We kidded ourselves a while. We said: 'They won't stay, [after some time] they will be gone,' but this isn't reality. And of course, the approach [to build] a multicultural [society] and to live side by side and to enjoy each other . . . has failed, utterly failed."

Merkel was referring to the Muslims from Turkey who began coming to Germany in 1961 as guest workers. Over the years, the government was reluctant to grant them citizenship, regarding them as temporary workers. However, fifty years later these workers still reside in the country. In 2010, there were about four million Muslim Turks living in Germany, forming Germany's largest immigrant group. However, for the most part the Turkish Muslims continue to live in their own enclaves, segregated from the general population. Many of them do not speak German and lack the skills and training necessary to thrive in Germany's advanced economy. They are also more dependent on the welfare system than other groups in Germany.

Merkel was careful to point out that immigrants were still welcome in Germany. For many European countries, an aging population and declining birth rates make immigration essential to meet the needs of the economy. In contrast, just a

Muslim women wearing various type of Islamic veils: a Hijab (top left), a Niqab (top right) a Tchador (bottom left) and a Burqa. AFP Photo/AFP/Getty Images/newscom.

few days before Merkel's speech, a German think tank released a study in which 30 percent of Germans said the country was "overrun with foreigners" who were in Germany mainly for the welfare benefits. This suggested that the public mood in Germany was hardly welcoming to either new or existing immigrants. The runaway success of a book published in September, in which Thilo Sarrazin, a prominent banker and former government minister, claimed that Muslim immigrants were of lower intelligence than ethnic Germans, highlighted the deep divide even further.

Public Displays of Islam

One of the issues that Germany, like many other European countries, is trying to address is whether Muslim women should be permitted to wear distinctive Muslim clothing such as the hijab and burqa.

The word "hijab" refers to the head covering worn by many Muslim women, a headscarf that covers the forehead, hair, and often the neck. In a broader sense, "hijab" refers to modesty and humility, which many Muslims define as covering all but the hands, feet, and face for Muslim women. Other forms of distinctive Muslim clothing include the burqa, a full-body covering with a thin mesh strip across the eyes, allowing the woman to see through the mesh, and the niqab, which shows only the eyes. Opinions on how hijab should be defined vary. Conservative scholars in the Muslim community generally advocate the burqa and cite verses from the Qur'an to support their views.

A veiled woman shows her face to a policewoman to verify her identity before casting her ballot at a polling station in Amman, Jordan, 9 November 2010. Muhammad Hamed/ Reuters.

Liberal scholars in the community tend to advocate a broader interpretation that does not require specific covering or veiling, but instead promotes modesty in general, also citing Qur'an scripture.

To complicate matters further, opponents of Islamic dress frame the issue within the context of women's rights. It is often assumed that in male-dominated Islamic societies women are compelled to wear veils and burqas. Many Muslim women, however, say they choose to do so; no one forces them to.

Those who object to face veils and full-body covering for Muslim women also cite security reasons for their opposition. For example, if an incident in a public building gives rise to a complaint or a criminal charge, security officers, law enforcement personnel, or members of the general public may be asked to identify people, a task made more difficult if any of the people involved were wearing a veil that covered the face. According to this argument, Muslim women are off-limits in investigations of potential criminals or terrorists because of their traditional beliefs.

The point is simply that public safety is a legitimate and primary concern in any society. In the United States, for example (where there is no ban on face-covering veils), many banks ask that people entering the premises remove all hats, hoods, or sunglasses. There is no religious or political element behind such a policy, which is simply followed in order to promote security. In addition, in Western societies today, many routine business practices, including acquiring or renewing a driver's license or public library borrower's card, require photographic identification in order to verify the identity of the applicant. Someone whose face is veiled, either in a photo or in person, will not be able to satisfy the requirements in such cases.

The French Burqa Ban

Head covering among Muslims in Western society has, since the 1970s, taken on political as well as religious meaning. For nearly two decades the issue of headscarves worn by female Muslims has been a topic of debate in French society. In France, religion is treated as a private matter; a 1905 law separates church and state. Students and employees who wanted to wear religious garments or symbols (such as crucifix necklaces or yarmulkes) were generally allowed to do so as long as the symbols were relatively unobtrusive. As the Muslim population increased in France and more young women entered schools wearing headscarves, this highly visible mode of religious expression became a source of debate, culminating in the 2004 French law banning conspicuous religious symbols (including yarmulkes and hijab) from schools and government institutions.

In June 2009, French President Nicolas Sarkozy sparked controversy when he endorsed banning the burqa in France, saying, "We cannot accept, in our country, women imprisoned behind a mesh, cut off from society, deprived of all identity. That is not the French republic's idea of women's dignity." As wearing the burqa

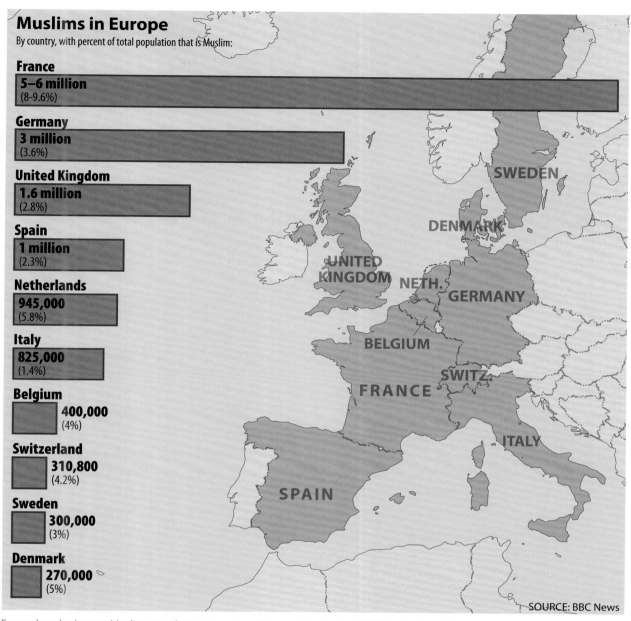

Muslims in Europe

By country, with percent of total population that is Muslim:

France
5–6 million
(8–9.6%)

Germany
3 million
(3.6%)

United Kingdom
1.6 million
(2.8%)

Spain
1 million
(2.3%)

Netherlands
945,000
(5.8%)

Italy
825,000
(1.4%)

Belgium
400,000
(4%)

Switzerland
310,800
(4.2%)

Sweden
300,000
(3%)

Denmark
270,000
(5%)

SOURCE: BBC News

France has the largest Muslim population in western Europe. Illustration/XNR Productions/Cengage Learning, Gale.

has become increasingly widespread in France's Muslim community, many in the government have worried publicly that women may not be adopting the burqa voluntarily. Further, they see the burqa as a threat to French secularism. Critics of the ban say that banning the burqa in France would further stigmatize Muslims, who already feel marginalized. France is home to five million Muslims, the largest Muslim population in Western Europe.

In January 2010, a parliamentary commission in France recommended that both the burqa and niqab be banned in all public places. Members of the commission said that the decision was based on the issue of women's rights and that 74 percent of French citizens supported such a ban. In July 2010, the lower house of the French Parliament voted overwhelmingly to ban full face and body coverings in public. The upper house approved the measure in September.

On 7 October 2010, the French constitutional court approved, with minor changes, a ban on full

A 31-year-old French Muslim woman, Anne, (assumed name), who was fined for wearing a niqab while driving, along with her husband Lies Hebbadj arrive for a news conference in Nantes, western France, 26 April 2010. Stephane Mahe/Reuters.

Islamic body coverings already passed by parliament. The court made an exception to the ban in the case of public places of worship. Unless blocked by the European Court of Human Rights, the ban is scheduled to take effect in 2011. Under the law, women wearing the full veil may be fined and those who force women to cover themselves face stiff fines and possible jail time. The law is supported by the French public by a margin of over four to one. The Pew Global Attitudes Project found in a survey that 82 percent approved of the law and only 17 percent disapproved.

In spite of the law's popularity at home, just three weeks after its passage, the French received an unpleasant reminder of how negatively the news was received in certain quarters in the world. The Arabic news network Al-Jazeera aired an audio recording of a speaker claiming to be al-Qaeda leader Osama bin Laden. In the recording, the speaker threatened to kill French citizens in retaliation for their support of the U.S. war effort in Afghanistan and for the law banning face-covering veils.

Turkish Secularism Threatened by Headscarves?

Turkey faces a different challenge regarding headscarves and politics. Strict secular laws dating back to the foundation of modern Turkey ban the wearing of headscarves in government institutions. Women are in general allowed to wear headscarves but students, teachers, and government employees are not. This strict secularism was instituted in the 1920s by Turkish leader Mustafa Kemal, known as Ataturk, who saw the strict separation of church and state as essential to his efforts to modernize Turkey.

In France, Muslims make up 7–8 percent of the population; in Turkey, 99 percent of the population identifies as Muslim. Turkey's law banning headscarves first received international attention in 1999 when a newly elected female member of parliament, Merve Kavakçi, attended her swearing-in ceremony wearing a headscarf. She was denied her swearing-in and later had her Turkish citizenship revoked, though for reasons unrelated to the headscarf. In 2008, Turkish president Abdullah Gul signed legislation removing a ban on wearing headscarves in Turkish universities, claiming the lifting of the ban did not clash with Turkey's secular laws. On 5 June 2008, however, Turkey's Constitutional Court ruled that removing the ban went against the founding principles of the Turkish constitution.

The issue remains contentious, and support has grown for the lifting of the ban. But in October 2010, the Turkish government failed to win parliamentary support to remove the ban on headscarves at universities. The secularists who opposed the lifting of the ban feared that to do so would erode the secular principles on which modern Turkey is founded. The government, on the other hand, argued the case from the viewpoint of promoting religious freedom.

Belgians Struggle to Find Balance

The issue of the hijab and burqa also proved controversial in Belgium. After experimenting for years with allowing students free choice over the issue of headscarves, state-run schools in Flanders, Belgium, banned all religious symbols, including headscarves, in 2009. School officials declared that they imposed the ban to ensure equality among students. The decision sparked protests from Muslim conservatives, and government representatives believe that the controversy will probably result in the formation of state-funded Muslim schools.

In April 2010, Belgium became the first European country to ban the burqa—which covers a woman's entire body—in addition to face-covering Islamic veils. The ban, which was presented as a women's rights issue and an affirmation of Western values, had broad political support that included an unusual political alliance between conservatives and feminists. Opponents of the ban in Belgium, who included Amnesty International, characterized it as an attack on religious freedom. Some people also pointed out that the law was

largely symbolic, since there are only about 200 women in Belgium who wear the burqa.

A Double Standard in Germany?

Germany has also grappled with the conflict between secular laws and religious expression in an increasingly diverse culture. In 2003, the Federal Constitutional Court in Karlsruhe ruled that teachers could be banned from wearing

A member of the pro-Islamic human rights organization of Ozgur-Der chants slogans in Istanbul, Turkey, 6 October 2007, during a protest against the headscarf ban in schools and universities. AP Images/Serkan Senturk.

The minaret of the Mahmud Mosque in Zurich, Switzerland, 29 November 2009. AP Images/Alessandro Della Bella.

wear their religious habits. Critics characterize the ban on headscarves as a form of discrimination against Muslims and against women.

In February 2009, the New York–based Human Rights Watch (HRW) produced a report titled, "Discrimination in the Name of Neutrality: Headscarf Bans for Teachers and Civil Servants in Germany." The title pointed to the central issue: the ban on headscarves is meant to ensure equality and neutrality. However, HRW argues, since in practice almost all the people who want to wear headscarves are Muslim women, the law in fact discriminates against them. HRW declared that such laws "contravene Germany's international obligations to guarantee individuals the right to freedom of religion and equality before the law. These laws . . . discriminate against Muslim women, excluding them from teaching and other public sector employment on the basis of their faith."

In its report, which was based on eighty-four interviews conducted in 2008, HRW pointed out that in some cases, teachers have faced disciplinary action or even been fired for refusing to remove their headscarves. The ban has also had other negative effects on female teachers:

> These restrictions have led some women to leave their home state or leave Germany altogether, to prolong maternity and other leave from their employment, or to leave teaching after years of studies and investment in developing their skills. Women concerned feel alienated and excluded, even though many had lived in Germany for decades or even their entire lives, or are German-born converts to Islam.

Based on their interviews, HRW found that many Muslim women who had been affected by the ban on headscarves felt that in some way the German authorities regarded them as objects of suspicion. One interviewee, an elementary school teacher who converted to Islam, had worn a headscarf in school for decades. She told HRW:

headscarves without infringing their religious freedom, if such bans were formally enacted in laws. Since then eight of Germany's sixteen states have enacted laws banning the wearing of headscarves by public school teachers and other civil servants. Some of these states, however, allow for symbols from such religions as Christianity or Judaism. Catholic nuns, for example, are allowed to

"One has the feeling 'we don't want you'. . . Where should I go? I belong here. . . . I would never have thought that would be possible."

Human Rights Watch called for German state governments to repeal legislation on religious dress and symbols. The rights group also said that cases in which a teacher's conduct is thought to infringe the principle of neutrality should be resolved through disciplinary procedures on a case-by-case basis rather than by a blanket law that only addresses appearance.

However, as of 2010, the eight states maintained their headscarf bans, based on the declared need to keep religious expression out of schools and so avoid unfairly influencing impressionable children.

Alarming Minarets

Headscarves are not the only "public display of Islam" that has met with disfavor in Europe. On 29 November 2009, Swiss voters had their say on a controversial proposal to ban the building of minarets, a common architectural feature of mosques. Switzerland is home to about 400,000 Muslims; though there has been little evidence of radical Muslim activity, the Swiss have expressed concern with what they perceive as an increasing Islamic presence in their country. While other European nations have focused on headscarves as a visible symbol of the growing presence of Muslims in their communities, the Swiss have focused on minarets. The Swiss government urged voters to reject the ban, fearing that it would hurt Switzerland's international reputation. However, the ban was passed with the support of about 57 percent of Swiss voters. Hafid Ouardiri, an Algerian-born Muslim living in Switzerland, lodged an appeal against the results of the referendum with the European Court of Human Rights in Strasbourg on 16 December 2009. Ouardiri wants the minaret ban declared incompatible with the European Convention on Human Rights. No decision on the ban had been reached as of November 2010.

Isolation and Assimilation

Mosques and headscarves have acted as lightening rods around the growing presence of Islam in the West. But each is also symbolic of the larger issue of accommodating the Islamic faith inside a western country. European countries have sometimes welcomed immigrants that fully embrace the host country's customs, but are uncomfortable with the existence of an insular community. Observant Muslims, much like the Amish in the United States, often feel that their very existence is dependent on maintaining separateness and strictly adhering to customs that visibly emphasize their difference. It is this tension between personal and national identity that is played out in the arena of religious symbols.

Western Influence in the Islamic World

As Western nations debate the issue of how to accommodate Muslim culture and lifestyle choices, Muslim nations are debating the extent to which they can accommodate Western culture and Western visitors. Although there is no large-scale immigration from the West into Islamic countries, Western culture is pervasive, conveyed through movies, television, books, music, consumer goods, advertising, and the Internet.

There are a wide variety of approaches to this issue in the Islamic world. In the eyes of many Muslims, Western culture is shallow and materialistic, associated with undesirable things: pornography, indecency, drugs, and social problems such as the breakdown of the family, leading to high divorce rates.

Some countries do everything they can to keep what they perceive as harmful Western influences out of their country. For example, Iran banned Western popular music from state-run television and radio stations in 2005. Many Islamic countries have special police for enforcing Shari'a law, which includes imposing standards of modesty in dress and behavior. Western visitors, especially women, are required to respect such local customs, and there can be adverse consequences if they do not. In 2009, a young Western couple was arrested in Dubai, in the United Arab Emirates, for kissing in a restaurant. They were tried and convicted of inappropriate behavior as well as illegal drinking and were sentenced to one month in prison. Some countries, such as Saudi Arabia, enforce a strict ban on the sale and consumption of alcohol.

In other parts of the Islamic world, however, the rules are not so strict. In a large city such as Istanbul, in Turkey—a Muslim country with a secular government and constitution—Western visitors are allowed to drink alcohol in public and behave much as they would in a Western city. Even in Iran, where the government adopts a strict anti-Western stance, many young Iranian people adopt Western styles of dress such as jeans and T-shirts, and women wear jewelry at home, although not in public. Although there is concern about the rise of Islamophobia in western countries in recent years, historically it is Islamic nations that have reacted negatively to non-Islamic influences in their society, and laws mandating appearance and behavior are commonplace in most Islamic nations. All inhabitants of these countries, including foreign-born residents and temporary visitors, are subject to these laws, regardless of their religious or cultural background.

Incendiary Cartoons

On Friday, 1 January 2010, Danish cartoonist Kurt Westergaard was enjoying a relaxing evening at home with Stephanie, his five-year-old granddaughter. Westergaard is the cartoonist whose depiction of the Muslim prophet Muhammad with a bomb in his turban caused a furious reaction in the Islamic world when it appeared in a Danish newspaper in 2005. Since that time Westergaard has received numerous death threats.

Westergaard's quiet evening was interrupted by the sound of breaking glass. It was soon apparent that an intruder had entered the house through a window. Fearing the worst, Westergaard ran to his designated "panic" room, a specially equipped bathroom, and called the police by pressing an emergency button. The intruder was armed with an ax and a knife, and he tried to break the door down, shouting and swearing as he did so.

Ten police cars arrived on the scene within minutes. The intruder rushed outside and smashed a police car window with the ax. The police shot him twice, and he received non-life-threatening injuries. He was arrested and later charged with attempted murder. The attacker turned out to be a Somali man with ties to a terrorist group.

The Infamous Danish Drawing

This violent incident brought the case of the Danish cartoons back into the public eye. The story began on 30 September 2005, when the Danish newspaper *Jyllands-Posten* (Jutland Report) published twelve cartoons depicting Muhammad. Several of the cartoons were deemed to be deliberately provocative caricatures of Muhammad, the founder of Islam. The one by Westergaard, for example, showed Muhammad with a lit bomb atop his head. Initially, protests against the cartoon by Muslim groups were peaceful and local, but within months reprints of the cartoons appeared in several European Union newspapers and online. An unexpected wave of massive, and sometimes violent, protests worldwide resulted in an estimated 50 to 150 deaths in January and February 2006.

In early September 2005, *Jyllands-Posten* had called for Danish artists to submit cartoon representations of the founder of Islam as they saw him. The newspaper wished to initiate a debate about self-censorship in the media with regard to Islam. The project was, in part, a reaction to the experience of a Danish writer who had been unable to find illustrators willing to provide portraits of Muhammad for his children's biography. The *Jyllands-Posten* editors assumed that illustrators

Muslims in Copenhagen, Denmark, protest against Danish newspaper *Jyllands Posten* for publishing a cartoon of the Islamic prophet Muhammad wearing a bomb-shaped turban with an ignited fuse, 15 October 2005. Dean Pictures/Francis Dean/newscom.

had declined because they feared reprisal from Muslims, though critics have since suggested that artists may have declined out of respect for Muslim religious beliefs. The newspaper held the position that satire and irreverence were central elements of journalism in the Danish tradition of freedom of expression. In the editor's opinion, taboos on any subject violated Denmark's traditions; he claimed that other religions were subject to the same open treatment in his newspaper.

The cartoons were highly offensive to many Muslims for a number of reasons. Sunni Muslims have a long tradition of prohibiting the depiction of Muhammad. To some, almost any depiction of the prophet amounts to blasphemy. For many other Muslims, the cartoons were offensive because they believed the pictures stereotyped Muslim people as ignorant terrorists and were disrespectful to the religion.

The publication of the cartoons drew protests from Danish Muslim leaders, who organized a peaceful demonstration of about 3,500 people in Copenhagen, asking for an apology from the *Jyllands-Posten*. The newspaper refused. On 19 October 2005, ambassadors from eleven Muslim countries asked to meet with Danish Prime Minister Anders Fogh Rasmussen to discuss the controversial cartoons. To the dismay of many Muslims, Rasmussen refused to meet with the ambassadors. A group of Danish Muslims then began a campaign to publicize the cartoon issue throughout the Middle East.

Protesters hurled stones and fire bombs as they climb over the gate of the Danish embassy in Tehran, 6 February 2006. This was the second attack on an embassy in the city over a Danish newspaper's publication of caricatures of the Prophet Muhammad. AP Images/Hasan Sarbakhshian.

A meeting of the leaders of fifty-seven Muslim countries convened in December in Mecca, Saudi Arabia, regarding the cartoons. The leaders condemned the cartoons as a desecration of the image of Muhammad. In January and February 2006, newspapers in Norway, Austria, France, Italy, Germany, and Spain reprinted the cartoons, declaring their support for the principle of freedom of expression. Reactions were prompt. Libya and Saudi Arabia withdrew their ambassadors to Denmark. Throughout the Middle East, Danish flags were burned and a widespread boycott of Danish products was established. Activists in the Palestinian territories made death threats against the cartoonists.

The fury over the cartoons escalated in February 2006, with massive, often destructive, demonstrations in Muslim countries in the Middle East, Africa, Indonesia, and the Philippines. Danish embassies in Indonesia, Syria, and Iran were attacked and some set afire. Demonstrations with more than 50,000 participants in Afghanistan and Pakistan raged out of control; in numerous incidents, protesters were killed by the police. Iran, Libya, Syria, and Lebanon all experienced violent protests, with deaths, injuries, property destruction, and arrests. Christian churches and Western businesses, including McDonalds and KFC restaurants, were attacked. Rioting also occurred in London, England; Brussels, Belgium;

and Madrid, Spain. Prime Minister Rasmussen called the rioting a "global crisis."

The violence waned by March 2006, with many moderate Muslim leaders calling for calm. Some commentators called the cartoon conflict a clash of cultures between the Muslim countries and the West. On one level, the concept of freedom of speech upheld by the Danish newspaper seemed to clash severely with the deeply held religious beliefs of many Muslims. On the other hand, many Western critics of the Danish newspaper's position argued that newspapers always exercise choice in what they publish and frequently avoid publishing stories that are disrespectful or painful to targeted groups unless there is a public benefit to the publication. Conversely, some Muslim journalists upheld the Danish newspaper's right to express itself freely.

Other observers contend that the controversy about the cartoons was political rather than cultural, occurring in a context of bitter resentments in the Middle East over the Iraq War and the ongoing conflict between the Israelis and the Palestinians. One group of commentators pointed out that, beyond being highly disrespectful to Islam, the Muhammad cartoons reflected what many perceive as a pervasive anti-Muslim sentiment in the West. In Denmark, strong anti-immigrant sentiments have shaped the nation's politics, and protesting Danish Muslim leaders contended that the nation's 200,000 Muslim immigrants faced a new brand of racial discrimination. The worldwide response to the cartoons among Muslims was attributed by some scholars to anger at what many Muslims perceive as Western discrimination against Islam.

On the other side of the argument, commentators upholding the Danish newspaper's position on free expression cited very different political causes of the violence. Several journalists and observers argued that extremists and some political leaders in Muslim countries had exploited the initially minor cartoon incident to inflame Muslim

A group organized by a Muslim leader protests cartoons published by a Danish newspaper, outside the Danish consulate in New York, 17 February 2006. The cartoon showed the Islamic prophet Muhammad wearing a bomb-shaped turban with an ignited fuse. AP Images/Dima Garvyrsh.

people against the West. Iran, at that time being isolated by the West for its alleged development of nuclear power, was accused by many, including the U.S. government, of using the cartoon incident to incite its people to rioting and violence aimed at the West.

Resentments over the cartoons smoldered among some groups over the next two years. In February 2008, Danish police arrested three suspects accused of conspiring to kill Westergaard. The *Jyllands-Posten* responded to this news by reprinting the cartoons, and many Danish newspapers followed suit.

The aftershocks of the cartoon controversy were still being felt in 2009, when Turkey, a predominantly Muslim nation and member of NATO (the North Atlantic Treaty Organization, a military alliance of Western powers), raised strong objections to the nomination of Rasmussen as the next head of NATO. Rasmussen's stance on the cartoon issue had angered Muslims. Turkey withdrew its objection to Rasmussen after U.S. president Barack Obama offered his assurances that Turkish representatives would play a prominent and active part in NATO affairs.

In 2010, with the attack on Westergaard at his home, the violence related to the 2005 cartoon reached into its fifth year. In May, the home of Lars Vilks, another Swedish cartoonist who had depicted Muhammad was attacked by arsonists. In 2007, Vilks depicted Muhammad with the body of a dog in a Swedish newspaper. In response, Muslim clerics in Iraq and Somalia declared a fatwa (decree of death) on Vilks, offering a reward to anyone who would murder him.

German Chancellor Angela Merkel stepped into the Muhammad cartoon controversy on 8 September 2010 when she presented Westergaard with a press freedom award. At the ceremony in Potsdam, Merkel stressed that "freedom of opinion" was part of European culture. Merkel's attendance at the ceremony was criticized as foolhardy by some commentators in the German press and was called insensitive by Germany's Central Muslim Council.

What If Everybody Draws Muhammad?

In April 2010, Comedy Central aired its 200th episode of the popular animated comedy series *South Park*, in which Muhammad was presented in a bear suit. The episode, which also featured Buddha, Jesus Christ, Moses, Krishna, Joseph Smith, and Lao Tzu, prompted immediate threats of violence by Islamist groups, including death threats. A New York–based group called Revolution Muslim "warned" the show's creators, Matt Stone and Trey Parker, that they "will probably wind up like Theo Van Gogh." Van Gogh was a Dutch filmmaker who, with Somali-born writer Ayaan Hirsi Ali, produced a film that was harshly critical of the treatment of women in Islamic countries. The film was shown on Dutch television in August 2004. Van Gogh received death threats and was shot to death on an Amsterdam street in November 2004 by a radical Muslim man.

Muhammad was also featured in the 201st episode of *South Park* this time obscured by a black box. All instances of Muhammad's name were "bleeped" out.

In October, a radicalized American Muslim named Adam Chesser pleaded guilty to several charges related to his active support of Al Shabaab, an ultra-Islamist Somali terrorist group. Chesser, a twenty-year-old native of Virginia, allegedly encouraged attacks on staff writers for *South Park*. He also posted the personal contact information of members of a Facebook group promoting "Everybody Draw Muhammad Day" to an Islamic militant site. Prosecutors said that Chesser's posting of this personal information of the Facebook group members would put their lives at risk "for many years to come." The group had begun the "Everybody Draw Muhammad Day" movement in 2010 to protest the fear-driven censorship of such programs as *South Park*. The movement's founders set 20 May as "Everybody Draw

Protesters march outside the Theodore Levin Federal Courthouse in Detroit, 8 January 2010. Inside Umar Farouk Abdulmutallab, the Nigerian suspect who allegedly tried to set off an explosive device aboard a U.S. airliner, pleaded not guilty to charges of trying to ignite an explosive on the plane on Christmas Day, 2009. AP Images/Carlos Osorio.

Muhammad Day" and encouraged followers to draw and display pictures of Muhammad on this day. The idea caught on, and the Facebook page soon had more than 71,000 followers. There were protests in Pakistan, and Facebook was blocked in that country until it voluntarily agreed to block the page for users in India and Pakistan.

The idea for "Everybody Draw Muhammad Day" originated from a cartoon by Molly Norris, a cartoonist in Seattle, Washington. In this drawing, which appeared on various Web sites in April, Norris facetiously showed six anthromorphized everyday objects, including a cup of coffee and box of pasta, each claiming to be the true likeness of Muhammad.

In late April 2010, Norris dissociated herself from the censorship controversy about Islam. Unfortunately, her disavowal of any involvement did not spare her the frightening consequences of having her name linked to "Everybody Draw Muhammad Day." She received numerous serious death threats, including one from Anwar al-Awlaki, a radical Muslim cleric who lives in Yemen, who issued a fatwa calling for her death. The fatwa was published in an English-language magazine aimed at young Muslims in the United States. On the advice of the Federal Bureau of Investigation, Norris changed her name and went into hiding. On 15 September 2010, the *Seattle Weekly*, where Norris's cartoons used to appear, made the following announcement:

The gifted artist is alive and well, thankfully. But on the insistence of top security specialists at the FBI, she is, as they put it, "going ghost": moving, changing her name, and essentially wiping away her identity. . . . She is, in effect, being put into a witness-protection program, except, as she notes, without the government picking up the tab.

Meanwhile, Kurt Westergaard, the seventy-five-year-old Danish cartoonist whose depiction of Muhammad first lit the fires of the censorship controversy, published an autobiography, *The Man Behind the Lines*, in November. The book includes a new version of the cartoon, in which Westergaard depicts himself looking at his 2005 cartoon with a bomb on his own head. Although the cartoonist said he would like to return to the days when he was just an ordinary artist, he added that he did not regret the publication of the offending cartoon or that of similar cartoons by other artists. He was quoted in a *Reuters* article as follows: "The cartoons have contributed to starting a necessary debate on freedom of speech. That has caused friction between Muslim and Western Christian democratic cultures and that is something we need to get through. But it should preferably happen peacefully."

Few people of goodwill on either side of the long-running, fractious encounter between Islam and the West would disagree with such sentiments, but if the simmering disputes over mosques, headscarves, and cartoons are any guide, it will not be easy to address these issues with peaceful goodwill on both sides. There are many politicians who have argued that Islam and Western secularism are wholly incompatible. Still, there are others who see a brighter future for relations between Islam and the West. As Susilo Bambang Yudhoyono, president of Indonesia, wrote in an *Economist* article titled "How to Let Islam and the West Live in Harmony" published 13 November 2009, "People all over the world are beginning to realise that co-operation yields dividends not only within civilisations but also between and among them. . . . A clash of civilisations is not inevitable. A confluence of civilisations is entirely possible. For millennia, our archipelago has been home to many currents of civilisation. This is why, in today's Indonesia, democracy, Islam and modernity can go hand-in-hand."

Research and Exploration

Ahmed, Akbar, *Journey into America: The Challenge of Islam*, Washington DC: Brookings Institution Press, 2010.

Ahmed is a scholar of Islam and in this book he explains what it is like to be a Muslim in the United States after 9/11. The book includes many interviews with American Muslims. Ahmed and his researchers traveled for a year, visiting seventy-five American cities.

Ali-Karamali, Sumbul, *The Muslim Next Door: The Qur'an, the Media, and That Veil Thing*, Ashland, OR: White Cloud Press, 2008.

Ali-Karamali grew up as a Muslim in the West, and in this book she explains the tenets of Islam in a straightforward and engaging manner. She also explains such topics as jihad, Islamic fundamentalism, and the status of women. Full of lively anecdotes, the book has been highly praised by reviewers.

"Daily Show: Michael Bloomberg," *The Daily Show with Jon Stewart*, 26 August 2010, http://www.thedailyshow.com/watch/thu-august-26-2010/michael-bloomberg

Jon Stewart interviews New York mayor Michael Bloomberg, who supports the planned construction of a mosque near the World Trade Center site and predicts during the show that the controversy will disappear after the midterm elections.

"France Recommends Ban on Veil," *AlJazeeraEnglish*, 26 January 2010, http://english.aljazeera.net/news/europe/2010/01/201012661032640718.html

In this video segment, people in France discuss France's ban on head-covering veils in public places.

Islamicity.com, http://www.islamicity.com

This site is an exhaustive resource on all aspects of Islam and includes text and video.

"Islam Struggles for Place in U.S. Religious Mosaic," *PBS Newshour*, 24 August 2010, http://www.pbs.org/newshour/bb/religion/july-dec10/islam2_08-24.html

In this twelve-minute segment, Gwen Ifill discusses the place of Islam in the United States with a Christian minister who is president of the Interfaith Alliance; an expert on religious militants; and a scholar of Islam.

Klausen, Jyette, *The Cartoons that Shook the World*, New Haven, CT: Yale University Press, 2009.

A book about the Danish cartoon controversy. Klausen argues that the reaction was manipulated by those with political interests in Denmark and Egypt, and also by Islamic extremists who wanted to bring down the government in Pakistan and other countries. The book itself has been controversial because Yale University Press removed all images from it, including the cartoons.

"Quran and Mosque Controversy," *CBS News*, 9 September 2010, http://www.cbsnews.com/video/watch/?id=6849235n.

This is a video segment in which Southern Baptist Convention's Dr. Richard Land and Rep. Keith Ellison (D-Minn.), a Muslim Congressman, discuss the planned burning of the Qur'an by a Florida pastor.

"Should Mosque Be Built Near Ground Zero in NYC?" *PBS Newshour*, 10 August 2010, http://www.pbs.org/newshour/video/module_byid.html?s=news01n4231qf34

This sixteen-minute segment includes interviews with four people, two of whom lost relatives in 9/11.

"Why an Islamic Center at Ground Zero," *Larry King Live*, 14 September 2010, http://www.cnn.com/video/#/video/bestoftv/2010/09/14/lkl.imam.ground.zero.mosque.cnn?iref=allsearch

Imam Feisal Abdul Rauf explains why his organization has chosen to build an Islamic Center so close to Ground Zero.

Mexico's Drug War

Stringer Mexico/Reuters.

It was like a scene from a horror film: The victim was chopped into seven pieces, his limbs and skull tossed into a box separate from his torso. Most horrifying of all, the man's face had been sliced off and stitched to the outer surface of a soccer ball. The grotesque creation was left near Los Mochis City Hall in Sinaloa state with a note that read, "Happy New Year, because this will be your last."

Three years into Mexico's drug war, murder had become an everyday occurrence for police and soldiers. But the scene in Los Mochis—located in the western coastal state of Sinaloa, far from the U.S. border—shocked even their jaded sensibilities. The victim, Hugo Hernandez, had been kidnapped in the neighboring state of Sonora for reasons unknown to police. The region is home base to the Sinaloa cartel, one of the most powerful drug trafficking organizations in Mexico.

The shocking murder is in some ways a fit-ting summary of the Mexican drug war: brutal, inexplicable bloodshed that can strike anywhere and at any time, with government officials seem-ingly unable to stem the tide of violence. In the early months of the war, with government forces trumpeting major arrests and seizures, a typical Mexican citizen might have been inclined to ask, "Are things better now?" Years later, with escalat-ing hostilities and no end in sight, a more fitting question might be, "Could things possibly get any worse?"

The War Begins

In late 2006, the Mexican government launched an all-out assault against the drug traf-ficking organizations that had in many ways taken over the country. The result was a long, bloody conflict that has yet to be resolved. As of Novem-ber 2010, more than 30,000 people have been killed in a seemingly endless string of assaults,

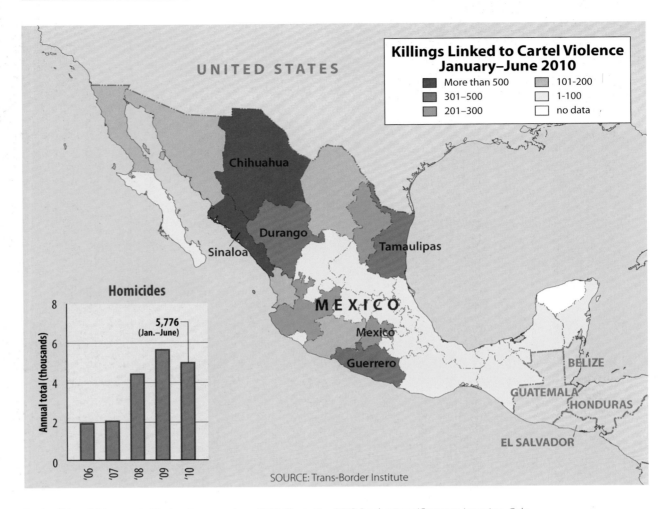

Killings Linked to Cartel Violence January–June 2010

More than 500	101-200
301–500	1-100
201–300	no data

Homicides

5,776
(Jan.–June)

Annual total (thousands)

'06 '07 '08 '09 '10

SOURCE: Trans-Border Institute

Regional homicide rates in Mexico, January - June 2010. Illustration/XNR Productions/Cengage Learning, Gale.

ambushes, shootouts, and executions. This is five times higher than the total number of American soldiers killed in Iraq and Afghanistan combined.

Mexico's drug war has a direct effect on the United States. Trafficking in Mexico leads to drug-related crimes and drug abuse north of the border, where Mexico's drug cartels have developed a growing presence. With the fates of the two nations intertwined, the United States has offered assistance to Mexico in its struggle to shut down the traffickers. However, the hardest task lies with the Mexican citizens, who must stand against corruption and unspeakable brutality for a chance at preserving their own future.

The Flow of Drugs and Money

The illegal drug trade operates as a complex web that spans the globe. Opium-based drugs such as heroin originate from poppies grown mostly in Afghanistan and other countries in South Asia. Marijuana, grown in small, controlled environments around the world, is also cultivated as a large-scale crop in areas such as northwestern

Migrants trying to pass through Mexico en route to the United States have fallen victim to drug violence. Pictured is the funeral of Miguel Carcamo in El Guante, Honduras, on 2 September 2010. He was killed by drug traffickers in Tamaulipas, probably because he refused to carry drugs across the U.S. border for them. Edgard Garrido/Reuters. ▶

Packs of marijuana stored in a drug smugglers' tunnel in Tijuana. The tunnel, discovered 3 November 2010, extended across the border into the United States. Stringer Mexico/Reuters.

made Mexico a key player in the drug trade. The majority of cocaine that enters the United States now arrives through Mexico. The drug traffickers responsible for the cocaine trade, however, also transport marijuana, heroin, methamphetamine, and other drugs along this route for distribution in the United States and Canada. Some human couriers, known as mules, use the vast expanse of unsecured border to sneak shipments to U.S. customers. Others use small airstrips in remote desert locations to launch small cargo planes across the border. In November 2010, a tunnel eighteen hundred feet long was discovered under the border between San Diego, California, and the Mexican city of Tijuana—and in warehouses on each end, agents seized more than twenty-five tons of marijuana. This was one of about seventy-five border-crossing tunnels discovered by authorities between 2006 and 2010.

Despite unusual transport methods like these, a significant percentage of the illegal drugs entering the United States passes through busy border checkpoints or ports. The drugs are usually hidden inside vehicles or within shipments of legal goods. Some traffickers coat the outside of the drug packages with foul or strong-smelling substances in an attempt to thwart drug-sniffing dogs.

Once inside the United States, the goods enter nationwide distribution networks run by drug syndicates. The profits make their way back to the traffickers in U.S. dollars, which are then converted into Mexican pesos through a money-laundering scheme known as the Black Market Peso Exchange. This is an important step, since the massive amounts of cash generated through drug sales would otherwise be impossible to hide

Mexico. Cocaine originates primarily in South America, where the coca plant—the base ingredient in cocaine—is easily cultivated. Local tribes have made use of coca plant leaves for centuries, both as a medicine and in religious ceremonies. The largest producers of cocaine are Peru, Colombia, and Bolivia. The majority of cocaine produced in South America is transported to and sold in the United States.

During the 1980s and 1990s, the main cocaine trafficking route was across the Caribbean and into Florida. This was the route used by Colombian trafficker Pablo Escobar, perhaps the most successful drug kingpin in the history of the world. As anti-drug efforts have stepped up in these areas, drug traffickers have shifted their route to the west, where Mexico shares a nearly two-thousand-mile-long border with the United States.

This close connection with the United States—the largest illicit drug market in the world—has

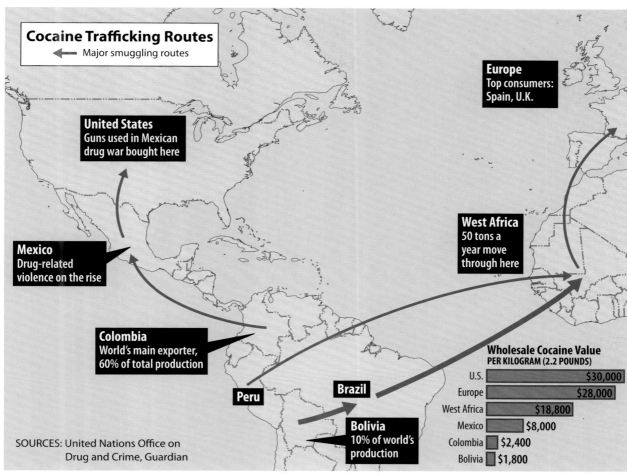

Cocaine Trafficking Routes
← Major smuggling routes

Europe
Top consumers:
Spain, U.K.

United States
Guns used in Mexican
drug war bought here

West Africa
50 tons a
year move
through here

Mexico
Drug-related
violence on the rise

Colombia
World's main exporter,
60% of total production

Peru

Brazil

Bolivia
10% of world's
production

SOURCES: United Nations Office on
Drug and Crime, Guardian

Wholesale Cocaine Value
PER KILOGRAM (2.2 POUNDS)

U.S.	$30,000
Europe	$28,000
West Africa	$18,800
Mexico	$8,000
Colombia	$2,400
Bolivia	$1,800

Cocaine is grown primarily in South America and trafficked from there to the United States and Europe. Illustration/XNR Productions/ Cengage Learning, Gale.

from banks and government investigators. One laundering scheme involves buying winning lottery tickets from the original ticket holders using drug funds, which allows the trafficker to convert illegal earnings into a government-approved payout.

The Major Players in the Mexican Drug Trade

The illegal drug trade in Mexico is controlled by drug cartels, groups of drug traffickers that each control drug-related business in a certain region. To maintain control over drug-related business in an area, heavily armed cartels use violence, terror, bribery, and blackmail to ensure that the production, transportation, and sale of their narcotics proceed smoothly and that no rival cartels can set up competing operations. Though cartels are in competition with one another, they have common interests against government and international police forces.

The first drug cartels arose in Colombia during the 1970s and 1980s, with Escobar's Medellín cartel being the most successful. As Mexico's importance in the flow of drugs to the United States increased, a former Mexican federal police agent, Miguel Ángel Félix Gallardo, rose to power as the leader of the Mexican drug trade. Throughout the 1980s, Gallardo expanded his operations from

How Drug Money is Laundered Via the Lottery

Wins lottery **Drug cartel claims lottery prize**

Sells lottery ticket to drug cartel for cash premium

Collects clean money

Drug traffickers use a variety of tricks to disguise the illegal origins of their money. One example is to find lottery winners and convince them to sell their winning ticket, so the trafficker can then turn it in for legal winnings. Illustration/XNR Productions/Cengage Learning, Gale.

simply transporting narcotics to distributing and selling them as well. In 1987, when the operation became too massive for Gallardo to handle on his own, he assigned different sections of the country to several families already involved in trafficking. These assignments represented the birth of the Mexican drug cartels.

Mexican cartels are usually named after their controlling family or their base of operations. The Sinaloa cartel, based in the western coastal state of the same name, is led by a trafficker who spent eight years in a Mexican maximum-security prison before escaping and resuming control of cartel operations. The Beltrán Leyva cartel, created in 2008 and operating in the same region, was formed by four brothers who had previously worked for the Sinaloa cartel but felt betrayed by its leader. La Familia is a cartel based in Morelia, Michoacán—where Mexican president Felipe Calderón was born and raised—that enjoys a better reputation than most. The group is noted for its support of the poor, and in November 2010,

it even offered to disband, provided the Mexican government could keep order in the region.

Arguably, the most violent cartels are found in the region along the Mexico-United States border. The Tijuana cartel controls the area where Tijuana meets San Diego, as well as the Baja California peninsula to the south. The Juárez cartel controls Ciudad Juárez, a city of about 1.5 million people located across the Rio Grande from El Paso, Texas. The Gulf cartel (Del Golfo) operates along Mexico's eastern coast, with important access to the Texas border at towns such as Nuevo Laredo. These border cartels are instrumental in physically transporting illegal drugs into the United States, and charge "access fees" to other cartels looking to traffic through their region of control. Because access to these border towns is crucial to the drug trade, the border cartels are merciless in retaining control of their territories.

Violence between cartels is common, and alliances between groups shift often enough that some longtime enemies have recently found themselves

Tattoo of "Saint Death" (Santa Muerte). The so-called saint is reportedly popular among Mexican drug traffickers. Daniel Aguilar/Reuters.

fighting on the same side. Each group has its own wing of armed enforcers that clash regularly over territorial disputes. Los Negros was once the armed wing of the Sinaloa cartel before joining up with the Beltrán Leyva cartel and eventually going independent. Los Zetas, a well-trained group created by former military and police officers, was once the enforcement arm of the Gulf cartel. In early 2010, a Gulf cartel member allegedly killed a prominent Zeta officer, leading Los Zetas to split from the Gulf cartel and align with the Beltrán Leyva cartel instead. The two groups, once allies and now enemies, then fought a bloody battle for control over Reynosa and other border towns along the Rio Grande Valley. This rift is part of a larger conflict that has divided Mexico's cartels roughly in half and pitted them against each other for ultimate control of the drug trade.

Corruption from Within

The cartels' rise to power in Mexico was made easier by rampant corruption throughout all levels of government. Gallardo, the godfather of the Mexican drug cartels, was himself a former agent for the Federal Judicial Police. In the early years of the drug cartels, it was common for judges, police officers, and politicians to receive bribes from traffickers; in return, the government officials looked the other way. Some even became close associates with traffickers or participated in the trafficking themselves. In the early 1980s, the governor of Sinaloa allegedly brought Gallardo to stay at his house, and after Gallardo was arrested in Culiacán in 1989, almost one-third of the city's police

Friends and family mourn during a funeral service for victims of a shooting massacre that took place at a family birthday party in Ciudad Juárez on 23 October 2010. Thirteen people were killed, most of them teenagers. A drug gang is believed to have made the attack, perhaps in a case of mistaken identity. Gael Gonzalez/Reuters.

Distribution of Profits of the $35 Billion U.S. Cocaine Market, 2008

70% U.S. mid-level dealers

15% U.S. wholesalers

13% International traffickers

Traffickers in the Andean countries 1%

Farmers in the Andean countries 1.5%

SOURCES: Derived from original calculations based on UNODC ARQ & Government reports

As shown here, most of the money made from the illegal drugs trade ends up in the hands of traffickers and other middlemen. Illustration/XNR Productions/Cengage Learning, Gale.

officers deserted their posts out of fear they would be implicated in his trafficking operations.

Mario Villanueva, the governor of the state of Quintana Roo from 1993 to 1999, was accused of working with the Juárez cartel even while he was still in office. Investigators alleged that he received almost $20 million to shield the cartel from law enforcement. Villanueva was protected from prosecution during his term, but as soon as his term ended, he fled; he was captured and convicted of money-laundering two years later. When his original sentence was completed, Villanueva was convicted of drug trafficking and sentenced to an additional thirty-six years in prison. In May 2010, he was extradited to the United States to face additional trafficking charges.

While Villanueva was hardly the only politician involved in trafficking, corruption has been most prevalent among the very officers sworn to uphold the law. Over the course of a two-year period in the 1990s, for example, more than one

out of every five federal judicial police officers was arrested for corruption related to drug trafficking. In 2007, the entire police force of the border town of Rosarito was disarmed after allegations that members of the force had attacked their own police chief on behalf of the drug cartels. Similarly, in December 2009, the entire police force of Tancítaro was disbanded after its officers proved unable or unwilling to deal with rampant drug-related crime in the area. Several other towns have also seen their local forces disbanded and replaced with federal peacekeepers.

However, even federal officers are prone to corruption. Two leading officials of the Mexican branch of INTERPOL were arrested on suspicion of working with traffickers in 2008. Even the acting commissioner of the Federal Police was arrested on charges of corruption in 2008, as was the former head of the country's anti-organized crime agency. In 2009, the head of public safety fired a team of lie-detector agents tasked with questioning police officers about corruption—after the

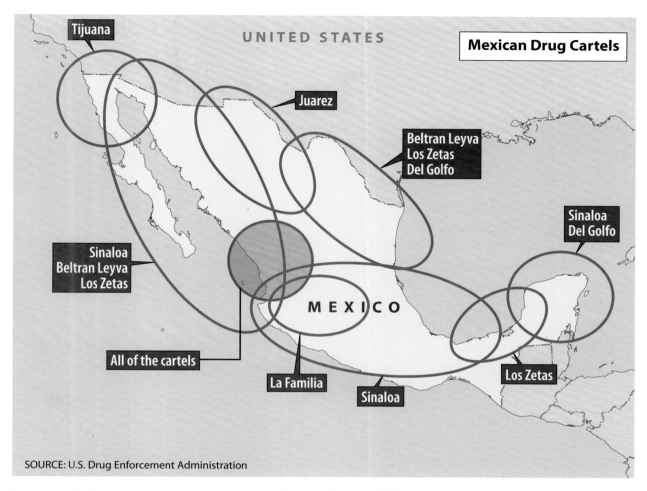

Mexican Drug Cartels

Tijuana

UNITED STATES

Juarez

Beltran Leyva
Los Zetas
Del Golfo

Sinaloa
Del Golfo

Sinaloa
Beltran Leyva
Los Zetas

MEXICO

All of the cartels

La Familia

Sinaloa

Los Zetas

SOURCE: U.S. Drug Enforcement Administration

Seven major Mexican drug cartels and their general areas of control. Illustration/XNR Productions/Cengage Learning, Gale.

members of the team were found to be cheating on their own tests.

But perhaps the most shocking example of corruption among Mexico's police forces occurred in 1985, with the murder of Enrique Camarena. Camarena was an undercover agent working for the U.S. Drug Enforcement Administration (DEA) in cooperation with the Mexican government. In 1984, he was instrumental in the destruction of a multibillion-dollar marijuana plantation located in the state of Chihuahua. Months later, he was kidnapped by corrupt Mexican police officers under the control of Mexico's drug kingpin, Gallardo. DEA officials spent weeks trying to uncover the truth about Camarena's disappearance but were repeatedly blocked by Mexican government officials. They eventually discovered that Camarena had been interrogated and tortured for nine hours—carefully kept alive by a cartel doctor throughout the entire torture session—and then murdered. The event caused a severe rift between American drug enforcement agents and their Mexican counterparts that lasted for many years.

President Calderón Declares War in Michoacán

With widespread corruption at local and federal levels of government, the drug cartels were virtually unstoppable throughout the 1990s and into the twenty-first century. Even as traffickers

U.S. Marine Corps pallbearers carry the casket holding the body of slain U.S. Drug Enforcement agent Enrique Camarena. AP Photo/ Lenny Ignelzi.

stepped up the violence, few were ever prosecuted, and the cartels sought their own justice against each other. In 2006, however, Felipe Calderón was elected president of Mexico, and he brought to office one important mission: end the economic, political, and social stranglehold of the Mexican drug cartels.

Calderón was born and raised in Morelia, Michoacán, later the base of operations for La Familia. He had seen firsthand the effects of drug trafficking and the corruption that allowed it to flourish. Just before Calderón took office in 2006, La Familia made its first dramatic power play for control of Michoacán: Several cartel members entered a night club and tossed five human heads on the dance floor, declaring that La Familia was a force of justice in the region.

Within two weeks of taking office, Calderón sent four thousand federal troops into his home state to stop the drug violence there. This act marked the beginning of Mexico's drug war. Soldiers conducted raids and took control of major roadways, prompting a violent response from La Familia. The conflict between soldiers and cartel members escalated, with thousands of additional federal troops working to cut off La Familia's trafficking routes entirely.

On 15 September 2008, drug cartel members tossed two hand grenades into a crowded plaza in Morelia. The explosions killed eight civilians and injured at least one hundred more. Three members of Los Zetas cartel were arrested in connection with the attack, but some continued to suspect La Familia as the perpetrators. Three months later, Alberto Espinoza, a high-ranking lieutenant in La Familia, was arrested on trafficking charges,

Mexican president Felipe Calderón, during Independence Day celebrations on 16 September 2010. AP Images/Claudio Cruz.

and officials asserted that La Familia had been behind the grenade bombing.

Federal forces continued their string of La Familia arrests with Rafael Cedeño, described as second-in-command of the cartel, in April 2009. Three months later, another lieutenant, Arnoldo Rueda, was taken into custody by federal police. Cartel forces responded with attacks against police stations throughout Michoacán that left more than a dozen dead. Several more high-ranking members of La Familia were arrested in the months that followed, and attacks against soldiers and police continued throughout 2010.

The true depth of La Familia's influence in the region was revealed in July 2009, when Julio César Godoy Toscano, a recently elected congressman, was accused of being a member of La Familia. Godoy evaded police long enough to be sworn into office, which granted him immunity from prosecution during his term. The most surprising part of the story is that Godoy is half-brother to Leonel Godoy Rangel, the governor of Michoacán, who has denied having any ties to La Familia.

An Army Unprepared

Michoacán is just one front in Mexico's drug war. Federal troops have been dispatched throughout Mexico to combat the escalating violence of the drug cartels. In total, approximately fifty thousand soldiers and twenty thousand federal police have been deployed. Even the largest cartels are estimated to contain only one to three thousand members, thus on paper, the opposing forces might appear unevenly matched. But the Mexican Army is spread thin, and any image of a well-armed and well-trained military force like the U.S. Armed Forces is optimistic at best: Mexican soldiers are underpaid and ill-equipped

Following a grenade attack on thousands of Independence Day revelers, police and rescue workers assist survivors. Morelia, Mexico, 15 September 2008. AP Images.

The swearing in of Julio César Godoy Toscano as federal congressman. Godoy is accused by some of being connected to drug trafficking. AP Images/Fernando Castillo.

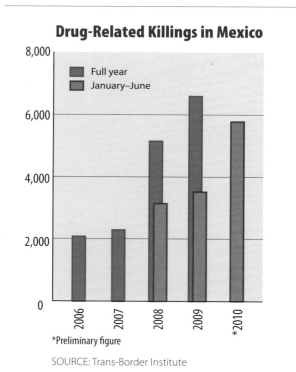

Drug-Related Killings in Mexico

- Full year
- January–June

*Preliminary figure

SOURCE: Trans-Border Institute

Drug-related murders since the election of Felipe Calderón. Illustration/XNR Productions/Cengage Learning, Gale.

to combat the advanced weaponry of the well-funded cartels.

One of President Calderón's first acts upon taking office was to increase pay for soldiers and limit pay for high-ranking government officials. He increased the base pay for full-time soldiers by almost 50 percent, to just under $500 per month. This was still less than half the base pay of new police officers in Mexico. The pay is so poor, in fact, that some drug cartels have distributed advertising flyers to hire soldiers for more pay than the government can provide. Mexico's own secretary of defense estimates that between 2001 and 2008 about a hundred thousand soldiers deserted their army posts.

Even those soldiers willing to endure the low pay face alarming obstacles that limit their effectiveness and put them at risk. In a 14 August 2009 editorial for the *New York Times*, Kelly M. Phillips, a former National Guard soldier and wife of a Mexican Army officer, tells of the barely functional

A recruiting poster by the Zetas drug cartel. It reads: "The Zetas want you, soldier or former soldier. We offer good salary, food and family care. Don't go hungry any longer." Stringer Mexico/ Reuters.

weapons issued to soldiers: "I had seen weapons in the same shape filled with concrete and used as dummies in training exercises in the United States." Phillips also relates her husband's experience with a soldier who, instead of being issued a bulletproof vest before being sent up against the cartel's gunmen, was simply given a life-jacket painted black.

The Other Half of the Drug Trade

On the other side of the conflict, the drug cartels are equipped with a wide assortment of machine guns, semiautomatic rifles, and grenade launchers to fend off army and police forces. Since legal weapons are difficult to obtain in Mexico, stopping the flow of these weapons has become a critical factor in ending the drug war violence. According to the Mexican government, the source of the weapons is not a mystery: Traffickers haul drugs into the United States and bring guns—many of which are legally purchased in gun shops near the border—back into Mexico. In addition, some arms provided by the United States to the Mexican Army are stolen by deserting soldiers and, like the soldiers themselves, become tools of the cartels.

The flow of U.S. guns into Mexico has been verified by no less an authority than the U.S. Bureau of Alcohol, Tobacco, Firearms, and Explosives (ATF). According to a 2008 statement by acting ATF director Michael Sullivan, of the weapons confiscated by the Mexican government that can be traced, at least 90 percent of them come from U.S. sources. Most of those were legally purchased from gun shops in Arizona, Texas, and California, and transferred from "straw buyers" with clean records to cartel members. The ATF has responded with Project Gunrunner, intended to stop the smuggling of weapons from the United States to Mexico. Agents have stepped up inspections of border-area gun dealers to make sure they obey existing gun laws and share information with U.S. prosecutors and Mexican government officials regarding weapons traffickers.

Despite the tracking efforts of the ATF, the majority of cartel weapons seized by the Mexican government cannot be traced at all. In addition, building criminal cases against U.S. dealers who sell to straw buyers has proven difficult, since straw buyers are, by definition, legitimate purchasers. U.S. president Barack Obama has voiced support for a proposed 1997 treaty that would reduce trafficking among the countries of North, Central, and South America, but the treaty has already been rejected once by Congress and would face serious opposition if brought to a vote again. Meanwhile, the Mexican government has

A police officer runs after an attack on patrol vehicles in Ciudad Juárez, 15 July 2010. AP Images.

stockpiled hundreds of thousands of guns taken from the cartels. After being cleared by investigators, the best weapons are turned over to federal forces to be used against the traffickers—one small attempt at leveling the playing field between the two sides.

Mexico's Army vs. the Drug Traffickers

Skirmishes between cartel gunmen and government forces have been mostly small-scale, but are frequently deadly. They have occurred throughout the country's thirty-one states but are concentrated along the coastal and northern border regions.

Operation Baja California was launched just weeks after Operation Michoacán, in early 2007. The operation involved aircraft and ocean vessels as well as land forces in an attempt to cut off the Tijuana cartel. Numerous local forces were disarmed pending corruption investigations, which caused a spike in crime as federal police tried to maintain order. In April 2007, a group of armed cartel agents tried to free a hospitalized criminal by taking over Tijuana General Hospital. They failed, but three people were killed in the resulting shootout.

In October 2008, federal police scored their biggest victory yet in Operation Baja California. After a three-hour shootout at his Tijuana home, government troops arrested Eduardo Arellano Félix, leader of the Tijuana cartel. In the months that followed, officers arrested several more high-ranking members of both the Tijuana and Sinaloa cartels, but the arrests did little to curb violence in Tijuana and the surrounding region. In October 2010, Mexican officials made the biggest marijuana bust in Baja California history, seizing more than one hundred tons of the drug with a street value in excess of $300 million.

The Beltrán Leyva cartel, run by four brothers, was also hit hard by federal troops. Alfredo Beltrán Leyva was arrested in Culiacán in January 2008, along with several of his lieutenants. His brother Arturo was killed on 16 December 2009 after two different shootouts in an upscale community south of Mexico City. The attack was staged by about two hundred Mexican Naval Infantry troops and also involved two helicopters and two tanks. Two weeks later, a third brother, Carlos, was arrested peacefully in Culiacán after

he was caught driving with a forged license. The remaining brother, Héctor, continues to elude police but remains as head of the cartel. Both the U.S. State Department and the Mexican government have offered multimillion-dollar rewards for information leading to his capture.

Terror in Tamaulipas

In Tamaulipas, a Mexican state bordering Texas, turf wars between the Gulf cartel and Los Zetas have turned once-thriving communities into war zones. The extent of cartel infiltration was made clear in November 2008, when federal police in the border city of Reynosa seized the largest illegal weapons cache in the history of the nation. The cache, believed to belong to members of the Gulf cartel, consisted of more than five hundred assault rifles, tear gas launchers, dynamite, and more than half a million rounds of ammunition.

In February 2010, citizens were driven from

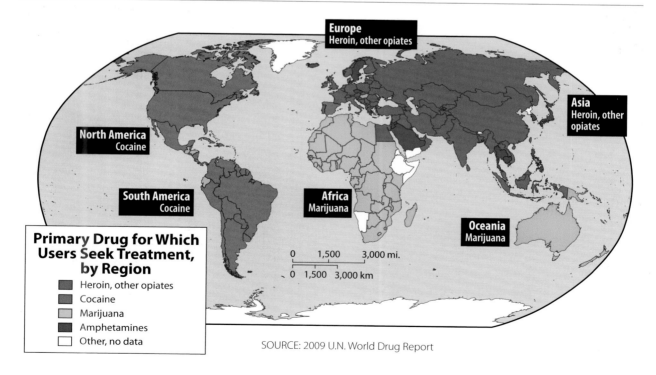

SOURCE: 2009 U.N. World Drug Report

Main problem drugs, by region. Illustration/XNR Productions/Cengage Learning, Gale.

Recent Large Drug Busts

- 4.4 tons of ecstasy or MDMA pills worth $288 million; hidden in 3,000 cans of tomatoes; Australia 2007; biggest ecstasy bust in history.

- $293 million of hashish found in trenches and bunkers in Afghanistan in 2008; reportedly meant for the Taliban.

- 13.8 tons of cocaine hidden in the River Mira (Colombia); valued at $350 million, 2005.

- 40,000 lbs of cocaine seized by US Coast Guard in 2007, worth $500 million dollars, the largest maritime bust in US history.

- 27 tons of cocaine seized by Colombian Navy in 2007, biggest bust in nation's history (at that time); valued at $500 million.

- 134 metric tons of marijuana seized by the Mexican Army in October 2010; largest bust in Mexican history; valued at over $340 million.

the streets by gun battles in border cities such as Reynosa and Matamoros that left at least sixteen dead. Schools cancelled classes and police on the U.S. side of the border warned American travelers against crossing into Mexico. Mexican federal troops arrived in the area and instituted a curfew, though the killing has not ceased.

Indeed, the cartels have begun targeting not just each other, but civilians and politicians in an attempt to show their strength and send a message. In June 2010, the leading candidate for governor of Tamaulipas was murdered along with six campaign workers just days before the election. In July, a Mexican Army soldier was killed in a shootout with cartel members. The following month, cartel agents terrorized the cities of Ciu-

dad Victoria and San Fernando with car explosions, most likely caused by grenade blasts. The cars were parked in front of police stations and a television station office.

In August 2010, seventy-two illegal immigrants from Central and South America were murdered by agents of Los Zetas cartel at a remote ranch about a hundred miles south of the U.S. border. The immigrants were making their way toward the border to cross illegally into the United States when cartel agents kidnapped them and demanded that they work as drug runners. When the immigrants refused, they were shot. The lone survivor, an eighteen-year-old native of Ecuador, managed to escape with injuries and notified authorities of the mass murder. Soon after, Los Zetas members murdered the two police officers assigned to investigate the massacre.

During the last week of August 2010, two mayors—one in Tamaulipas and one in the neighboring state of Nuevo León—were murdered by Los Zetas agents. Six police officers were arrested for playing a part in the Nuevo León murder; they confirmed that the mayor was murdered because Los Zetas agents believed he was sympathetic to the Gulf cartel. Two months later, the entire fourteen-officer police force of Los Ramones in Nuevo León quit after a group of cartel gunmen opened fire on the police station for twenty minutes and lobbed several grenades at the building. Amazingly, no officers were harmed in the attack.

On 5 November 2010, the violence in Tamaulipas came to a head when government troops engaged in a massive shootout against cartel gunmen in Matamoros, just across the border from Brownsville, Texas. The day-long battle resulted in at least forty-seven deaths, including that of a journalist. Crime reporter Carlos Alberto Guajardo, called in on his day off to cover the shootout, was killed when he got too close to the action. According to some accounts, Guajardo was killed by bullets from soldiers amid the chaos.

Tons of marijuana being incinerated by the Mexican Army, after they seized a record 134 tons of the drug on 17 October 2010. Stringer Mexico/Reuters.

After the dust settled, Mexican military officials confirmed that Antonio Ezequiel Cárdenas Guillén, better known as Tony Tormenta, one of two leaders of the Gulf cartel, was among the dead. Tormenta had been included on the DEA Most Wanted list, and both the U.S. and Mexican governments had offered multimillion-dollar bounties for information leading to his arrest.

Juárez on the Brink

Ciudad Juárez is by some accounts the most important drug trafficking corridor along the border. It is no surprise that the Sinaloa cartel would challenge the longtime turf rulers, the Juárez cartel, in an effort to take control of the city. The resulting conflict has been one of the bloodiest in Mexico's drug war. Bodies, sometimes beheaded or mangled from torture, turn up almost daily as warnings to those who would defy the traffickers on either side of the battle.

This cartel violence caused Ciudad Juárez to be ranked as the 2009 murder capital of the world. In February of that year alone, 250 people were killed in the city, prompting President Calderón to send in thousands of additional troops to restore and maintain order. It was also in February

Culpan a ex procuradora Patricia González de trabajar para la Línea

larednoticias   214 videos   Subscribe

In this scene from a video posted on YouTube, kidnappers force Mario Gonzalez to state that he and his sister Patricia were involved in the drug trade while she was attorney general of Chihuahua. Source: YouTube.

that cartel agents demanded that Juárez police chief Robert Orduna step down; if he did not, they vowed to kill a police officer every forty-eight hours until he changed his mind. After ten days of Orduna's continued resistance, five officers had been murdered, and Orduna agreed to resign.

In May 2009, Eric LeBaron, a sixteen-year-old living in a Mormon community, was kidnapped and held for ransom by cartel members in the rural Chihuahua region known as Galeana. The victim's older brother, Benjamín LeBaron, was a dual American-Mexican citizen determined to stop the violence of the cartels. Rather than pay the ransom, Benjamín rallied the community in a protest against the kidnappers. A week later, after realizing they would not receive the ransom, the kidnappers released Eric. Two months after the kidnapping, Benjamín and his brother-in-law Luis Carlos Widmar were dragged from their homes late at night and executed as retribution for defying the cartel.

On 2 September 2009, armed men entered a drug rehabilitation clinic in Ciudad Juárez and gunned down eighteen patients. Some sources reported that the murdered patients had links to the Juárez cartel. Two weeks later, gunmen stormed another rehab clinic and killed ten more patients. Some government officials claim that the rehab clinics have become recruiting centers for the cartels. According to Dr. Tony Payan, a political science professor at the University of Texas at El

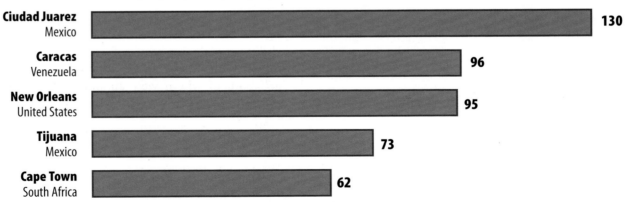

Deadly Cities
WORLD'S HIGHEST MURDER RATES
Murders per year per 100,000 people

Ciudad Juarez Mexico	130
Caracas Venezuela	96
New Orleans United States	95
Tijuana Mexico	73
Cape Town South Africa	62

SOURCE: Mexico's Citizen's Council for Public Security

Cities with the world's highest murder rates in 2009, according to the Citizens' Council for Public Security. Illustration/XNR Productions/Cengage Learning, Gale.

Paso, "In the end, the people who end up in these centers are involved in the business" (*Los Angeles Times*, Ellingwood, 4 September 2009).

In April 2010, an unnamed U.S. intelligence officer told the Associated Press that the Sinaloa cartel had won control of the city from the Juárez cartel. However, in July 2010, a car explosion killed two police officers and two others; the Juárez cartel claimed credit and suggested that the local police were controlled by the Sinaloa cartel. The violence peaked on September 9, which proved to be one of the deadliest days in the city's history with twenty-five dead in numerous attacks. Shortly after the attacks, officials found graffiti suggesting the attacks were aimed at the Sinaloa cartel. Clearly, the battle remains unresolved.

Principles, Not Guns

Residents of the border region near Juárez are so fearful of cartel violence that the municipality of Práxedis Guadalupe Guerrero went for a full year without a police chief. Police chiefs and mayors had been frequent targets of cartel violence, and none of the few remaining officers wanted the job.

In October 2010, someone finally stepped forward and offered to fill the post. The applicant was twenty-year-old female college student and mother Marisol Valles Garcia. After being sworn into office, Valles Garcia explained at a press conference her reason for accepting the job: "I took the risk because I want my son to live in a different community to the one we have today. I want people to be able to go out without fear, as it was before" (*New York Post*, Mangan, 21 October 2010).

Despite the fact that many police officers on the force have been murdered—and the local mayor was gunned down months before—Valles Garcia, a criminology major, stated that she will not carry a weapon while on the job. "The weapons we have are principles and values, which are

Marisol Valles Garcia at work in Práxedis G. Guerrero, Mexico. Only twenty years old, Valles Garcia became police chief when no one else would take the position in this violent border town. Stringer Mexico/Reuters.

the best weapons for prevention," she said in an interview with CNN en Español (*USA Today*, Winter, 20 October 2010). Valles Garcia also expressed a desire to create a predominantly female police force that would focus on improving security by rebuilding relationships in the community.

Just weeks after Valles Garcia took office, the young woman was joined in her crusade by two housewives in the towns of Villa Luz and El Vergel, both of whom were appointed as chiefs of police for their respective communities south of Ciudad Juárez.

Blood Spills across the Border

With Ciudad Juárez just across the Rio Grande from El Paso, one might assume that the bustling Texas city would be a likely place for spillover violence from the Mexican cartels. But despite its size and location, El Paso boasts one of the lowest homicide rates in the United States, with only one murder in the first half of 2010. This low rate may be due to the constant presence of drug enforcement and immigration agents stationed in and around the city. While the distinction between the United States and Mexico is clear in El Paso, in other areas the border is more porous, and the Mexican cartels have encroached upon U.S. territory with their bloodthirsty tactics.

David Hartley was a veteran of the border region. He and his wife Tiffany lived in the border town of McAllen, Texas, and had previously lived on the other side of the border in Reynosa, Mexico, until the violence of the drug war drove them back to U.S. soil. Like the Hartleys, Falcon Lake straddles the border between the two nations; the sixty-mile-long lake, created by a reservoir on the Rio Grande, is divided down the middle by concrete markers representing the United States-Mexico border.

The lake is famous for bass fishing, but it has also recently acquired a reputation for piracy. In the spring and summer of 2010, several U.S. fishermen and boaters reported incidents in which they were approached by gunmen from the Mexican side of the lake and either robbed or threatened. Some of these incidents took place in Mexican waters, but at least one was reported on the U.S. side of the border markers.

On 30 September 2010, the Hartleys took their Jet Skis across the lake to the Mexican side to view a famous old church that was partially submerged when the reservoir was created. According to Tiffany, before they could return to the U.S. side, two boatloads of gunmen approached and opened fire. David was struck in the head and killed, while Tiffany fled across the lake. According to a witness, the gunmen pursued her into U.S. waters but could not catch her before she reached U.S. soil.

Despite intensive searches of the U.S. side of

American couple David and Tiffany Hartley before he was reportedly murdered on a border lake on 30 September 2010. Splash News/newscom.

the lake, David's body has yet to be found. Since the shooting happened in Mexico, the investigation had to be left in the hands of Mexican investigators. After suggesting to a television news station that two suspects in the murder were members of the Los Zetas cartel, one of the investigators went missing. Days later, his head arrived in a suitcase at a local Mexican Army garrison.

A similar fate awaited Martin Alejandro Cota-Monroy, who was found decapitated in his apartment on 10 October 2010. However, there was one important difference between his case and that of the Hartleys: Cota-Monroy was murdered in a suburb of Phoenix, Arizona, nowhere near the border. Violence among illegal immigrants in Arizona has grown in recent years, but the beheading

Murdered Mexican Mayors, 2010

	Date	Town	State
1.	Feb. 17	Guadalupe y Calve	Chihuahua
2.	Feb. 22	El Mezquital	Hidalgo
3.	April 28	Zapotitlán Tablas	Guerrero
4.	June 19	Guadalupe	Chihuahua
5.	June 20	San José del Progreso	Oaxaca
6.	June 30	Santo Domingo de Morelos	Oaxaca
7.	Aug. 16*	Santiago	Nuevo León
8.	Aug. 29	Hidalgo	Tamaulipas
9.	Sept. 8	El Naranjo	San Luis Potosí
10.	Sept. 23	Doctor Gonzalez	Nuevo León

*Kidnapped on Aug. 16, found dead two days later.

SOURCE: McClatchy Washington Bureau

Public officials cannot escape the violence that plagues Mexico. As one example, ten mayors were murdered during the first ten months of 2010. Illustration/XNR Productions/Cengage Learning, Gale.

of Cota-Monroy marks the first known appearance of grisly cartel tactics in the United States. Investigators have speculated that the murder was carried out by traffickers looking to send a message. David Gonzales, a U.S. marshal working in Arizona, stated of the brutal murder: "It's only a matter of time that more of the violence is going to bleed over into the United States, and I think we'll see more of these types of crimes occur" (*East Valley Tribune*, Sakal, 29 October 2010).

A Threatened Press

More than thirty journalists have been killed or gone missing since Calderón took office, and Reporters Without Borders has named Mexico the most dangerous country in Latin America for members of the press. The risk has led to self-censorship among some news outlets in an attempt to keep the cartels from targeting their staff.

In July 2010, four journalists in the Laguna metropolitan area of northern Mexico were kidnapped by cartel agents, presumably aligned with the Sinaloa cartel. The kidnappers demanded that a local television station air several videos showing Los Zetas cartel members discussing their influence over local police and politicians. The station aired the videos, but the journalists were not released.

In September 2010, a photographer for the largest daily newspaper in Ciudad Juárez, *El Diario de Juárez*, was shot by cartel gunmen as he left the office building for lunch. He was the paper's second journalist murdered in as many years and prompted an unusual plea from the paper's staff, a front-page editorial written directly to the cartels and titled "What Do You Want From Us?" Although the paper's staff viewed the move as an attempt to ensure the safety of their reporters, critics have condemned it as evidence of an utter failure of the freedom of the press. Within days of the Juárez plea, President Calderón announced a plan to provide better federal protections for journalists.

Public Perception of the Drug War

Mexico has a long history of corruption in its government, and certain crimes—such as bribery—might be viewed by the public as simply a way of life. Dishonest police, judges, and politicians provided poor examples for citizens looking to succeed. In this sense, the jobs offered by the drug cartels were not all that different from so-called legitimate careers. According to Transparency International, Mexico's Corruption Perceptions Index—a measure of how much corruption is perceived to exist among government officials—has increased substantially since the 1980s yet remained low in 2010.

Some cartels cultivated reputations as supporters of the poor, who take money from wealthy Americans and use it to enrich their local communities. It is this heroic, rebellious image of the drug trafficker that drove some songwriters to create *narcocorridos*, or drug ballads. Although drug ballads can be traced back several decades, the genre exploded in the 1990s with the increase in actual drug traffickers in Mexico. The songs usually portray the business as both glamorous and dangerous, and some are direct tributes to real-life drug lords. Tragically, many of the top *narcocorrido* performers became aligned with certain cartels and were murdered by rival traffickers.

The behavior of soldiers and federal police has also led to a negative perception of them among some Mexican citizens. Human rights organizations have filed numerous complaints on behalf of citizens who were beaten, raped, or otherwise abused by government troops in search of cartel members. These human-rights issues have proven severe enough to affect the funding the Mexican government receives from the United States.

The Colombian Solution

The drug war in Mexico has led many to look to Colombia as a model for battling the cartels. During the 1980s and 1990s, Colombia was the center of the drug trafficking world. In 2000, the United States announced additional aid to help the Colombian government combat drug traffickers. Plan Colombia, as it was known, focused on strengthening the Colombian military and on eradication of the coca crops used to make cocaine. Under the plan, it is estimated that around 2.5 million acres of drug crops have been destroyed. In addition, Colombian police and soldiers have received training from American military personnel as well as equipment such as surveillance planes and interceptor boats to catch traffickers.

Though some have criticized the plan's emphasis on military tactics, cultivation and production of cocaine eventually showed a decline by 2008. Colombia has since ceded its title as the world's number-one producer of cocaine to

Mexican journalists display images of their colleagues who have been murdered by drug traffickers, during a protest in Mexico City on 7 August 2010. Ronaldo Schemidt/AFP/Getty Images/newscom.

Peru. Drug-related violence in Colombia, once ranked as the worst in the world, has also been scaled back considerably, though the country's murder rate is still among the world's highest per capita. The number of kidnappings—considered a favorite tactic among traffickers—in Colombia dropped an astounding 95 percent between 2000 and 2009.

But some skeptics argue that Colombia's success has come at the expense of other Latin American nations. As cocaine production has decreased in Colombia, it has increased in neighboring countries, specifically Peru and Bolivia. As drug-related violence has decreased in Colombia, the violence in Mexico, Venezuela, and Guatemala

and drug-sniffing dogs and has also worked to stop the flow of guns from the United States into Mexico. The total amount of aid authorized through 2010 was over $1.8 billion, of which nearly 1.6 billion was designated for Mexico.

Although it has jokingly been called "Plan Mexico" by critics, the Mérida Initiative focuses less on military aid and more on improving the infrastructure of Mexico's police forces. In addition, the funds can be cut off if Mexican soldiers and officers are found to violate human-rights laws. This is an important clause in the agreement, as Mexican police and soldiers have been accused of numerous human-rights violations by groups such as Human Rights Watch. Mexican police have also been trained to engage in torture as part of their interrogation techniques against suspected drug traffickers.

In September 2010, the U.S. government announced that it would withhold more than $26 million in aid due to Mexico's failure to improve human-rights protections for its citizens. In part, the U.S. State Department called for a commitment to try accused military personnel in civilian courts, rather than relying on military courts to dispense justice.

Economic Impact of the Drug War

The drug war has proven devastating in both its human toll and its economic toll. Street violence has shut down countless businesses in border regions, and the damage to buildings and property has climbed into the millions.

In addition, the country's lucrative tourism industry has all but vanished as the U.S. and other governments have issued travel advisories warning their citizens to stay away. Traditionally, tourism makes up more than 8 percent of Mexico's gross domestic product. But in Tijuana alone between 2005 and 2008, tourism dropped by 90 percent, devastating local businesses and vendors.

has increased dramatically. Any effort to enact a Plan Colombia in Mexico, skeptics argue, would at best shift the problem to a different area. In addition, despite the improvements the country has seen, Colombia remains one of the world's main locations for drug trafficking and cocaine production.

Plan Mexico?

In 2008, the U.S. Congress signed into law the Mérida Initiative, aimed at helping Mexico and other Central American nations fight the powerful drug cartels. Through this initiative, the United States has provided equipment such as helicopters

The front page of *El Diario* newspaper of Ciudad Juárez, Mexico, 19 September 2010. The editorial asks "What Do You Want From Us?" It is directed at drug gangs who have murdered two of *El Diario*'s reporters since 2008. © *El Diario de Juárez,* 19 September 2010. Reproduced by permission.

In November 2010, an official from Pemex, Mexico's state-owned petroleum company, stated that drug violence has disrupted production of natural gas in the country's northern region. The losses total around $350,000 per day, or more than $10 million per month. These massive losses, calculated for just one facet of a single business enterprise, represent a small fraction of the economic damage created by the battle against the drug cartels.

The U.S. Role in the Drug War

Through the Mórida Initiative and through its own international anti-drug efforts, the United States has assisted the Mexican government in its fight against the cartels. This assistance includes several successful raids within the United States as well as additional border support.

Project Reckoning was an international anti-drug operation carried out with the cooperation of the United States, Mexico, Italy, and Guatemala. The fifteen-month operation led to the September 2008 arrest of 176 suspected drug traffickers in several countries. Among these suspects were three alleged leaders of the Gulf cartel. As of that date, Project Reckoning agents had seized about 37,000 pounds of cocaine, 1,000 pounds of methamphetamine, 51,000 pounds of marijuana, $60 million in U.S. currency, and nearly 200 weapons and vehicles.

Operation Xcellerator was a joint effort by drug enforcement agents in the United States, Mexico, and Canada that concluded in February 2009. The target of this operation was the Sinaloa cartel and its distribution channels in the United States and Canada. Operation Xcellerator resulted in 755 arrests and $60 million in seized cash. Agents also seized more than twelve tons of cocaine, eight tons of marijuana, 1.3 million Ecstasy pills, and several planes and boats.

In October 2009, U.S. agents concluded a four-year operation against La Familia known as Project Coronado. The final series of raids took place in nineteen Mexican states and led to more than three hundred arrests. In total, Project Coronado resulted in 1,186 arrests and seizures of more than eleven tons of drugs, as well as $33 million in seized U.S. currency and several hundred weapons and vehicles.

In May 2010, President Obama pledged to station an additional twelve hundred National Guard troops along the United States-Mexico border to combat traffickers. In June 2010, President Obama also requested emergency funding from Congress to hire an additional one thousand Border Patrol agents. That same month, drug raids in Texas and Oklahoma led to more than fifty arrests, including that of an alleged high-ranking member of the Sinaloa cartel.

Despite these efforts, Mexican government officials have repeatedly called for two additional actions by the U.S. government to help end the drug war. First, it wants stricter gun-control laws in the United States to limit the number of firearms that end up in the hands of the cartel enforcers. Mexico has some of most restrictive gun laws in the world; the United States has some of the least restrictive gun laws in the world. While the exact percentage is the subject of heated debate, there is no doubt that a large proportion of the thousands of firearms used in violent acts by Mexican drug cartels were purchased in the United States. Second, the Mexican government wants greater drug treatment funding for U.S. citizens to reduce the market for illegal drugs.

The second demand cuts to the heart of the Mexican drug war's roots. The United States is the largest market for illegal drugs in the world; if not for the great demand by U.S. citizens, there would be no lucrative market for Mexico's cartels to fight over. In February 2010, President Obama proposed a 3.5 percent increase in federal funding for drug treatment and prevention programs.

Gun Control and Drug Treatment: Will Americans Cooperate?

The Mexican government wants the United States government to stem the flow of guns to drug cartels by enacting stricter gun laws and reduce demand for illegal drugs in the United States by offering users effective addiction treatment. But are Americans willing to cooperate?

Gun control is a contentious political issue in the United States. According to a 2009 Pew Research poll, popular opinion in the United States is fairly evenly divided on the topic of gun control. But the Americans who support gun ownership rights do so strongly, citing their constitutional right "to keep and bear arms." Gun rights supporters vehemently resist all at-tempts by lawmakers to restrict gun sales. As a result, American politicians often shy away from gun control issues.

Illegal drug use became a pressing social problem in the United States in the 1960s and 1970s. After that, public opinion on how best to deal with the problem evolved. The 1980s saw the beginning of the so-called War on Drugs that featured stiff, mandatory legal penalties and jail sentences for both the possession and sale of narcotics. Prisons filled and overflowed with drug offenders, but drug use continued to rise through the 1990s. By 2008, three-fourths of Americans deemed the War on Drugs a failure. In the twenty-first century, doctors, law enforcement officials, and politicians increasingly argued that effective drug addiction prevention and

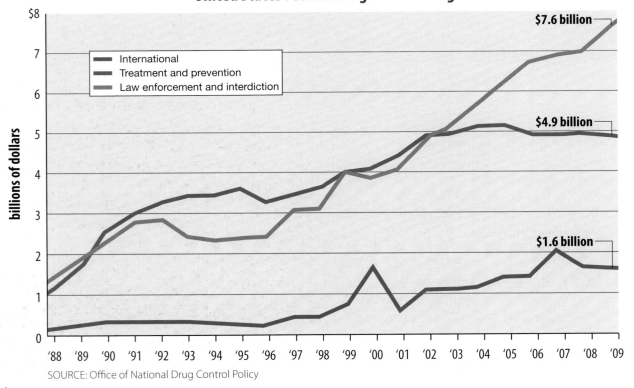

United States Federal Drug Control Budget

This chart shows U.S. federal government funds spent to combat illegal drugs between 1988 and 2009. Illustration/XNR Productions/ Cengage Learning, Gale.

Mexican Drug Seizures, in Pounds

Methamphetamine

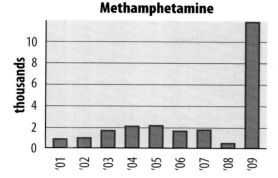

Opium gum*

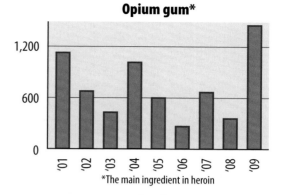

*The main ingredient in heroin

Marijuana

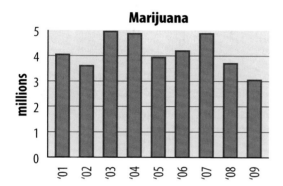

Cocaine

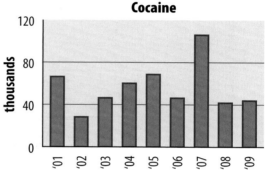

SOURCE: U.S. State Department

Drug seizures in Mexico. Illustration/XNR Productions/Cengage Learning, Gale.

treatment, not long prison sentences, would help curb demand for illegal drugs. Several opinion surveys have found that a majority of Americans also favor treatment over prison for nonviolent drug users. However, treatment can be expensive, there is no guarantee of long-term success, and Americans have not been willing to fund major drug treatment initiatives.

Research and Exploration

"Above the Influence: Drug Facts." *Above the Influence*, 2010, http://www.abovetheinfluence.com.

> This site, sponsored by the Office of National Drug Policy, includes a detailed interactive guide to a wide variety of drugs and their effects.

"Ciudad Juárez: The War on News." Huerta Muñoz, Carlos. *Border Stories*, 2008, http://borderstories.org/ciudad-juarez-the-war-on-news.

> This short documentary deals with the dangers facing journalists and publishers who attempt to cover the ongoing developments in the drug war. The video focuses on a journalist who was forced to flee temporarily to the United States after receiving death threats from cartel members.

"Drug Violence in Mexico (Interactive)." Reuters, 2010, http://www.reuters.com/article/interactive/idUSTRE69B6KF20101013?view=large&type=worldNews.

> This interactive feature shows the entire organization of a typical drug cartel and offers an animated map that shows the flow of drugs through Mexico.

"Failed Drug War: U.S. and Mexico Losing Battle

Against Cartels." *Associated Press*, 2010, http://hosted.ap.org/specials/interactives/_national/drug_war/?SITE=CODEN&SECTION=HOME.

This comprehensive feature focuses on the financial and human costs of the drug war, with data on drug use trends, arrests and convictions of alleged cartel members, and the amount of money the United States has spent on drug control efforts.

"Mexican Cartels: Drug Organizations Extending Reach Farther into U.S." *Associated Press*, 2009, http://hosted.ap.org/specials/interactives/_international/mexican_cartels/index.html?SITE=AP.

This feature by the Associated Press contains many interactive maps covering locations of reported violence, regions of cartel control, and more. The site also features videos highlighting the violence in Tijuana and Tamaulipas.

"Mexico Points Finger at U.S. for Drug War." Greenberg, Peter. *CBS News*, 2010, http://www.cbsnews.com/video/watch/?id=7049563n&tag=contentMain;contentBody.

In this exclusive CBS News video interview, President Calderón asserts that the United States must acknowledge the part it plays in fueling Mexico's drug war, both through its consumption of illegal drugs and its accessible weapons market.

"Mexico's Drug War (blog)." Longmire, Sylvia. Typepad blog site, 2010, http://borderviolenceanalysis.typepad.com/.

This blog, maintained by an intelligence expert specializing in Latin American issues, offers both news and analysis of the latest events in the Mexican drug war.

"Mexico's Drug War: A Rigged Fight?" Burnett, John, and Marisa Peñaloza. *National Public Radio*, 2010, http://www.npr.org/templates/story/story.php?storyId=126890838&ps=cprs.

This audio program investigates the Mexican government's claims in its drug war fight and asserts that the government itself appears to be choosing sides among the cartels.

"Murder in Monterrey Interactive: How the Shooting Unfolded." Rañoa, Raoul. *Los Angeles Times*, http://www.latimes.com/la-me-monterrey.fl,0,642374.flash.

This Flash-based interactive feature recounts the 2008 cartel murder of a Monterrey police commander and his wife with detailed location diagrams and a timeline of the event.

"Narco Terms." Buggs. *Borderland Beat*, 2009, http://www.borderlandbeat.com/2009/04/narco-terms.html.

This comprehensive glossary provides definitions for terms (many in Spanish) that are commonly used when discussing Mexico's drug cartels.

"Narcocorridos: The Songs of Mexico's Drug War." Muessig, Ben. *AolNews*, 2010, http://www.aolnews.com/weird-news/article/narcocorridos-the-songs-of-mexicos-drug-war/19579177.

This feature on Mexico's drug ballads and their performers includes several videos of famous songs in the genre, including "Cuerno De Chivo" ("Horn of Goat"), a song about a weapon—the AK-47—that is often used by drug traffickers.

"Tijuana Violence (Photos)." Barletti, Don. *Los Angeles Times*, 2008, http://www.latimes.com/la-fg-tijuana25-oct25-pg,0,4996579.photogallery.

This arresting gallery of images from 2008 captures the grisly reality of life in a border town torn apart by drug cartel violence.

© Sebastião Salgado/(Contact Press Images)

Migrants, Immigrants & Refugees

Attitudes towards immigrants have shifted and changed throughout history, but the answers to two basic questions have informed virtually every nation's debate on immigration: who should be allowed in, and who should not. In 2010, controversy surrounding immigration issues dominated the media, not only in the United States but around the globe. Unparalleled calls for enhanced border protection came from all corners of the world, including traditionally immigrant-friendly nations, while anti-foreign sentiment seemed to be spiraling out of control.

How a Girl with Green Sneakers Became the Face of Failed Immigration Policy

In *The Death of Josseline: Immigration Stories from the Arizona-Mexico Borderlands* (Beacon Press, 2010), Tucson-based journalist Margaret Regan calls attention to the treacherous conditions faced by undocumented immigrants crossing the U.S.-Mexico border and highlights the complexities of the immigration issue in the United States. Fourteen-year-old Josseline Hernandez was one of 183 migrants who died in southern Arizona in 2008. She and her younger brother were en route from El Salvador to Los Angeles via Mexico. Their mother was an undocumented immigrant working at a low-paying job in California. She had paid an unscrupulous "coyote," or smuggler for hire, to

A memorial marker for Josseline Hernandez, who died en route from El Salvador to join her mother in Los Angeles. Image copyright by Margaret Regan, 2010. Taken from her book *The Death of Josseline: Immigration Stories from the Arizona-Mexico Borderlands.* Beacon Press: 2010.

oversee the children's crossing at the Arizona border and reunite the family in Los Angeles.

Josseline, her brother, and several adults traveled together with the same coyote on that cold, damp night in January 2008. They made it into the United States as a group, but along a particularly hazardous stretch of trail through Arizona's Tumacacori Wilderness, Josseline became weak and began to vomit. "The coyote decided to leave this child behind in the wilderness," Regan told Neal Conan in an interview for NPR's *Talk of the Nation* (24 February 2010). "Nobody else stayed with her either. The other adults in the group, everyone left this kid behind." Josseline would never reach her mother.

After collapsing on the rocky Tumacacori trail,

Josseline told her brother to keep going—to get to their mother. Three days later, when the younger brother finally got to L.A., he told his mother that Josseline was ill and alone somewhere in Arizona. "I suspect she was probably already dead by that time, weak as she was when she'd been left behind," Regan told Conan. Josseline's bright green sneakers helped authorities identify her body three weeks later.

SB 1070: Arizona's Strict New Immigration Law

The wrenching story of Josseline Hernandez, and many others like her, reveal the flaws in U.S. immigration policy. In the spring of 2010, tens of thousands of immigrants and activists rallied in Washington, D.C., pressing the government to support fair and humane immigration legislation that allows migrating families to stay together. Shortly thereafter, on 23 April 2010, Arizona's governor Jan Brewer signed a highly controversial immigration bill into law.

The law—better known by its Senate Bill number, SB 1070—was designed to deter undocumented Mexican immigrants from entering or remaining in Arizona. The United States is the destination of choice for almost all immigrants leaving Mexico, and a report released by the Pew Hispanic Center reveals that 60 percent of all unauthorized immigrants in the United States come from Mexico. Since California tightened its borders, Arizona has become a main entry point for undocumented immigrants seeking a way into the United States—not only from Mexico, but from Central American nations like El Salvador, as Josseline's story so vividly illustrates.

SB 1070 makes it a misdemeanor to travel in the state of Arizona without immigration papers. Further, it requires police to verify an individual's citizenship if "reasonable cause" exists to detain that person for another potential crime.

A truck full of illegal immigrants at the border between Mexico and the United States. Sarah Coran/Getty Images.

Fears of racial profiling arose among Arizona's Hispanic population after the passage of SB 1070, as did concern that grounds for "reasonable cause" might be broadly interpreted to allow for police harassment of Hispanics no matter what their immigration status. A week after Governor Brewer signed the bill into law, CBS News reported that 60 percent of Arizonans supported the law and believed it would decrease crime in their state. However, data from the U.S. Department of Justice fail to support a link between crime and immigration; in fact, violent crime in Arizona in 2009 had fallen to its lowest rate in forty years. Ironically, immigration from Mexico fell dramatically when the United States economy went into recession in 2007 and the economic slowdown made jobs scarce. Mexican census statistics showed a 25 percent drop in immigration to the United States in 2008, mainly attributable to the declining job market.

Threats of Economic Fallout in Arizona

Days after the law's passage, Mexican president Felipe Calderón slammed SB 1070 as discriminatory. The law sparked worldwide outrage and speculation that Arizona might lose more than $7 million per day if Mexican citizens boycotted the state. Each day, an estimated 65,000 Mexicans cross the Arizona border legally as workers or tourists, and fallout from the law, it was theorized, could seriously jeopardize that daily revenue flow.

The Mexican government issued a travel advisory on 27 April 2010: the advisory warned Mexican citizens about the potential dangers of travel to Arizona and charged that the state's adoption of the strict immigration enforcement law created "a negative political environment for migrant communities and for all Mexican visitors." The official declaration of the Mexican Foreign Ministry stated that it would be safe to assume that "every

Mexican citizen may be harassed and questioned without further cause at any time."

Long before the Arizona controversy, United States president Barack Obama had announced plans to reform immigration laws in the country. The issue has been a bone of contention in U.S. politics for years, and there have been several attempts at reforming immigration law, including initiatives in 2006 and 2007. Following the passage of SB 1070, Obama

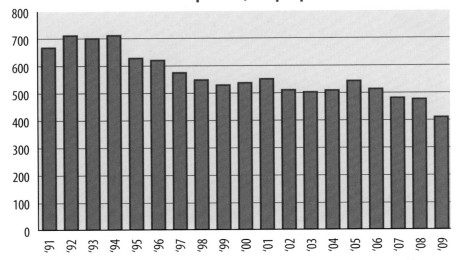

Violent Crimes per 100,000 people in Arizona

SOURCE: FBI, Uniform Crime Reports
as prepared by the National Archive of Criminal Justice Data

Arizona violent crime is at its lowest in twenty years. Illustration/XNR Productions/Cengage Learning, Gale.

sought to ease Mexican concern over U.S. immigration policy on 18 May 2010, when he met with President Calderón in Washington. Calderón and his wife were on a two-day state visit. In public comments after the two leaders met, Obama repeated his objections to the Arizona law and his commitment to federal immigration reform. The next month, President Obama met with the Congressional Hispanic Caucus to discuss strategies for reviving a comprehensive immigration reform bill in 2010. Regardless of its intent, Arizona's immigration law resulted in a controversy that gave

Mexican farmers protest the Arizona Senate Bill 1070, which is against illegal immigrants. © Alex Cruz/Collection/Corbis.

President Obama meets with the Congressional Hispanic Caucus, 29 June 2010. Official White House Photo by Pete Souza.

the immigration issue new impetus. The president later used a televised speech at American University to make the case for immediate action on immigration reform.

Hung Up by Legal Challenges

Shortly after the passage of SB 1070, the U.S. Department of Justice filed suit against Arizona, charging that its law was unconstitutional because it erroneously gave the state of Arizona authority over immigration policy. According to U.S. law, the federal government—not the individual states—has sole authority to regulate immigration. Pro–SB 1070 officials in Arizona argue that the federal government failed to enforce existing laws to protect the state's borders, thus turning the Arizona-Mexico line into a gateway to the North; they maintain that Washington's inaction left Arizonans with no choice but to take the law into their own hands.

On 28 July 2010, U.S. federal judge Susan Bolton issued an injunction blocking key parts of the Arizona law that had been scheduled to take effect the very next day. Arizona immediately announced that it would appeal the judge's decision. While a decision by the appeals court was not made by the end of 2010, preliminary reports indicated that the judges are most concerned with balancing the notion of reasonable cause against requirements to enforce immigration law. The question remains: Without genuine cause to believe that an individual has committed a crime, are state and local police officers still required to act on the suspicion that someone is in the United States illegally?

Border Vigilantes

Vigilantism is alive and well in twenty-first-century America.

Five years before the governor of Arizona signed that state's immigration bill into law, then-President George W. Bush warned about the dangers of vigilante action against migrants attempting to enter the United States illegally.

The states of California, Arizona, New Mexico, and Texas lie on the 1,950-mile-long border between the United States and Mexico. Every day, 65,000 Mexican workers and tourists cross Mexico's border with Arizona legally; about 2.5 percent of that number—or roughly 1,600 people a day—try to slip across that same border illegally. In 2004, members of a group called the Minuteman Project began a campaign to stop illegal- immigrants from crossing over into the United States.

The group takes its name from the Revolutionary War–era

A bullet-riddled sign warning of possible illegal immigrant and smuggling activity near the Arizona/Mexico border. Gila Photography/Shutterstock.com.

militiamen who stood ready to fight for the colonies' rights at a minute's notice. This Minuteman Project refers to a voluntary patrol that made international headlines in 2004 and 2005, after announcing their plans to spot and track undocumented immigrants attempting to cross the desert land that separates the United States from Mexico. These self-appointed immigration enforcers say they

were driven to such action by the U.S. government's failure to stem the "invasion" occurring at the border—particularly a 23-mile-long stretch of border between Arizona's Cochise County and Mexico.

The Minuteman Project was originally conceived as a month-long effort to post 1,000 volunteers—many of them armed, many of them former members

The Language of Immigration

Contemporary immigration issues generate considerable discussion and debate, so much so that the Washington, D.C. –based Migration Policy Institute sponsored an online project to sort through data. Called the Migration Information Source (www.migrationinformation.org), this online resource includes a glossary of nearly seventy migration-related terms used both by scholars and by the media.

The term *migration* refers to the movement of people worldwide. Individuals who move away from their homeland are generally referred to as *immigrants*. Migrating people are said to *emigrate* from a sending state or nation (their homeland) and *immigrate* to a receiving state or nation (their destination). Migration may be voluntary or involuntary; if the decision to migrate is driven by fear—fear of persecution, violence, or even death—the migrating people are known as *refugees*. An even further distinction is made between of the U.S. military—at the most heavily trafficked section of the Arizona border. "People are going to set up their lawn chairs, put on some sunscreen and start looking for suspicious activity," said Chris Simcox, one of the Minuteman Project leaders, in a 2005 *New York Times* interview. "We're doing the job President Bush refuses to do."

Its opponents portray the project as a modern-day lynch mob. Ray Borane, the mayor of one border town in Cochise County, told the *Washington Post*: "They [the Minutemen] are going to draw every misfit, every renegade, everyone with an ax to grind about ethnic preference," adding, "They are not welcome here."

Immigration officials immediately expressed concern that the presence of the Minutemen might spark violent confrontations at the border and escalate international tensions. Fears that extremists would join the ranks of the Minutemen became palpable when Aryan supremacist groups began voicing online support for the project.

The Minuteman Project took credit for pressuring the Department of Homeland Security into adding more than 500 border patrol agents to the area and increasing the air surveillance along the Arizona border, even though the federal government dismissed the timing of these ramped-up efforts as mere coincidence.

According to Jennifer Allen, executive director of Border Action Network, a membership-based organization that works to advocate immigrant rights, the U.S. government was wrong to allow anti-immigrant groups to operate along the border. In 2005, the Network filed a petition stating the federal government should be held responsible for human rights abuses against undocumented immigrants. "We tried everything possible to get local, state and federal officials to address rights violations and criminal behavior of these groups who act like they are above the rule of law," Allen said. "We found that no one had the courage or political will to prosecute them. In some cases, we found collusion between the government and vigilantes" ("Inter-American Commission to Hear Case vs. Border Vigilantes," Border Action Network, 01 October 2009). Following one particularly troubling case involving the death of a Hispanic man and his child in Arivaca, Arizona, in the summer of 2009—allegedly at the hands of a border vigilante—the Inter-American Commission on Human Rights agreed to hear the Border Action Network's case.

Actions by vigilante groups persisted into late 2010, with the rise of a new, heavily outfitted militia in Arizona led by former marine Jason "J.T." Ready. Ready has admitted to upholding Nazi-like beliefs of white supremacy, including the notion that nonwhites should leave the United States.

those people who cross an international border in their quest for refuge versus those who do not: *internally displaced persons* seek asylum away from their home region but within the political boundaries of their country of origin.

Migratory Roots

The movement of people within and beyond their national borders is not a new trend. In fact, the act of migration is as old as humanity itself, tracing its roots to the first people who inhabited Earth. Archeologists believe the likely spot where humans originated was somewhere in eastern or southern Africa. These early peoples made their way out of Africa by land to southern Asia about 1.8 million years ago. From there, over the course of thousands of years, they migrated to the northern and eastern sections of Asia. Scientists speculate that their path followed the migration routes of animal herds.

Haitan refugees living in a makeshift camp in Place St. Pierre, Haiti, 2010. Alison Wright/National Geographic Stock.

The overland trek was possible because much of the planet's ocean water was frozen in polar ice caps, and the continents as we now know them had not yet shifted into their present locations. During periods when sea levels were lower, land bridges connected northeastern Asia with present-day Alaska and Canada, allowing for migration to and settlement of what we now know as the Americas.

The early humans sought living spaces that matched their needs: ample land suitable for hunting and gathering, a generous supply of fresh water, fertile soil for farming, a livable climate, and protection from predators. While the motivations behind modern movements of populations might seem far more complicated than the forces that drove the first humans to migrate, decisions about where to live always center on some very basic and perennial concerns—namely, survival, safety, and the fulfillment of social and economic needs.

Migration, then, can be viewed as one of the defining forces in human history. One of the most potent examples of early migratory influence can be found in the composition of the English language. In essence, English is an amalgam reflecting influences from the multitude of peoples, often invaders, who have migrated to Britain over the ages—Latin from the Romans; Germanic from the Angles; Norse from the Vikings; and French from the Normans. The migrants or invaders brought their own linguistic traditions with them, merging them into the existing local language.

"Push" and "Pull" Factors

Throughout history, motivations for migrating have fallen into one of two categories defined by immigration scholars: *push factors* and *pull factors*.

Push Factors

As the name suggests, push factors are the key reasons that prompt people to leave their country of origin. One push factor that frequently drives individuals from their homeland is economics. When faced with insurmountable poverty, people migrate to areas that offer prospects for better-paid work. The economic push factor also operates within a nation's borders, several examples of which are available in the history of the United States.

Prior to the era of the world wars, more than three-quarters of all blacks in the United States lived in the southern states. Migration to the North began around 1920 and reached its peak, with an influx of more than five million people, around World War II. The United States was fast becoming an industrial giant, and a huge labor force was needed in the North. Around the same time, a large segment of southern black farmers found themselves out of work following the introduction of the mechanical cotton picker, marking the beginning of the end of the sharecropper

Bias in Immigration Reporting

The marked increase in coverage of the immigration situation in the United States has prompted calls for an end to the use of negative stereotypes by the media. The International Center for Journalists and the National Association of Hispanic journalists consider the term *illegal aliens*—as well as the shortened form, *illegals*—particularly objectionable: the word *alien* conjures up thoughts of strange and hostile beings, while the ungrammatical transformation of "illegal" into a noun demonizes people rather than their alleged crimes. Both organizations have appealed to the press to use the terms *undocumented immigrant* or *undocumented worker* in stories related to immigration.

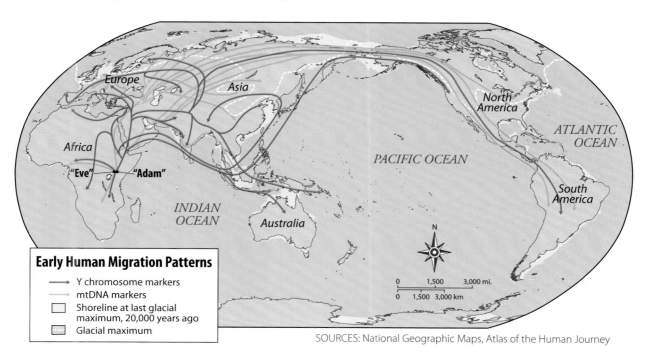

Early Human Migration Patterns

→ Y chromosome markers
→ mtDNA markers
☐ Shoreline at last glacial maximum, 20,000 years ago
▦ Glacial maximum

SOURCES: National Geographic Maps, Atlas of the Human Journey

The pattern of migration for our early ancestors to various parts of the world. Illustration/XNR Productions/Cengage Learning, Gale.

system. This change left black farm workers with few employment prospects in the South.

With a growing demand for unskilled labor in the North—and a reasonable expectation that there would be a reduction in the social and economic oppression that had marred the supposed gains of post–Civil War emancipation—African Americans headed to northern U.S. cities in record numbers. On Chicago's South Side alone, the black population quintupled by 1930. In all, between 1910 and 1970, about 6.5 million African Americans migrated to the northern United States.

In an ironic twist, the states in the North suffered a huge exodus of workers in the 1970s. The decline of manufacturing jobs in the automotive and steel industries triggered a voluntary economic migration of American workers from the North to the South. Large corporations saw the chance to increase their profits by moving production facilities out of the so-called Rust Belt states in the northeastern and mid-western United States and relocating to the South. With labor unions holding little sway in the South, the states in the Sun Belt offered a far more hospitable environment for industry. Lower labor costs allowed American-run companies to better compete with Asia's burgeoning manufacturers. Cheaper land and a lower overall cost of living in the South sealed the deal for corporate leaders, and a record number of new production facilities set up shop in the Sun Belt. Workers from the North followed the jobs to the southern states, which saw a significant increase in their populations.

Closely connected to the concept of economic migration is the need to escape from the ravaging effects of natural or human-caused disasters. The exodus from Ireland to Britain and the United States in the mid-nineteenth century was fueled by the unrelenting hunger and disease resulting from the Irish potato famine of the 1840s. Another push factor, the flight from religious persecution, advanced the formation of New World settlements in the seventeenth century and the eventual founding of the United States. Religious intolerance also led to the large-scale migration of

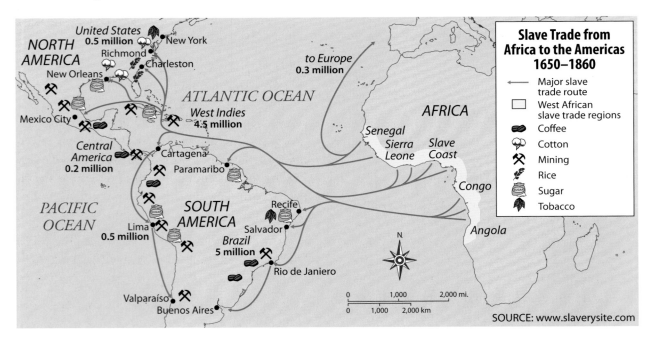

The primary routes travelled by enslaved West Africans between 1650 and 1860. Many slaves were delivered to the West Indies, Central America, and South America. Illustration/XNR Productions/Cengage Learning, Gale.

Jews from the former Soviet Union to Israel beginning in the 1970s.

In other corners of the world, push factors include escape from politically, racially, or ethnically based forms of oppression, or discrimination on the grounds of gender or sexual orientation. Corruption in the Haitian government under the ruthless Jean-Claude "Baby Doc" Duvalier set off a massive wave of Haitian immigration to the shores of southern Florida in the late 1970s and early 1980s. Likewise, the infamous Mariel Boatlift from Cuba stemmed from extreme dissent within the island nation. Fed up with opposition to his regime, the Communist leader Fidel Castro allowed 125,000 Cubans to sail for Miami from Mariel Harbor in 1980. He called the refugees *escoria,* meaning "trash" or "scum" in Spanish, and declared that he was glad to be rid of them.

Pull Factors

So-called pull factors, on the other hand, are what make an intended destination particularly attractive. Some immigrants seek a warmer climate (such as a Canadian retiree moving to Florida); others relocate for transnational marriage or other family reasons; and some move to enhance their cultural life (as when a Briton searches for *la dolce vita,* or "the sweet life," in Italy). Economic opportunity, religious tolerance, and lack of class restrictions have long been pull factors that attract migrants to the United States.

Immigration and the New World

Modern migration patterns began to be established around the sixteenth century, following the discovery of the so-called "New World" (the Americas and, later, Australasia). Immigration subsequently flowed from one continent to another at an unprecedented rate in human history. There were many different kinds of immigrants:

- European colonizers and settlers, often sponsored by their home countries

- forced migrants, especially people kidnapped into slavery and sent from Africa to the Americas

- and when that was prohibited in the nineteenth century, indentured or "coolie" labor from Asia.

Forced Migration Builds a Nation

One of the most significant westward immigration waves occurred between 1650 and 1860, when an estimated 10 to 12 million Africans were abducted and shipped to the New World as slaves. The process began slowly, with approximately 300,000 slaves brought to the Americas prior to the seventeenth century. Conditions on slave ships were horrific. The crowding was so severe that there was barely enough air to breathe and no room for the slaves to stand up. The kidnapped Africans were chained together in rows and literally wedged by the hundreds on the ships' decks, which were filthy because they lacked adequate toileting facilities. Crammed side-by-side for the duration of "the Middle Passage" (as their one-way journey to servitude came to be called), they endured these conditions for an average of six to eight weeks, the time it took for the journey from Africa to America in good weather.

During the eighteenth century, more than six million slaves were imported to America. Historians point out that these numbers represent African men, women, and children who survived the brutal conditions of the forced migration. Hundreds of thousands more—possibly one of every five, by some accounts—died of disease or starvation aboard the slave ships, or were killed in failed escape attempts.

Immigration in the Nineteenth Century

Immigration is frequently a response to a hard-faced economic need. In the nineteenth century, millions of immigrants—first from western Europe, then increasingly from southern and eastern Europe—began arriving on America's shores,

"Slaves below Deck." This painting by Lieutenant Francis Meynell of the British Royal Navy depicts the hold of a captured slave ship in 1846. The Granger Collection, New York.

seeking a better life for themselves and future generations. Technological progress hastened the rate of migration. Throughout the 1800s, with the advent of the steamship, the number of people migrating to the United States increased rapidly, reaching around 50 million by the century's end.

Who Ended Up in the United States?

Early immigrants to the United States came in waves. In 1825, Great Britain declared that England was overpopulated: Old British laws prohibiting emigration were replaced by new laws encouraging it. At the same time, the first migrants from Norway set out for America. A list of petitions for U.S. naturalization from the first half of the 1800s included names like Robert Blackburn, a "fancy chair maker" from Rothwell, near Leeds, England; Robert Brown, a Scottish stone cutter; J.J. Johanisen, a Norwegian portrait painter; and the Reverend Jeremiah Keily, from County Cork, Ireland.

Crop failures began plaguing subsistence farmers throughout Europe in the 1840s, leaving them destitute. In Ireland, a fast-moving blight rotted potatoes on their stalks; in just two years' time, between 1845 and 1847, the devastating potato famine led to an alarming decrease in Ireland's population. More than a million Irish people died of starvation. By 1854, one to two million Irish immigrants moved to the United States to seek a better life.

The Irish joined a large population of Germans who had arrived in the United States over the course of two centuries. An influx of Poles, Italians, Greeks, and eastern European Jews followed. They found work as carpenters, caterers, hairdressers, and jewelers, and as skilled laborers in the garment industry and manufacturing. Their plan was to establish themselves in the new land—find employment, locate a place to live, save some money—and eventually send for their relatives back home.

Meanwhile, Over in Australia

Australia's wool industry boomed in the 1820s, creating a huge demand for labor and sparking an increase in people seeking to migrate from Britain. Many Irish farming families fled to Australia to escape starvation during the 1840s. A decade later, the gold rush triggered another wave of immigration; hundreds of thousands of immigrants landed in Australia around this time, including many Chinese.

Australia was a haven for Chinese immigrants who faced prejudice in the United States and restrictions on their eligibility for U.S. citizenship. The first Chinese Exclusion Act was passed by the United States Congress in 1882, following outcries from American workers who feared that lower-paid Chinese workers would take their jobs.

America at the Turn of the Twentieth Century: A Melting Pot?

The history of the United States is unlike that of any other country in the world. Sparsely populated in the sixteenth century, it had attracted tens of millions of people from all corners of the world by the twentieth century. Americans who had lived in the United States for generations began to wonder when or if the continued migratory inflow would end.

The mix of languages, cultures, and religions contributed to the "melting pot" theory of U.S. immigration. The belief was that newly arrived groups would eventually learn English and forge a new identity as Americans; this, however, was not always the case. Immigrants from the same country tended to settle together, the new arrivals learning from the old. Language barriers were perpetuated by clubs and church congregations organized along ethnic lines. Insulated and sometimes isolated, the vibrant nationalities that comprised the new nation did not always "melt" as expected.

Quotas

To address concerns about unlimited immigration, the United States Congress prohibited migration from Asia altogether and passed the first of several quota acts on immigrant populations from Europe in 1921. Quotas were based on percentages of existing populations in the United States by place of origin in a given year. The system resulted in a drastic decrease in overall immigration to the United States, with the number of people allowed in from southern and eastern Europe suffering the largest cuts.

International Refugees in the Twentieth Century

A primary motivator for people seeking refuge in a foreign land is to avoid the violence that targets them because of their race, religion, nationality, or social or political convictions. Refugees feel compelled to seek protection outside their country of origin due to a genuine fear of persecution or death at the hands of aggressors. Although refugees have existed since the earliest human civilizations, it was not until the two world wars in the twentieth century that international treaties and agencies began to tackle this problem.

The World Wars

After World War I, millions of people were displaced in Europe and Asia. The League of Nations Office of High Commissioner for Refugees was established in 1921, headed by Norwegian scientist and diplomat Fridtjof Wedel-Jarlsberg Nansen. The Nansen Office, as it came to be called, issued 450,000 international passports to refugees. These were honored by more than fifty countries. In the postwar years, the program was highly successful, providing assistance to 500,000 Greeks who resettled from Asia Minor to Greece and to 500,000 Turks who resettled from Greece to Turkey, and helping the 1.4 million Russians who had fled their country after the Russian Revolution of 1917.

As the Nazi party gained power in Germany in the early 1930s, Jews and others who feared the new government began to emigrate. By 1938, when it was clear that the Nazis aimed to eliminate Jews from Germany, a mass exodus began that continued until the end of 1941, when Germany sealed its exits and prohibited any further flights. Most of the Jews who left Germany went to Britain, North America, or Palestine. But due at least in part to a severe economic depression that was occurring worldwide at the time, many nations feared massive influxes of immigrants. At the time that Jewish refugees desperately needed asylum, many countries, including the Soviet Union, Britain, Canada, and the United States, erected immigration barriers severely restricting the admission of immigrants. The League of Nations offered little help. Without legal means of staying in one country, many European Jews were forced to move from place to place in Poland, Russia, and other areas. Hundreds of thousands of these refugees died during World War II.

The United Nations

When the UN was established after the war, dealing with the refugee problem was one it its highest priorities. In 1948, the UN issued the Universal Declaration of Human Rights, which included the right "to seek and to enjoy in other countries asylum from persecution." The UN International Refugees Organization (IRO) helped

Restrictions of Immigration to the United States

Immigration policy in the United States was basically unrestricted until 1882, when Congress passed the Chinese Exclusion Act, barring Chinese laborers from entering the country. Originally working as miners during the California gold rush, the Chinese went on to become a formidable economic force in the United States. In the 1860s, they helped build the first transcontinental railroad in North America— a project vital to the development of the U.S. economy. Still, the Chinese were largely viewed as outsiders who "stole" American jobs and drove down wages.

All Asian immigration to the United States was banned between 1924 and 1943, when President Franklin D. Roosevelt convinced Congress that it was in America's best interest to repeal the exclusionary laws against China, an American ally during World War II.

Increasingly restrictive immigration policies followed an influx of European immigrants from Ireland and Italy—mainly poor and Catholic—in the 1800s and early 1900s. A steady flow of Catholics from southern Europe in the last two decades of the nineteenth century was accompanied by a surge in the number of eastern European Jews that continued into the twentieth century. Opposition to the growth of the non-Protestant population in the United States swelled. In fact, disdain for Italians in the early 1900s paralleled the anti-Mexican sentiment prevalent in many parts of the nation during the early twenty-first century, when Mexicans

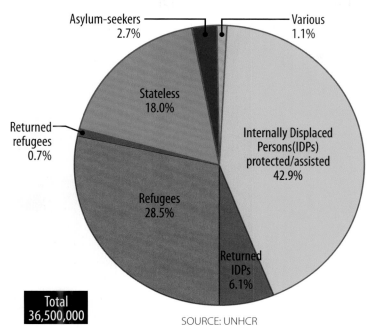

Total Population of Concern to UNHCR by Category, End-2009

Asylum-seekers
2.7%

Various
1.1%

Stateless
18.0%

Returned refugees
0.7%

Internally Displaced Persons(IDPs) protected/assisted
42.9%

Refugees
28.5%

Returned IDPs
6.1%

Total
36,500,000

SOURCE: UNHCR

Breakdown of the 36.5 million people of concern to the United Nations' High Commissioner for Refugees. Illustration/XNR Productions/Cengage Learning, Gale.

1.5 million European and Asian refugees. It was dismantled in 1951, when the United Nations Convention Relating to the Status of Refugees—the cornerstone of international law on refugees—was adopted.

Since 1951, the Office of the United Nations High Commissioner for Refugees (UNHCR) has been responsible for protecting international refugees. It helps to establish "durable solutions" to the problems created by mass movements of people resulting from civil disturbance or military conflict. The UN encourages countries to admit refugees and provide resettlement opportunities for

outnumbered all other immigrants to the States. In major American cities, contempt for Italian laborers was reflected in storefront "help wanted" signs that read, "Guineas [a racial slur for "Italians"] need not apply."

A dramatic change in immigration patterns followed the passage of the Immigration Act of 1924, which revised the terms of the Immigration Act of 1921 by establishing strict quotas based on national origin. Immigration from southern and eastern European nations plummeted with the implementation of these quotas, as seen in

Italy's immigration history. According to the U.S. Bureau of the Census, a whopping 222,260 of the 805,228 immigrants entering the United States in 1921 were from Italy. Four years later, however, a much smaller pool of immigrants arrived (just 294,314), with only 6,203 of them originating from Italy.

Policies favoring immigrants from northwestern Europe over those from southeastern Europe remained in effect until 1965. The national quota system seemed to clash with the ideology of the burgeoning civil rights movement in

1960s America. A new law, the Immigration Act of 1965, liberalized U.S. immigration policy, setting immigration limits by hemisphere rather than country and facilitating the entry of recent immigrants' family members.

Immigration scholars credit the 1965 act with boosting the numbers of Central American and Asian migrants to the United States in the decades that followed. According to demographics experts, if current trends continue, half the U.S. population will be of Central American or Asian descent by the year 2050.

Palestinians mark the 61st anniversary of Nakba, when hundreds of thousands of Palestinian people fled or were driven out of their homes when Israel was created. AP Images/Adel Hana.

them. It also helps refugees settle in their new homes.

In 1948, the UN addressed the Palestinian refugee situation in the Middle East. In the year-long war that followed Israel's declaration of independence in 1948, more than 700,000 Arabs living in Palestine (80 percent) fled the country, fearing attacks by Israeli fighters. Palestinians refer to this event as the *nakba,* Arabic for "disaster." Many Palestinians took refuge in camps near the west bank of the Jordan River and in a southern coastal area known as the Gaza Strip. The UN created a new organization, the United Nations Relief for Palestinian Refugees, later called the United Nations Relief and Works Agency for Palestine Refugees in the Near East (UNRWA), which assisted more than 1.5 million Palestinian refugees

through the early 1970s. At the turn of the century, an estimated five million displaced Palestinians made up about one-fourth of the world's refugees. They are considered the oldest and largest refugee population in the world today.

In the mid-1970s, tens of thousands of Vietnamese people fled the Vietnam War and conditions that resulted from the conflict. The UN-HCR assisted more than 36,000 Vietnamese boat people in the South China Sea and also took over relief efforts among Cambodian refugees in transit camps in Thailand. In 1982, the UNHCR turned its attention to the 1.2 million African refugees in Somalia, Sudan, Djibouti, Kenya, and the Horn of Africa. The majority of these refugees were escaping conditions of famine in

Some of the World's Most Important Current Migration Routes

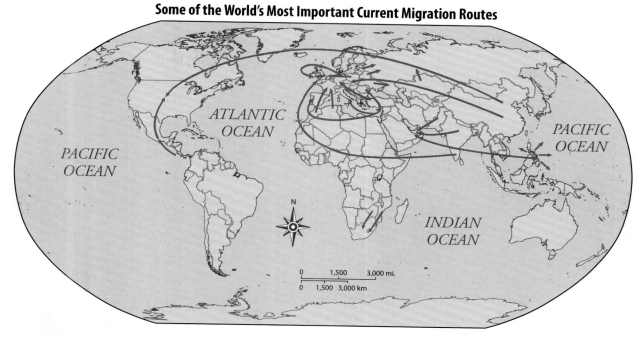

SOURCES: National Public Radio; The Economist

Modern routes of migration around the world. Illustration/XNR Productions/Cengage Learning, Gale.

underdeveloped African countries.

Also in the early 1980s, the UNHCR helped 2.9 million refugees leave Afghanistan, where war with the Soviet Union was ongoing, to resettle in Pakistan. Although millions of Afghan refugees have been able to return home in the intervening years, in 2007 the UNHCR reported about 1.9 million refugees from the war-torn country remained scattered throughout seventy-two countries—mostly in Pakistan and Iran.

Globalization and Immigration Trends

Patterns of international immigration have been shaped by increasing global interdependence and the changing nature of world politics. Globalization is a term used to describe the increasing trend toward free trade, open borders, and the free movement of capital and goods—and sometimes people—across those borders. The globalization surge that began in the late 1990s is the largest

one the world has witnessed to date, with flows of investment across international borders topping the $12 trillion mark.

End of the Cold War Leads to Immigration Boom

After World War II, a state of extreme political tension known as the Cold War arose between the United States and the Soviet Union. No declarations of war were made between the two countries during the Cold War, but the ideological differences between Americans and Soviets crystallized. The U.S. government came to view the Soviets as a menacing force in world affairs. Americans championed democracy, while the Soviets espoused the virtues of communism.

With central and eastern European countries under its thumb, the Soviet Union managed to quell dissension in its satellite states for decades. In the United States, fear of communist conspiracies abounded in the postwar years, and a nuclear arms race with the Soviet Union ensued. During

Uzbek refugees who fled from Kyrgyzstan live in a refugee camp on the border at the Uzbek village of Erkishlok. AP Images/Anvar Ilyasov.

the late 1980s, a revolutionary tide swept over the Eastern Bloc nations, and the Cold War came to a close with the dissolution of the Soviet Union in 1991. Increased political openness and freedom of movement ensued in the former Soviet nations, along with the promise of free elections and hope for economic reform throughout the region.

The Cold War's end—coupled with the formation of the European Union (EU) in 1993, its subsequent expansion, vigorous economic gains in the early 2000s, and the relaxation of EU member nations' border controls—resulted in an immense rise in legal and illegal immigration. Undocumented immigrants adopted ever more ingenious and dangerous methods to reach the West. An upsurge in conflicts throughout Africa and the Middle East also caused a sharp rise in the number of people seeking safety and political asylum in European countries and North America.

At the same time, legal short-term migration of workers from Eastern European countries such as Poland helped boost the economies of richer EU countries. Clearly, as journalist Harry de Quetteville put it in a 23 October 2008 article for the London *Telegraph*, "Poles have brought with them . . . a no-nonsense ethic that mines a deep nostalgia in Britain for an age of hard-working simplicity." In the same article, Paul Statham, a University of Bristol sociology professor, called the Polish migration to the United Kingdom "a mass arrival of people with traditional values that have been eroded here [in the UK]."

The 1990s and Beyond: Globalization and Its Wild Effects on Immigration

The remarkable $12 trillion of international investment that fueled the global economy in the late 1990s and early 2000s had far-reaching and

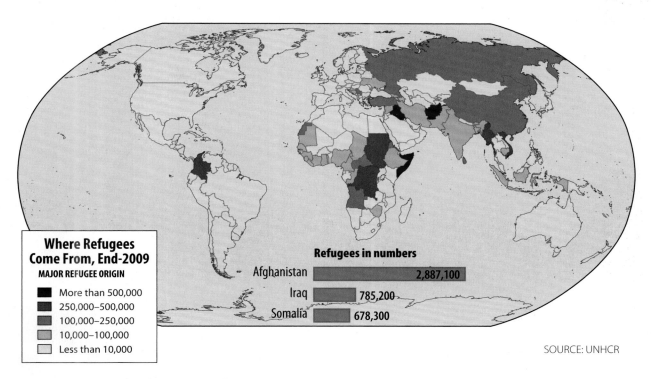

Where Refugees Come From, End-2009

MAJOR REFUGEE ORIGIN

- More than 500,000
- 250,000–500,000
- 100,000–250,000
- 10,000–100,000
- Less than 10,000

Refugees in numbers

Afghanistan — 2,887,100
Iraq — 785,200
Somalia — 678,300

SOURCE: UNHCR

Major source countries for refugees in 2009. Illustration/XNR Productions/Cengage Learning, Gale.

unanticipated effects. In March 2005, following sharp increases in immigration to the West, the United Nations High Commissioner for Refugees actually reported a third year of steep *declines* in immigration. Improvements in the economies of countries like Poland and Ireland were largely responsible. The number of refugees and people seeking asylum in industrialized countries went down as well. Observers attributed the reduction to a decrease in refugee-producing armed conflicts, along with a rise of more stable and humane governments throughout the world.

But a reversal of these encouraging trends began in 2008: international trade began to shrink that year, and the decline continued through most of 2009. This global recession wiped out many hard-won improvements in the world's interconnected economies.

As jobs became scarce in 2008 and 2009 even in wealthy nations, governments moved to limit new immigration by reducing quotas and making

it more difficult for firms to hire immigrant labor, according to a 2009 report by the Organization for Economic Cooperation and Development. From the United States and the European Union to Asia and even Australia, the first decade of the twenty-first century saw an increase in calls for better border protection and stiffer enforcement of existing immigration policies. Disturbingly, acts of violence against immigrant workers and students appear to be on the rise. For instance, Indian immigrants have recently been the targets of gang violence in Australia, a nation long known for its open borders and acceptance of immigrants.

Fears Grow, Attitudes Change

The issue of contemporary immigration (since the onset of the global recession) tends to evoke strong feelings that range from impassioned support and empathy to anger and rage. In very few countries do the famous sentiments expressed on the Statue of Liberty ("Give me your tired, your

Bangladeshis in hiding in Melilla. Many people try to immigrate illegally to Europe via Melilla, an exclave of Spain on the coast of North Africa. Rafael Marchante/Reuters.

poor / Your huddled masses yearning to breathe free . . .") still ring true. The cause for this swing in opinion is connected to money. Just like their nineteenth-century predecessors, twenty-first-century immigrants are motivated by economics. Seeking a better life for future generations of their families, they arrive in industrialized nations prepared to take on laborious, dirty, and unskilled but necessary jobs that few in the native population will accept.

For instance, day laborers from Mexico perform backbreaking work on U.S. farms for a small fraction of the pay given nonimmigrant workers. Spanish farmers say their strawberries would rot in the fields if not for the seasonal Romanian pickers who harvest them. Still, some immigrant

populations face hostility and racial intolerance in their new homelands. Indeed, large segments of the population in some industrialized countries are so opposed to allowing more immigrants into their countries that immigration, whether legal or illegal, has become a defining electoral issue. Efforts aimed at determining the optimal level of annual immigration allowed by a country are now a political priority.

In addition to low wages and harsh working conditions, some immigrants are subject to physical abuse by employers. About one million Indonesians work in Malaysia as maids and physical laborers. In 2009, scandal erupted when pictures of a scarred Indonesian maid were broadcast on television. The woman had allegedly been the victim of years of physical abuse at the hands of her employer. The Indonesian government claims that abuse of Indonesian maids in Malaysia is widespread, and it has announced that it will halt the immigration of domestic workers to Malaysia until the two governments can agree on labor reforms to protect the workers.

The Balancing Act

Effective management of immigration poses numerous problems for governments of both rich and poor countries. For rich nations, the dilemma does not end with deciding who should be allowed in; it extends to finding a workable way of keeping the rest out. In poorer countries, the better-educated and more naturally entrepreneurial members of the population tend to leave in search of a better life in richer countries. This can cause a "brain drain" in the countries of origin.

Civic Alliance of Roma members protest the French government's expulsion of Roma migrants. Radu Sigheti/Reuters.

Brain drain refers to a large emigration from an area by people with vital professional skills and knowledge in such fields as medicine, technology, business, law, and administration, who seek

Migrant workers in Turkey collect onions during harvest time. © Reuters/Corbis.

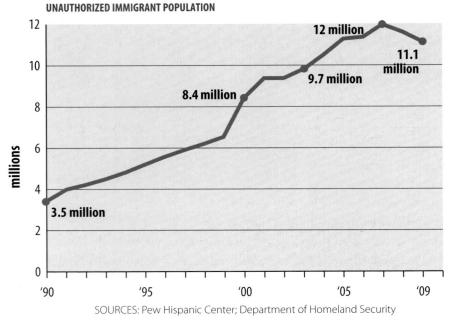

Drop in Inflow of Illegal Immigrants to the U.S.

UNAUTHORIZED IMMIGRANT POPULATION

3.5 million

8.4 million

9.7 million

12 million

11.1 million

millions

'90   '95   '00   '05   '09

SOURCES: Pew Hispanic Center; Department of Homeland Security

An estimate of illegal immigration to the United States from 1990 to 2009. Illustration/XNR Productions/Cengage Learning, Gale.

better conditions in a more prosperous country. This phenomenon compounds the developing country's unfulfilled potential and lack of development, resulting in a vicious circle, in which the best of the next generation will also want to leave.

The New Push and Pull:
Keep Out—Unless, of Course, You're a Genius

Immigration reform advocates in the United States argue that the nation has lost control of its borders; they demand a legislative remedy for the situation. A similar trend is under way in Western Europe as EU nations grapple with the social, economic, and political effects of immigration. Lured by the promise of better jobs and a higher standard of living, immigrants from Latin American and Eastern European countries set out for Spain, France, Ireland, Britain, and Germany starting in the 1990s. Many, however, are now returning to their home countries. Ireland alone saw fifty thousand immigrants leave its borders between

April 2008 and April 2009. Other countries, including Spain, are even paying immigrants to go back to their home countries.

The situation in Ireland offers a dramatic example of the connection between immigration trends and economic conditions. Beginning in the mid-1990s, Ireland underwent a period of rapid economic and social change. The nation's economy shifted from manufacturing and food production to global technology and services. As a result, Ireland's labor force grew, and an overall population increase of 18 percent occurred between 1999 and 2008. This rapid growth in population was attributed largely to immigration.

The economic crisis of 2008–2009 coincided with record decreases in immigration to Ireland and Spain, according to a 2010 report by the Migration Policy Institute titled *Migration and Immigrants Two Years after the Financial Collapse: Where Do We Stand?* Ireland's economy was particularly susceptible to the destabilizing factors that characterized the recession. A reduction in investments from foreign-owned firms sent the nation's economy into a tailspin. Job security became the number-one priority for Irish citizens; public outcry led to a tightening of government restrictions on non-Irish workers. Ireland's fourteen-year reign as one of the leading migratory destination countries in the world ended in 2009.

A similar story unfolded in Spain with the onset of the recession. Decades of growth and prosperity for Spain led to huge increases in the immigrant population: from 1999 to 2008, one of every three immigrants to Europe settled in Spain—some legally, some illegally. Immigrants from Romania and Morocco, more than 750,000 and 600,000 respectively, made up about 25 percent of the newly arrived people in Spain. By 2010, however, the rate of unemployment among Spanish-born citizens reached 20 percent; immigrants to Spain fared even worse, with an unemployment rate of 30 percent. In an effort to put its people back to work, the Spanish government sought to restrict the entry of non-Spanish workers.

A comparable situation has emerged in Germany, as well. In a story for NPR titled "In Germany, Voices against Immigration Grow Louder," Eric Westervelt described

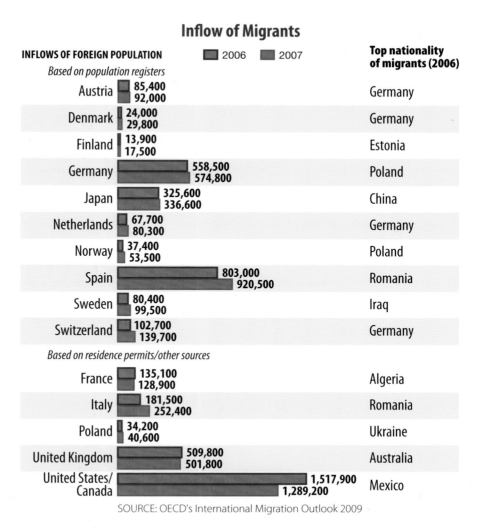

Inflow of Migrants

INFLOWS OF FOREIGN POPULATION ■ 2006 ■ 2007

Top nationality of migrants (2006)

Based on population registers

Country	2006	2007	Top nationality of migrants (2006)
Austria	85,400	92,000	Germany
Denmark	24,000	29,800	Germany
Finland	13,900	17,500	Estonia
Germany	558,500	574,800	Poland
Japan	325,600	336,600	China
Netherlands	67,700	80,300	Germany
Norway	37,400	53,500	Poland
Spain	803,000	920,500	Romania
Sweden	80,400	99,500	Iraq
Switzerland	102,700	139,700	Germany

Based on residence permits/other sources

Country	2006	2007	Top nationality of migrants (2006)
France	135,100	128,900	Algeria
Italy	181,500	252,400	Romania
Poland	34,200	40,600	Ukraine
United Kingdom	509,800	501,800	Australia
United States/Canada	1,517,900	1,289,200	Mexico

SOURCE: OECD's International Migration Outlook 2009

Migrant inflows into Organisation for Economic Co-operation and Development (OECD) countries. Illustration/XNR Productions/Cengage Learning, Gale.

the ill effects of strict immigration policies on the nation's businesses. Anti-immigration action on the part of the German government has been so extreme that it may be causing more harm than good for German businesses. More than 1,100 of Germany's 1,600 high-tech companies reported having difficulties filling open positions in 2010.

Conditions in Germany mirror a reversing trend in migration throughout Europe: a phenomenon known as "elite" immigration status. Although unauthorized immigrant flows dropped significantly in 2009, the Migration Policy Institute noted that admission of highly skilled immigrants—those said to have "extraordinary abilities"—are rising to unprecedented levels in some countries. Proposed immigration caps in the EU have scientists, researchers, and academics in Western nations concerned that bright minds from around the world will be denied access to their countries. In particular, recent measures to lower immigration into Britain from 200,000 people annually to just 50,000 have set off a panic among the nation's scholars, who fear that future advancements in British science (and, therefore, economic progress for the entire United Kingdom) may be at risk.

Refugees in Crisis

With economic instability comes political instability. According to the 2009 Global Trends report released by the United Nations High Commissioner for Refugees in June 2010, an estimated 43.3 million people had been uprooted, exiled, or otherwise displaced from their homes because of persecution or armed conflict by the end of 2009, an increase of 1.3 million from 2008. This number includes a global total of more than 15 million refugees and asylum seekers, and 27 million internally displaced persons (IDPs). Such a high number of IDPs had not been reported since 1994, and experts say that although the shaky world economy may not be entirely to blame, it has certainly had an impact on the situation.

A Startling Trend

People who flee in fear of persecution or turmoil have a right to seek asylum in other nations, but those countries do not have to grant it. Since the 11 September 2001 (9/11) terrorist attacks in the United States, many countries have passed anti-terrorism laws that restrict refugee rights. Within six weeks of 9/11, President George W. Bush signed the USA Patriot Act into law. This sweeping legislation was designed to make it easier for the U.S. government to investigate terrorist threats and crack down on illegal immigrants suspected of having ties to terrorist organizations. The act loosened rules concerning detention, interrogation, and deportation, leading some critics to argue that it unfairly targets and vilifies law-abiding immigrants of Middle Eastern descent

Racial Profiling

The 9/11 attacks stirred the pot of racism in the United States. Many people felt that following the attacks, people of Middle Eastern descent became targets for racial profiling. The Middle East, more accurately described as Southwest Asia, is predominantly Muslim.

The 9/11 attackers all originated from Middle Eastern countries, and trained in Al Qaeda camps in Afghanistan. They were Muslims with extreme views which motivated them to make the attack. Because of this, after 9/11 some Americans began to assume—incorrectly—that all Middle Easterners and Muslims pose a threat to the United States.

A 2003 U.S. Department of Justice factsheet on racial profiling attacks the practice as "discriminatory" and "dehumanizing":

America has a moral obligation to prohibit racial profiling. Race-based assumptions in law enforcement perpetuate negative racial stereotypes that are harmful to our diverse democracy, and materially impair our efforts to maintain a fair and just society. [Furthermore,] racial profiling... taints the entire criminal justice system [because it] rests on the erroneous assumption that any particular individual of one race or ethnicity is more likely to engage in misconduct than any particular individual of other races or ethnicities.

While the language in the aforementioned factsheet seems clear enough, it has had little impact on post-9/11 perceptions of Muslims held by some in the United States or on the widespread but mistaken assumption that Southwest Asia is rife with anti-American terrorist networks. In March 2004, a report by the N.Y. Advisory Committee to the U.S. Commission on Civil Rights pointed out that the backlash from 9/11 reaches far beyond stereotyping: it has led to the creation of "no fly" lists, broad-based wiretapping and communications monitoring, financial assets control, tightened rules regarding detainment and deportation, even disputes about due process in immigration proceedings. And anti-Muslim attitudes apparently die hard. In August 2010, nearly nine years after 9/11, an unsuspecting New York City taxi cab driver had his face and arm slashed by a passenger who had asked him if he was Muslim. The attack is believed to have been connected to the proposed building of a mosque near the former site of the Twin Towers—commonly referred to as Ground Zero—in Manhattan.

Afghan migrants who set up "The Jungle" camp in Calais, France, protest as police move in to break up the camp. Daniel Fouray/Photopqr/Ouest France/newscom.

living in the United States.

In some cases, refugees have been sent back to the countries from which they fled, where they faced the possibility of further persecution or even death. At the turn of the twenty-first century, the wealthiest nations were in many cases the least likely to help refugees. According to Human Rights Watch, Asia hosts 45 percent of the world's refugees, while Africa hosts 30 percent, Europe hosts 19 percent, and North America hosts about 5 percent.

High unemployment rates and sluggish economies throughout Europe from 2008 to 2010 sparked an array of anti-asylum measures. Consider, for example, the controversial move made by the French government in September 2009, when officials announced the closure of a migrant camp in the port of Calais known as "the jungle."

Calais is located just across the English Channel from Britain, making it a magnet for refugees seeking entry into the United Kingdom.

Prolonged conflict in their home countries led many Afghans and Iraqis to the port of Calais, and the settlement of 1,800 migrants there became a thorn in the side of French immigration officials. To discourage the resettlement of migrants in Calais, French authorities reduced the camp to rubble. Although the French claimed that the immigrants from the camp would be allowed to apply for asylum, few did. Instead, many ended up back on the streets of Calais, preferring a life on the run from French authorities—sometimes hiding in the woods, in train cars, or under bridges with little or no protection from the elements—to a return trip home.

A group of Afghan refugee girls collect water from a hand pump next to their camp in Pakistan. AP Images/Muhammed Muheisen.

The IDP Crisis in Africa

The Geneva-based Internal Displacement Monitoring Centre cited Africa as the region hardest hit by internal displacement, with Sudan, the Democratic Republic of the Congo, and Somalia reporting a total of 8.3 million IDPs (*Internal Displacement: Global Overview of Trends and Developments in 2009,* May 2010).

The Tragedy of Sudan

Except for ten years in its fifty-five-year history as an independent state, the northeast African country of Sudan has been embroiled in civil war. The nation's first civil war, which lasted for seventeen years, began in 1956 as a result of religious differences, an uneven distribution of wealth and resources, and claims that southern Sudan's interests were being ignored by the northern-led,

Arab-dominated central government. A fragile peace was established between 1972 and 1983, but a second civil war broke out when the central government assumed control of southern military forces and undertook efforts to Islamicize the South.

Another peace settlement promising a more equal share of wealth and power was reached in Sudan in 2005, but human rights tragedies persisted. Five years of unparalleled violence in the western region of Darfur led to the displacement of half the region's population. In what is widely described as an act of genocide, the Janjaweed—an Arabic militia force backed by the Sudanese government—murdered an estimated 400,000 people in Darfur.

Although the Sudanese president, Omar al-Bashir, declared the war in Darfur over in February

2010 and won reelection two months later in the nation's first multiparty election in two decades, a unified Sudan is an unlikely possibility. Reports of widespread voter intimidation, safety concerns, censored media coverage, and other irregularities undermined the credibility of the April elections, and in July, a warrant for al-Bashir's arrest on charges of war crimes was issued by the International Criminal Court. Southern Sudan was scheduled to hold a referendum in January 2011 about a likely separation from the Muslim-dominated north.

Ongoing Strife in the DRC

The Democratic Republic of the Congo (DRC), located in central Africa, has been ravaged by war since the mid-1990s. By the end of 2009, fighting between UN peacekeeping forces and armed militants had led to millions of deaths, and the number of displaced civilians stood at 1.9 million. The internally displaced women and children of Africa—often living on the fringes of society in makeshift camps while armed conflicts in their home regions drag on—are particularly vulnerable to rape and other forms of abuse. Such is the case in the DRC, where rape and murder occurs at an alarming rate. Children are often abducted by militia groups and forced to fight in the relentless conflict. Food shortages and abysmal living conditions combined with a lack of adequate health care and educational opportunities contribute to intractable poverty and disease.

A "Living Nightmare" in Somalia

In Somalia in early 2009, a brief break in the fighting between government forces and a militant Islamic insurgency group in Mogadishu offered false hope for the region's IDPs and refugees. By April, hundreds of thousands of civilians were forced to flee to camps that humanitarian aid workers call a "living nightmare" and "unfit for humans." In the Dadaab refugee camp in Kenya, 300,000 Somalis were living at a site originally intended for 90,000 people, and forces on both sides of the conflict were accused of recruiting refugee children into their ranks.

A thirsty child drinks from a water pump in the Shaddad IDP Camp Shangle Tubaya village in North Darfur. Ho New/Reuters.

In Afgooye, 30 kilometers south of Mogadishu, 400,000 people were crowded into what observers say is the densest concentration of refugees in the world.

With little food or water and only one toilet for every 200 people in area camps, the health of the refugee population declined. The UN estimated that a quarter of Somalia's displaced and refugee children were severely malnourished. In a particularly bold move, insurgents in southern and central Somalia forced UN agencies to leave the area. Conditions worsened even further after kidnappings and attacks on other international aid workers led humanitarian agencies to pull out their staff. The fighting in Somalia, which continued in late 2010, has affected three generations of Somali people, many of whom grew up and had their own children without ever seeing the land of their ancestors.

The Kampala Convention

In an effort to establish standards for protection and support of IDPs throughout Africa, the Convention for the Protection and Assistance of Internally Displaced Persons in Africa, more widely known as the Kampala Convention or the Kampala Declaration, was adopted by the African Union on 23 October 2009. However, the declaration will not become binding until fifteen of the fifty-three AU member states ratify it. As of late 2010, twenty-nine countries had signed it, but only two—Uganda and Sierra Leone—had ratified it.

IDPs Outside of Africa: Pakistan, Colombia, and Iraq

The three largest internally displaced populations outside of Africa in 2009 were in Pakistan, Colombia, and Iraq. Three million new displacements in Pakistan resulted from massive government attacks against the Taliban, an ultra-Islamist insurgent group, between the spring of 2009 and the spring of 2010. Although some Pakistanis were able to return home when the fighting subsided, many found themselves displaced again shortly thereafter due to a general lack of safety in their home regions, the destruction of their property during earlier displacement, and the renewal of armed violence between security forces and the Taliban.

Again, families headed by women found themselves in the most danger. A particularly disturbing finding was revealed in the Amnesty International report *"As If Hell Fell on Me": The Human Rights Crisis in Northwest Pakistan*, published in June 2010: Many displaced women in the region—unable in many cases to obtain proper identification papers because of gender bias, and unacknowledged as heads of their households in a male-dominated society—had been forced into prostitution in order to survive.

In late July and early August 2010, just a month after that report was released, northwestern Pakistan was dealt another blow: The area experienced devastating flooding. Four million people were forced from their homes and at

The aftermath of the 2010 Pakistani floods leave two young Pakistani children covered with flies as they live in miserable conditions. AP Images/Mohammad Sajjad.

least 1,600 were killed. The floods of 2010 only compounded the refugee situation, as people in Pakistan struggled for a dwindling share of humanitarian relief. Aid that had been reaching the nation's war-induced IDPs was diverted to people displaced by flooding.

In the South American nation of Colombia, decades of conflict resulted in a migratory loss of 10 percent of its population. New armed groups replaced the old in a seemingly endless struggle with government troops. The number of Colombian IDPs continued to grow throughout 2009, as fighting spread to previously unaffected regions of the country. According to the UN High Commissioner for Refugees, a majority of the refugees have no desire to return home. Ongoing guerilla warfare, unexploded landmines, and new threats from gangs involved in the country's highly profitable drug trade make Colombia unsafe for returning civilians.

The situation in Iraq remains at crisis levels, as well. According to Amnesty International, the Iraq War, which began in 2003, has produced an estimated 2.5 million refugees and an additional two million IDPs. A significant number of Iraqi

Cuban refugees wait on a flight deck of the U.S. Coast Guard cutter *Dauntless* as two fishing boats full of additional refugees enter the harbor at Key West, Florida, on 21 May 1980. AP Images/S. Helben.

refugees fled to Jordan and Syria, but some have applied for asylum in Europe or the Americas.

In October 2009, the UN Refugee Agency criticized the recent trend of rejecting asylum requests by European nations. The high commissioner noted that the United Kingdom, Denmark, and Sweden had forced refugees to return to Iraq, even though "serious human rights abuses"

in the conflict-ridden region make it crucial for refugees to be given international protection. The abuse of Iraqi civilians continues, and according to the Internal Displacement Monitoring Centre, the movement of displaced persons has been severely limited by checkpoints, barriers, curfews, and other security measures. Additionally, the withdrawal of American troops in August 2010 led to fears of an impending humanitarian crisis for Iraqi civilians.

Recent Immigration-related Developments in Asia

No-Nonsense Policy in the United Arab Emirates

Announcements made in 2009–2010 by the Ministry of the Interior in the United Arab Emirates (UAE) reflect a clear desire to limit immigration to the region. The UAE is located east of Saudi Arabia on the Persian Gulf. About three-quarters of its population is composed of immigrants, and foreign workers make up more than half the labor force.

Between 2004 and 2006, large numbers of Asian workers migrated to the UAE to fill jobs in the then-booming construction industry. However, by 2009, the effects of the global recession had slowed construction projects to a crawl. High-level jobs in the business sector were affected as well, and the unemployment rate among citizens and foreigners soared. Migrant workers, mostly from India, lost their visas when they lost their jobs and were forced to leave the country.

At the same time, the UAE stiffened existing immigration laws, heightened security, and instituted high taxes on remaining foreign workers in order to finance the training of indigenous workers. Other steps were taken by the government to discourage immigrants from entering the UAE, including crackdowns requiring the authentication of documents, an expensive new degree verification process, mandatory cultural-knowledge testing for foreigners, routine fingerprinting and iris scans, and single-entry-only visitor visas.

Sri Lanka's Defeated Tamils

Sri Lanka is an island nation located in the Indian Ocean southeast of India. The roots of its internal struggles lie in a longstanding battle for political rights that pitted minority Tamil insurgents against the Sri Lankan government. The twenty-five-year-long civil war ended in 2009, with the Sri Lankan government claiming triumph over the Tamils. But Sri Lanka's final, bloody offensive left an estimated 280,000 civilians displaced. The real death toll remains unknown because aid workers and journalists were barred from the region during the last (and deadliest) weeks of fighting. In May 2010, the International Crisis Group claimed to have evidence that the Sri Lankan government knowingly shelled supposed safe zones occupied by civilians.

Since the war's end, ethnic Tamils have been arriving in Canada in increasing numbers. Many have sought refugee status through official channels, but hundreds have attempted to enter Canada illegally as part of what the Canadian government has called "human smuggling." In August 2010, a ship carrying 490 illegal Tamil immigrants seeking asylum arrived in Canada. Opinion polls at the time showed that most Canadians believed the immigrants should be turned away. In October, the Canadian government proposed a law that would stiffen penalties against anyone transporting more than fifty people into Canada illegally. The migrants themselves would also face jail time and other penalties under the proposed

Indian migrant laborers pack their bags to return home. The construction company that brought them to the United Arab Emirates for work closed unexpectedly and left them and hundreds of others stranded without jobs or resources. AP Images/Kamran Jebreili.

Walls of Segregation

SOURCES: United Nations, U.S. Customs and Border Protection, www.berlin-wall.org

Israel-West Bank
Length: 703 km (436 mi.)
Security barrier (network of electrified fence and concrete walls) to prevent Palestinian terrorists from entering Israel; ongoing construction

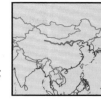

China's Great Wall
Length: 6,000 km (3,738 mi.)
Wall originally was in sections, built by warring states to keep out invaders; Emperor Qin Shihuang (221–206 B.C.) linked the sections to create the Great Wall

Berlin Wall
Length: 155 km (96 mi.)
Concrete wall divided the German city; erected in 1961 by former Communist East Germany as an "anti-fascist protection wall"; taken down in 1989

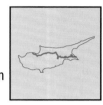

Cyprus
Length: 180 km (112 mi.)
Turkish invasion in 1974 divided the island; the U.N. buffer zone consists of a variety of formal and informal barricades

North-South Korea
Length: 240 km (151 mi.)
Demilitarized zone established in 1953 makes this one of the world's most militarized frontiers, fortified with a concrete wall, electric fence, razor wire and mines

U.S.-Mexico
Length: 3,141 km (1,951 mi.)
High fence and heavy patrols to prevent illegal immigration; not one continuous structure, but grouping of short physical walls that stop and start, secured in between with "virtual fence"

Walls created to provide security, segregate populations, and prevent illegal entry throughout the world. Illustration/XNR Productions/Cengage Learning, Gale.

law. Critics objected that the planned legislation would turn refugees into criminals. Supporters argued that Canada welcomes asylum seekers and immigrants but that proper rules must be followed in order to address security concerns and manage the strain on immigration systems.

Han Movement in Western China

With 1.35 billion people, China is the most populous nation in the world. Over 90 percent of the population is Han Chinese. Since 1950, the Chinese government has orchestrated an enormous Han migration to Tibet, a region of central Asia that mainland China calls its own. For many Tibetans, however, their homeland is an independent country occupied by China. The UN and various human rights organizations have expressed concern over many Chinese practices in the region, particularly its crackdowns on dissent. Some Tibetans fear that their already diluted language and culture will be overridden by the Han influx. In 2007, nongovernmental organizations (NGOs) testified before the United Nations Human Rights Council that systematic Han settlement of Tibet is a form of ongoing "cultural genocide." The Chinese government denies systematic Han settlement of Tibet. Meanwhile, with Chinese migrants outnumbering Tibetans in certain areas, Tibetan workers are becoming increasingly marginalized in their own land.

More recently, ethnic violence erupted in China's Xinjiang region between Muslim Uighurs and the ever-growing Han population. Xinjiang houses China's nuclear weapons program and shares borders with conflict-filled nations like Afghanistan and Pakistan. The Chinese government has been trying to increase its control over this huge area by moving the Han people in and decreasing the proportion of Uighurs there. Following a bloody clash in the summer of 2009, the Chinese government cut off cell phone and Internet access in response to online rumors of an ethnic clash in the region. Muslims say the stifling policies are an attempt to destroy their culture.

Prospects for the Future

At the 2010 UN Conference on Trade and Development, the recovery from the global economic recession was characterized as "fragile." However, in a press release dated 26 March 2010, the World Trade Organization predicted a 9.5 percent expansion in world trade by the end of the year.

The impact of an economic revival on global migration patterns remains to be seen. However, President Obama tried to put immigration in perspective for Americans when he said:

> For all the noise and anger that too often surrounds the immigration debate, America has nothing to fear from today's immigrants. They have come here for the same reason that families have always come here—for the hope that in America, they could build a better life for themselves and their families. Like the waves of immigrants that came before them and the Hispanic Americans whose families have been here for generations, the recent arrival of Latino immigrants will only enrich our country.

> http://www.ontheissues.org/2008/barack_obama_immigration.htm

Research and Exploration

Amnesty International (AI). http://www.amnesty.org/en/refugees-and-migrants.

AI is one of the best-known humanitarian organizations on the planet. Its comprehensive site includes coverage of human rights issues in 150 countries. The link listed here leads directly to a discussion of refugees, migrants, and IDPs.

Bulliet, Richard W., Pamela Kyle Crossley, Daniel

R. Headrick, Lyman L. Johnson, and Steven W. Hirsch. *The Earth and Its Peoples: A Global History to 1550.* 4th edition. Boston, Mass.: Houghton Mifflin, 2009.

This is the first volume in an acclaimed two-volume set that offers a human-centered view of world history.

"Darfur Is Dying." http://darfurisdying.com/.

Designed by a group of students from the University of California and sponsored by mtvU, Reebok, and the International Crisis Group, this first-person video game offers realistic insights into the day-to-day struggles of the refugees in Sudan's Darfur region.

"A Refugee Camp on the Web." Doctors Without Borders. http://doctorswithoutborders.org/events/refugeecamp/guide/index.cfm.

Doctors Without Borders is an independent humanitarian organization composed of medical professionals from around the world who supply emergency aid to those in need. "A Refugee Camp on the Web," a site maintained by the U.S. section of Doctors Without Borders, simulates the real-life experiences of millions of desperate people who have been uprooted by war, violence, and disease.

"Free Tibet Campaign." http://www.freetibet.org/about/migration.

Founded in 1987, Free Tibet is unaffiliated with any government agency. It is funded solely by donations from members and supporters. Its Web site seeks to educate the public about the situation in Tibet through continually updated news stories, publications, and campaigns that encourage activism. The site's online store features gifts crafted by Tibetan artisans and "Free Tibet" merchandise.

"Immigration Data Hub." Migration Policy Institute (MPI) Web site. http://www.migrationinformation.org/datahub/.

MPI is an independent, not-for-profit organization dedicated to the study of migration patterns and issues worldwide. The "Immigration Data Hub" give users instant access to migration-related facts, statistics, and maps.

"Immigration Issues: Myths and Realities." PBS-TV's Independent Lens. www.pbs.org/itvs/thecity/immigration1.html.

This PBS Q&A page outlines some immigration facts from fiction.

Internal Displacement Monitoring Centre (IDMC). *Internal Displacement: Global Overview of Trends and Developments in 2009.* Geneva, Switzerland: IDMC, May 2010. http://www.internal-displacement.org/.

This report by the IDMC, in conjunction with the Norwegian Refugee Council, analyzes trends in global displacement and examines durable solutions for their causes.

"Media." International Organization for Migration (IOM) Web site. http://www.iom.int/jahia/Jahia/media/lang/en.

The IOM is an intergovernmental agency committed to humane migration policy. Its Web site includes news releases, stories, photos, a video vault, and a continuously updated "Migration in the News" feature.

Papademetriou, Demetrios G., Madeleine Sumption, and Aaron Terrazas, with Carola Burkert, Steven Loyal, and Ruth Ferrero-Turrión. *Migration and Immigrants Two Years after the Financial Collapse: Where Do We Stand?* Report for the BBC World Service. Washington, DC: Migration Policy Institute, October 2010. http://www.migrationpolicy.org/pubs/MPI-BBCreport-2010.pdf.

This 126-page report addresses the unemployment gap that exists between migrant workers and native-born workers in Germany, Ireland, Spain, the United Kingdom, and United States.

"Video Galleries: Moving Pictures." United Nations High Commissioner for Refugees (UNHCR). http://www.unhcr.org/pages/4ac9fdae6.html.

The UN Refugee Agency documents its work through moving videos of refugees' struggles for survival.

On 1 February 1998, the United States Department of Defense came under attack by an unknown foe. Air Force, Navy, and Marine Corps computer networks were breached. Hundreds of computers were hijacked. All of the targets were part of key defense networks. The cyber attacks continued for more than three weeks, seemingly coming from sites all around the world—Israel, the United Arab Emirates, Germany, France, and Taiwan. The strikes occurred just as tensions in the Persian Gulf were rising and the U.S. government was considering military action against Iraq, leading generals to wonder: could Iraq be striking first?

The Department of Defense, FBI, the Air Force Office of Special Investigations, NASA, the U.S. Department of Justice, the Defense Information Systems Agency, the NSA, and the CIA together quickly established a task force and launched an investigation code-named "Solar Sunrise" to stop the attacks and determine their source. And find

the source they did: the attackers were not Iraqis, or foreign spies, or terrorists. They were three teenage boys, two from California and one from Israel. All were sentenced to probation.

"Solar Sunrise" was an alarming wake-up call for the world's mightiest military. It was also an ironic turn of events, because the United States Department of Defense had invented the Internet—or, more precisely, ARPANET, the computer network that formed the foundation of the Internet. ARPANET was launched in 1969, mainly as a communication medium for a handful of scientists and military personnel. By the early 1990s, thanks to the High Performance Computing and Communication Act of 1991, championed by Senator—and later Vice President—Al Gore, ARPANET evolved into a "web" of public and private computer networks and databases, or what Gore called the "information superhighway."

By 1998, it was clear to many world leaders

One of the teens who hacked into the Pentagon's computers in 1998 was Ehud Tenenbaum, also known as the "Analyzer." Later drafted into the Israeli Army, he appeared in this newspaper advertisement that says "In order to get far, you need the best equipment." Reuters.

that the information superhighway was both a blessing and a curse. The global communications revolution had materialized, bringing with it a host of complicated questions about the nature of war and peace in the twenty-first century.

Threats to Security

Computer security experts seek to protect corporations and governments against two main types of threat: the theft of classified, confidential, or proprietary information, and the disruption of computer systems' normal operation.

Identity Theft and National Security

Until the last few decades, identity theft was most frequently associated with a thief rummaging through trash or dumpster diving to find people's discarded personal information. Phone schemes, bogus interviews, and postal theft were (and still are) other ways to gain valuable personal information. With the advent of the Internet, however, identity theft became much easier for criminals to accomplish. According to the FBI, identity theft is the fastest growing crime in the United States and, according to some law enforcement officials, one of the fastest growing crimes in the world. The highest known rates are in the United States. Identity theft is also one of the fastest growing categories of complaints to the Federal Trade Commission (FTC). FTC statistics show that each year nine million Americans are victims of identity theft; in 2007, this resulted in $49 billion in losses to businesses and financial institutions.

While identity theft often proves to be a huge inconvenience to its individual victims, it can also be a major national security threat. Although most cases of identity theft involve financial crimes against individuals, identities are sometimes stolen for other purposes, including espionage and political assassinations.

In January 2010, a high-ranking leader of a Palestinian political group who was apparently involved in weapons procurement for the terrorist

Held in Hungary in September 2010, the Hacktivity conference brought together cyber experts and officials to discuss Internet security. Bruce Schneier, a U.S. computer security specialist, talked about the "Internet generation gap." Attilia Kisbenedek/AFP/ Getty Images/newscom.

organization Hamas was assassinated at a Dubai hotel. Dubai's chief of police believes that the killing was organized and carried out by the Mossad, Israel's secret police. Israel has denied the charge. The suspects carried British, Irish, French, German, and Australian passports. Though it was originally assumed that the passports were expert forgeries, it turned out that the passports were real, and the actual persons depicted on the passports were, according to investigators, victims of identity theft.

In July 2010, the United States launched an effort to issue new birth certificates to all 3.9 million residents of Puerto Rico and another 1.4 million Puerto Ricans who live in the United States who were born before 1 July 2010. The move was triggered by widespread identity theft targeting Puerto Ricans. In 2007, there was a series of burglaries in which thieves broke into Puerto Rican schools and stole students' birth certificates. In Puerto Rico, official copies of birth certificates are required as identification by schools, clubs, and other organizations, and the certificates are kept on file. The FBI estimates that about twelve thousand people have been victims of the Puerto Rican identity theft ring. U.S. State Department statistics indicate that 40 percent of fraudulent U.S. passport applications are created using Puerto Rican documents. The new birth certificates will have enhanced anti-fraud features.

Members of the Free Burma Coalition hold masks of imprisoned pro-democracy leader Aung San Suu Kyi as they protest outside the Myanmar embassy in Manila, the Philippines, 21 July 2009. Recent research from the Berkman Center for Internet and Society at Harvard University shows that human rights groups are frequently victims of web attacks designed to silence them. Nat Garcia/AFP/Getty Images.

Hackers and Botnets: "We Are Losing This War Badly"

When the Council of Europe drafted its international treaty on cybercrime in 2001, it was not simply a proactive or preventive move to combat cybercrime. Rather, it was a recognition that defense against Internet-based attacks was beyond the crime-fighting abilities of individual countries. Global cooperation was required if there was to be any chance of combating criminals who were armed, not with guns, but with computing savvy and technical skills.

Attacks on government and corporate targets by individual computer hackers and cybergangs for hire across borders have grown in frequency and complexity since 2001. Brazil, Japan, Poland, and Russia are frequent launching points for such attacks, but most originate in the United States, South Korea, and China. When most people think of cybercrime, they envision the individual hackers who have made international headlines over the years for breaking into seemingly impregnable computer systems. There was the sixteen-year-old American hacker Jonathan James, who in 1999 managed to break into the U.S. Department of Defense's Web site. There was German hacker Sven Jaschan, who wrote two highly destructive computer viruses called "worms" that affected 70 percent of the Internet in 2004. Hackers have a variety of motivations. Some are simply mischief makers who want a challenge. Others seek profit by stealing and exploiting valuable data, such as financial information and credit card numbers. Politically motivated hackers may target government agencies to shut down their computer systems or obtain classified information.

While tales of hacker exploits may make for good headlines, it was the faceless threat of botnets that had most government and corporate IT managers concerned in the first decade of the twenty-first century. Botnets are collections of software program agents that run through the Internet autonomously looking for security weaknesses in individual computers. The goal is to turn these computers into zombies and use them to launch attacks from far-flung locations. Botnets

Denial of Service Attack

A common cyber attack is the denial-of-service attack (DOS). In a DOS attack, a program running on thousands of desktop computers connected to the Internet intentionally sends many demands for service to a target computer or network. If the target is unable to cope with the sudden increase in requests, the attack will deny service to legitimate users, effectively shutting down the target system.

A DOS attack usually proceeds by hijacking desktop computers whose users are unaware of the attack. However, the computers may be recruited openly. For example, in the summer of 2009, social networking sites including Twitter began encouraging people to join a DOS attack against the government of Iran, as part of the worldwide protests against its disputed election results.

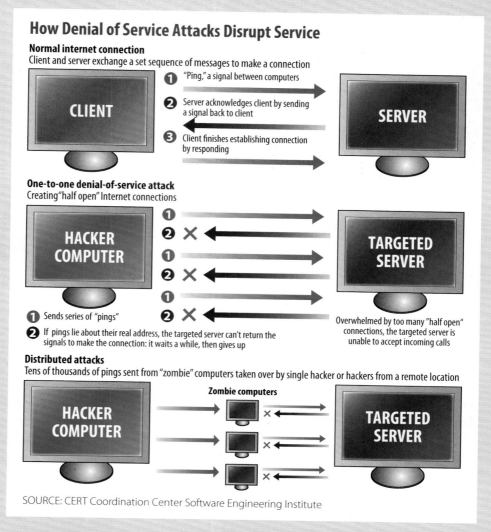

How Denial of Service Attacks Disrupt Service

Normal internet connection
Client and server exchange a set sequence of messages to make a connection
1 "Ping," a signal between computers
2 Server acknowledges client by sending a signal back to client
3 Client finishes establishing connection by responding

CLIENT — SERVER

One-to-one denial-of-service attack
Creating "half open" Internet connections
HACKER COMPUTER — TARGETED SERVER
1 Sends series of "pings"
2 If pings lie about their real address, the targeted server can't return the signals to make the connection: it waits a while, then gives up
Overwhelmed by too many "half open" connections, the targeted server is unable to accept incoming calls

Distributed attacks
Tens of thousands of pings sent from "zombie" computers taken over by single hacker or hackers from a remote location
HACKER COMPUTER — Zombie computers — TARGETED SERVER

SOURCE: CERT Coordination Center Software Engineering Institute

Denial of Service attacks attempt to take servers out of action by overwhelming them with requests for information. Illustration/XNR Productions/Cengage Learning, Gale.

Cyber Attacks: Top Ten Countries of Origin

	Country	Number of Attempted Cyber Attacks
1	United States	441,003,516
2	South Korea	24,238,369
3	China	20,622,543
4	Japan	14,296,108
5	Russia	12,273,320
6	Canada	10,646,203
7	Taiwan	6,302,941
8	United Kingdom	5,961,606
9	France	5,484,868
10	Germany	5,009,834

NOTE: Study analyzed locations of attempted cyber attacks on SecureWorks' 2,800 global clients between January and June 2010.

SOURCE: SecureWorks

Countries of origin for cyber attacks, as reported by online security firm SecureWorks. Illustration/XNR Productions/Cengage Learning, Gale.

can be used for many purposes, including sabotaging and disabling corporate Web sites, interfering with e-mail by sending out "spam" (junk) messages, and stealing sensitive data. In essence, botnets do what hackers do, but they do it on a much wider scale; battling the botnets has become the main challenge of today's IT managers. But as computer security expert Rick Wesson lamented in a 2007 *New York Times* interview, "We are losing this war badly." Gadi Evron, a computer security researcher based in Israel, agreed: "The war to make the Internet safe was lost long ago, and we need to figure out what to do now."

From a corporate perspective, the stakes in the battle against botnets are primarily financial. Security threats are estimated to cost larger enterprises nearly $3 million annually. Governments worry that botnet attacks, by terrorists or other nations, on computer systems related to transportation, infrastructure, the economy, and the military could cost not just money, but lives.

In 2009 and 2010, increased cooperation among corporations, computer security experts, law enforcement officials, and Internet Service Providers (ISPs) led to some successful "takedowns" of major botnets. After the takedown of the Mariposa and Waledac botnets in March 2010, Rik Ferguson, a security consultant at Trend Micro, told the *Register,* "We have had significant victories against several botnets in the past but that hasn't stopped the growth in malware or the growth in spam or in information theft. So, while we continue to win significant battles, winning the war will need closer cooperation between governments [and] law enforcement agencies on an ongoing basis rather than on an operational basis."

WikiLeaks: Muckraking or Mischief-Making?

Clearly the possibility that state secrets could be compromised by a sophisticated cyber attack is a high-priority security concern for world governments. The U.S. federal government spent $8.3 billion on protection against cyber attacks in 2010, and is projected to spend nearly $12 billion annually by 2014.

But, as the U.S. government found repeatedly in 2010, state secrets can also be compromised by relatively low-tech means: someone can leak them. Any combination of passion, politics, and profit can motivate someone with access to classified information to give or sell it to an outside party. When that outside party is WikiLeaks, the whole world soon comes to know what world leaders hoped was held in strictest confidence.

WikiLeaks is a nonprofit, Sweden-based organization that makes sensitive and classified information available to the public via its Web site, wikileaks.org. The administrators of the site focus on documents that expose actions they view as

Yearly Reported Losses Due to Cybercrimes

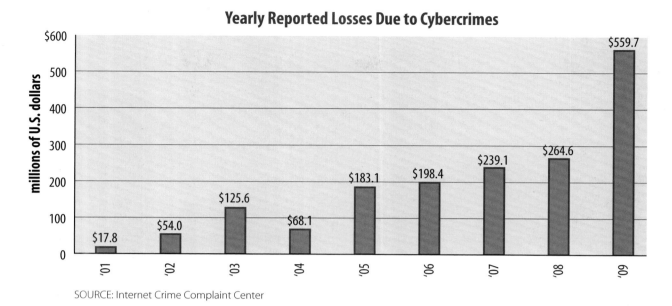

SOURCE: Internet Crime Complaint Center

Reported business losses due to criminal online activity have skyrocketed over the last decade. Illustration/XNR Productions/ Cengage Learning, Gale.

criminal or unethical, particularly actions committed by governments or corporations. In this sense, WikiLeaks set itself up in the tradition of the muckrakers of the nineteenth and early twentieth centuries: journalists who exposed government and corporate corruption in order to spur reform.

The material available on WikiLeaks is donated by anonymous individuals. WikiLeaks takes great pains to ensure that those who leak the documents remain anonymous for their own protection, and these donors are often unknown even to the administrators of the site. Since its launch in 2006, WikiLeaks has become recognized as one of the world's leading sources of leaked information, and has changed the way that many view modern investigative journalism.

WikiLeaks was founded by Julian Assange, an Australian with a long history as a computer hacker. Early in his career, even as he illegally gained access to information in corporate and military computers, he was known for his hatred of corporate and government secrecy, but at the same time for his condemnation of destructive hacking. Though most of the WikiLeaks servers are located in Sweden, volunteers working for the organization come from a number of countries, and Assange himself moves offices frequently. Part of the reason for this is security, since many of the documents featured on the site reveal political, military, and corporate secrets that Assange believes might make him a target of reprisal.

Several WikiLeaks publications made headlines in 2007, 2008, and 2009. In 2007, the organization published a classified document detailing U.S. Army protocol for handling detainees at the controversial Guantánamo Bay Detention Center in Cuba. In 2008, WikiLeaks published the contents of an e-mail account belonging to Sarah Palin, who was then campaigning as the Republican vice presidential candidate. Also in 2008, WikiLeaks released thousands of pages of internal documents from the Church of Scientology. In 2009, WikiLeaks published hundreds of secret United Nations documents.

WikiLeaks founder Julian Assange poses with a copy of the *Guardian* newspaper during a press conference in London. Andrew Winning/Reuters.

Leaks of U.S. Military Information

WikiLeaks gained greater attention in April 2010 when it released video footage of a controversial incident in the Iraq War. On 12 July 2007, two journalists from the news agency Reuters and an unknown number of Iraqi civilians were killed when two U.S. Apache helicopters fired on a group of suspected insurgents in the district of New Baghdad, and subsequently destroyed a nearby building with missile strikes. Initial reports from the U.S. military labeled all the Iraqi victims as armed insurgents, and portrayed the deaths of the reporters as an accident.

In early 2010, WikiLeaks received an encrypted copy of video footage of the incident taken from a camera on one of the Apache helicopters. After spending several months cracking the encryption and analyzing every frame of the video, the site released the footage. Although some possible weapons can be seen on the ground, the video does not show anyone engaged in combat.

After the first attack, the video reveals, U.S. soldiers mistakenly identified a wounded journalist and unarmed civilians as threatening targets, and gunned them down.

In July 2010, just a few months after releasing the 2007 missile strike video, WikiLeaks posted a collection of more than 91,000 documents related to the U.S. military conflict in Afghanistan. The collection, called the Afghan War Diary (or AWD), features reports from soldiers in the region.

The AWD documents contain admissions of civilian casualties and so-called "friendly fire" incidents caused by error or miscommunication. In many cases, these incidents had not been reported in the mainstream news media. The documents also suggest that Pakistan, believed to be assisting the United States in its fight against Afghan insurgents, has actually been helping the Taliban, the ultra-Islamist insurgent group against which the United States and its allies are fighting. Some critics have condemned the release of the AWD documents as an irresponsible breach of military security.

WikiLeaks claims to have no official political agenda beyond the "anti-secrecy" philosophy of its founder, and its anonymous contributors have exposed targets across the political spectrum. Some argue that leaks of classified information could endanger military forces operating in areas like Iraq and Afghanistan. Still, even critics acknowledge that for better or for worse, WikiLeaks has quickly and profoundly changed the face of modern reporting.

In October 2010, WikiLeaks released 400,000 classified U.S. documents related to the war in Iraq. It was, at the time, the largest leak of classified material in U.S. history. The leaked documents detail several cases of abuse and torture of Iraqi detainees by Iraqi security forces. They also show that the U.S. government maintained records of civilian casualties, although it denied keeping an official count, and that the Iranian government was linked to Shiite militias in Iraq. The leaked documents also present evidence that three American hikers arrested by Iranian Revolutionary Guards were actually in Iraqi territory when they were arrested. The two male hikers are still imprisoned in Iran as of January 2011; the female hiker was released for medical reasons.

Leaks of State Department Communication

WikiLeaks released an even bigger and more embarrassing collection of classified U.S. government documents on 28 November 2010. Hundreds of thousands of sensitive State Department cables and other documents were published by a handful of news providers to whom WikiLeaks gave an advance look at the documents. Many of

In this image taken from a classified U.S. military video that was posted by WikiLeaks, troops aboard a U.S. Apache helicopter fire down on civilians in Iraq on 12 July 2007. The military thought the civilians, which included two Reuters photographers, were insurgents. WikiLeaks/Reuters.

Secret Conversation Between General Petraeus and Yemeni President Revealed

The following text is excerpted from a secret diplomatic cable sent from the U.S. Embassy in Yemen on 4 January 2010. WikiLeaks revealed the cable to the public on 28 November 2010. This passage recounts a conversation between Yemeni President Ali Abdullah Saleh and U.S. General David Petraeus. AQAP is Al-Qaeda in the Arabian Peninsula. USG is U.S. Government. The ROYG is the Republic of Yemen Government.

... President Obama has approved providing U.S. intelligence in support of ROYG ground operations against AQAP targets, General Petraeus informed Saleh. Saleh reacted coolly, however, to the General's proposal to place USG personnel inside the area of operations armed with real-time, direct feed intelligence from U.S. ISR platforms overhead. "You cannot enter the operations area and you must stay in the joint operations center," Saleh responded. Any U.S. casualties in strikes against AQAP would harm future efforts, Saleh asserted. Saleh did not have any objection, however, to General Petraeus' proposal to move away from the use of cruise missiles and instead have U.S. fixed-wing bombers circle outside Yemeni territory, "out of sight," and engage AQAP targets when actionable intelligence became available. Saleh lamented the use of cruise missiles that are "not very accurate" and welcomed the use of aircraft-deployed precision-guided bombs instead. "We'll continue saying the bombs are ours, not yours," Saleh said, prompting Deputy Prime Minister Alimi to joke that he had just "lied" by telling Parliament that the bombs in Arhab, Abyan, and Shebwa were American-made but deployed by the ROYG....

the documents contained candid and unflattering assessments of world leaders made by U.S. diplomats. Other revelations in the documents were awkward but not altogether surprising. For example, a leaked document reveals that Saudi Arabia urged the U.S. government to take military action against Iran. "Cut off the head of the snake," King Abdullah urged in 2008. While it is well known that the Sunni-dominated Arab countries of the Middle East eye Shiite-dominated, non-Arab Iran with suspicion, heads of state rarely voice this sentiment publicly. The White House condemned the release of the documents as irresponsible, dangerous, and harmful to U.S. diplomatic efforts around the world.

Among the other headline-grabbing revelations were the following:

- Yemen, which battled a growing al-Qaeda presence in 2009 and 2010, covered up U.S. military attacks by agreeing to claim responsibility for them, so as not to inflame further anti-American feeling in the Middle East: "We'll continue saying the bombs are ours, not yours," Yemeni President Ali Abdullah Saleh told General David Petraeus in January 2010.

- The U.S. envoy to Rome, Elizabeth Dibble, called Italian president Silvio Berlusconi "feckless, vain, and ineffective as a modern European leader."

- Hillary Clinton, the U.S. Secretary of State, asked diplomats to acquire—perhaps illegally—personal information and even DNA samples of United Nations Security Council members.

- The U.S. government wanted to close the infamous Guantánamo Bay Detention Center so badly they were willing to pay foreign countries millions of dollars to shelter the detainees.

Some news commentators drew comparisons between the State Department leaks and the 1971 publication by the *New York Times* of a classified

Defense Department study of U.S. military involvement in the Vietnam War. The study, which was entered into the Congressional record by Democratic senator Mike Gravel, became known commonly as the "Pentagon Papers." The Pentagon Papers showed that successive U.S. presidents, from Harry S Truman to Lyndon B. Johnson, had deliberately and systematically lied to the American public about military actions in Vietnam.

However, while the leaked communication doubtless strained diplomatic relations around the world, many commentators pointed out that there were actually few outright surprises in the leaks. In fact, as *Time* columnist Fareed Zakaria argued in his 2 December 2010 article "WikiLeaks Shows the Skill of U.S. Diplomats," instead of exposing criminality or corruption in the U.S. government, the documents actually reveal U.S. diplomats to be quite diligent and capable. Zakaria wrote:

> The WikiLeaks documents . . . show Washington pursuing privately pretty much the policies it has articulated publicly. Whether on Iran, Afghanistan, Pakistan or North Korea, the cables confirm what we know to be U.S. foreign policy. And often this foreign policy is concerned with broader regional security, not narrow American interests. Ambassadors are not caught pushing other countries in order to make deals secretly to strengthen the U.S., but rather to solve festering problems.

Eminent British historian Timothy Garton Ash agreed, saying during an interview on NPR on 1 December 2010, "Well, it [the contents of the leaked material] revises upward my personal opinion of the State Department. In other words, what I've seen about how they report, and how they operate, is really quite impressive."

U.S. politicians were not inclined to take the leak of classified government documents as a compliment. In December 2010, the top Democratic and Republican leaders of the Senate Intelligence

Saudi Officials True Sentiments on Iran Exposed

On 17 April 2008, U.S. diplomat Michael Gfoeller met with Saudi Arabian government officials and royal family members to discuss policy toward Iraq, a meeting described in a secret cable to the State Department. When WikiLeaks made the cable public, it revealed that the Saudis' private sentiments about Iran are much harsher than their public statements would indicate:

...The King, Foreign Minister, Prince Muqrin, and Prince Nayif all agreed that the Kingdom needs to cooperate with the US on resisting and rolling back Iranian influence and subversion in Iraq. The King was particularly adamant on this point, and it was echoed by the senior princes as well. Al-Jubeir recalled the King's frequent exhortations to the US to attack Iran and so put an end to its nuclear weapons program. "He told you to cut off the head of the snake," he recalled to [Gfoeller], adding that working with the US to roll back Iranian influence in Iraq is a strategic priority for the King and his government....

Committee consulted with the Justice Department about charging Assange with spying under the Espionage Act.

Cyber Attacks, Rape Charges, and Other Perils for WikiLeaks

In an intriguing turn of events, just as news outlets were publishing parts of the leaked State Department documents, the WikiLeaks site itself was brought down by a sustained denial-of-service cyber attack. "The Jester"—either a hacker or a group of hackers—claimed responsibility for the attack, and said they were targeting WikiLeaks for endangering U.S. troops. The site was functioning

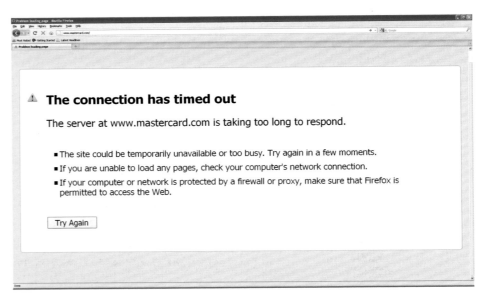

On 8 December 2010, hackers affiliated with WikiLeaks crashed the Web sites of several credit card companies, including MasterCard. The act was in response to credit firms withholding donations to the WikiLeaks Web site. Reuters.

again within a day, but was knocked out again, temporarily, by "the Jester" on 2 December 2010. Assange blamed the U.S. government for the attacks.

Assange himself is the subject of a controversial rape investigation. Swedish officials announced on 1 September 2010 that they were pressing forward with an investigation of claims by two women who said they were raped by Assange in August. Assange claims the charges are part of a smear campaign against him, as the *Washington Post* reports. Speculation immediately began that Assange was the victim of a "honey trap," a classic espionage trick in which an intelligence agency uses attractive female agents to compromise a subject. "There have been headlines all over the world about my being accused of rape. They won't just disappear," Assange acknowledged to Stockholm's *Aftonbladet* newspaper. "And I know by experience that WikiLeaks' enemies will continue to bandy around things even after they have been renounced. I don't know who is behind this, but we have been warned that, for example, the Pentagon plans to use dirty tricks to spoil things for us."

Swedish officials issued an international arrest warrant for Assange on 20 November 2010, and on 2 December refused to allow him to appeal it. Assange, who was hiding in the United Kingdom, voluntarily turned himself in to British police on 6 December.

Assange may actually come to wish he were safely housed in a Swedish prison if intelligence gathered by the U.S. National Security Agency (NSA) proves to be true. NSA operatives believe that WikiLeaks and Assange have been under tight surveillance by Russia's Federal Security Service (FSB), the successor agency of the infamous Committee for State Security (KGB) of the Soviet era. Assange told a Moscow newspaper in October 2010 that he had damaging information about the Russian government and Russian businesses, and that the information would be published "soon." According to a U.S. law enforcement agent interviewed by Philip Shenon in his 30 November 2010 article "Moscow's Bid to Blow Up WikiLeaks" for the *Daily Beast*, "We may not have been able to stop WikiLeaks so far, and it's been frustrating. The Russians play by different rules. . . . [They] will be ruthless in stopping WikiLeaks." (Assange claims to have an encrypted document with incriminating evidence on major world figures that will be released if anything happens to him or his family.)

Cyberwars of the Future

Mischievous hackers can cost companies millions of dollars. WikiLeaks can clearly embarrass governments and hamper foreign relations. But the biggest threat posed by the Internet is that it could be used as an instrument of war. Developed nations are increasingly reliant on computer networks, making them more and more vulnerable to attack. As Richard Clarke, counterterrorism advisor to Presidents Bill Clinton and George W. Bush, explained in a 19 April 2010 interview on the NPR-broadcast program *Fresh Air,* "A cyber attack could disable trains all over the country. It could blow up pipelines. It could cause blackouts and damage electrical power grids so that the blackouts would go on for a long time. It could wipe out and confuse financial records, so that we would not know who owned what, and the financial system would be badly damaged. It could do things like disrupt traffic in urban areas by knocking out control computers. It could, in nefarious ways, do things like wipe out medical records." A potent threat, indeed.

Cyberspies and Cyberskirmishes

As of 2010, no known "cyberwars" had broken out between any two countries. There have, however, been some suspected "cyberskirmishes." In Estonia in 2007, unknown parties brought down multiple government, police, banking, and media Web sites with denial-of-service attacks from April until June. The attack was provoked by the government's removal of a Soviet-era memorial from the capital, leading some Estonians to assert that Russia or Russian agents within Estonia were behind the attack. No proof existed to support such a claim, and Russia denied responsibility. Howard Schmidt, a former White House

Cybersecurity Coordinator, explained Estonia's predicament in a 24 May 2007 article in *Information Week* titled "Estonian Attacks Raise Concern over Cyber 'Nuclear Winter'": "Estonia has built their future on having a high-tech government and economy, and they've basically been brought to their knees because of these attacks. Whether this is done by one nation against another or one group against a nation, it's a concern." Georgia, too, was stricken by a cyber attack in 2008 that coincided with the Russian military's advance into the breakaway Georgian region of South Ossetia, leading Georgia to blame Russia. Again, Russia denied responsibility. The experiences of Estonia and Georgia were not lost on the United States: in 2009, Defense Secretary Robert Gates approved the creation of the U.S. Cyber Command (US-CYBERCOM), which is headed by U.S. Army General Keith Alexander. According to a October 2010 Fact sheet issued by the U.S. Department of Defense, "USCYBERCOM plans, coordinates, integrates, synchronizes, and conducts activities to: direct the operations and defense of specified Department of Defense information networks and; prepare to, and when directed, conduct full-spectrum military cyberspace operations in order to enable actions in all domains, ensure US/Allied freedom of action in cyberspace and deny the same to our adversaries."

In the first decade of the twenty-first century, cyberspying on commercial and government computer systems in the United States occurred on a daily basis. In fact, U.S. counterintelligence agents reported in 2007 that 140 foreign intelligence agencies regularly attempted to infiltrate the computer systems of U.S. government agencies and U.S. businesses. Many such attacks allegedly originated in China and Russia. The United States has repeatedly accused the Chinese government of hacking into the computers of the U.S. Departments of Defense, Commerce, and State, seemingly for the purpose of espionage. In 2007, hackers using computers located in China briefly shut down a computer network in the Pentagon

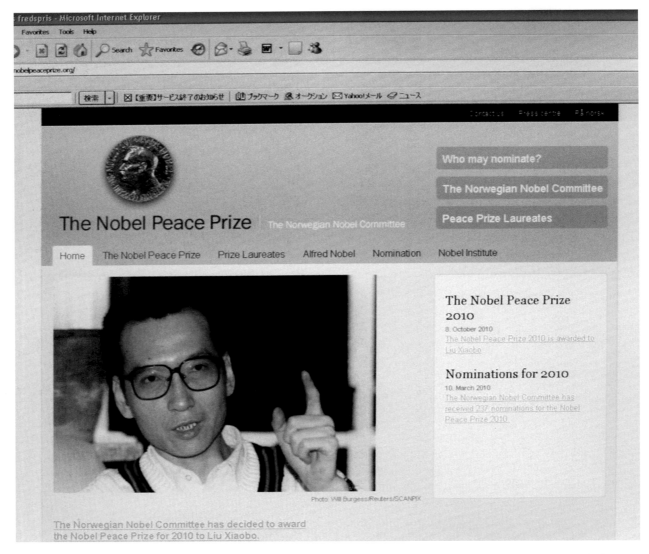

The Nobel Peace Prize Web site came under attack in October 2010, according to Norwegian officials, after imprisoned Chinese dissident Liu Xiaobo won the award. China strongly objected to the selection before the site was hacked. The attack was traced to an IP address at a university in Taiwan. AP Images/Kyodo.

serving the office of the Secretary of Defense. The government of China denied backing the attack. In 2007, the British security agency MI5 warned three hundred banks, legal firms, and other corporations in the United Kingdom that their computers had been breached and their secret data stolen by Chinese agents working through the Internet. In 2008, the U.S. Congress approved a $17-billion, five-year program to enhance national computer security.

Terrorism on the Internet

Anonymity is one of the appeals of cyberwarfare, and of cybercrime in general. The anonymous attacker(s) can cause considerable damage with very little risk to themselves. In theory, this would make cyberwar an especially attractive option for terrorists.

International intelligence officials have difficulty in determining exactly what proportion of crime on the Internet is connected with terrorism.

It is clear that there are strong connections, but they tend to be small in scale. Terrorists might, for example, resort to identity theft to acquire fake passports, or credit card numbers for purchasing weapons. In June 2007, three British residents, Tariq Al-Daour, Waseem Mughal, and Younes Tsouli, were convicted of inciting murder via the Internet. They had used the Internet to steal credit card numbers and personal information from about 37,000 people, then used the information to buy supplies and airline tickets for radical Islamic terrorists. They made a total of more than $3.5 million in fraudulent charges. It was certainly a major financial fraud for three individuals, but hardly a devastating attack against a nation.

Direct links between terrorist groups and hackers capable of launching sophisticated cyber attacks are more difficult to confirm. Experts estimate that a coordinated attack against multiple computer networks could take two or more years to plan and execute. A more complex attack that would cause wide-scale disruption could take six or more years. However, they warn that the fact that cyber attacks are difficult to plan should be no reason for confidence. Past terrorist attacks, including the 11 September 2001 attacks on the United States by al-Qaeda, required extensive coordination and years of planning, so there is no reason to assume that terrorist groups lack the ability to prepare an effective cyber attack.

Terrorists may, however, lack interest in such attacks because they don't create the same drama as conventional attacks with human casualties. Said James Adams, CEO of the Ashland Institute for Strategic Studies, "Al-Qaeda doesn't see cyberterrorism as achieving significant military goals. They see the world in a rather old-fashioned way, where bombings and shootings have direct impact and scare people."

To Defend Against It, First Define It

The United States and many other nations, while denying that they launch peacetime cyber attacks, officially plan to carry out and defend

Taken from a video posted on YouTube in February 2010, these images allegedly show an Iranian opposition protester being arrested and beaten by police. Various entities have accused Iran of trying to create an information blockade by jamming phones, the Internet, and satellite television. AFP/Getty Images/newscom.

against wartime cyber attacks. In 2004, the United States announced the formation of a group called the Network Attack Support Staff, which is charged with keeping cyberwarfare assets up to date. In 2008, the Bush administration announced that it had established a secret cyberwar strategy. On 29 May 2009, in a speech announcing the results of a top-to-bottom review of the U.S. federal government's cybersecurity measures, U.S. President Barack Obama called the threat of cyber attacks a serious economic and national security challenge.

The United Nations has been working toward

Chinese blogger Zhang Shihe, also known as Tiger Temple, is a critic of internet censorship in China. Here, he reads a Web article about Google and whether it will leave the Chinese Market in spring 2010. AP Images/Gemunu Amarasinghe.

a comprehensive agreement on cyberwar since 2000. The problem is that the international community is divided over what exactly constitutes cyberwar or cyberweaponry. The United States and Russia, old Cold-War foes, remain particularly at odds. The United States sees cyberwar mainly as anything that threatens to shut down the computer networks that keep the country functioning. Accordingly, the United States favors an international cyberwar treaty that would encourage international law enforcement cooperation to catch and prosecute anyone guilty of attacking vital industries. It is the computer networks themselves that the United States wants to protect.

Russia, however, perceives an additional threat: the threat of political dissent or propaganda disseminated via the Internet. It favors an international treaty on cyberwarfare that would include increased government oversight of the Internet and Internet communication. In fact, Russian diplomats at the United Nations have pushed for an international cyberwarfare agreement that would ban "information terrorism," which could be interpreted as any information meant to undermine another country's political system.

China, India, Brazil, and several other countries support the Russian position. In fact, the threat posed by outside information is a serious concern for rapidly globalizing China. The Chinese government employs at least thirty thousand full-time workers to censor the Internet and routinely imprisons people for trying to access forbidden Web sites or post dissenting views to the Web. This is not mere paranoia on the part of these governments, however: established regimes have some reason to worry. For example, the opposition to

A map of global Internet traffic created by the Cooperative Association for Internet Data Analysis using a program called Skitter. Pink areas are located in the United States, dark blue is the United Kingdom, light blue is Italy, green is Sweden, white is unknown locations. CAIDA/Photo Researchers, Inc.

the administration of Iranian president Mahmoud Ahmadinejad used the Internet to mobilize a massive political movement—later dubbed the "Green" movement, led by Mir Hossein Moussavi—that mounted a strong challenge to Ahmadinejad in the June 2009 presidential elections.

Ahmadinejad won, but opposition leaders said the vote was rigged and Moussavi's supporters took to the streets by the thousands to protest. By strictly controlling the flow of information into and out of Iran, and by authorizing brutality on the part of security forces, Ahmadinejad was able to maintain control and suppress the opposition.

The careful control of information has always been a key feature of international relations, even in Western societies with free-speech guarantees. Important deals are made behind closed doors. In the age of WikiLeaks, secrecy is a thing of the past in affairs of state. Secrecy is not, however, a thing of the past in terms of national defense, when cyberattackers can wreak havoc behind a veil of anonymity. Balancing the rights of citizens to seek and share information via the Internet with the duty of governments to protect their citizens is the key challenge of what policy analysts have come to call "twenty-first-century statecraft." Some governments will choose to restrict the flow of information on the Internet in the name of self-preservation. Others will adjust, come to terms with, and even capitalize on the communication potential of the Internet. As Anne-Marie Slaughter, director of policy planning for the U.S. State Department, argues, "The emerging networked world of the twenty-first century . . . exists above the state, below the state, and through the state. In this world, the state with the most connections will be the central player, able to set the global agenda and unlock innovation and sustainable growth. . . . Of course, the world will still contain conflict. Networks can be as malign and deadly as they can be productive and beneficial. . . . But on the whole, the positive effects of networks will greatly outweigh the negative." ("America's Edge: Power in the Networked Century," *Foreign Affairs*, 1 January 2009.)

Research and Exploration

Clarke, Richard and Robert Knake. *Cyberwar: The Next Threat to National Security and What to Do About It.* New York: Ecco, 2010.

The former counterterrorism advisor to U.S. presidents Bill Clinton and George W. Bush, Richard Clarke, offers his vision of the threat of cyberwar and what citizens can do to protect themselves.

Cooperative Cyber Defence Center of Excellence, http://www.ccdcoe.org/

One of NATO's "centers of excellence" for training on technically sophisticated aspects of NATO operations, located in Estonia. The organization's Web site offers information on its activities and its assessments of the legal and military challenges involved in cyber conflict.

Cyber, War and Law, http://www.cyberwarandlaw .com/

The author of this blog, which tracks developments in cyberwarfare, is Dondi West, a mathematician, computer scientist, and lawyer. West follows issues in cyberwarfare while at the same time focusing on how law in this vague but quickly expanding field is evolving.

Halpin, Edward F., et. al., eds. *Cyberwar, Netwar and the Revolution in Military Affairs.* Basingstoke, England and New York: Palgrave Macmillan, 2006.

This book contains a collection of essays on the difficulty of balancing human rights and Internet security.

National Cyber Security, http://nationalcybersecurity .com/

This Web portal contains frequently updated news and information on the broad topic of cyber security.

U.S. Department of Defense: Cyber Security, http:// www.defense.gov/home/features/2010/0410 _cybersec/

This U.S. Department of Defense Web site contains news and information related to the department's cybersecurity efforts.

U.S. Department of State: Internet Freedom in the Twenty-First Century, http://www.state.gov/r/pa/ scp/fs/2010/136702.htm

This fact sheet by the U.S. State Department outlines the department's commitment to preserving what it calls "the five key freedoms of the Internet age."

WikiLeaks, http://wikileaks.ch/

This is the home page of the infamous Internet organization that exposes official secrets. It is a visually simple gateway (the first page never has more than a few items), but behind it is a vast collection of formerly secret information. It includes a prominent link for any readers who wish to add their own leaks.

INDEX

Note: Page references followed by *t* indicate information contained in tables. *Italicized* page references indicate information contained in illustrations and photographs.

A

Abdullah, Abdullah, 10

Abdullah, King (Saudi Arabia), 180, 302, 303

Abdulmutallab, Umar Farouk, *227*

Abu Bakr, 191

Accounting mismanagement, 75–76, 92

Adjustable rate mortgages (ARMs), 68, 72

Afghan Ministry of Counter Narcotics (MCN), 20

Afghan National Army, 17, 27–28

Afghan National Security Council, 18

Afghanistan
emigration and refugees, 12, 206, 275, *277, 283, 283, 284*
geopolitical history, 2, 4–7
language and ethnic groups, *26,* 26–28, 192
location, 2, 5, *6, 171*
Soviet conflict, 5, *5,* 6–7, 19, 275

Afghanistan, government
elections, 10, 17, *17,* 25–26
history, 4

interim, 2001, 20

Islamic Republic of Afghanistan, 8

Karzai and U.S. relations, 9, 14, 18, 19

regions not under control, *21,* 22

Afghanistan War, 1–33, 212
Afghan public opinion, 12, 32*t*
American public opinion, 24, 24*t*
Bush policy, 2, 7–8, 9
civilian casualties, *8,* 8–9, 10, 12, *12, 16,* 22*t,* 23, 300
international coalition, 7, 8, 11, 13–14, 31–32
Obama policy, 1–2, 9–10, 10–11, 14, 23–25, 28–29, 31–32
terrorist and insurgent activity, 1–2, *2, 7,* 8–9, 10, 11–13, *13,* 22*t,* 28–30, 31–32, *32*
timelines, 2, 4–5
training, Afghans, 13, 17, 21
troop deaths, 10*t,* 13, 31–32
troops totals, 13–14, 14*t,* 23–24, 32
U.S. actions, WikiLeaks coverage, 300–301
U.S. spending, 31*t,* 32

Africa
refugees, 274–275, 276, 284–286
slavery, 159, *268, 269, 270*
See also specific nations

African-Americans
American Muslims, 206

migration patterns, 267–268

Agriculture. *See* Farmers and farming

Ahmadinejad, Mahmoud, *180,* 189
information control policy, 309–310
Iran nuclear program, 171–172, 173, 179, *179,* 181
Israel policy, 195–196

AIDS rates, 157

AIG (American Insurance Group), 75, 76, 77

al-Bashir, Omar, 284–285

al-Qaeda. *See under* Q

Al Shabaab (terrorist group), 226

al-Yazid, Mustafa Abu, 192

Alabama
anti-Catholic sentiment, Birmingham, 212
Gulf oil spill, economic effects, 119–120, 121, *121*
Gulf oil spill pollution, *102,* 112, *113*

Alaska. *See Exxon Valdez* oil spill (1989)

Algeria
emigration, 281*t*
oil reserves, 132*t*

Ali ibn Abu Talib, 191

Allen, Thad, 108, *125*

Alternative energy sources. *See* Renewable energy

American Bankers Association, *93*

American imperialism, 161–162

American Recovery and Reinvestment Act (2009), 79

American Society for Muslim Advancement (ASMA), 202

Amnesty International, 219, 286, 290

Amoco Cadiz (tanker) oil spill (1978), 101*t*, 127

Amputation, 139, 161

Anadarko Petroleum (corporation), 123

Anglo-Afghan Wars (1839-1842; 1878-1880), 4

Annabi, Hedi, 138

Anti-Americanism, 190, 207

Anti-ballistic missile systems, 179

Anti-Catholic sentiment, 210–213, *211*

Anti-communism, 207

Anti-Defamation League (ADL), 203

Anti-Islam sentiment. *See* Islamophobia

Anti-terrorism laws, 282

Apollo 13 mission, 58–59, *59*

Arab-Israeli conflict, 192–196, 207, 225, 274, *274*

Arab nationalism, 192

Arabs (ethnic group), 192–193

Arellano Félix, Eduardo, 244–245

Aristide, Jean-Bertrand, 162–163

Arizona
crime rates, 250–251, 261, 262*t*
economy, 261
illegal immigration stories, 259–260
immigration laws, 260–263, *262*
immigration vigilantism, *264,* 264–265
Mexican drug war and, 243, 250–251

Armies. *See* Afghan National Army; Mexico; U.S. Army

Arms race, 181–183, 183*t*

Arms trafficking and seizures, *235,* 243–244, 245, 253, 255

ARPANET, 293

Artibonite River (Haiti), 147

Asia
emigration and immigration, 206, 269, 271–272, 273, 274, 278–279, 287–289
financial markets, 77, *78*
South Asian tsunami, 2004, 153–154
U.S. debt ownership, 91*t*

Assange, Julian, 299, *300,* 301, 303, 304–305

Assassinations and assassination attempts, 31, 161, 162–163, 294–295

Assimilation and assimilation theory,
206–208, 213, 214, 221, 271

Asylum seekers, 273*t*, 282, 283, 286–287, 288–289
See also Refugees

Ataturk, 218

ATF (U.S. Bureau of Alcohol, Tobacco, Firearms, and Explosives), 243

Atomic bombs, 181–182, *196*

Atoms for Peace program, 177

Austerity programs, plans and reactions, 81, 82–83, *83, 84,* 84–85, 89, *90*

Australia
Afghanistan troops forces, 14
emigration, 281*t*
immigration policy, 271, 277

Austria
immigration, 281*t*
retirement age, 85*t*
unemployment rates, 81*t*

Automobile use, United States, 123–124

Automotive industry, 94

Azeris (ethnic group), *193*

B

Bahrain, 180

Bailouts
automotive industry, 94
financial industry, 75, 76, 77, 92, 93
Greece, 81–82, 89
Ireland, 94

Ban Ki-moon, 138, 154, 169

Bangladesh, emigrants, 206, *278*

Bank of America, 73

Bank of Japan, 77

Bankruptcies, banks, 67, 72, 74, 77

Banks. *See* Bankruptcies, banks; Investment firms

Barak, Ehud, 180

Barbour, Haley, *125*

Barrios Rojas, Yonni, *57,* 57–58

Bashir, Omar al-, 284–285

Basij (Iran security force), 189

BBC (British Broadcasting Corporation), 155, 160

Bear Stearns, 75

Belgium
economic protests, *69*
headscarf laws, 219
Muslim populations, *217,* 219
retirement age, 85*t*

Beltrán Leyva drug cartel, 236, 237, *239,* 245

Benjamin, Regina, 116

Berlin Wall, 289, *289*

Berlusconi, Silvio, 302

Bernanke, Ben, 76

Bias in reporting, 267

Biden, Joe, 176

bin Laden, Osama, 7, *32,* 218

Bingham Canyon Mine (Utah), 61

Birds, Gulf oil spill damages, 97, *97,* 110, 115, 116, *117*

Birmingham, Alabama, 212

Birnbaum, Elizabeth, 122

Birth certificates, 295

Birth rates, 214

Bitumen, 131

Black market medicines, 17, *162*

Black Market Peso Exchange, 234–235

Blogs and bloggers
China, *308*
Haitian earthquake coverage, 155

Bloomberg, Michael, *203,* 203–204

Blowout preventers (BOP) (oil drilling), 98, 100, 103, *103, 105,* 106, *106,* 107, *107, 128*

Blue Mosque (Turkey), *213*

Bobo, Rosalvo, 161

Boehmer, Maria, *213*

Bolivia
Chilean relations, 54, *55*
drug production and trade, 234, *235,* 252

Bolton, Susan, 263

Bombings
Afghanistan, 1, 8–9, 10, 12–13, 31
Mexican drug war, 240–241, *241,* 245, 246, 249
nuclear, WWII, 181, *196*
al-Qaeda, *32*

Border Action Network, 265

Borders, geographic, 259
Chile-Bolivia, 54
European Union, 276
global walls of segregation, 194, 289, *289*
Mexico-U.S., and drug trafficking, *233,* 234, *234,* 236, 237, 246, 249–251, 255
Mexico-U.S., and gun trafficking, 243, 255
Mexico-U.S., and immigration, *233,* 246, 250–251, 259–263, *264,* 264–265, 289, *289*

Botnets, 296, 297–298

Bottom kill technique (oil spill containment), 107–108

BP (corporation), 97, *126*, 127
    cleanup of oil spill, 108, 109, 121, 125
    costs and payments, 109, 119, 120–121, 123, 125–126
    exploration plans, 120
    halting of oil leak, 100, 105–108, 125
    public relations, 100, 103, 109, 119, 126–127
    sub-contractors, 123, 125

BP oil spill (2010). *See* Gulf oil spill (2010)

Braer (tanker) oil spill (1993), 127

"Brain drain," 279–280, 281

Brazil
    economic standing, 86–87, 86*t*
    oil reserves, 132*t*
    U.S. debt ownership, 91*t*

Brewer, Jan, 260, 261

Bribery
    Afghani culture, 15
    Afghanistan government cases, 18
    Mexican drug war corruption, 237–238, 251
    See also Corruption, government and police

BRIC nations, 86–87, 88, 308

British Broadcasting Corporation (BBC), 155, 160

British East India Company, 4

British imperialism, 4–5, 186, 206–207

Brown, Gordon, 80, 93

Bubbles (economics), 70–71

Budget deficits
    Greece, 81, 82, 83
    United States, 91

Building codes, 158

Bullheading technique, 106–107, *108*

Burma, *296*

Burqas, 215, *215*, 216–218, 219

Bush, George H.W., 153–154

Bush, George W.
    Afghanistan military policy, 2, 7–8, 9
    anti-terrorism policy, 282
    cyberwar strategy, 307
    economic policy, 77, 91
    Haitian relief fundraising and work, 153, *154*
    immigration policy, 264, 265
    Iran policy, 179, 181, 190
    Iraq military policy, 8

Bushehr, Iran nuclear facility, 185, *185*

Byzantine Empire, 206

C

Cable News Network (CNN), 155

Calderón, Felipe
    Arizona immigration law opinion, 261, 262
    Mexican drug war and, 236, 239–241, *241*, 242, 247, 251

Camarena, Enrique, 239, *240*

Camp Hope (San José mine, Chile), *47*, 48, 54, 56–57

Canada
    Afghanistan War forces, 7, 10, 14
    drug enforcement, 255
    economic standing, 86*t*
    Haitian relief donations, 152*t*, 157
    immigration, 272, 281*t*, 288–289
    oil reserves, 132*t*
    retirement age, 85*t*
    U.S. debt ownership, 91*t*

Capping, Gulf oil spill, 101, 105–107, *107*, *108*

Carcamo, Miguel, *233*

Cárdenas Guillén, Antonio Ezequiel, 247

Caribbean Community, 154–155

Caribbean Geologic Conference, 2008, 141–142

CARICOM, 154–155

Cartels, drug trade, *239*
    See also Mexican drug war; specific cartels

Carter, Jimmy, 6–7, 190

Cartoons. *See* "Everybody Draw Muhammad Day" (Facebook 2010); *Jyllands-Posten* Muhammad cartoons controversy (2005-2006)

Castro, Fidel, 269

Catholicism
    Crusades, 206
    discrimination, 210–213, *211*

Catts, Sidney J., 211

Cayne, Jimmy, 75

Cedeño, Rafael, 241

Celebrity, psychological aspects, 48–50

Censorship and information control
    Internet, China, 308, *308*
    Iran, *307*, 309–310
    Russia, 308
    self-censorship, Islamic topics, 222, 225

Center Rock Inc., 38, 53

Central America
    emigration, 259–260, 273
    slave trade, *268*
    See also specific nations

Central Asia, *6*
    See also Geopolitical history

Central Emergency Response Fund (CERF) (United Nations), 155

Central Intelligence Agency (CIA)
    Afghanistan War, 24–25
    Afghans on payroll, 18
    Internet security investigations, 293
    Iran actions, 186

Chemical dispersants. *See* Dispersants

Chesser, Adam, 226

Chile
    Bolivian relations, 54, *55*
    mining accidents, 35, 61*t*, 62–63
    Navy, 39
    See also Chilean miners' rescue

Chile earthquake (2010), *158*, 158–159

Chilean miners' rescue, *40*, *48*
    families of miners, *42*, *44*, 47–48, *48*, 54, *56*, 56–57, 62
    individual miners' stories, 50–53, *53*, 53–54, *55*, *57*, 57–59
    media coverage and fame, 35, 48–50, *50*, 57–59
    medical needs and attention, 38, 40, 41, 43, 45, *46*, 50, 58, 59, 60
    mine structure, 40–41, *41*
    miner survival and activities, 38, 40, *41*, 41–47, *42*, *46*, 52–53
    psychological aspects, 41–47, 48, 50
    rescue plans and methods, 35–40, *39*, *40*, 40–41, *41*, *51*, *52*, 53, *56*, 59–61
    timeline, 42–43

China
    economic standing, 86–87, 86*t*, 87*t*
    emigration, 271, 272, 281*t*
    espionage, 305–306, *306*
    financial markets, 77
    Great Wall, 289, *289*
    Han migrations, 289–290
    Internet policy and censorship, 308, *308*
    Iran diplomatic relations, 174, 175, 180–181, 184
    mining accidents, 61*t*, 62, 64, *64*
    nuclear weapons possession, 183, 183*t*, 184
    oil reserves, 132*t*

Tibet relations, 289

U.S. debt ownership, 91*t*

Chinese Exclusion Act (1882), 271, 272

Chivers, C.J., 12–13

Cholera, 146–151, *147, 150, 151,* 166, *166,* 167

Christian expansionism, 206

Church-state separation

France, 216, 217, 218

Germany, 220, 221

Turkey, 218, 219

Citizen journalism

Haitian earthquake coverage, 155

Iran protests, *307*

Ciudad Juárez, Mexico, 247–249, 248*t*, 251, *254*

Civic Alliance of Roma, *279*

Civilian casualties

Afghanistan War, *8,* 8–9, 10, 12, *12, 16,* 22*t*, 23, 300

Colombia, 286

Democratic Republic of the Congo, 285

Iraq War, 300, 301, *301*

Mexican drug war, 231–232, *233, 237,* 240, 246, 248, *248*

Somalia, 285

Sri Lanka, 288

Sudan, 284

Clarke, Richard, 305

Claude, Redjeson Hausteen, 141, *141*

Cleanup, 2010 Gulf oil spill

costs, 109, 121–122, 125

methods, 108–114, *112, 114, 117, 118*

Clinton, Bill, 153–154, *154,* 162, 204

Clinton, Hillary, 176–177, 302

Clinton Bush Haiti Fund, 153

CNN (Cable News Network), 155

Coal mining accidents, 61, 63, *63,* 64, *64*

Coast Guard. *See* U.S. Coast Guard

Coastal erosion, 114

Coastline, Gulf states, 97, 110, 112, *113,* 115

Cocaine

drug treatment programs, *245*

market value and profits, *235, 238*

production, 234, 252

seizures and busts, 246, 255, 257*t*

trafficking routes, 234, *235*

CODELCO, 36, 59

Cold War, 5–6, 182, 207, 275–276

Colombia

drug busts, 246

drug production and trade, 234, 235, *235,* 252–253, 286

internally displaced populations, 286

mining accidents, 61*t*

Colonialism. *See* Imperialism and colonialism

Columbus, Christopher, 159

Communism, 207, 275

Compensation programs, disasters, 119, 120

Comprehensive Nuclear Test-Ban Treaty (1996), 184

Computer networks, 297, 305, 307, 308

Computer security. *See* Internet security

Computer servers, 297

Computer viruses, 174, 296

Congress, U.S.

financial regulation and reform, 92, 93, 94

global financial crisis, 67–68, 75, 77, *92*

Gulf oil spill, *126,* 127

immigration policy, 262, *263,* 271, 272, 273

Mexican drug war policy, 243, 253, 255

midterm elections (2010), 90–91, 200, *200,* 201, 213

WikiLeaks response, 303

Congressional Hispanic Caucus, 262, *263*

Containment booms (oil spills), 110

Containment domes (oil spills), 103–104, *104,* 104–105

Controlled burns, Gulf oil spill, 108, 110, *112*

Convention for the Protection and Assistance of Internally Displaced Persons in Africa, 285–286

Convention on Cybercrime (2001), 296

Copper mining, 35, 40, 54, 61

See also Chilean miners' rescue

Corexit (chemical dispersant), 111

Corporate information and computer security, 294, 296, 298, 299, 299*t*, *304,* 305, 307

Corporate power, United States, 122, 124, 127

Correa, Rafael, 89

Corruption, government and police

Afghanistan, 10, 14–18

Haiti, 164–165, 269

Iran, 186

Mexico, 237–239, 241, *242,* 251

United States, government-corporate relations, 122, 124

world index, 14, *15,* 251

Corruption, military, 17, 301

Cota-Monroy, Martin Alejandro, 250–251

Council of Europe, 296

Council on American-Islamic Relations (CAIR), 201, 205

Countrywide (mortgage lender), 68, 70, *70,* 72–73

Coups and coup attempts

Ecuador, 2010, 89

Haiti, 1915 and 1991, 161–162

Iran, 1953, 186

Coyotes (human smugglers), 259–260

Credit crunch

causes, 75, 76

effects, 77, 78–79

Credit default swaps, 75–76

Creole culture, 159

Crime rates and immigration, 250–251, 261, 262*t*

Crude oil

properties, 113, 116

U.S. production, 124

See also Gulf oil spill (2010); Oil spills

Crusades, 206

Cuba

emigration, 269, *287*

Guantánamo Bay (U.S. Detention Center), 299, 302

Haitian relief donations, *160*

Haitian-U.S. immigration, 164

slave trade, 159

"Cultural genocide," Tibet, 289

Cummings, Elijah, 68

Cybercrime. *See* Internet security; specific crimes

Cyberterrorism, 298, 305, 306–307

Cyberwarfare, 305–310

Cyprus, 289, *289*

Czech Republic, retirement age, 85*t*

D

Darfur, Sudan, 284–285, *285,* 290

DEA (U.S. Drug Enforcement Administration), 239, *240,* 247

Dead zones, seas, 113

Dean, Howard, 203

The Death of Josseline: Immigration Stories from the Arizona-Mexico Borderlands (Regan), 259–260, *260*

Deauville Deal (EU economic plan), 89

Debt cancellation, 150

Debt concealment, 82

Deep-sea drilling. *See* Offshore drilling; Ultra-deepwater drilling

Deepwater Horizon rig, 97–101, *98, 99,* 110, *128*

See also Gulf oil spill (2010)

Deepwater spilled oil, 109–110

Deficits. *See* Budget deficits; Trade deficit, U.S.

Demilitarized Zone (DMZ), 289, *289*

Democracy. *See* Elections

Democratic Republic of the Congo, 284, 285

Demonstrations. *See* Protests and demonstrations

Denial of service attacks, 297, 303–304, *304,* 305

Denmark
immigration, 225, 281*t*, 287
Jyllands-Posten Muhammad cartoons controversy, 222–226, *223, 224, 225,* 228
Muslim populations, *217,* 222, 223
NATO relations, 226
retirement age, 85*t*
unemployment rates, 81*t*

Department of Defense (DOD). *See* U.S. Department of Defense

Department of Energy (DOE), 123, 131

Department of Health and Human Services (HHS), 119

Department of Homeland Security (DHS), 265

Department of Justice (DOJ), 282, 293

Department of State (United States), 179, 295, 301–303, 305, 310

Department of the Interior. *See* U.S. Department of the Interior

Developing nations, oil exploration and pollution, 130

DHS (U.S. Department of Homeland Security), 265

El Diario de Juárez (newspaper), 251, *254*

Diarrheal diseases, 145, 146, 148, 149, 150

Dibble, Elizabeth, 302

Diphtheria, 146

Diplomatic relations
Iran, 169, 171, 172–173, 174–175, 179–181, 196–197
nuclear non-proliferation, 172, 184, 196–197
U.S. State Department, and WikiLeaks, 179, 301–303, 310
See also U.S. Department of State

Diseases. *See* AIDS rates; Cholera; Diarrheal diseases; Diphtheria; Public health issues

Dispersants
oil spill cleanup and pollution, 108, 109, 110–112, 113–114, 117
photographed, 102
seafood consumer concerns, 120

Displaced persons (DPs). *See* Internally displaced persons (IDPs); Refugees

Distributed denial of service attacks, 297

Doctors Without Borders, 139, *140,* 167, 290

Dolphins, 116, 119

Domestic worker abuse, 278–279

Dominican Republic, 149, 157, 159

DOS attacks. *See* Denial of service attacks

Dot.com bubble, 70, 71

"Double dip" recessions, 81, 88

Dove World Outreach Center, *204,* 205

Dow Jones Industrial Average, 67, 70*t*, 77, 93

Drilling, in Chilean miners' rescue, 36–39, 40–41, *41,* 53

Drug addiction
Afghanistan and Pakistan, *20,* 20–21
global, and treatment sought, *245*

Drug ballads, 252

Drug rehabilitation and treatment
global, *245*
Mexican drug war patients and incidents, 248–249
United States, 255, 256–257, 256*t*

Drug seizures
as insignificant, 231
large busts, 246, 255
Mexican discoveries, 234, *234,* 245, *247*
Mexican totals/rates, 257*t*

Drug trafficking and trade, 232, 234
Afghanistan, 18–22, 232, 246
Mexican drug cartel methods, 235–238, 245
Mexican drug cartels map, *239*

routes, 234, *235,* 247
South and Central America to U.S., 234, *234,* 246, 252–253

Dudley, Bob, 127

Dutch art, *71*

Duvalier, François, 162

Duvalier, Jean-Claude, 162, 269

E

Earthquakes, 158, 159
See also Chile earthquake (2010); Haiti earthquake (2010) and aftermath

Economic crisis of 2008. *See* Global economic crisis

Economic migration, 267–268, 269–270, 271, 278, 279–280

Ecosystems, Gulf of Mexico, 113–114, 115

Ecstasy (drug), 246, 255

Ecuador coup attempt (2010), 89

Egypt, 194

EIA (Energy Information Administration), 123, 131

Einstein, Albert, 181

Ekofisk oil spill (Norway, 1977), 128–129

El Paso, Texas, 249–250

El Salvador, emigration, 259–260, *260*

ElBaradei, Mohamed, 171

Elections
Afghanistan, 10, 17, *17,* 25–26
Eastern Europe, 276
Haiti, 162–163, 166–167
Iran, 297, 309–310
Jordan, *216*
Sudan, 284–285
United States (2010), 90–91, 200, *200,* 201, 213
United States (2012), 91
women voters, *216*

Electoral Complaints Commission (ECC), Afghanistan, 10

Elphinstone, William, 4

Emigration. *See* Immigration

Energy consumption
China, 63–64, 180–181
fossil fuels, 63–65, 130–131
mining's role, 63–65
United States, 123–124, 130, 131

Energy independence goals, 130

Energy industry. *See* Oil industry

Energy Information Administration (EIA), 123, 131

English (language), 266

Enriched uranium. *See* Uranium enrichment; Yellowcake uranium

Enriquillo-Plantain Garden Fault, 142, *143*

Environmental disasters. *See* Gulf oil spill (2010); Oil spills

Environmental justice issues, 130

Environmental Protection Agency (EPA), 111, 116

Environmental regulations
  developing nations, oil exploration, 130
  Gulf oil spill issues, 100, 122–123, 124, 127
  mining, 61
  reforms, 122–123, 127
  See also Corporate power, United States; Environmental Protection Agency (EPA)

EPA. *See* Environmental Protection Agency (EPA)

Equal Employment Opportunity Commission (EEOC), 209–210

Erosion
  coastal, 114
  deforestation effects, 157

Escobar, Pablo, 234, 235

Espinoza, Alberto, 240–241

Espionage
  Internet security and information theft, 294–295, 305–306
  methods, 304
  WikiLeaks considerations, 303

Estonia
  cyber skirmishes, 305
  emigration, 281*t*

Ethnic and language groups. *See* Language and ethnic groups

Europe
  central banks, in economic crisis, 74, 77
  economic crisis: countries details, *69, 78,* 80–86, 88–89, 94
  emigration, 268–269, 269–273
  EU formation, 276
  financial markets, 77
  financial regulations, 92–93
  immigration, *213,* 213–215, 221, 225, 276, 278, *279,* 280–281, 281*t,* 283, 287
  Muslim communities and relations, *213,* 213–215, 216–221, *217,*

222–226, *223*
  recession and austerity plans, 81, 82–83, 84–85, 89, *90*
  See also specific nations

European Court of Human Rights, 218, 221

European Monetary Union, 82

Eurozone, 81–82, 83

"Everybody Draw Muhammad Day" (Facebook 2010), 226–227

Evictions, *73,* 165

Explosions. *See Apollo 13* mission; Bombings; Gulf oil spill (2010); Mining accidents and explosions; Oil spills

Exxon Valdez oil spill (1989)
  economic harms, 120
  environmental outcomes, 114, *129*
  health harms, 117, 118
  size, 101, 127, *128*

F

Facebook, 226–227

Falcon Lake (Texas/Mexico), 250

La Familia drug cartel, 236, *239,* 240–241, 255

Fannie Mae, 77

Farmers and farming
  Afghanistan opium crops, 19–20, 21–22
  European protests, *69*
  Irish crop failures, 268, 270–271
  migrant labor, 278

Faults (plate tectonics), 141, 142, *142, 143,* 159

Federal Bureau of Investigation (FBI)
  Gulf oil spill inspections, 107
  Internet security and crime, 293, 294, 295

Federal Reserve, U.S., 74, 75, 77

Federal Trade Commission (FTC), 294

Feinberg, Kenneth, 119

Financial Accounting Standards Board (FASB), 92

Financial crisis of 2008. *See* Global economic crisis

Financial regulation
  credit default swap loopholes, 75–76
  economic crisis reactions and corrections, 77, 80, 92–94

Finland
  economic crisis and recession, 81
  immigration, 281*t*

retirement age, 85*t*

First Anglo-Afghan War (1839-1842), 4

Fisher, Brandon W., 38, 53

Fishing industry, and Gulf oil spill, 97, 109, 119, 120–121

Fission, 181–182

Flooding, 64, 147, 148, 286, *286*

Florida
  foreclosures, *76*
  Gulf oil spill, economic effects, 119–120, 121
  Gulf oil spill pollution, 102, 112, *113,* 115

Flowrates, Gulf oil spill, 100–101, 100*t*

Food chain studies, 114

Foreclosures
  hard-hit states, *76,* 79
  protests, *93*
  U.S. filing rates, 72, 72*t,* 76

Foroughi, Mohammad-Ali, 186

Fortis (financial firm), 77

Fossil fuel production and use, 63–65, 130–131

France
  Afghanistan War forces, 10, 13, 14
  austerity plans and protests, 84, *84,* 86, *90*
  colonialism and imperialism, 159, 161–162, 206–207
  economic crisis and recession, 83–86
  economic standing, 86*t*
  European Union debt relief policy, 89
  Haitian relief donations, 152*t*
  immigration policy, *279,* 281*t,* 283, *283*
  Iran diplomatic relations, 174, 175, 179
  Islamophobia, *212*
  Muslim communities and relations, *212, 213*–214, 216–218, *217, 218,* 224
  nuclear weapons possession, *182,* 183, 183*t*
  oil spills, 101*t,* 127
  retirement age, 84, 85*t,* 86
  secularism, 216, 217, 218
  unemployment rates, 81*t,* 83

Fraud, computer crimes, 294–295, *295,* 296–297, 307

Fraud, elections
  Afghanistan, 10, 17, 25–26
  Haiti, 166–167

Freddie Mac, 77

Free Burma Coalition, *296*

Free Tibet Campaign, 290

Freedom of expression. *See* Head coverings, Muslim women; *Jyllands-Posten* Muhammad cartoons controversy (2005-2006)

Freedom of speech, 310

Friendly fire incidents, 300

    See also Civilian casualties

FTC (U.S. Federal Trade Commission), 294

Fuel rods, *173*, 185

Fuld, Richard S., 67–68, *68*

G

G-7 nations, 150

G-20 nations, 80, 93

Gallardo, Miguel Ángel Félix, 235–236, 237–238, 239

Garton Ash, Timothy, 303

Gasoline consumption, U.S., 123–124

Gasoline prices, 133

Gates, Robert, 305

Gaza Strip, 194, 274

General Motors (GM) bailout, 94

Genocide

    "cultural," Tibet, 289

    Holocaust, 194, 195, 272

    Sudan, 284

Geology

    Chilean mining environments, 35, 40–41

    tectonic regions and ridges, 141–142, *142, 143,* 159

Geopolitical history

    Afghanistan, 2, 4–7

    Arab-Israeli conflict, 192–196, 207, 225, 274, *274*

    Iran, 190–192

    Ottoman Empire, 192, 206–207

Georgia (nation), 305

Geotec SA, 38

Germany

    Afghanistan War forces, 10, 13, 14

    austerity plans, *90*

    Berlin Wall, 289, *289*

    economic standing, 86*t*, 281

    emigration, 211, *211,* 271, 272, 281*t*

    European debt relief opinions/plans, 82, 89

    Haitian relief donations, 152*t*

    headscarf laws, 219–221

    immigration, *213, 214,* 214–215, 281,

281*t*

    Muslim communities and relations, *213,* 213–214, *214, 217,* 219–221, 226

    retirement age, 85*t*

    unemployment rates, 81*t*

    World War II, 129, 194, 195, 272

Gfoeller, Michael, 303

Gingrich, Newt, 202–203

Global economic crisis, 67–94

    aftermath, 86–91, 86*t,* 93–94

    causes, 67–77, 91–93, 94

    emigration and immigration effects, 261, 277, 282, 283, 287, 290

    lead-up and warning signs, 67, 73–74

    timeline, 74–75

    See also Recessions

Global financial indexes, 77

    See also Dow Jones Industrial Average

Globalization and immigration, 275–280

Godoy Toscano, Julio César, 241, *242*

Golborne, Laurence, *45*

Gold rushes, 271, 272

Goldman Sachs

    Greece dealings, 82

    profits, 92, 93

    Senate hearings, 2010, *92*

Del Golfo cartel. *See* Gulf drug cartel

Gonzalez, Mario, *248*

Google, *308*

Gore, Al, 293

Government Accountability Office (GAO), reports, 121

Government deficits. *See* Budget deficits

Government oversight. *See* Congress, U.S.; Environmental regulations; Financial regulation

Gravel, Mike, 303

Great Britain

    emigration, 268, 270

    imperialism, 4–5

    See also United Kingdom

"Great Game," 4–5, 186

Great Migration (United States), 267–268

Great Wall of China, 289, *289*

Greece

    austerity measures, 82–83, *90*

    debt-concealing tactics, 82

    economic crisis, 81–83, 88–89

    postwar migration patterns, 272

    protests, 82, *83*

retirement age, 85*t*

Green energy jobs, 89

"Green movement" (Iran), 309

Greenspan, Alan, 77

Gross domestic product (GDP), 78–79, 87–88

"Ground Zero" site and mosque, *202,* 202–205, *203, 203t, 207,* 210, 282

    See also September 11, 2001 terrorist attacks

Guajardo, Carlos Alberto, 246

Guantánamo Bay, Cuba

    Haitian-U.S. immigration, 164

    WikiLeaks coverage (U.S. Detention Center), 299, 302

Guatemala

    drug enforcement, 255

    drug trade violence, 252–253

    economic crisis effects, *79*

Guest worker programs, 214

    See also Migrant workers

Gul, Abdullah, 219

Gulf Coast Claims Facility, 119

Gulf currents, 115

Gulf drug cartel, 236, 237, *239,* 245, 247, 255

Gulf of Mexico ecosystem, 113–114

Gulf of Mexico oil spills

    accidents 2001-2010, 127

    annual seepage, 115*t*

    Ixtoc I (1979), 101, 101*t*

    See also Gulf oil spill (2010)

Gulf oil spill (2010), 97–133

    accident and explosion, 97–100, *98, 99, 128*

    capping, 101, 105–107, *107, 108*

    cleanup costs, 109, 121–122, 123, 125

    cleanup efforts, 108–114, *112, 114, 117, 118*

    economic impact, *102,* 119–122, *121,* 123

    environmental impact, *102,* 109–114, *111,* 115–118, *116,* 119

    flowrates, 100–101, 100*t*

    leak containment efforts, 100, 101, 102, 103–108, *104, 105, 106, 107, 108*

    media coverage, 102–103, 109, 115

    repercussions, 123–127

    restoration following, 113, 121, 125

    responsibility, 100, 122–123

    size and significance, 97, 100–102, 101*t,* 115*t,* 124

spill containment efforts, 108, 110, *114*

timeline, 110–111

Gun control, 255, 256

Gun violence, Mexican drug war, 231–232, *237*, 243, 244–245, 246, 250, 255

H

H-bombs, 182

Hacking, computers. *See* Internet security

Haise, Fred W., 58

Haiti earthquake (2010) and aftermath, 135–167, *138*

death toll, 135–136, 139*t*, 150

earthquake dynamics, *138*, 140–142, *142, 143, 157*

health challenges/complications, 139, 145–151, *162, 166,* 167

infrastructure, *137*, 141, 151, 152, 157, 160, *163,* 166

media coverage, 135, 141, 155–156

predictions, 141–142

recovery and reconstruction, 143, 145, 150–153, *154,* 154–155, 159

refugees, 143–145, *144,* 146, 147, 148, 149, 152, *153,* 165, *266*

rescue work, 135, *136,* 141, *141,* 156

timeline, 144–145

Haiti-United States relations, 154, 161–164

Haitian history, 159, 161–164, 269

Halliburton (corporation), 98, 123, *126,* 127

Hama Massacre (Syria, 1982), 192

Hamad, King (Bahrain), 180

Hamas, 195, 294–295

Han Chinese, 289–290

Hang Seng Index (China), 77

Haqqani, Jalauddin, *29*

Haqqani group, *29, 30,* 31

Hartley, David and Tiffany, 250, *250*

Hatch, Orrin, 204

Hate crimes

anti-Muslim, 199–200, 209, 282

immigrants as victims, 210, 265, 277, 278–279, 282

Hayward, Tony, 126–127

Hazaras, 26

Head coverings, Muslim women, 189, *215,* 215–221, *216, 218, 219*

Health issues

Afghanistan health status, 16–17

human health, Gulf oil spill, 116–119

medical and public health challenges, post-Haiti earthquake (2010), 139, 140, 145–150, *147, 150,* 161, *162,* 166, *166*

"Hearts and minds" struggle, Afghanistan War, *12,* 12–13

Hekmatyar group, *30*

Helmand province, Afghanistan, 10, 11–13, *21,* 21–22

Hengxinyuan mine (China), 64

Hernandez, Josseline, 259–260, *260*

Heroin

drug treatment, *245*

production, 18, 232

trafficking, 234

usage and addiction, *20,* 20–21

See also Opium

Hezb-e-Islami Gulbuddin (HIG), 31

Hezbollah, 129–130, 190, 195

High Performance Computing and Communication Act (1991), 293

Hijab, 215, *215,* 219

Hiring Incentives to Restore Employment (HIRE) Act (2010), 89–90

Hiroshima and Nagasaki, Japan bombings (1945), 181, *196*

Hispaniola (island), 142, *143,* 149, 157, 159

See also Dominican Republic; Haiti earthquake (2010) and aftermath

Holland. *See* Netherlands

Holocaust, 194, 195, 272

Holocaust denials, 195

Home foreclosures. *See* Foreclosures

Home ownership rates, 67, 91

Homelessness

Haitian earthquake aftermath, 135, 138, 143–145, *144,* 146, 147, 148, 149, 152, *153,* 165

South Africa, *80*

Homicides, Mexican drug war, *231,* 231–232, *232, 233,* 237, *237,* 239, 242*t,* 246, 247, 248, 250–251, 251*t,* 254

Hong Kong, 91*t*

Hostage situations, *188,* 190

House of Representatives, U.S. *See* Congress, U.S.

Housing crisis. *See* Foreclosures; Mortgage crisis; Real estate bubble; Subprime mortgage loans

Human health issues. *See* Health issues

Human rights abuses

Afghanistan, 7

China, 289

Democratic Republic of the Congo, 285

Haiti, post-earthquake, 140

immigrants, 265, 278–279, 287

Internet attacks, *296*

Iran, 186, *307,* 309–310

Iraq, 287, 301

Mexico, 252, 253

Myanmar, *296*

Pakistan, 286

Somalia, 285

Sudan, 284

Human Rights Watch, 220–221, 253, 283

Human smuggling

Asia-Canada, 288

Mexico-U.S., 259–260

Hungary, retirement age, 85*t*

Hunger and famine

Africa, 274–275

Ireland, 268, 270–271

slave trade, 269

Hurricane Katrina (2005), 103, 118

Hurricane Tomas (2010), 147, 148, *148*

Hussein, Saddam, 192

Hydrates, *104,* 104–105, *128*

Hydrogen bombs, 182

Hydrostatic kill technique, 106–107, *108*

Hypoxic regions, seas, 113

I

IAEA. *See* International Atomic Energy Agency (IAEA)

Iceland

bank nationalization, 77

recession, *78*

unemployment rates, 81*t*

Identification, photographic, 216, *216,* 294–295

Identity theft, 294–295, 307

Ijaw people (Nigeria), 130

Illegal immigration

Arizona law: SB 1070, 260–263, *262*

Asia-Canada smuggling, 288–289

crime and immigrant populations, 250–251, 261, 262*t*

Haiti-U.S., 161, 163–164

Mexico-U.S., 246, 250–251, 259–263, *261*, 289, *289*
post-Cold War, 276
terminology, 267
U.S. rates and totals, 280*t*
vigilantism, *264*, 264–265
See also Immigration
Immigration, 259, 277–281, 281*t*
Arizona law: SB 1070, 260–263, *262*
crime rates and, 250–251, 261, 262*t*
Europe, *213*, 213–215, 221, 225, 276, 278, 279, 280–281, 281*t*, 283, 287
Haitians, to North America, 159, 161, 163–164, 269
history, 268–277
language and terminology, 264–265, 267
media coverage, 267
Mexican drug war and would-be immigrants, *233*, 246, 250–251
Puerto Ricans, identity theft, 295
safe haven policy, 164
trends and predictions, 273, 275–281, 290
U.S. rates and totals (illegal), 280*t*
See also Illegal immigration; Migrant workers; Migration, human; Refugees
Immigration Act (1921, 1924, and 1965), 273
Immigration reform, 262–263, 280
Immunizations. *See* Vaccines
Imperialism and colonialism
Crusades, 206
Europe, in Middle East, 192, 206–207
France, 159, 161–162, 206–207
Great Britain, 4–5, 186, 206–207
Russia, 4–5, 186
Spain, 159
United States, 161–162
India
economic standing, 86–87, 86*t*
emigrant workers, 277, 287, *288*
financial markets, 77
nuclear weapons possession, 183, 183*t*, 184
worker protests, *88*
Indigenous peoples, 130, 159
Indonesia
emigrants, 278–279
history, U.S. relations, 207
Islam and culture, 228
Industrialization

China, and energy needs, 62, 63–64, 180–181
mining safety and, 61–62, 63–64
U.S. history, 267–268
world history, 130–131
Information control policy. *See* Censorship and information control
Information security
espionage, 294, 305–306
theft, 294, 296–297, 298, 307
WikiLeaks, 23, *23*, 298–305, 310
See also Internet security
Inspections, weapons. *See* International Atomic Energy Agency (IAEA); Iran nuclear program
Insurgency, Afghanistan. *See* Taliban
Inter-American Commission on Human Rights, 265
Interim Haiti Recovery Commission (IHRC), 152
Internal Displacement Monitoring Centre (IDMC), 284, 287, 291
Internally displaced persons (IDPs), 264–265, *273*, 282, 284, 285–287, 288
International Accounting Standards Board, 92
International aid
Afghanistan, 12, 16–17, 22, 29, 29*t*
Africa, 285
Colombia, 252
Haiti, 20th century, 162
Haiti 2010 earthquake: financial, 138–139, 150–152, 152*t*, 153, 154, 155, 156, 157
Haiti 2010 earthquake: international recovery coordination, 135, 141, *141*, 143, 152–153, 154–155, 156, 161, 167
Haiti 2010 earthquake: medical, 139, *140*, 141, 143, 145–150, 161, *162*, *166*, 167
Mexico, 252, 253, 255
South Asian tsunami, 2004, 153–154
See also Medical aid
International Atomic Energy Agency (IAEA)
international role, 183, 184, 185
Iran monitoring and positions, 169–172, 173, 174–175, 177, 178, 179, 185, 197
International Council on Security and Development (ICOS), 12
International Monetary Fund (IMF), 82,

83, 86, 94, 138
International Organization for Migration (IOM), 291
International Refugees Organization (IRO) (United Nations), 272–273
International Treaty on Cybercrime (2001), 296
Internet
Chinese control, 290, *308*
fundraising method, 156, 157
history, 293–294
traffic, visual representation, *309*
See also Internet security
Internet businesses, stocks, 70, 71
Internet security
conferences and conventions, *295*, 296, 307–308
costs and losses totals, 298, 299*t*, 306
espionage, 294, 305–306
hacking and computer crimes, 293, *294*, 294–298, 298*t*, 303–304, *304*, 305–306
history and development, 293–294, 296, 298
See also National security; WikiLeaks
INTERPOL, 238
Investment firms
bailouts, 75, 76, 77, 92, 93
European dealings, 82
profits, 92–93
role in financial crisis, 68, 74–76, 77, 92–93
salary caps, 93
testimony on financial crisis, 67–68, *68*, 75, *92*
See also specific firms
Iran
Afghan refugees, *171*, 275
American hostage crisis, *188*, 190
economic standing, 189–190
election results and protests (2009), 297, 309–310
history and U.S. relations, 177, 186–190, 196, 207
information control and human rights, 186, *307*, 309–310
Iraq War and, 301
Islamic Revolution, 186–188, 190, 192
Islamic Revolutionary Guards Corps, 175
Jyllands-Posten (newspaper) protests, *224*, 226

language and ethnic groups, *193*
location, *21, 171,* 186
Muslim sects, 190, *191,* 192
oil reserves, 132*t*
sanctions, 171, 174, 175, *176,* 179, 180–181, 189, 190
Saudi Arabia relations, 180, 302, 303
Western influences, 186, 187, 189, 190, 221, 222
See also Iran nuclear program
Iran-Iraq War (1980-1988), 129, 189, 190, 192
Iran nuclear program, 169–197
facilities, 169, *170, 171,* 172, *173,* 176, 177, 185, *185*
international relations and inspections, 169–173, 174–181, 197
sanctions, 171, 174, 175, *176,* 179, 180–181
status, 170–175, 185, 196–197
timeline, 188–189
Iraq
Iran-Iraq War (1980-1988), 129, 189, 190, 192
Muslim sects, 190, *191*
oil reserves, 132*t*
Persian Gulf War, 101*t,* 130, 192
refugees and emigration, *277,* 281*t,* 286–287
Tammuz nuclear reactor, *194*
Iraq War, 2003-
refugees and internally displaced, 286–287
U.S. actions, WikiLeaks coverage, 300, 301, *301*
U.S. invasion, 8, 212
U.S. withdrawal, 287
Ireland
austerity plans, 81
economic crisis and recession, 81, 94, 280
emigration, 19th century, 210, *211,* 268, 270–271, 272
immigration, 280
retirement age, 85*t*
iReport (Cable News Network), 155
Isfahan, Iran uranium conversion plant, *173*
Islam in the West, 199–228
Europe, *212, 213,* 213–226, *214, 217, 218, 220, 223*
United States, 199–210, *200,* 209, 209*t,* 210–211, 213, *225, 227,*

282–283
Western influences and Muslim world, 206–207, 221–222, 224
Islam (religion), 191, 201, 209*t,* 210, 213
See also Islamic history
Islamic community centers, 210
Florence, Kentucky, 202
Murfreesboro, Tennessee, 199–200, 210
New York City, *202,* 202–205, *203,* 203*t,* 210, 282
Sheboygan County, Wisconsin, 201
Temecula, California, 201–202
See also Mosques
Islamic history, 190–191, 206–207, 223
See also Islam (religion)
Islamic law, 201, 221–222
Iran, 171, 188–189
Pakistan, 9
Taliban Afghanistan rule, 7
United States, 201, 211
Islamic Revolution (Iran), 186–188, 190, 192
Islamic Revolutionary Guard Corps, 175, 189
Islamists and Islamism, 192
Afghanistan, 1970s-1980s, 6–7
Iran, 186, 187, 188–189, 190
Somalia, 285
Sudan, 284
See also Taliban
Islamophobia, 200–202, 222
politicians' campaigns, 199–200
sentiment in Western culture and policy, 203, 204–205, 209, 210–211, 212, *212,* 213, 225, 282
Israel, 192
creation and Arab-Israeli conflict, 192–196, 207, 225, 274, *274*
immigration, 195, 268–269
Iran weapons programs and, *174,* 175–177, 179, 180, 185, 190, *194,* 195
Israel-West Bank border, 194, 195, 289, *289*
Mossad, 295
nuclear weapons possession, 175, 176, 183, 183*t,* 184–185
population, 192
U.S. relations, 176–177, 178–179, 190, 196
wars and skirmishes, 129–130, *177,*

194, *194,* 195, 196
world view, 195–196
Italy
austerity plans, *90*
drug enforcement, 255
economic standing, 86*t*
emigration, 272, 273
immigration, 281*t*
Muslim populations, *217*
retirement age, 85*t*
U.S. diplomatic relations, 302
Ixtoc I oil spill (1979), 101, 101*t,* 128

J

Jalalabad, Afghanistan, 4
James, Jonathan, 296
James, Raymond, 157
Janjaweed, 284
Japan
economic standing, 86*t*
financial crisis and banking system, 77, *78*
Haitian relief donations, 152*t*
Hiroshima and Nagasaki bombings, 181, *196*
immigration, 281*t*
nuclear power and weapons technology, 185
retirement age, 85*t*
unemployment rates, 81*t*
U.S. debt ownership, 91*t*
Jaschan, Sven, 296
JBS Swift company, 209–210
Jean, Wyclef, 157
Jerusalem, 206
"The Jester" (Internet hacker), 303–304
Jews
immigration and emigration, 195, 268–269, 271, 272
Israel as homeland, 193–194
WWII holocaust, 194, 195, 272
Jindal, Bobby, 120
Job creation
Obama policy, 89–90
small businesses, 79
Job losses
credit crunch and small businesses, 79
effects on immigration, 261, 277, 287
Greece, 83
hardest-hit fields, 79–80
South Africa, *80*
United States, 121–122

See also Unemployment

Jones, Terry, *204,* 205, *205*

Jordan, 195

    Six-Day War (1967), 194

    women's dress and elections, *216*

Journalists. *See* Media coverage issues;
    Press

JP Morgan Chase, 75, 92, 93

Juárez, Mexico, 247–249, 248*t,* 251, *254*

Juárez drug cartel, 236, 238, *239,*
    247–249

Junk shot technique (oil spill contain-
    ment), 105, *106*

Jyllands-Posten Muhammad cartoons
    controversy (2005-2006), 222–226,
    223, 224, 225, 228

K

Kabul, Afghanistan

    history, 4, 5, *5,* 8

    terror attacks, 1–2, *2*

Kampala Convention, 285–286

Kandahar, Afghanistan, 8, 14, *18*

Kandahar Offensive, 28–29

Kandahar province, Afghanistan, 19,
    21, 22

Karzai, Ahmed Wali, 19

Karzai, Hamid

    assassination attempts, 31

    corruption, 17–18, 19

    domestic/ethnic/tribal relations, 27,
    27, 28, 29–31

    drug eradication programs, 21

    election, 10, *11*

    U.S. relations, 9, 14, 18, 19, 23

Kavakçi, Merve, 218–219

Kemal, Mustafa, 218

Kennedy, John F., 162, 213

Kerry, John, 14, 18

Khamenei, Ayatollah Ali, 171, *178,* 189

Khatami, Mohammad, 189

Khomeini, Ayatollah Ruhollah,
    186–189, *187,* 190, 192

Kidnappings

    African militias, 285

    Colombian drug trade, 252

    Mexican drug war, 231, 248, *248,* 251,
    251*t*

Know-Nothing movement, 210

Koran. *See* Qur'an

Kranz, Eugene Francis, 59

Kreyol (Haitian language), 159–160

Kurds (ethnic group), 192, *193*

Kuwait

    oil reserves, 132*t*

    Persian Gulf War and oil supplies,
    101*t,* 130

Kyrgyzstan, refugees, *276*

L

Labor strikes, Europe, 84, *84,* 86, *87, 89*

    See also Protests and demonstrations

Laden, Osama bin, 7, *32,* 218

Lake Pontchartrain, 102

Land ownership, Haiti, 164–165

Language and ethnic groups

    Afghanistan, *26,* 26–28, 31

    Arabs, 193–194

    English, history, 266

    Haiti, 159–160

    Iran, *193*

    Tibet/China, 289

    United States, 208, 271

    See also Sunni/Shiite Muslims, history
    and tensions

The Late Show with David Letterman,
    50, 77

Layne Christensen Company, 38

League of Nations, 271–272

Leaks, media. *See* WikiLeaks

Leases, oil drilling, 100, 122, 127, 133

Lebanon, 129–130, 175, 190, 194

LeBaron, Eric and Benjamín, 248

Legal systems and Islamic law, 201, 211

Lehman Brothers, 67–68, *68,* 77

Letterman, David, *50, 77*

Libya

    European foreign relations, 224

    oil reserves, 132*t*

    oil spill, 1980, 101*t*

Literacy rates, Haiti, 157, 160

Liu Xiaobo, *306*

Logar province, Afghanistan, 2, *3*

Long-range missiles, *174,* 178, *178,* 180

Lotteries, 235, *236*

Louisiana

    Gulf oil spill, economic effects, 97,
    119, 120–121

    Gulf oil spill pollution, 97, 102, 110,
    112, *113, 114,* 115

    Hurricane Katrina (2005), 103, 118

Lovell, James A., 58

Lower marine riser package (LMRP) cap
    containment system, 105–106, *107*

M

Mahmud Mosque (Switzerland), *220*

Major Crimes Task Force (Afghanistan),
    18

Malaysia, immigration and human
    rights, 278–279

Mamani, Carlos, 53–54, *55*

The Man Behind the Lines (Westergaard),
    228

Manhattan Project, 181

Mariel Boatlift (Cuba, 1980), 269

Marijuana

    drug treatment, *245*

    production, 232, 234, 239

    seizures, Mexico, *234,* 245, *247,* 255,
    257*t*

    trafficking, 234

Marine animals

    dispersants' effects, 111

    food chains and ecosystems, 114, 115

    Gulf oil spill damages, 97, *97,* 110,
    115–116, *117, 118,* 119

Marine Well Containment Company
    (MWCC), 127

Marja, Afghanistan, 11–13, 21–22

Marshes and wetlands, 97, 102, 108,
    110, 115, 117

Mazar-e-Sharif, Afghanistan, 8

McCain, John, 77, 203

McChrystal, Stanley, 10–11, 23

McKay, Lamar, *126*

MDMA (Ecstasy), 246, 255

Médecins Sans Frontières (Doctors With-
    out Borders), 139, *140,* 167, 290

Medellín drug cartel, 235

Media coverage issues

    bias in reporting, immigration, 267

    Chilean miners' rescue, 35, 48–50, *50,*
    57–59

    developing nations' lack of coverage,
    130

    Gulf oil spill, 102–103, 109, 115

    Haiti earthquake, 135, 155–156

    journalists, in Mexican drug war, 246,
    251, 252–253, *254*

    Jyllands-Posten Muhammad cartoons
    controversy (2005-2006), 222–226,
    223, 224, 225, 228

    self-censorship, Islamic topics,
    222–223, 225

    See also WikiLeaks

Medical aid

    Afghanistan, 12, 16–17

Chilean miners' rescue, 38, 40, 41, 43, 45, *46,* 50, 58, 59, 60
Haitian earthquake relief and challenges, 139, *140,* 141, 143, 145–150, *147, 150,* 161, *162, 166,* 167
Medical isotope production, 173
Medvedev, Dmitry, 179, *179,* 184
Melilla, Spain, *278*
Melting pot theory and practice. *See* Assimilation and assimilation theory
Mental health issues
Chilean miners, 42–50
environmental disaster-related, 118–119
Merkel, Angela, 13, 93, *213,* 214, 226
Methamphetamine
drug treatment, *245*
seizures, Mexico, 255, *257t*
trafficking, 234
Metula oil spill (1973), 127
Mexican drug war, 231–257
arms trafficking, 243–244, *245,* 253
cartels, 231, 235–237, *239,* 240–241, 242, *243,* 245–249, 251–252
corruption, 237–239, 241, *242,* 251
economic impact, 253, 255
history, 231–232, 239–240
public perception, 251–252
seizures, 234, *234,* 245, *247,* 255, *257t*
trafficking routes, 234, *235,* 247
U.S. soil, 250–251
Mexico
Army, 240, 241–243, *243,* 244–247, 253
economic standing, *86t,* 253, 255
emigration, *233,* 246, 250–251, 259–263, *264,* 264–265, 272–273, *281f*
environmental damages, 114
human rights abuses, 252
Navy, 245
retirement age, *85t*
United States relations, 232, 234, 236, 243, 255–256, 261–262, 263, 289, *289*
See also Mexican drug war
Meynell, Francis, *270*
MI5 (United Kingdom), 306
MI6 (United Kingdom), 186
Michoacán, Mexico, 240, 241
Microbes, 113–114
Middle East region, *171*
economic standing, *86t*

emigration and immigration, 206, 214, 276, 282–283, 286–288, *288*
ethnic groups, 192–193
geopolitical history, 190–192, 206–207
Iranian nuclear weapons, *174,* 175–177, 178–179, 179–180, 302, 303, 309
Muslim sects, 190, *191,* 192
nuclear weapons-free zone, 184–185
oil reserves, 131, *132t*
Palestine/Israel territories, 207, 274, *274*
Mignon, Abraham, *71*
Migrant workers
Europe and Asia, 214, 276, 278–279, *279, 288,* 288–290
Mexicans, in U.S., 261, 264, 278
Middle East, 287–288
victims, *233,* 259–260
Migration, human
history, 265–269, *267*
international protection, 164, 273, *273*
patterns, 265–266, *267,* 269, *275*
terminology, 264–265, 267
See also Immigration; Refugees; Slavery
Migration Policy Institute, 264, 280, 281, 290–291
Military security, 293, 296, 299, *300,* 300–301, 303–304, 305
Minarets, *220,* 221
Minerals Management Service (MMS), 122–123, 127
Mining accidents and explosions, 35, 61–62, *61t, 63,* 63–64
See also Chilean miners' rescue
Minuteman Project, 264–265
Miot, Joseph Serge, 138, *140*
Missiles, *174, 178, 178,* 179, 180
Mississippi
Gulf oil spill, economic effects, 121
Gulf oil spill pollution, 112, *113*
Mitsui (corporation), 123
MMS (Minerals Management Service), 122–123, 127
Moderate Resolution Imaging Spectroradiometer (MODIS) photography, 102
Mofaz, Shaul, 175–176
Money laundering, 234–235, *236*
Morales, Evo, 54
Morel, Cecilia, 54
Mórida Initiative, 253, 255

Morocco, emigration, 281
Mortgage-backed securities, 74–76
Mortgage crisis, 67–68, 70, 71–74, 79
See also Investment firms; Subprime mortgage loans
Mortgage defaults, 72, 74
See also Foreclosures
Mortgage lending standards, 68, 72, 91
Mosques
community education and relations, 210
community opposition, 200, *200,* 201–202, 282
Mahmud Mosque (Switzerland), *220*
minarets, *220,* 221
Sultanahmet Mosque (Turkey), *213*
See also Islamic community centers
Mossad, 295
Mossadegh, Mohammed, 186
Mottaki, Manouchehr, 174–175
Moussavi, Mir Hossein, 309
Mozilo, Angelo, 70, *70*
Mubarak, Hadia, 213
Muhammad (prophet), 191
"Everybody Draw Muhammad Day," 226–227
Islamic depiction standards, 223
Jyllands-Posten cartoons controversy (2005-2006), 222–226, *223, 224, 225*
Sunni/Shiite relations and, 190–191
Mujahideen, 6–7, 8
Multiculturalism, 214
Murder rates, *232t,* 247, *248t,* 250, 252
See also Homicides, Mexican drug war
Murfreesboro, Tennessee, 199–200, 210
Music
drug ballads, 252
Western and pop culture, 221
Muslim populations, global
China, 289–290
Europe, 213–215, *217,* 221
racial profiling, 209, 282
sects, 190, *191*
Sudan, 284, 285
United Kingdom, 200, 201
United States, 199–210, 282
women's head coverings, *215*
See also Islam in the West; Western influences and Muslim world
Muslims in the West. *See* Islam in the West
Myanmar, *296*

N

Nagasaki and Hiroshima, Japan bombings (1945), 181, *196*

Nakba (Palestine), 194, 274, *274*

Nansen, Fridtjof Wedel-Jarlsberg, 271–272

Narcotics. *See* Drug addiction; Drug seizures; Drug trafficking and trade; Mexican drug war; Opium

NASA

  Apollo 13 rescue, 58–59, *59*

  Chilean miners' rescue aid, 39, 46, 50, 59

  Gulf oil spill photography, 102, 115

  Internet security investigations, 293

Natanz, uranium enrichment site, 174

National Oceanic and Atmospheric Administration (NOAA), 109, 112, 115, 119, 120

National security

  global, and Internet security, 293–294, *294*, 296–298, 307–308, 310

  global, and WikiLeaks, 298, 299, 302, 303, 304–305

  nuclear weapons concerns, 184

  U.S., and Internet security, 293, 294–295, 296–298, 305–306, 307, 310

  U.S., and WikiLeaks, 298, 301–303

  See also Borders, geographic; Military security

National Security Agency (NSA), 293, 304–305

Nationalization of banks, 74–75, 77

NATO

  Afghanistan drug eradication programs, 21

  Afghanistan War involvement and strikes, 8, *8*, 10, 11, 12, 22*t*, 23, 25, 29, 32

  Pakistan presence and strikes, 9, *9*, 25

  Turkey-Denmark relations, 226

Natural disasters. *See* Haiti earthquake (2010) and aftermath; Hurricane Katrina (2005); Hurricane Tomas (2010); Pakistan floods (2010); South Asian tsunami (2004)

Los Negros drug cartel, 237

Netanyahu, Benjamin, 176, 195

Netherlands

  Afghanistan War forces, 13, 14

  austerity plans, *90*

  immigration, 281*t*

Muslim populations, *217*

  retirement age, 85*t*

  17th-century financial crisis, *71*

  unemployment rates, 81*t*

Networks, computers, 297, 305, 307, 308

New Century Financial (mortgage lender), 74

New York City. *See* "Ground Zero" site and mosque

New Zealand

  mine explosions, *63*, 64

  retirement age, 85*t*

Newman, Steven, *126*

NIE. *See* U.S. National Intelligence Estimate

Nigeria

  oil industry and spills, 130

  oil reserves, 132*t*

Nikkei Index, 77, *78*

9/11. *See* September 11, 2001 terrorist attacks

Niqab, 215, *215*, 217–218, *218*

NNPT. *See* Nuclear Non-Proliferation Treaty

Nobel Peace Prize

  recipients, 184, *296*, *306*

  Web site security attack, *306*

Non-Aligned Movement, 184

Norris, Molly, 227–228

North Africa region

  economic standing, 86*t*

  emigration, 214, *278*

  ethnic groups, 193

  oil reserves, 131, 132*t*

North Atlantic Treaty Organization. *See* NATO

North Korea

  Demilitarized Zone (DMZ), 289, *289*

  nuclear weapons possession, 183–184, 183*t*

  sanctions, 184

  weapons technologies, 180, 184, 196

North-south migration (United States), 268

Northern Alliance (Afghanistan), 7–8, 27

Northern Rock bank, 74–75

Norway

  emigration, 270

  Haitian relief donations, 152*t*

  immigration, 281*t*

  oil spills, 128–129

  retirement age, 85*t*

  unemployment rates, 81*t*

NPT. *See* Nuclear Non-Proliferation Treaty

NSA. *See* National Security Agency (NSA)

Nuclear fission and fusion, 181–182

Nuclear Non-Proliferation Treaty, 172, 183, 184, 196–197

Nuclear power, 169, 171, 174, 179, 183, 185

  See also Iran nuclear program

Nuclear programs. *See* Iran nuclear program; Nuclear weapons

Nuclear weapons

  Iran programs and suspicions, 169–171, 172, 173, 174, 177–178, 179–180, 185, 186, 192, 195, 196

  non-proliferation treaties, 172, 183, 184, 196–197

  rogue states, 184, 192

  technology history, 177, 181–182, 183, 185

  testing, 174, 181, 182, *182*, 183, 184

  usage, 181, *196*

  world nuclear powers, 175–176, 181, 182–183, 183*t*, 196–197

O

Obama, Barack

  Afghanistan military policy, 1–2, 9–10, 10–11, 14, 23–25, 28–29, 31–32

  drug treatment policy, 255

  drugs and arms trafficking policy, 243, 255

  economic policy, 79, 89–90, 93–94, 307

  election, 90

  energy policy, 124–125, 127, 130

  environmental policy, 125, 126, 127

  foreign policy, Afghanistan, 18, 19

  foreign policy, Arabian peninsula, 302

  foreign policy, Iran and Israel, 176, 179

  "Ground Zero" mosque opinion, 203

  Gulf oil spill and, 97, 124, 125, *125*, 127

  Haitian relief fundraising, 153

  immigration policy, 262–263, *263*, 290

  Iran sanctions and foreign policy, 175, *176*, 177–178, 179, 181

  national security policy, 307

  nuclear policy, 184

Pakistan military policy, 9, 24–25

Occupied Territories, 194, 195, 289, *289*

Ocean currents, 115

Ocean floor oil, 109–110

Office for the Coordination of Humanitarian Affairs (OCHA) (United Nations), 152–153

Offshore drilling

BP/Gulf oil spill, 97–98, 120, *120,* 124–125

history, oil spills, 128–129

leases and safety regulations, 100, 122, 127

Nigeria, 130

oil reserves, 131

U.S. energy policy, 123–124

world locations, 124*t*

See also Gulf oil spill (2010)

Ogoni people (Nigeria), 130

Oil collection domes. *See* Containment domes (oil spills)

Oil consumption. *See* Energy consumption; Gasoline consumption, U.S.

Oil industry

Ecuador's struggles, 89

Iran, 186

Mexico, drug war influence, 91

nationalized programs, 89

Nigerian exploration and spills, 130

Russian resources, 87

United States regulation, 100, 122–123, 124, 127

U.S. debt ownership, 91*t*

See also Energy consumption; Gulf oil spill (2010); Oil reserves; Oil spills; Organization of the Petroleum Exporting Countries (OPEC)

Oil pipelines, 129

Oil prices, 131, 133

Oil reserves, 131–133, 132*t*

Oil sands, 131

Oil Spill Liability Trust Fund, 121, 125

Oil spills

developing nations, and lack of attention, 130

history, global, 101*t*, 127–130

tankers, 101*t*, 127–128, 129

See also Exxon Valdez oil spill (1989); Gulf oil spill (2010)

Ojeda, José, 38, *51*

Oklahoma, 201

Online businesses, stocks, 70, 71

OPEC (Organization of the Petroleum

Exporting Countries), 131, 133

Operation Baja California, 244–245

Operation Michoacán (Mexico), 240–241

Operation Moshtarak (Afghanistan), 10–11, 21–22

Operation Xcellerator (Mexico), 255

Opium

production, *18,* 19, 19*t,* 20, 20*t,* 21, 22, 232

seizures, Mexico, 257*t*

trade, 18–22, *20, 21,* 232

Oppenheimer, J. Robert, 181

Orduna, Robert, 248

Organization of the Petroleum Exporting Countries (OPEC), 131, 133

Ottoman Empire, 192, 206–207

P

Pahlavi, Mohammad Reza, 186, 187, 188, 190

Pahlavi, Reza Shah, 186

Pakistan

Afghan refugees, 275, *284*

emigrants, 206

intelligence organization, 23

nuclear weapons possession, 183, 183*t,* 184

al-Qaeda in, 8, 24

strife and internally displaced populations, 192, 286, *286*

Taliban relations, 8, 9, *9,* 286, 300

U.S. actions, Afghanistan War, 9, 24–25

Pakistan floods (2010), *286*

Palestine

Arab-Israeli conflict, 194, 207, 225, 274, *274,* 289, *289*

history, 195, 206, 207, 272

statehood, 194

Palin, Sarah, 202, 299

Park51 Project. *See* "Ground Zero" site and mosque

Pashtuns, 26, 27, 28, 31, *193*

Passport security, 294–295

Patriot Act (2001), 282

Paulsen, Henry, 77

Peace conferences and talks

Afghanistan, 29–31

Arab-Israeli conflict, 194

Pemex (Mexican oil company), 101, 255

Pena, Edison, *50*

Pensions, eligibility. *See* Retirement age

Pentagon Papers, 302–303

Per-capita GDP, 87–88

Persia, 186

See also Iran

Persian Gulf War

damages, *194*

oil sabotage, 101*t,* 130

sectarian violence, 192

Persians (ethnic group), 192, *193*

Personal information, security, 294–295, 296–297, 299, 307

Peru

drug production and trade, 234, 252

mining accidents, 61*t*

Petraeus, David, 23, 302

Petroleum industry. *See* Oil industry

Phoenix rescue capsule (Chilean miners' rescue), *39,* 39–40, *40, 51, 52,* 53, 59–61

Photographic identification, 216

Photojournalism and event photography

Gulf oil spill, 102

Haitian earthquake, 141, *141,* 155–156

Iran political protests, *307*

Pike River mine, New Zealand, *63,* 64

Piñera, Sebastian, *36, 49,* 53, 54, *55,* 57, 62

Pipeline accidents, 129

Plan A, Chilean miners' rescue, 36

Plan B, Chilean miners' rescue, 36, 37–38, 40–41, 53

Plan C, Chilean miners' rescue, 36–37

Plate tectonics. *See* Tectonic regions and ridges

Plutonium, weapons-grade, 177, 181, 184, 185

Poland

Afghanistan troops forces, 14

emigration and migrant work, EU, 276, 281*t*

immigration, 281*t*

mining accidents, 61*t*

retirement age, 85*t*

unemployment rates, 81*t*

Police forces

Afghanistan, 13, 15, 18, *18,* 21, 27, 29

Colombia, 252

Mexico, corruption in drug war, 235, 237–239, 246, 251

Mexico, efforts in drug war, 238, 240, 241, *244,* 244–245, 246, 248, 249, 253

Political prisoners, *296, 306,* 308

Political protests. *See* Protests and demonstrations

Pollution

oil exploration in developing countries, 130

oil spills' environmental effects, 109–112, 113–118

Polycyclic aromatic hydrocarbons (PACs), 116

Population issues

BRIC nations, 87

China, 289

European trends, 214–215

Haiti 2010 earthquake, migrations, 145, 160–161

Muslim sects, 190, *191*

U.S. trends, 205–209, *208,* 273

See also Illegal immigration; Immigration; Migration, human

Port-au-Prince, Haiti, 136, 138, *138, 142, 144,* 145, 148, *163, 165*

See also Haiti earthquake (2010) and aftermath

Portugal

austerity plans, *90*

labor protests, 86

retirement age, 85*t*

Potato famine, Ireland, 268, 270–271

Predatory lending, 68, 72–73, 91

Press

bias in immigration reporting, 267

Haitian earthquake coverage, 135, 155–156

Jyllands-Posten Muhammad cartoons controversy (2005-2006), 222–226, *223, 224, 225,* 228

Mexican drug war coverage and victims, 246, 251, *252–253, 254*

self-censorship, Islamic topics, 222–223, 225

WikiLeaks role, 298–301, *300*

Prestige oil spill (2002), 127–128

Préval, Elisabeth, *140*

Préval, René, 135, 138, *140, 154*

Probert, Tim, *126*

Project Coronado (Mexico, 2006-2009), 255

Project Reckoning (Mexico, 2007-2008), 255

Protestants, anti-Catholicism, 210–213

Protests and demonstrations

Belgium (economic strife), *69*

France (austerity measures), 84, *84,* 86

France (migrants policy), *279*

Greece (austerity measures), 82, *83*

Haiti (cholera), *149,* 150

Haiti (election results, 2010), 166

Iceland (economic strife), *78*

India (economic reforms), *88*

Iran (election results, 2009), 297, *307,* 309–310

Iran (Revolution), 187, 190

Myanmar human rights, *296*

Russian Internet policy, 308

Spain (economic strife), 86, *87*

Turkey (headscarf laws), *219*

Turkey (U.S. Islamophobia), *205*

United States (anti-foreclosures), *93*

United States (anti-Muslim), 201–202, *204,* 204–205, *205*

United States (anti-offshore drilling), *120*

United States (immigration policy), 260

United States (Muslim understanding), *225, 227*

worldwide (*Jyllands-Posten* Muhammad cartoons controversy), 222, 223, *223, 224,* 224–225, *225,* 225–226

Prudhoe Bay oil pipeline, 129

Public health issues

Gulf oil spill, 116–119

Haiti 2010 earthquake aftermath, 140, 145–150, *147, 150,* 166, *166*

Puerto Rico, 295

Pull factors, immigration, 266, 269

Push factors, immigration, 266–269

Q

al-Qaeda, *32,* 192

2001 terror attacks, 7, 202, 282, 307

Afghanistan and Taliban, 7, 8, 29, 30, 31, 32–33, 192

nuclear weapons, 192

tactics, 307

Yemen and Arabian Peninsula (AQAP), 302

Qajar, Ahmad Shah, 186

Qatar, oil reserves, 132*t*

Qom, Iran nuclear facility, 169, *170, 171*

Quotas, immigration, 271, 273

Qur'an, 191

context and interpretation, 201

protest burnings, *204,* 205, *205*

women's veiling and dress, 215–216

R

Racial profiling, 209, 261–262, 282

Rasmussen, Anders Fogh, 223, 225, 226

Real estate bubble, 68, 70, 71–72, 91

Recessions, 81

global, *78,* 79, 80, 81–86, *90,* 94

United States, 79–80, 81, 88, 261

Recruitment, drug cartels, 242, *243,* 248–249

Red Cross, 156

Refugee and relief camps

Africa, 285, *285*

Cuba, 164

European displaced persons, 195

France, 283, *283*

Haiti, 135, 138, 143–145, *144,* 146, 148, 149, *164,* 165, *266*

Israel/Palestine, 274

Pakistan, *284*

Southeast Asia, 274

Uzbekistan, *276*

Refugees

Afghanistan, 12, 275, *277,* 283, *283, 284*

Africa, 274–275, 284, 285, *285*

Colombia, 286

Haiti, post-2010 earthquake, 135, 138, 143–145, *144,* 146, 147, 148, 149, 152, *153,* 165, *266*

Haiti, 1980s and 1990s classifications, 163–164, 269

historical treatment and world conflicts, 271–274, 282–283

internally displaced persons (IDPs), 264–265, *273,* 282, 284, 285–287, 288

Iraq, 286–287

Jews, WWII, 195, 272

Kyrgyzstan/Uzbekistan, *276*

Pakistan, 286

Palestine, 194, 274, *274*

sources and totals, 274–275, *277,* 282, 283

South Asia, 274

types, 264–265, 271, *273,* 282

UN High Commissioner for Refugees, 164, 273, *273,* 274–275, *277,* 282, 286, 291

Regan, Margaret, 259–260, *260*

Regulations, environmental. *See* Environmental regulations

Regulations, financial. *See* Financial regulation

Regulations, safety. *See* Safety regulations

Reid, Harry, 203

Relief aid. *See* International aid; Medical aid

Relief wells (oil spill containment technique), 104, 107–108

Religious discrimination. *See* Anti-Catholic sentiment; Head coverings, Muslim women; Islamophobia

Religious faith, *44*

Religious persecution
    Catholics, 210–213
    immigration push factor, 268–269
    Muslims, 199, 200–202, *204,* 204–205, *205,* 206, 209–210
    See also Jyllands-Posten Muhammad cartoons controversy (2005-2006)

Remotely-operated vehicles, 100, *106, 108, 109*

Renewable energy
    potential among fossil fuels, 64–65
    traditional sources, 131
    as U.S. goal, 130

Reporters Without Borders, 251

Reserves, oil, 131–133, 132*t*

Retirement age
    France, 84, 85, 86
    global comparisons, 85*t*
    Greece, 82

Reza, Mohammad. *See* Pahlavi, Mohammad Reza

Reza Khan, 186

Reza Shah, 186

Riser Insertion Tube Tool (RITT) (Deepwater Horizon oil leak), 105

Rodriguez, Manuel, 59–61

Roma peoples, *279*

Roman Catholicism. *See* Catholicism

Romania
    Afghanistan troops forces, 14
    austerity plans, *90*
    emigration, 278, 281, 281*t*

Romney, Mitt, 203

Roosevelt, Franklin D., 272

Routine, in daily life, 45–46

Rueda, Arnoldo, 241

Rushdie, Salman, 190

Russia
    cyber skirmishes and espionage, 305, 308
    economic standing, 86–87, 86*t*
    emigration, 272
    Federal Security Service and

WikiLeaks, 304–305
    imperialism, 4–5, 186
    Iran diplomatic relations, 174, 175, 179, *179,* 180, 184
    nuclear weapons possession and policy, 182, 183, 183*t,* 184
    oil reserves, 132*t*
    U.S. debt ownership, 91*t*

S

Sabotage
    Islamic community centers, 200
    oil supplies, 101*t,* 129–130

Sachsen Landesbank (mortgage lender), 74

Safavid Empire, 192

Safe haven conventions, 164, 273

Safety equipment, offshore oil drilling
    blowout preventers, 98, 100, 103, *103, 105,* 106, *106,* 107, *107, 128*
    containment domes, 103–104, *104,* 104–105
    Deepwater Horizon failures highlighted, *103, 104, 128*

Safety measures, earthquake zones, 158

Safety regulations
    mining, 61, 62, 65
    offshore oil drilling, 100, 122, 127

Saint-Domingue (colonial Haiti), 159

Sajjil-2 missiles, *174*

Salary caps, 93

Salazar, Ken, 122–123, 127

Saleh, Ali Abdullah, 302

Salehi, Mohammad, 18

Salinas, Marta, 57–59

Sam, Jean Vilbrun Guillaume, 161

San Esteban Primera Mining Company, 62

San José mine, Chile, 35, 40, *41,* 62
    See also Chilean miners' rescue

San Sebastian Film Festival (Spain), *87*

Sanitation issues, Haiti, 135, 138, 143, 145, 146–150, *147,* 151, 160

Santa Muerte (Saint Death), *237*

Sarkozy, Nicolas, 84, 93, 179, 216, *279*

Sarrazin, Thilo, *214,* 215

Satellite photography, 102, 115

Saudi Arabia
    Haitian relief donations, 152*t*
    Iran policy and U.S. communications, 180–181, 302, 303
    Islamic law, 201, 222

oil exports, China, 180–181
    oil reserves, 132*t*

Saving habits, 79

SB 1070 (Arizona anti-immigration law), 260–263, *262*

Scams, 294

Schneier, Bruce, *295*

Schramm Inc., 37

Sea animals. *See* Marine animals; Sea turtles

Sea turtles, 110, 115, 116, *118*

Seafood industry, and Gulf oil spill, 97, 109, 119, 120–121

Second Anglo-Afghan War (1878-1880), 4

Second mortgages, 70, 71–72

Secularism, 228
    Arab nationalism, 192
    France, 216, 217, 218
    Turkey, 218–219

Securities and Exchange Commission (SEC), 76

Security, Internet. *See* Internet security

Segovia, Maria, 56–57

Seismographs, *157*

Self-censorship, 222, 225

Self-regulation, industries, 122

Senate, U.S. *See* Congress, U.S.

Separation of church and state
    France, 216, 217, 218
    Germany, 220, 221
    Turkey, 218, 219

September 11, 2001 terrorist attacks, 7, *32,* 202, 206, *207,* 282, 307
    commemoration protests, *204,* 205
    immigration and racial profiling, 282
    Muslim communities and, 202, 203, 206, *207,* 209
    victims' families, 203

Sernageomin, 62

Servers, computers, 297

Sexual assault
    accusations, Julian Assange, 304
    African refugees, 285
    Haiti, post-earthquake, 140

Shabaab, Al (terrorist group), 226

Shah of Iran. *See* Pahlavi, Mohammad Reza

Shahab-3 missiles, 178, *178*

Shanghai Composite Index, 77

Shari'a. *See* Islamic law

Shiite/Sunni Muslims, history and tensions, 180, 190–192, *191,* 302

Sinaloa drug cartel, 231, 236, 237, *239,* 247, 249, 251, 255

Singh, Manmohan, 87

Six-Day War (1967), 194, 195

Skimming, post-oil spills, 105, 108, 110

Slavery
  colonial Haiti, 159
  forced migration and Middle Passage, 269, *270*
  trade routes, *268,* 269

Sleep-wake patterns, 46, 47

Small businesses, 78–79

Social media
  Haitian earthquake coverage and relief, 155, 156–157
  Iran citizen journalism, *307*
  Mexican drug traffickers' use, *248*

Social security programs, 84
  See also Retirement age

"Solar Sunrise" investigation, 293, *294*

Somalia
  emigrant workers, 209–210
  refugees, *277,* 284, 285

Soppe, Richard, 53

Sougarret, André, 36

South Africa
  economic crisis and race, *80*
  nuclear weapons possession, 183
  oil spills, 101*t*

South America
  drug production, 234, 235, *235,* 252–253
  slave trade, *268*
  See also specific nations

South Asian refugees, 274

South Asian tsunami (2004), 153–154

South Korea
  Demilitarized Zone (DMZ), 289, *289*
  financial crisis, 77
  retirement age, 85*t*

South-north migration (United States), 267–268

South Park (television program), 226

Southwest Asia. *See* Middle East region

Soviet-Afghan War (1979-1989), 6–7, 19

Soviet Union
  Afghanistan invasion, (1979), 5, *5,* 6, 19, 275
  Jewish emigration, 268–269
  nuclear weapons possession, 182, 183
  relations with U.S./Cold War, 5–7, 182, 207, 275–276

Spain
  Afghanistan, troops in, 14
  austerity plans, *90*
  economic standing, 86*t*
  exploration, 159
  Haitian relief donations, 152*t*
  immigration and migrant work, 278, 280–281, 281*t*
  Melilla, *278*
  Muslim communities and relations, 213–214, *217*
  oil spills, 127–128
  retirement age, 85*t*
  unemployment rates, 80–81, 81*t,* 281

Spam (e-mail), 298

Special Investigative Unit (Afghanistan), 18

Sri Lanka, civil war and immigration, 288–289

St. Lorenzo, *44*

State Department. *See* U.S. Department of State

Static kill technique (oil spill containment), 106–107, *108*

Stimulus spending
  global, 74, 77, 80
  United States, 74, 77, 79, 91, 94

Stock markets, 67, 70, 71, 77, *78*

Strategic Arms Reduction Treaty (START), 184

Strauch, Eduardo, 49–50

Stress. *See* Mental health issues

Strikes. *See* Labor strikes, Europe; Protests and demonstrations

Sub-Saharan Africa, economic standing, 86*t*

Submerged, spilled oil, 109–110, 116

Subprime mortgage loans, 68, 70, 71, 72–74, 77

Sudan, 284–285, *285,* 290

Sullivan, Martin, 75

Sultanahmet Mosque (Turkey), *213*

Sunjiawan mine (China), 64

Sunni/Shiite Muslims, history and tensions, 180, 190–192, *191,* 302

Supertanker oil spills, 101*t,* 127–128

"Surges," Afghanistan War, 1–2, 9–10, 10–11, 11–12, 23–24, 29, 32

Suu Kyi, Aung San, *296*

Swat Valley, Pakistan, 9, *9*

Sweden
  Haitian relief donations, 152*t*
  immigration, 281*t,* 287

Muslim populations, *217*
  retirement age, 85*t*
  unemployment rates, 81*t*
  WikiLeaks, 298–299, 304

Sweeney, Charles P., 212

Swigert, John L., 58

Switzerland
  immigration, 281*t*
  mosques and minarets, *220,* 221
  Muslim populations, *217,* 221
  retirement age, 85*t*
  unemployment rates, 81*t*

Syria, *177,* 192, 194, 196

T

Taiwan
  Internet attacks, 293, 298*t, 306*
  U.S. debt ownership, 91*t*

Tajiks, 26, 27

Taliban
  Afghanistan diplomacy, 28, 29, 30–31
  Afghanistan government and history, 2, 7, *7,* 19, 192
  Afghanistan insurgency and attacks, 1–2, *2, 7,* 8–9, 10, 11–13, *13, 22t,* 28–30, 32, 300
  Afghanistan opium production and trade, 18, 19, 19*t,* 20
  ethnic makeup, 28, 31, 192
  leaders, *29*
  in Pakistan, and Pakistan relations, 8, 9, *9,* 25, 31, 286, 300
  al-Qaeda and, 7, 8, 32–33

Tamaulipas, Mexico, 245–246

Tamil populations, Sri Lanka, 288–289

Tammuz nuclear reactor (Iraq), *194*

Tar sands, 131

TARP (Troubled Assets Relief Program), 77

Taxation
  austerity plan components, 85, 89, 90
  businesses (Europe), 82
  foreign workers, 287
  value-added tax (VAT), 82–83

Tchador, *215*

Technology stocks, 70, 71

Tectonic regions and ridges, 141–142, *142, 143,* 159

Teller, Edward, 181

Temporary Protected Status (TPS), immigration, 161

Tenenbaum, Ehud, 293, *294*

Tennessee, Muslim communities, 199–200, 210

Terrorists and terrorism
Afghanistan as haven, 2, 29
Afghanistan War attacks, 1, 2, *2*, 11, 31
anti-terrorism laws' effects on immigrants, 282
Internet use and crimes, 298, 305, 306–307
Iran support, 190
nuclear weapons and, 184, 192
Pakistan as haven, 8, 9
plots foiled, *227*
suspicion of and discrimination to Muslims, 200–201, 209, 223, 282–283
U.S. embassy attacks, *32*
women's dress and, 216
See also al-Qaeda; Hamas; Hezbollah; September 11, 2001 terrorist attacks

Test-Ban Treaty (nuclear weapons), 184
Text messaging, 156
Theft
Internet scams and crimes, 294–295, 296–297
military corruption, 17
Theory of relativity (Einstein), 181
Third-party uranium enrichment, 172–173, 175
Tibet, 289, 290
Ticona Yanez, Ariel, 54
Tiger Temple (blogger), *308*
Tijuana drug cartel, 236, *239*, 244–245
Tobar, Vincenot, 62
Top kill technique (oil spill containment), 105, *105*
Tormenta, Tony, 247
Torrey Canyon (tanker) oil spill (1967), 101*t*, 127
Torture
Iraq War, 301
Mexican drug war, 239, 247, 252, 253
Tourism
Gulf oil spill effects, *102*, 119–120, 121, *121*
Gulf states industry, 121
Mexican drug war effects, 253
Trade deficit, U.S., 88
Trafficking. *See* Arms trafficking and seizures; Drug trafficking and trade; Human smuggling
Trans Alaskan oil pipeline, 129

Transocean (corporation), 97, 100, 108, 123, 125, *126*, 127
Transparency International, Corruption Perceptions Index, 14, *15*, 251
Tribal groups. *See* Language and ethnic groups
Trinidad, 1979 oil spill, 101*t*
Tropical storms. *See* Hurricane Katrina (2005); Hurricane Tomas (2010)
Troubled Assets Relief Program (TARP), 77
Tsunami, South Asia (2004), 153–154
Tulip "bubble," Holland (1630s), *71*
Turkey
Afghanistan troops forces, 14
Cyprus relations, 289
emigrants, 214
immigration, 272, *279*
mosques, *213*
protests, *205, 219*
retirement age, 85*t*
secularism, dress, and customs, 218–219, 222
Turtles, 110, 115, 116, *118*
Twitter
Haitian earthquake coverage, 155, 156
political denial-of-service attacks, 297

U

UAE. *See* United Arab Emirates
Uighur populations, China, 289–290
Ukraine, emigration, 281*t*
Ultra-deepwater drilling, 124, 124*t*
See also Deepwater Horizon rig; Offshore drilling
Unconventional oil sources, 131
See also Offshore drilling
Underwater photography, 102, *106, 109*
Unemployment
Europe, 80–81, 81*t*, 83, 281, 283
Iran, 189
U.S., Gulf oil spill effects, 121–122
U.S. legislation, 89–90
U.S. rates, 80, 81*t*, 88, 89*t*
youth rates, 83, 189
UNICEF (UN Children's Fund), 146
Unified Command, Gulf oil spill response, 108–109
Unions, 61–62, 84, 85, 86, 268
United Arab Emirates
immigration policy, 287–288, *288*
Iraq relations, 180

Islamic law, 222
oil reserves, 132*t*
United Kingdom
Afghanistan War forces, 7, 8, 10, 11, 13, 14
austerity plans, *90*
bank nationalization, 74–75, 77
economic standing, 86*t*
global economic crisis, 80, 81
Haitian relief donations, 152*t*
immigration, 276, 281, 281*t*
Muslim communities and relations, 200, 201, 213–214, *217*
national security, 306, 307
nuclear weapons possession, 183, 183*t*
oil spills, 101*t*, 127
retirement age, 85*t*
unemployment rates, 81*t*
U.S. debt ownership, 91*t*
United Nations (UN)
Afghanistan War policy, 8
African aid and peacekeeping, 285
Arab-Israeli conflict, resolutions, 194–195
Conference on Trade and Development, 290
Convention Relating to the Status of Refugees, 164, 273
cybersecurity policy, 307–308
formation and history, 207, 272–274
Haitian earthquake headquarters destruction, 136, 138
Haitian earthquake relief work, 135, 138, 145, 146, 148, 152–153, 154, 155
Haitian earthquake security work, 139–140
High Commissioner for Refugees (UNHCR), 164, 273, *273*, 274–275, 277, 282, 286, 291
Human Rights Council issues, 289
International Refugees Organization (IRO), 272–273
Iranian nuclear program and, 169–172, 173, 174–175, 177, 178, 179, 181, 197
North Korean nuclear program and, 184
nuclear non-proliferation work, 184
Office on Drugs and Crime (UNODC), reports, 14–16, 19*t*, 20–21, 20*t*, 22
Relief and Works Agency for

Palestine Refugees in the Near East (UNRWA), 274

Stabilization Mission in Haiti (MINUSTAH), 163

WikiLeaks coverage, 299

See also International Atomic Energy Agency (IAEA)

United States

crime rates, 250, 261

debt, foreign holdings, 91*t*

diplomatic relations, 301–303, 310

drug market, 234, *238*, 246, 255, 256–257

drug trafficking policy and aid in combating, 243, 252, 253, 255–257, 256*t*

economic standing, 86*t*, 88, 91, 208

energy consumption, 123–124, 130, 131

energy policy, 122, 123–125, 127, 130, 131

foreclosure rates, 72*t*

foreign policy and Cold War, 5–6, 182, 207, 275–276

foreign policy and WikiLeaks, 301–303

gun laws, 255, 256

Haitian relief donations, 152, 152*t*, 153–154, 156, 157

immigration policy, 206, *211*, 260–265, 270, 271, 272–273, 280*t*, 281*t*, 282–283, *287*, 290

Israel relations, 176–177, 178–179, 190, 196

mining accidents, 61*t*, 63

Muslim communities and relations, 199–210, 209*t*

nuclear weapons possession and policy, 181, 182, 183*t*, 184

oil reserves, 132*t*

petroleum industry regulations, 100, 122–123, 124, 127

population makeup, *208*, 273

retirement age, 85*t*

unemployment rates, 80, 81*t*, 88, 89, 89*t*

See also Afghanistan War; Iraq War, 2003-; Obama, Barack

Universal Declaration of Human Rights, 272

Up-reaming drilling technique, 36

Upper Big Branch mine (West Virginia), 63

Uranium-235, 181, 183

Uranium enrichment

Iran facilities, 169, 170, *170, 171,* 172, *173,* 174

Iran production, 170–171, 172, 173–174, 175, 177

process, *172, 173,* 175, 183

third-party, 172–173, 175

Uruguayan Air Force Flight 571 disaster, 49–50

Urzua Iribarren, Luis Alberto, 50, *52,* 52–53, *53,* 59, 60

U.S. Army

Afghanistan presence, 1–2, *3, 12*

change of command, 22–23

cybersecurity, 305

WikiLeaks coverage, 299

U.S. Bureau of Alcohol, Tobacco, Firearms, and Explosives (ATF), 243

U.S. Bureau of Ocean Energy Management, Regulation, and Enforcement, 122–123, 127

U.S. Coast Guard

drug busts, 246

Gulf oil spill work, 100, 102, 110, 127

U.S. Congress. *See* Congress, U.S.

U.S. Cyber Command, 305

U.S. Department of Defense

Internet history, 293–294

Internet security attacks and initiatives, 293, *294,* 296, 305–306

Pentagon Papers, 302–303

U.S. Department of Energy, 123, 131

U.S. Department of Health and Human Services, 119

U.S. Department of Homeland Security, 265

U.S. Department of Justice, 282, 293

U.S. Department of State, 179, 295, 301–303, 305, 310

U.S. Department of the Interior

investigations and reports, 122

Minerals Management Service (MMS), 122–123, 127

U.S. Drug Enforcement Administration (DEA), 239, *240,* 247

U.S. Energy Information Administration (EIA), 123, 131

U.S. Fish and Wildlife Service, 116

U.S. Geological Survey (USGS), 142

U.S.-Haiti relations, 154, 161–164

U.S. invasion of Iraq (2003), 8

U.S.-Mexico relations

drug war, 232, 234, 236, 243, 250–251, 255–256

immigration, 261–262, 263, 289, *289*

U.S. National Intelligence Estimate, 174, 177–178

U.S.-Soviet relations, 5–7

User-generated content. *See* Citizen journalism; Social media

Uzbekistan

oil spill, 1992, 101*t*

refugees, *276*

Uzbeks, 26

V

Vaccines

corruption in distribution, 17

Haitian needs, post 2010 earthquake, 146

Valenzuela, Susana, *57,* 57–59

Valles Garcia, Marisol, 249, *249*

Value-added tax (VAT), 82–83

Van Gogh, Theo, 226

Vega, Alex, *40*

Veils. *See* Head coverings, Muslim women

Venezuela

drug trade violence, 252–253

oil reserves, 131, 132*t,* 133

Vibrio cholerae (cholera bacterium), *150*

Vietnam War (1959-1975)

Pentagon Papers and information sharing, 302–303

refugees, 274

Vigilantism

border security, U.S., *264,* 264–265

Iran, 189

Vilks, Lars, 226

Villanueva, Mario, 238

Villaroel, Richard, 52

Vincent, Sténio, 162

Violence against women

African refugees, 285

Haiti, post-earthquake, 140

servitude and abuse, 278–279

Viruses, computer, 174, 296

Volatile organic compounds (VOCs), 116

Voodoo, 161

W

Wall Street. *See* Investment firms

Walls of segregation, global, 194, 289, *289*

War of the Pacific (1879), 54

War on Drugs (United States), 256–257

Warlord rule, Afghanistan, 7, 19

Washington Mutual, 77

Water sanitation, Haiti, 135, 138, 143, 145, 146–150, *147,* 151, 160

Waxman, Henry, 68

Weapons trafficking. *See* Arms trafficking and seizures

West Africa
  drug trade, *235*
  slave trade, *268,* 269

West Bank, 194, 195, 289, *289*

Westergaard, Kurt, 222, 226, 228

Western influences and Muslim world, 186, 187, 189, 190, 206–207, 221–222, 224

Wetlands and marshes, 97, 102, 108, 110, 115, 117

White supremacists, 265

WHO. *See* World Health Organization (WHO)

Widmar, Luis Carlos, 248

WikiLeaks, 23, *23,* 179–181, 298–305, 310, 311

Women's rights abuses. *See* Human rights abuses; Violence against women

Women's rights and Islam, 201, 215–221

Woodward, Bob, 24–25

Workplace discrimination, 209–210

World Bank, 138–139

World Health Organization (WHO), 139, 146, 148, 149

World Trade Center site. *See* "Ground Zero" site and mosque; September 11, 2001 terrorist attacks

World Trade Organization (WTO), 290

World War I
  displacement and relocation, 271–272
  geopolitics following, 192, 206–207
  Muslim soldiers, *212*
  U.S. involvement, 211

World War II
  Holocaust, 194, 195, 272
  Iran alliances, 186
  nuclear weapons use, 181, *196*
  oil tanker sabotage, 129

X

Xenophobia, 190, 225, 259, 272–273, 281, 290
  See also Islamophobia

Xinjiang region, China, 289–290

Y

Yazid, Mustafa Abu al-, 192

Yéle Haiti Foundation, 157

Yellowcake uranium, *172*

Yemen, 302

Yom Kippur War (1973), 194

Youth unemployment, 83

YouTube, *248, 307*

Yudhoyono, Susilo Bambang, 228

Z

Zakaria, Fareed, 303

Zapatero, Jose Luis Rodriguez, *87*

Zardari, Asif Ali, 9

Zelenik, Lou Ann, 200, *200*

Los Zetas (Gulf drug cartel), 237, *239, 243,* 245, 250, 251

Zhang Shihe, *308*

Zionist movement, 194